D0883953

"... a restless disposition, an unbounded desire of riches, and an
excessive love of independence . . . are the very elements which insure a
long and peaceful future in the republics of America."

Alexis De Tocqueville, *Democracy in America*

THE
TUNA/PORPOISE
CONTROVERSY

August Felando

Harold Medina

THE
TUNA/PORPOISE
CONTROVERSY

**HOW TUNA FISHERMEN WERE
CAUGHT IN THE GOVERNMENT'S
NET AND FOUGHT TO SURVIVE**

**August Felando
Harold Medina**

WESTERN SKY PRESS
San Diego, California

TABLE OF CONTENTS

LIST OF ACRONYMS

AIDCP	Agreement on the International Dolphin Conservation Program
ATA	American Tunaboat Association
CDFG	California Department of Fish and Game
CFR	Code of Federal Regulations
CYRA	Commission's Yellowfin Regulatory Area
EEZ	Exclusive Economic Zone
EPO	Eastern Pacific Ocean
ETPO	Eastern Tropical Pacific Ocean
FR	Federal Register
IATTC	Inter-American Tropical Tuna Commission
ICCAT	International Commission for the Conservation of Atlantic Tunas
LMR	Living Marine Resources
MMC	Marine Mammal Commission
MMPA	Marine Mammal Protection Act
MSFCMA	Magnuson-Stevens Fishery Conservation and Management Act
NMFS	National Marine Fisheries Service
NOAA	National Oceanic and Atmospheric Administration
PFMC	Pacific Fishery Management Council
PRF	Porpoise Rescue Foundation
SPTT	South Pacific Tuna Treaty
SWFC	Southwest Fisheries Center (NMFS)
SWR	Southwest Regional (NMFS)
UNLOS	United Nations Law of the Sea
USIC	United States International Trade Commission
USTF	United States Tuna Foundation
WCPFC	Western and Central Pacific Fisheries Commission

PREFACE

This book presents our views on a controversy related to the destruction of an industry that was born in Southern California during the early 1900s--the catching and processing of tuna.

We think it is important to tell the story of how American tuna fishermen learned how to use the tuna/porpoise enigma, and how this use has promoted the sustainability of the yellowfin tuna resource in the eastern Pacific Ocean (EPO). We hope that this story will, in time, raise public inquiry and Congressional oversight as to the wisdom of the two laws that were enacted by Congress in 1990. In particular, the law that concerns the labeling of canned tuna as "dolphin safe." This is a "feel-good" labeling rule that claims to tell the truth to the U.S. consumer that the tuna in the can was caught by methods that are "marine mammal-safe" but not the truth that the promotion of this labeling rule throughout the tuna fishery in the EPO would endanger the sustainability of tuna resources and cause devastating waste of juvenile tunas and other living marine resources.

We describe the background of this dispute, with emphasis on how the fishermen's experiences, talents, motivations, and sacrifices developed the gear and procedures to catch tunas associated with porpoise, with minimal harm to the porpoise. Also discussed is the complex web of government actions, such as the Senate and House Committee legislative and oversight hearings, debates on the floor of the House and Senate, administrative law judge decisions on proposed agency regulations, federal judicial decisions and orders, and findings by the International Trade Commission that entangled the industry and eventually drove it to near extinction.

The book explains why the controversy is the result of a mystery of nature, the fact that in the eastern Pacific Ocean medium to large yellowfin tuna obediently follow the "leaders" of a porpoise school. Confronted by man's inability to separate the tunas from the porpoise so as to catch only the tunas in their nets, the fishermen developed ways to herd and capture portions or all of tuna/porpoise schools with their purse seines. Although they did their best to free the porpoise, initially there were significant mortalities and injuries of porpoise.

Today, tuna canneries, which not too long ago serviced tuna fleets that landed their catches in Southern California, Hawaii, Oregon, American Samoa, and Puerto Rico, are no longer in operation. The tens of thousands of jobs, directly and indirectly related to a tuna canning industry, are now located beyond the shores of United States. In addition to the loss of jobs and the almost total reliance by the U.S. consumer on imported tuna products, the loss of the tuna industry has contributed greatly to a diminished role for the United States government as a member of international fishery commissions concerned with the conservation and management of tuna resources. This is because when a nation's citizens are consumers, but not producers, of tuna, the government of that nation has little, if any, influence on how the tunas are to be conserved, managed, and allocated by international fishery commissions.

God said, "Let us make man in our own image, in the likeness of ourselves, and let them be masters of the fish of the sea . . . ."   Genesis, 1: 26

PART 1

TUNA CLIPPER CAPTAIN [1]

HAROLD MEDINA,

CAPTAIN'S SON

After arriving in San Diego, California, from the high seas off Mexico during the summer of 1935, the crew of the U.S. flag Tuna Clipper SAN SALVA-DOR, including eight-year-old Harold Medina, was examined in the vessel's galley by U.S. customs agents. To the question as to his place of birth, Harold correctly answered, "I was born in my grandmother's home." His father and captain of the SAN SALVADOR, "Machado" Medina, explained to the agents that Harold's birth occurred in San Diego on March 9, 1927, and that his son was completing his first tuna fishing trip.

Circa 1933, Captain Machado Medina using his sextant at sea.

For Harold, it remains to this day a memorable maiden fishing trip. He remembers the excitement of the purchase of fireworks by his father during the vessel's entry into the port of Ensenada, Mexico. He recalls the thrills aboard the SAN SALVADOR on the Fourth of July, when firecrackers and rockets were detonated. So numerous were the fireworks, that the crew had to pull up the ship's deck boards to remove the residue. He also recalls his first baptism in the ocean, an unexpected dunking that occurred while the vessel was fishing off Roca Partida, Baja California. A two-pole yellowfin tuna weighing over 30 pounds swallowed the hook at the end of the line on Harold's bamboo fishing pole, pulling him and his pole off the fishing rack. An alert fisherman in the nearby fishing rack grabbed the legs of the crying and sinking Harold and pulled him safely aboard. Harold learned that tuna fishing was exciting, but risky for the young and unskilled.

During this first voyage fishing for tuna, Harold also discovered the need to be careful when exploring a Tuna Clipper. Because of limited refrigeration space, cartons of food supplies were placed in the vessel's shaft alley. Harold was playing about the ship, and decided to climb a ladder located on the live bait tank, just aft of the shaft alley. As he climbed to the top of the ladder, he reached for a corner of a box secured to a tank containing live bait. In this box was a heavy metal meat grinder that was used to crush food for live bait. As Harold pulled on the box, it came toward him, forcing him to fall backward from the top of the bait tank through the main hatch opening leading to the shaft alley, some 18 feet below. Harold landed backward on the cardboard boxes containing bread. He looked up and saw the grinder box perilously wedged in the shaft alley opening directly over his head. Boyish curiosity aboard a ship gives birth to personal risks. Finally, he recalls the time when he changed the vessel's chronometer in the chart room to "local time," believing that the timepiece was incorrectly keeping time and that he was being helpful. Upon discovering this well-intentioned mistake, his father—who was also the ship's navigator—patiently explained that the chronometer was keeping time for another time zone and why this "time" was used in navigating to far-away places. From his father, Harold learned that it was adventurous to be in command of a Tuna Clipper.

Circa 1935, Crew using pole and line with live bait to catch tuna.

As each summer passed aboard the SAN SALVADOR, Harold developed skills and knowledge about working and living with the crew aboard his father's Tuna Clipper. As a teenager, his body was strengthened by pulling tuna aboard and by unloading them at San Diego canneries. The resulting strength and teamwork ethic helped Harold become an outstanding tackle on his high school football team.

Much happened to the Tuna Industry before Harold's first voyage with his father in 1935. During 1932-1933, at a time when an economic depression was engulfing the world, the Industry was suffering from an increasing flood of low-cost frozen and canned tuna imported from Japan. Fortunately, the federal government took timely tariff action to prevent the economic collapse of the California Tuna Industry. However, the effects of the depression had ruined almost all vessel investment plans of canners and fishermen. The economic viability of the California Tuna Industry had been badly shaken, as evidenced by the fact that the entry of new Tuna Clippers during a five-year period during the 1930s merely equaled removals. As of December 31, 1936, the high-seas tuna fleet numbered only 49 vessels. By 1935, confidence was clearly developing in the industry due to the public's acceptance of canned tuna. Fortunately, the depression had not destroyed the essential core of the Industry. San Diego tuna fishermen, supported by tuna canners and shipyard owners, had regained confidence in the idea that a prosperous fishing future required newer and larger vessels. The success of the San Diego captains who operated the newly-built clippers: the 122' CONTE BIANCO (Louis Castagnola), the 127' CAPE SAN VINCENT (Vincent Gann), and the 136' CABRILLO (Joe Medina), were influential in furthering this vision. This second major surge of fleet investment resulted in the entry of 32 new baitboats, of which 15 were built in 1937. By December 31, 1940, the fleet numbered 70 vessels, a historic high. Among these were some older Tuna Clippers built and owned by non-citizen Japanese fishermen.[2]

The tuna fishing families of Portuguese, Italian, and Japanese descent living in San Diego, supported by San Diego canners and shipyard owners, were again the principal risk-takers in building newer, larger, and more-efficient high-seas tuna baitboats.[3] The Italian, Japanese, and Dalmatian fishermen of San Pedro were building new purse-seine vessels for the fast-developing California sardine fishery. In addition, fishing failures by respected San Pedro owners who were experimenting with super-large tuna purse seiners had reduced interest by the Dalmatians in the distant-water tuna fishery.[4] Other events were impacting the Japanese fishing communities, particularly in the Los Angeles area. During 1938, the U.S. Attorney in Los Angeles filed legal actions against Japanese immigrant vessel owners and their co-owners.[5]

Other events and sights occurring during this period were causing persons involved in the California tuna and sardine fisheries to express the opinion that war between the United States and Japan was a real possibility. In July 1938, San Pedro commercial fishermen pledged their 42 vessels for use in case of war.[6] In March 1939, the trade journal *Pacific Fisherman* reported the charge of the Office of the U.S. Attorney in Los Angeles "that Japanese tuna clippers have followed the U.S. Fleet into the Caribbean Sea, where the Navy's war games were being held last Month." The spying charge was denied by an organization representing the owner that employed Japanese immigrants aboard 21 Tuna Clippers operating from San Diego.[7] During 1940 and early 1941, the Navy and Army purchased more than 50 West Coast-based commercial fishing vessels for patrol, minesweeping, and training work. In mid-1940, Tuna Clippers departing for Central and South American fishing areas were required to obtain permission to do so from the Secretary of the Treasury. Tuna Clippers were reporting that U.S. Navy destroyers were on "neutrality patrol" and strictly inspecting every vessel traveling between San Diego and Panama. By the fall of 1941, Tuna Clippers fishing off the Galapagos Islands were reporting that U.S. Navy-trained wireless operators were working a powerful radio station on Isla Isabela in the Galapagos Islands. By October 1941, shipyards and fishermen were complaining about delays in receiving parts, materials, and supplies. Tuna-fishing gear from Japan, such as bamboo poles and hooks, were no longer being shipped to suppliers in San Diego.

Following the Japanese attack on Pearl Harbor, the country needed vessels and seaman. The Government ordered all Tuna Clippers at sea to make port in California or the Panama Canal Zone.[8] On December 13, 1941, the Tuna Clipper ALERT, under the command of San Diego Captain Jose Silva, was attacked by U.S. military aircraft off the Pacific coast of Costa Rica and forced to enter the port of Puntarenas. Upon entering Panama, some Tuna Clippers were acquired by the U.S. Navy and used to protect the Canal Zone. Crewmembers of these vessels failing to prove U.S. citizenship were held in custody. On February 15, 1942, nearly 600 San Diego tuna fishermen attended a meeting with Navy representatives. The fishermen were asked to enlist and serve aboard former Tuna Clippers that were being acquired by the U.S. Navy. By February 17, the Navy had chartered 16 Tuna Clippers; most of their crew and officers were former tuna fishermen.[9] At about the same time, Japanese fishermen and their families living on Terminal Island and San Diego were relocated to internment camps. Innovative and productive tuna fishing communities developed by the Japanese immigrants in Terminal Island and San Diego were destroyed.[10] The first group of Tuna Clippers taken by the Navy was sent to waters in the Gulf of Panama for "picket" duty, protecting the Panama Canal. Other groups of clippers were being manned for duty in Hawaii, Samoa, and other South Pacific areas. Within eight months after the attack on Pearl Harbor, 52 Tuna Clippers were acquired by the military. All but a few of the Tuna Clippers were designated by the Navy as Yard Patrol (YP) vessels. They were given hull numbers, and became affectionately known by sailors and marines in the South Pacific as "Yippies." The Army used Tuna Clippers as tugs or supply ships. Twenty-one former Tuna Clippers serving as YPs never returned to the tuna fishery. Four were sunk by enemy action; others were lost due to storms or accidents. Some were deliberately destroyed by the U.S. military after the surrender of Japan.

In early 1942, the U.S. Navy requisitioned the SAN SALVADOR from Harold's father.[11] It and other Tuna Clippers were used for various purposes in South Pacific naval operations. After the transfer of their vessels to the U.S. Navy, Harold's father, known in the tuna fleet as "Machado," and his uncle, Frank Medina, converted two small vessels to tuna baitboats, the BETTY L. and the ROSEMARIE. During the summers of 1942-1944, Harold fished aboard these vessels. He recalls a fateful event that occurred during that period. He was a passenger, with another crewmember, in the speedboat used to catch live bait, sitting on the hatch cover secured over the inboard gasoline engine. As the speedboat came alongside the ROSEMARIE, Harold jumped aboard from the speedboat. Just after climbing onto the main deck, he turned around to witness the speedboat's engine explode, sending its hatch cover overboard.

At age 18, Harold used his recorded sea time aboard Tuna Clippers to obtain an able-bodied seaman's (ABS) certificate. To prepare for the certificate's examination, he studied at the Crawford Navigation School in San Pedro, California. Afterward, he joined the Seafarer's International Union, AFL, and shipped aboard the "black oil" tanker, CATHWOOD. This vessel made trips to a number of west coast ports, from Los Angeles, California, to Vancouver, British Columbia. His next job was aboard the gasoline tanker SAN DIEGAN as a quartermaster or person who attends the ship's helm. It was a very difficult vessel to steer, but Harold performed his job much to the satisfaction of its captain. During his 18 months in the Merchant Marine, he learned how to work with other crewmembers, how to respect the ship's officers and obey their orders, and various skills of seamanship. His most memorable lesson: Do your job, but don't place yourself in jeopardy; always use "one hand for the seaman." He recalls two incidents that occurred aboard the SAN DIEGAN that illustrate this self-protection rule for merchant seamen.

In order to repair a block on the mast of the SAN DIEGAN, it was necessary for Harold to use a boatswain's chair that was controlled by another crewmember. To place the block around another cable, Harold had to let one hand go to grab another cable. At the very moment of this hand change, the crewmember slackened the boatswain's chair line, causing the chair to drop a few feet and making Harold fall backward. Fortunately, his knees were secured to the chair seconds before his hand made contact with another boom-lifting cable. By holding onto this cable, he saved himself from a 30-foot drop to the deck below. Harold had violated the rule of keeping "one hand for the seaman." It was a lesson he never forgot.

While unloading gasoline from the SAN DIEGAN to shore facilities in the port of San Diego, the mate ordered Harold to fill the bow ballast tank with seawater. This action would help trim the vessel, since the bow of the SAN DIEGAN had risen after the gasoline cargo was pumped ashore. Harold used an electric water pump located in the bow area to pump seawater. The cover on the pump's enclosure was of ¼" steel and secured together every two inches with ½" bolts. After Harold started the pump and walked about 20 feet toward mid-ship, a loud explosion occurred, followed by smoke coming from the bow. The steel cover over the pump was blown into the area of the forepeak, smashing the paint locker. Harold found a fire extinguisher, and then rushed to the bow. Only smoke without flames was found. Whenever recalling this event, he questions his response to this emergency, explaining that he should have been running away from the vessel as quickly as possible. The cargo of gasoline—thousands of gallons—was still aboard; miraculously, the SAN DIEGAN and Harold escaped being blown sky high.

"My Merchant Marine experiences taught me to be forever vigilant about the many dangers to life and limb that lurk about a vessel when working with others at sea. They gave a special meaning to my memories of close calls that occurred during my summer cruises aboard Tuna Clippers."

After leaving the SAN DIEGAN, Harold went fishing for albacore off Southern California with his uncle, Manuel Monise, aboard the MAHAMA.[12] This small vessel, about 48 feet in length, had the carrying capacity of about 15 tons of frozen tuna. On the first night of the first trip, Harold suffered the pains of trying to work and sleep in rough seas on a vessel that was much less comfortable than the merchant marine vessels he had worked on. He still recalls the fumes from the diesel engine located just below his bunk and the tightness of the quarters for the two men. During this first night, Harold became seriously seasick, and couldn't sleep all night. The next day, his body and mind adjusted to this new experience. Within days, Manuel and he quickly loaded the vessel, using both pole-and-line with live bait and trolling gears.

Uncle Frank Medina, Captain and Managing Owner of the newly-built tuna clipper BERNADETTE, asked Harold to join the crew on a full-share basis.[13] During 1947, Harold made three trips; two were each about 90 days in duration, but the third was completed after only 30 days. The first two trips were made in the Pacific waters off Central America, primarily off Costa Rica. These voyages were difficult and long because most of the schools of tuna encountered rejected human efforts to be stimulated into a feeding frenzy, an experience not uncommon to tuna baitboat fishermen. During the third trip, the fish were concentrated in the Gulf of Tehuantepec, and much easier to catch.

Harold was assigned to work in the engine room as an oiler, and it became a learning experience that was of great benefit to his future work as a Captain and Managing Owner. Since age 13, Harold had become familiar with the workings of speedboat engines. His mentor was his uncle, Tony Monise, an experienced tuna fisherman. He was patiently taught to carefully maintain and overhaul the engines, part by part. Unlike the SAN SALVADOR, the BERNADETTE was an "all brine vessel;" the tunas were not individually iced by the crew but packed into fish wells filled with cooled ocean water. From Chief Engineer Tony Silva, he learned how to properly maintain and operate the vessel's main and auxiliary diesel engines and its brine well refrigeration equipment.

Harold treated his experience aboard the BERNADETTE as merely an extension of his merchant marine training. He had not understood why his merchant marine work habits were not wholly applicable on fishing vessels. On a tuna baitboat, the fishermen and ship-owner share the profit of a fishing trip, so the harder the fishermen work the more money they make, on average. On merchant vessels, the crew is paid wages for the voyage by the ship-owner, so they have no motivation to work extra hard. This short-term misunderstanding explains Harold's initial work habits aboard the BERNADETTE. He thought that he only had to perform routine duties in the engine room and in the fishing racks. No more, no less. Later, Harold realized that his Uncle Frank should have fired him for not performing his implied duties as a share fisherman. Aboard the merchant vessels CATHWOOD and SAN DIEGAN, he had performed only those tasks expressly ordered. Since he was not asked by Uncle Frank to search for the tunas, he did not volunteer to perform this important task. Later, after becoming a Captain, Harold made sure that the crew was always wholly engaged in the purpose of the voyage as a team and as co-venturers, working together in searching for the tunas and baitfish and performing with enthusiasm and pride the other implied duties of at-sea maintenance and repair of the vessel, its machinery, and its fishing gear.

A "key" man aboard the BERNADETTE was "Señor Manuel." He was valued by Uncle Frank for his ability to sight, follow, and capture both bait and the tunas. His eyesight was exceptional, and his judgment reliable. Señor Manuel would not leave the Bridge or Mast until he was satisfied that Uncle Frank had identified the location and movements of the tuna schools. Uncle Frank entrusted Harold with the important duty of taking a bottle of whiskey to the galley after a good day of fishing. Harold was instructed to make sure that Señor Manuel was given a water glass filled to the brim with whiskey, and to give one "shot" only to each of the other members of the crew. Señor Manuel would finish his whiskey with one gulp, as though drinking water. Then, he would quietly retire to his bunk for the night.

Aboard the BERNADETTE, Harold was exposed to lessons taught by master fishermen. When fishing for baitfish—anchovetas or sardines—Señor Manuel would be located on the bow of the speedboat operated by Harold. Obeying Señor Manuel's hand signals, Harold would guide the speedboat to find and follow the school of baitfish. The bait net would be released when ordered by Señor Manuel. This baiting experience with a master fisherman was another lesson for Harold. By observing Uncle Frank, Harold learned how to maneuver a Tuna Clipper in "working" tuna/porpoise schools. He saw that Uncle Frank would make sure that the bait was being tossed where the main body of the tuna school was located, and that the vessel was moving, in terms of speed and direction, in concert with that portion of the porpoise school seemingly controlling the movements of the tunas.

After loading the final brine well with tuna, the crew immediately began to clean the BERNADETTE, and continued to do so until the vessel's arrival in San Diego. The engine room crew would clean, polish, paint, and repair the equipment below the main deck, while the deck crew worked on the structures and equipment on the main and upper decks. After completing their third and final fishing trip of the year and while awaiting unloading instructions by the cannery in San Diego, Harold recalls how he and other crewmembers of the BERNADETTE made a special visit to the Tuna Clipper MAYFLOWER, a sister ship. They critically compared its appearance with that of the BERNADETTE. Competition in the San Diego Tuna Fleet among the crews was not limited to fishing success, but also in how their vessels were properly maintained as "homes away from home." As the crew of the BERNADETTE departed San Diego with pride in their vessel's beauty and hope for its fishing success, so did they labor to greet their families with their vessel's stateliness when arriving fully loaded with tuna.—a custom faithfully followed by Harold as a Captain of Tuna Clippers.

---

[1] The term "Tuna Clipper" refers to large (>100 feet in length), ocean-going "tuna baitboats." "Tuna Baitboats" are commercial fishing vessels that use live bait and bamboo or fiberglass poles with attached hook and line gear to catch the tunas. Many of the early tuna fishermen came to San Diego from New England fishing ports where the term "Clipper" became identified with large, ocean-going vessels. As large tuna baitboats were built to fish tunas from California to the Galapagos Islands, the term "Tuna Clippers" became identified with these vessels. The term "Tuna Clippers" has not been widely used to identify "Tuna Seiners" or tuna vessels using purse-seine gear to catch the tunas.

[2] This was the result of controversial legal actions initiated by the U.S. Attorney of Los Angeles. The following Tuna Clippers were built by Japanese immigrants prior to 1932; a change in their ownership interests made documentation as vessels of the United States

legal: SOUTHERN CROSS (1929); CIPANGO (1929); PANAMA (1930); MARICO (ex ASAMA 1930) ; COLUMBUS (1930), and ALERT (1930).

[3] During 1935-1938, the Medina brothers built the 136' CABRILLO; the 145' QUEEN MARY, the 148' NORMANDIE; Manuel Rosa and Associates built the 138' BELLE OF PORTUGAL; the 139' PICAROTO; the 141' AZOREANA; Manuel and Joe Monise, respectively, built the 140' VICTORIA and the 141' ENDEAVOR; San Diego Tuna Canners and Shipyards built the 140' AMERICAN BEAUTY; the 116' YANKEE; the 112' QUEEN AMELIA; the 124' CHALLENGER, and the 119' PROSPECT. The former yacht of author Zane Grey, which cruised new sport fishing grounds in the South Pacific was converted to a tuna baitboat by W.R. Dobbs and Associates in San Pedro and retained the name FISHERMAN II.

[4] Two failures by San Pedro purse-seine fishermen of Dalmatian descent to experiment in the high-seas tuna fishery were influential. After experiencing poor fishing, the 121' PARAMOUNT, a new steel-hulled tuna purse seiner built in 1937, was sold in 1940 for conversion to a tuna baitboat. A former 156' steel hull Navy tug built in 1919 was converted to a tuna purse seiner in 1940, and named the FALCON. After a very unsuccessful maiden voyage of six months, the vessel was converted to a tuna baitboat, and then acquired by the U.S. Navy in August 1942. Neither vessel returned to the tuna fishery, the PARAMOUNT was sunk at Okinawa in October 1945, and the FALCON was destroyed by the U.S. Navy in 1946. The term "Tuna Clippers" is used herein to identify both baitboats and purse seiners that are of U.S. flag documentation and of 100 gross tons or greater.

[5] "Problem of Aliens, . . . numerous charges have been made, specifically concerning Japanese tuna boats on the West Coast. Navy officials are said to look askance upon the presence of many alien fishing boats and crews in Los Angeles and San Diego harbors, where a large section of the U.S. naval fleet is stationed, regarding as undesirable and of possible danger." *Pacific Fisherman*, April 1935, p. 27.

A photo taken on August 14, 1935, in Bahía Magdalena, Baja California, showed 15 Tuna Clippers at anchor. The following 8 Clippers based in California ports flew the Japanese flag: SAN LUCAS, ENTERPRISE, HESTON, COLUMBUS, ALERT, OSPREY, ASAMA, and PANAMA. *Pacific Fisherman*, March 1935, p. 19, "Alien Subterfuge Charged."

See: Articles on actions taken by a U.S. Attorney against Japanese immigrant owners of commercial fishing vessels, as follows: *Pacific Fisherman*, June 1935, p.16, "Aliens Must Dispose of Shares in Boats of U.S. Registry;" *Pacific Fisherman*, July 1938, p. 25, "Three More Seiners Libelled as Aliens;" *Pacific Fisherman*, August 1938, p.25, "More Seiners Libelled by U.S. on Grounds of Illegal Registry;" *Pacific Fisherman*, September 1938, p. 35, "25 Fishing Vessels Seized by U.S. on Grounds of Alien Ownership," *Pacific Fisherman*, December 1939, p.35, "Japanese fishing Boats Shifted to U.S. Owners."

[6] *Pacific Fisherman*, July 1938, p.29, "San Pedro Seiners Pledged for War Use."

[7] *Pacific Fisherman*, March 1939, p. 25, "Spying Charge Denied."

[8] For a description of how the Japanese fishermen and their families residing on Terminal Island were treated by various federal agencies on December 7, 1941, and how the families responded to the 48-hour eviction notice, effective February 27, 1942, which was

authorized by FDR's Executive Order 9066, dated February 19, 1942: Yamashita, Kanshi Stanley (Lt. Colonel, U.S. Army, Ret.) University of California, Irvine, "Terminal Island: Ethnography: Its Dissolution and Reorganization to a Non-spatial Community," A dissertation submitted in partial satisfaction of the requirements for the degree of Doctor of Philosophy in Comparative Culture: 139-140.

[9] Each of the 16 Clippers was equipped with four Navy telephone sets; all CW sets aboard Clippers were retained. To efficiently man the 16 Clippers, a request was granted to enlist M2 Reserves, three chief petty officers per vessel, warrant machinists and boatswains, and two warrant officers per vessel. The plan was to have 14 men per vessel. No guns or depth charges were placed aboard these 16 Clippers. Source: National Archives-Pacific Region (Laguna Niguel) Telephone conversation between Captain E.W. Morris and Commander W.J. Morcott, Commandant's Office, Eleventh Naval District, San Diego, California, February 17, 1942. ND11/L8-3(a) Serial B(SD)-947.

See: Newspaper reports on WW II activities of tuna clippers converted to U.S. Navy Yard Patrol vessels (YPs): "Eight Tunaboats Kept by Navy; Five Released," *San Diego Union*, 06 January 1942, p. 7; "Blue Water Men of Tuna Fleet Write Sea Saga of Democracy," *San Diego Union*, 23 July 1943, p. B-1; By John Bunker, "Tuna Skippers Bare Wartime Role" *The San Diego Evening Tribune*, 26 February 1957, p. B-1; By John Bunker, "Tuna Boats Fuel Midway Guns" *The San Diego Evening Tribune*, 27 February 1957, p. B-1; By John Bunker, "Skipper Tells Of No. 1 Morale Run" *The San Diego Evening Tribune*, 01 March 1957, p. a-10; By John Bunker, "American Tunaboats Were In the Thick of WWII," National Fisherman, September 1970, p. 6-B; By Joe Brown, "As the Yippees Went to War" *San Diego Union*, 10 July 1960, pp. a-43 and a-46; By Tim Shepard, "Yippee There Went the Tunaboats to War," *San Diego Union*, 06 August 1967, p. G-2; By Ken Hudson, "Tuna Fleet Had World War Two Role," *San Diego Union*, 7 June 1977, p. B-1.

See: Interviews of tuna fishermen who served aboard YPs during World War II, and presentation of government documentation concerning pre-WW II interest of the U.S. Navy in the military value of tunaboats and other California commercial fishing vessels: University of San Diego, San Diego, "The "Pork Chop Express" San Diego's Tuna Fleet 1942-1945, A thesis submitted in partial satisfaction of the requirements for the degree of Master of Arts in History by Daniel M. Shapiro (1993).

[10] Yamashita, Kanshi Stanley (Lt. Colonel, U.S. Army, Ret.), University of California, Irvine, "Terminal Island: Ethnography: Its Dissolution and Reorganization to a Non-spatial Community," A dissertation submitted in partial satisfaction of the requirements for the degree of Doctor of Philosophy in Comparative Culture: 46, 57, note 7. "The interviews of some of the former Terminal Islanders all relate the bitter and unforgettable days and months . . . There were a few whose boats had been leased, but since the physical community of East San Pedro (Terminal Island) had been completely demolished, housing had to be found in the surrounding communities of Long Beach, Wilmington, or San Pedro. In contrast to the large number of **Nikkei** fishermen before the war, only a few resumed fishing . . . . The proximity of the three fish canneries in Long Beach to the trailer camp and the willingness of the operators to hire Japanese provided an opportunity for some of the *Issei* and a few *Nisei* women to work on the packing line.

Immediately after WW II, it has been claimed that only the following 10 commercial fishing vessels were operating from Southern California ports by citizens of Japanese descent: NANCY ROSE, STELLA MARIS, JEANETTE C, REDEEMER, WESTERN EX-PLORER, EL CAPITAN, UBUYU MARU, PATRIOTIC, JOHNNY BOY, and PACIFIC. This report claims that during 1936-1942, there were 79 vessels listed as being operated by "Terminal Islanders," and that 145 vessels were operated by "Terminal Islanders," during 1915-1936. Tatusmi, Yukio, Toshiro Izumi, Massaharu Tanibata, Kisaye N. Sato, Kenji Yamamoto, Tatsuo Shioji, and Bob Ryono, "Terminal Islander 25th Anniversary Brochure (1971-1996)," pp.48-57.

[11] The Federal Government requisitioned about 2,500 vessels of 1000 gross registered tons or less for use during the war. Title was acquired for about 2,000 vessels, and about 500 more were acquired on a bareboat charter basis. This fleet included fishing vessels, tugs, barges, small tankers, launches, cruisers, and yachts. The Navy, Army, and Coast Guard requisitioned about 600 fishing boats for emergency use. By the fall of 1944, approximately 142 chartered fishing vessels had been released by the War Shipping Administration. *Fisheries Market News*, Department of the Interior, Fish and Wildlife Service, (September 1944) Vol. 6, No. 9, p. 23.

A copy of a provision in a two-page "Bare-Boat Charter of Tuna Vessels" issued in San Diego stated: "Bare-boat charter requires the vessel to be returned to the owner in a condition at least as good as taken less ordinary wear and tear based on use of vessel for Naval purposes, or the United States shall pay to the owner an amount for reconditioning to place the vessel in such condition." Source: National Archives-Pacific Region (Laguna Niguel). "Commandant's Office, Eleventh Naval District, San Diego California, February 17, 1942, BARE-BOAT CHARTER OF TUNA VESSELS. ND11/L8-3(a) Serial B (SD)-948 for signature by W.J. Morcott, Copy for Chief of Staff." Of the 52 tuna Clippers acquired by the U.S. Military, the number taken under a Bare-Boat Charter is presently unknown.

[12] The name "MAHAMA" was based on the first two letters of Mary, Harold, and Marjorie; the wife, son, and daughter of M. Machado Medina.

[13] *Pacific Fisherman*, May 1946, pp. 61-62, "BERNADETTE---Able and Admirable Medina Clipper." Profile photo of vessel and photo of individuals involved in launching ceremony.

2

CAPTAIN, F/V **ALPHECCA,**
TUNA BAITBOAT

Fishing Record

During a 13-year period (April 1948 to August 1960), Harold commanded the ALPHECCA as a tuna baitboat on 42 fishing trips, recording a catch of 10,258 short tons of tuna (about 25 million cans of tuna) or over one million tunas during 2,884 days at sea. Although his fishing operations ranged from Baja California to waters off Chile, his favorite fishing grounds were located at the Galapagos Islands. He experimented with, and learned to fly, an onboard amphibian airplane in locating schools of tuna and baitfish. In 1949, Harold permitted a Federal Government biologist to make a fishing trip aboard his vessel for purposes of scientific study. During 1959, tuna biologists of the Inter-American Tropical Tuna Commission (IATTC) were also permitted aboard his vessel on two trips to study his fishing operations, tag tunas, and conduct other scientific studies related to tuna conservation and management.

Due to the loss of the SAN SALVADOR during military service in World War II, Harold's father was given an option to purchase a decommissioned U.S. Navy vessel. The SAN SALVADOR, renamed by the Navy as YP-

The ALPHECCA, a former US Navy vessel converted to a tuna baitboat.

281, foundered in the mid Pacific near the International dateline on January 9, 1944. The versatility of the converted Tuna Clippers to operate in the South Pacific for military purposes was proven very early during the war. They could carry perishable cargoes in their refrigerated fish wells, and also fuel and ammunition. They could carry troops into shallow waters of atolls, and their wood hulls provided immunity to most mines. For these and other reasons, the Navy built 30 vessels patterned after the Tuna Clipper design. In 1947, the YP-639 was purchased from the U.S. Navy for conversion to a Tuna Clipper baitboat by the Medina family and the San Diego tuna canner, Westgate Sea Products Co. Because of his familiarity with certain stars as navigational aids, Harold's father named the vessel ALPHECCA. During the vessel's conversion in San Diego at Campbell Shipyard, Harold helped to modify the engine room to tuna vessel standards.

First Generation Tuna Captains

During the 1948 maiden tuna fishing voyage aboard the ALPHECCA, Harold was taught how to navigate by his father and "Paper Captain" Frank V. Theodore. He learned how to take a sun line sight and to use the Bowditch tables[1], but was not taught how to take a star sight. As the vessel was prepared for the second voyage, Harold was named its new Captain. His father explained that it was the time "for the American generation to take over the business." Harold argued that he did not have sufficient navigational skills or command training. Machado answered that Harold had enough experience, training, and testing. Machado's decision to make his 21-year-old son Fish Captain was a cause of wonder within the close-knit tuna fishing community in San Diego. However, within a short time, others followed Machado's lead. Soon, many of Harold's boyhood friends became first-generation captains by succeeding their foreign-born fathers.

First Trip as Captain

Harold's navigational skills were quickly tested on his maiden voyage. While the vessel was approaching Cabo San Lucas, Baja California, Harold was struggling with poor visibility conditions while trying to determine his location. The radar seemed to show that he was heading into land masses. In response, Harold was continually changing course to avoid these radar images. He became seriously concerned about the safety of the vessel and more doubtful of his navigational ability. His use of the radar was convincing him that he was heading into danger until he discovered by observation the close relationships of radar targets and the presence of oncoming rain squalls. His earlier anxieties and fears had been caused by incorrectly interpreting the radar targets as land masses, rather than as rain squalls.

After receiving reports of a "Big Run" at the Galapagos Islands, Harold decided to make a 14-day trip to that destination. Both seiners and baitboats were making tuna catches in the vicinity of Isla Fernandina and off Cabo Berkeley, Isla Isabela. Baitfish were plentiful. Upon arrival, Joe Marques, Captain of the NORMANDIE, invited him to come aboard for a meeting. Captain Marques commanded the largest Tuna Clipper in the fleet, and his success in fishing at the Galapagos Islands for both tuna and baitfish was legendary. For over two hours, Captain Marques used his confidential fishing charts to show Harold the area's best fishing and baiting locations. This instruction was unique, and Harold has been forever appreciative of this Captain's kindness and friendship. The following day, Harold obtained bait and joined other vessels in the search for the tunas. Within a few days, it became clear that the "Big Run" was suddenly and unexpectedly over. Harold reluctantly decided to leave and search for the tunas off Costa Rica and Panama. After about 90 days, low supplies and crew fatigue forced the vessel's return to San Diego with about 175 tons, 100 tons short of a full load. During the trip, the disappointed and stressed Harold lost over 15 pounds. The trip's misfortunes had created personal doubts and concerns about his ability to successfully command the ALPHECCA.

On the third trip, Harold's father joined the ship. The voyage turned out well, and Machado was satisfied with his son's work and fishing judgments. He asked Harold to take command on the fourth trip. Again, Harold headed for the Galapagos Islands, after receiving reports of good fishing. Fishing was highly successful; Harold concluded that it was a "turnaround trip." Thereafter, Harold's father never found it necessary to accompany Harold on the ALPHECCA. Harold's confidence in fishing at the Galapagos Islands increased through the years. About two-thirds of the ALPHECCA'S fishing trips under his command were made at these islands. He became as familiar and confident in navigating about these islands as if he were in San Diego Harbor. The Galapagos Islands region was personally enjoyable because it was a "warm-water fishing area" in contrast to the turbulent and cold water off Baja California. It was also a good fishing location for both baitfish and tunas, which produced uncommon economic advantages. Generally, tuna fishing occurred on the high seas off Mexico and Central America, while fishing for baitfish occurred in bays and estuaries. The need to leave the fishing grounds on the high seas and return to baiting grounds along the coast were costly in time and fuel, and they could cause the vessel to miss the "fishing cycle."

Harold learned much in commanding a crew of 11 to 13 men during this 13-year period (1947-1959). Crew changes aboard the ALPHECCA averaged only about one man per year. This low rate of turnover was in part due to a fundamental principle adopted by Harold. In obedience to his "Golden Rule," Harold would not ask any crewmember to do anything that he would not do himself. Further, he would usually be directly involved in whatever the crew was doing. Harold worked constantly to learn as much as possible about all of the workings of the baitboat operation. He became competent in maintaining and repairing the ship's machinery, engines, and other mechanical systems; knowledgeable in the use of navigational aids; skillful in sighting and catching baitfish; talented in crafting fishing poles and bait nets; artful in working tuna and tuna/porpoise schools; competitive in the fishing racks, and proficient in navigation and in maneuvering the ALPHECCA. He even learned how to fly a seaplane placed aboard the vessel during the mid-1950s for use in searching for bait and tuna schools.

The Captain's Duty: Find the Tunas

During the 13-year operation of the ALPHECCA as a tuna baitboat, the tuna grounds for California-based vessels ranged in an irregular seaward band along the hemisphere's coastline from San Diego, California, to about Antofagasta, Chile. The dependence upon baiting grounds limited baitboat operations to waters relatively close to the coast and offshore islands and banks. Weather conditions also constrained searching operations, especially during the summer "hurricane" season that prevailed in the area from Guatemala to northern Baja California. For instance, baitboats of less than 200 tons capacity would fish in the Gulf of California, from Guaymas to the Islas Tres Marias to Cabo San Lucas during November to May. Fishing off the Pacific coast of Baja California was usually best during June, July, August, and September when warm waters were pushed northward by the tropical storms and hurricanes. These storms would cause dangerous sea conditions off the Mexican coast from the Gulf of Tehuantepec to areas inside and about the Gulf of California. Before June and after October, the Middle American Trench, which extends from Cabo Corrientes, Mexico, to the Golfo de Tehuantepec, would be fished by tunaboats. In this area, they would find numerous yellowfin schools mixed with porpoise. During the first six months of the year, tuna schools, especially skipjack, were found in waters within sight of giant volcanoes located in Honduras and Nicaragua. In this area, tuna baitboats found that tunas mixed with porpoise were especially abundant during the periods of January to May and October to December. The region from Costa Rica to Colombia also produced excellent fishing on floating debris for about six months.

Tuna Searching

Aboard the ALPHECCA, Harold and the crew were constantly searching for signs of tuna schools. Bird activity was the key clue for those using the high-powered, surplus military binoculars installed on the bridge. Schools of tuna, mixed with porpoise, always attracted birds. Floating debris was also a target of this search because small fishes were usually found milling about the debris, including tree stumps and branches, which is why tuna fishermen coined the term "log fishing." For yet unexplained reasons, tunas were also found with other objects, such as rope, wooden hatch covers, tanks, or partially submerged dead whales. Eye fatigue in using the military binoculars was a factor that caused search watches to be of short duration. By the early 1950s, the San Diego tuna fleet was experimenting with helicopters and seaplanes for use in searching for live bait and tuna schools. The ALPHECCA first used a Piper Cub during 1955. It was carried on the canopy above the bait tank, and was lifted to and from the ocean with the ship's boom. In 1956, the use of this fishing tool aboard the ALPHECCA ended when the seaplane flipped over and sank while being lifted aboard.

Tuna Fishing Banks

Bountiful tuna grounds or "banks" have been named after Tuna Clippers, *e.g.* NORMANDIE, PICAROTO, PARAMOUNT, BERNADETTE, NAVIGATOR, GOLDEN GATE, RANGER, UNCLE SAM, LUSITANIA, and ALPHECCA. Other fishing banks have been named after Tuna Captains who discovered their locations, *e.g.* Morgan (Harold), Rosa (Victor), and Brito (Lou). Some are identified by a physical characteristic, *e.g.* Ecuador's "Guayaquil Bank," Peru's "14-fathom spot," Mexico's "450-fathom spot," and "Finger Bank." Some fishing banks have names given for obvious reasons, such as "Cadillac Bank" and "Hurricane Bank."[2] All of the major islands in the eastern Pacific Ocean (EPO) have been searched by U.S. Tuna Baitboats for the presence of tuna and live bait.[3]

In early 1929, the HERMOSA, based in San Pedro, California, was the first tunaboat to fish at Isla Cocos, Costa Rica. The identity of the first California Tuna Clipper to fish at the Galapagos Islands has not been established with certainty, but it is clear that fishing first took place there in late 1929. Captain Frank Medina told the author Felando that the ADVENTURER was the first tuna clipper to fish for tuna at the Galapagos Islands, but no government information to confirm this claim has not been found. Reports in fishery magazines published in 1930 make mention of the first San Diego- based Clippers making trips to the Galapagos Islands after receiving reports that tunas were caught there by a San Pedro-based Clipper in 1929. Some reports claim that this vessel was the HERMOSA, and others imply that it was the ADVENTURER. Tuna Captains have always been secretive as to their tuna fishing locations. This was particularly true during the early years when the fleet expanded its pursuit of the tunas beyond Mexico. Scientists employed by the California Department of Fish and Game established a program to obtain fishing information from many Tuna Captains after assuring them that the fishing data would remain confidential. These government records may be the only source of reliable data to establish the identity of the first Tuna Clipper to fish at the Galapagos Islands.

ALPHECCA'S Best Fishing Day and Trip

The best fishing day was the taking of 85 tons (over 4,800 two-pole yellowfin) on Guayaquil Bank, Ecuador. Harold recalls that he was maneuvering on the tuna school from sunrise to sunset. Fishing was interrupted because of the need to load the fish wells with the tunas that filled the deck behind the fishing racks. But for this delay, Harold claims that the eight-man fishing team would have caught over 100 tons, or about 5,700 two-pole yellowfin.

Harold's best fishing trip, in terms of effort, value of catch, tonnage landed, and duration of the voyage, occurred at the Galapagos Islands, near Isla Rabida. Each day, about 25 tons of heavy one-pole yellowfin were landed and refrigerated, followed by the movement to nearby baiting grounds for replenishment of the boat's bait supply. During the last week of the fishing trip, the vessel was drifting and enjoying a morning of exciting one-pole fishing. Harold left his position at the Bridge and went into the fishing racks. While fishing, Harold noticed that the vessel was very close to the island; he ran to the Bridge and

Captain Harold Medina at the wheel on the baitboat ALPHECCA.

found that the vessel was in very shallow water. He started the main engine to pull away from the island. As the vessel moved ahead, it collided with a submerged rock, causing the ALPHECCA to roll to its starboard side. When it rolled to the port, the stacked tuna washed over the bulwarks into the ocean. Then, Harold saw that the bow was rising and falling and that the stern was also moving up and down. Deciding that the vessel was free from the ocean bottom because of the tuna falling overboard, Harold "kicked it slowly ahead." Later, crewmembers dove to confirm that a rock pinnacle had gouged the vessel's hull. Shortly afterward, the ALPHECCA "topped off" its load, permitting Harold to record his first and only grounding experience at the Galapagos Islands.

Harold's Favorite Fishing Area: Galapagos Islands

The vast majority of the ALPHECCA"S fishing trips occurred in this region. Harold was of the opinion that fishing at the Galapagos Islands could be good at any time of the year.

The first U.S. Tuna Clippers fishing off the Galapagos Islands found that they had to dive and manipulate the bait net about the rocky bottom in order to capture a school of baitfish. Within a decade, the catching of live bait changed from "free diving" to the use of diving equipment. The ALPHECCA was equipped with the standard diving tools used to catch bait at the Galapagos Islands, and this fact also influenced Harold's first decision to fish at the Islands. The voyage was not only Harold's maiden voyage as a Captain of a Tuna Clipper; it was also his first use of a diving helmet. A school of sardines was found swimming about the main engine of the sunken San Diego tunaboat TRIUNFO. The bait net had to be placed around the sunken remains of the engine. With the help of the crew, Harold put on the diving helmet and shoulder weights. Rather than grasping the lead line of the bait net to slowly move down to the bottom, Harold was alongside the vessel when lowering his head downward toward the sunken engine. To Harold's surprise, he quickly sank helmet and head first, "as fast as a torpedo" to the bottom some 24 feet below. Fortunately, he escaped serious injury, but not embarrassment.

Two divers are required to handle the Bait Net, working as follows: one diver would pull the net away from the rocks as the other would pull the lead line and slack net toward the net's center. When so working, sharks would often appear and become a serious threat to the divers. Harold recalled the incident involving two "white-tip" sharks in the bait net while he and another diver were working in the net. The sharks ranged in length from about 8 to 9 feet. As the sharks maneuvered within the net, Harold noticed a rapid upward movement to the surface by his partner. In reaction to this unexpected maneuver, Harold decided to carefully continue with his working of the net. Later, the other Diver explained that his escape from the net was prompted by fear of being attacked by the two sharks. Unlike other vessels, the ALPHECCA did not experience shark attacks during baiting operations at the Galapagos Islands. When sharks were found in the ALPHECCA'S bait net, they were removed alive without risk to the fishermen.

Sardines were the most important live bait fished at the Galapagos Islands. The "bohunks" would be about six inches in length and the "pinheads" from two to three inches in length. Tuna Clippers also used a flat fish called "salima" as live bait. During his many years of fishing at the Galapagos Islands, Harold would experience only a few days of delay in locating and catching baitfish. Unlike fishing for tuna along the coasts of Mexico and Central America, both baitfish and tuna were available at the Galapagos Islands, which reduced the "dead time" required to catch bait and return to the fishing grounds.

Harold participated in a 10-member "Code Group" composed of young Captains who were also boyhood friends. Annually, the Captains would meet to evaluate the effectiveness of their organization, changing the code, and sometimes removing a member for violations of the "Code." Captains in Harold's Code Group were selected and retained because of their success in discovering new fishing areas and willingness to tell the truth about their daily fishing results.

As part of the process in deciding where best to fish, Harold would perform the following daily navigation tasks: (1) take a morning fix one-half hour before sunrise; (2) two morning running fixes; (3) a noon sight; (4) two afternoon running fixes before sunset, and (5) an evening sight. A summary of this information, along with the ALPHECCA'S current fishing activity, would be sent to the vessels of the Code Group during a pre-arranged daily 15-minute radio exchange. Harold would decode the information received, and then decide whether to remain in the area or move to a new area reported by a member of the Code Group.

In order to concentrate on his duty to find tunas, Harold employed an engineer (called in the Fleet as the "Chief") to ensure that the ship's machinery was always in good working order. Further, and most importantly, the Chief was responsible for proper storage of the catch. On the ALPHECCA, both at sea and at anchor or tied up at a dock, the Chief was the most important member of the crew. To reduce the days spent in port between trips and in making trip turnarounds efficient, a good Chief was essential. As the ALPHECCA was homeward bound, the Chief prepared the engine room work list. He supervised the engine room repair work in port, and worked directly with shipyard employees and other repairers. Harold's experience in the engine room aboard the BERNADETTE was of great value in working with the Chief aboard the ALPHECCA. Harold often labored in the engine room with the Chief, both at sea and in port. In this way, Harold increased his ability to deal effectively and efficiently with his ship's mechanical problems. The result was more productive time fishing for the tunas.

Unlike handling information on where and how the tunas were biting, Skippers in the fleet were shrewdly cooperative with others in providing reliable intelligence on availability of bait. The need to obtain bait during a fishing trip was common to all baitboat captains; it was the one task that had to be performed before a captain commenced intense and war-like competition on the tuna grounds. Enough risks existed in searching and catching the tunas, so why impose further hardships on your peers by denying them information on "getting bait." Besides that, you might be in the same position someday. It was a friendly gesture that could later pay dividends.

To illustrate some of the unfriendly gestures resulting from the competitive spirit of Tuna Clipper Captains by providing deceptive information as to where the tunas were biting, Harold recalls the following events:

Upon entering Bahia James, Isla San Salvador, early in the evening, he spotted the Tuna Clipper MARY E. PETRICH at anchor. He decided to anchor the AL-PHECCA close behind so that he would be able to conveniently visit the ship and ask about fishing conditions. That evening he took the small skiff and went aboard the MARY E. PETRICH. As he headed for mid-ship, he smelled the presence of freshly caught tuna, and asked a crewmember working on the main deck about fishing. This crewmember told him that they were not doing much, and then turned away to continue his work. However, Harold noticed fish slime about the crewmember's freshly-washed neck. Harold then talked to the Captain of the MARY E. PETRICH, and was again told that fishing had met with little success. Harold advised this Captain that he planned to look for bait on grounds near Cabo Nepean and maybe check out fishing conditions at Isla Rabida or Isla Jarvis. In fact, Harold moved to a location that would make it possible for him to discreetly observe the movements of the MARY C. PETRICH. Upon spotting the MARY E. PETRICH travel toward Isla Isabela, he pushed the eight-knot AL-PHECCA in pursuit. The MARY E. PETRICH was a newly-built vessel with a cruising speed of 13 knots, and considered to be one of the fastest vessels in the Fleet. In time, Harold's suspicions were proven correct; the trailing ALPHECCA found the MARY E. PETRICH fishing among numerous biting schools of skip-jack. Later, another incident illustrating the competitive spirit within the fleet involved these two vessels. Both were homeward bound and fully loaded. At the cannery, the unloading schedule was based upon the principle of first come, first served. Abeam Isla Jeronimo, Baja California, the ALPHECCA was overtaken by the MARY E. PETRICH. While the two vessels were moving alongside and within earshot, the crew of the MARY E. PETRICH scornfully tossed toilet paper at the crew aboard the laboring ALPHECCA. When the ALPHECCA arrived near Point Loma early the next morning, it found the MARY E. PETRICH at anchor outside the harbor's entrance. It had arrived too early to tie alongside the dock operated by the U.S. Customs Service. Until entry was approved or "cleared" by U.S. Customs, no person was allowed to leave a vessel that had left a port of the United States and touched a foreign port during its voyage. The turtle-like moving ALPHECCA continued onward to San Diego Harbor and won the race to the U.S. Customs dock for clearance.

Craftiness and deceit were also practiced by some of Harold's relatives. Joe Machado, a cousin and Captain of the Tuna Clipper QUEEN MARY, was a member of Harold's Code Group. For three consecutive days, Joe was reporting to Harold that he was not having much success, but kept advising Harold that he had not moved from a location off Punta Albermarle for three days. Later, Harold discovered that the reason that Joe was not moving was that the QUEEN MARY was having considerable fishing success. Harold and his first cousin Carl Medina, Captain of the MAY QUEEN, were fishing on a shallow spot next to Roca Esta, on the west side of Isla San Cristobal (Isla Chatham). At first, fishing was excellent, and then, within a few days, there were "no signs" of fish. Harold left the area and traveled to the "Lava Flows" off Isla Santa Isabela. Harold and Carl were members of same Code Group. However, it became apparent to Harold that Carl was not providing reliable daily catch information. When Harold would report a 35-ton catch day, Carl would report a 40-ton day. Carl was always doing about 5 tons a day better than Harold. When fishing became slow off the "Lava Flows," Harold went back to the shallow spot next to Roca Esta, San Cristobal, the location where he and Carl had found excellent fishing. The ALPHECCA was alone, and Harold was reluctant to contact Carl and did not want to alert other vessels to his location. Yet, under the rules of the Code Group, he was obligated to contact Carl and inform him of his fishing success. The radio aboard the AL-

PHECCA had a transmitter of 1000 watts, but by removing the antenna the radio call could be heard only by boats relatively close to the ALPHECCA. Nevertheless, by making this effort, Harold could truthfully say that he had made an effort to radio a fellow Code Group member. He felt that the burden was now on Carl to hear his radio call. Harold did not change this radio tactic until the ALPHECCA was nearly loaded. On a day that the vessel was at anchor to work on the main engine, Harold was listening to a radio conver-

Circa 1956, Crew of ALPHECCA using pole and line with live bait to catch tuna.

sation between Carl and another Captain, Joey Lewis. With his powerful 1000-watt radio and antenna in place, Harold called Carl. Carl did not return the call. Joey Lewis heard Harold's call and told Carl that Harold was calling. Carl told Joey that he didn't want to talk to Harold. Harold then transmitted in "plain language" the fact that he was off the west side of San Cristobal, and that he expected to load up his vessel the following day and be homeward bound. Harold also declared that he had tried to make radio contact with Carl, but that Carl either did not hear the call or did not want to respond to it. According to the rules prevailing, Harold's action in calling Carl had excused him from being charged with "shafting" a fellow member of the Code Group. This was the last effort by Harold to communicate fishing information with Carl. Afterward, Harold and Carl were no longer members of the same Code Group. The next day, the Tuna Clipper COMMODORE was alongside the anchored ALPHECCA. They had overheard Harold's radio transmission to Carl. Harold told Captain Sam Navarro to stand by and that he would take him to the shallow spot where he expected to load-up his vessel.

Off Cabo Woodford, Isla Isabela, Harold was fishing in company with the tuna clipper ECUADOR, commanded by his boyhood friend Eugene Cabral. Good fishing signs prevailed in the area, but the tunas could not be tempted into a "feeding frenzy." During the afternoon of the day that Harold expected the arrival of the QUEEN MARY from Panama, Captain Cabral decided to scout a different fishing location. Unlike Harold, he had no reason to stay in the area. The QUEEN MARY, commanded by Harold's first cousin Joe Medina, was bringing much-needed diesel fuel and supplies for the ALPHECCA. Cabo Pinzón, Isla Duncan, was the agreed point of transfer. At the time that Harold saw the tip of the mast of the ECUADOR on the distant horizon, the tunas started a "feeding frenzy" for the crew of the ALPHECCA. Harold did not call Captain Cabral and tell him of the change in fishing conditions, as the ECUADOR was not a member of Harold's Code Group. According to the rules prevailing, Harold's action was proper; Harold had not given Captain Cabral "the shaft."

Harold's boyhood friend, Captain Roland Virissimo, of the HORNET, was fishing successfully on BERNADETTE BANK but transmitting in plain language on the radio that he was having no success in finding fish and that he was scouting for signs. Harold was about halfway to BERNADETTE BANK when told by Roland that there were no fish on the Bank. Harold and Roland were not members of the same Code Group. After conversing with Roland, he decided to reverse course and head back to Isla Santa Maria. Later, Harold discovered that at the time of his conversation with Roland, the HORNET was experiencing fantastic fishing success, even though almost out of bait. The skipjack schools were in such a biting frenzy that they would remain alongside even though the chum was comprised of only a few fish at a time. At Isla Santa Maria, Harold found no bait or biting tuna. Roland had "shafted" Harold for a second time. Roland's action to misrepresent tuna fishing conditions when conversing with a competitor was "common practice" in the fleet, and was recognized by all skippers as "part of the game" being played at sea.

A classic case of being "shafted" by your fellow Code Group Member: The NORMANDIE, commanded by the legendary Captain Joe Marques, was on the radio asking Captain Eugene Cabral of the ECUADOR about fishing conditions. Both were members of the same Code Group. Captain Cabral told Captain Marques that he was not catching any fish. Shortly after this radio conversation, the NORMANDIE'S seaplane flew over the ECUADOR and sighted the port stern rail full of tuna and the crew in the racks pulling tuna at full speed.

The "Chubasco" Surprise

Tropical storms, which occur in the EPO north of the Equator from June to October, are first generated off the coasts of Nicaragua or Guatemala. They travel a northward path toward Mexico, chugging off the coast as they grow and gain more power. When reaching Hurricane strength (64 or more knots on the Beaufort scale), some have been very destructive to Mexican ports. American tuna fishermen have long named these storms "Chubascos.[4]

As Chubascos near the entrance to the Gulf of California, some will enter the Gulf, but most will travel northward, and then head west toward the Islas Revillagigedo (Socorro, San Benedicto, Roca Partida, and Clarion). Most of them will eventually head toward the Hawaiian Islands. Sometimes, a Chubasco will gravitate to the mid-section of the west coast of Baja California before making its left turn. In 1939, one Chubasco, having Hurricane strength, neared Southern California before heading west toward Hawaii.

In July 1957, the ALPHECCA was working off Baja California. Fishing was slow, so Harold decided to head toward tuna fishing grounds aptly named "Hurricane Bank." This fishing spot is located some 100 miles northwest of Isla Socorro. As the ALPHECCA was traveling about 150 miles northeast of the shallow bank, the weather was calm, with a deep and large southwest swell. The ship's barometer was moving at about 29.85 inches. It was the time of the year when Hurricanes would be visiting this area, so his decision was risky. One crewmember, "Tiny," decided to have some fun with the cook, who was making his first tuna fishing trip. "Tiny" went into the galley and advised the cook that he should immediately put on his life jacket, warning that if the ALPHECCA is struck with stormy weather the waves will first hit the mid-section of the vessel and wipe out the galley. Later that day, Harold entered the galley and found the cook wearing his life jacket while he worked. When asked why he was wearing a life jacket, the cook explained that the vessel would soon be in a bad storm, that the large waves would first hit the galley and that the life jacket would provide safety. Harold decided not to discuss the matter further, guessing that crewmembers were having some fun with a naive and impressionable cook. At dinnertime, Harold decided not to go to the galley but remain on the Bridge. The cook joined Harold on the Bridge, asking why Harold was not eating. Harold replied that he was not hungry. Later, the cook brought Harold some coffeecake, advising that he should have something to eat before the storm enveloped the vessel.

The next morning the 128' ALPHECCA was fishing for tuna on "Hurricane Bank." At about daybreak, fishing was particularly good. The tuna were being hooked and tossed aboard at good rate and the sea conditions were acceptable. At about noon, Harold noticed a fast and substantial change in the weather. Within an hour, the ALPHECCA was in heavy seas and weather, and Harold had to maneuver the vessel so as to accommodate the huge waves. By four in the afternoon, the ALPHECCA was in a Chubasco with Hurricane strength. The Barometer had dropped to 28.65 inches. It was the lowest pressure that Harold had ever seen in over 10 years at sea. The wind was gusting as high as 120 knots. Waves were reaching heights of at least 25 feet and easily breaking over the bow, smashing into the deckhouse, the Bridge, and the pilothouse.

Harold recalled: "It was not a happy time." The Chief Engineer called me while I was on the Bridge, advising me that a lot of water was coming down the smoke stack into the engine room and threatening the electrical switchboard. I grabbed two crewmembers, including "Tiny," and we headed out onto the deck with canvas to cover the openings of the smoke stack. The wind was so strong that the canvas was forced onto the stack and we could not move it into a different position. I went down to the engine room to see what could be done to stop the water from destroying the ship's electrical system. I could see the water coming down the smoke stack, working its way toward the switchboard. I grabbed a collision mat from the bow storage and nailed this double canvas mat (10 feet by 10 feet) to the overhead beams separating the smoke stack and switchboard. This quick fix forced the water to fall onto the main engine below and then flow into the bilge for pumping back into the ocean. "It worked very well."

When Harold returned to the Bridge, he was told that smoke was coming from the Chief's room. It was necessary to open the pilothouse door to go to the decks below and check out the Chief's room. As Harold opened the pilothouse door, the wind pulled the door from his hand and it slammed onto the doorstopper, splitting about five inches off the end of a solid, two-inch door. As Harold struggled down the ladder and opened the door leading to Chief's room, again the door was taken from his hands by the wind and then smashed onto the stopper, splitting inches off the end of the door. No fire was seen in the Chief's room. Harold went back to the Bridge, and asked two crewmembers to go to his room and bail and dump the water into the toilet. The door leading to the Captain's room was locked with a blanket stuffed into the broken end of the door. However, the waves were hitting the cabin with such force that the wedged blanket would be forced back into the room allowing more water into the cabin. Two other men were placed in the crewmembers' section of the deckhouse, where four bunks were located, and two men were placed into the crewmembers' section, where eight bunks were located. These four crewmembers were engaged in bailing out the flow of water into this part of the deckhouse. The crew's critical battle to survive the storm lasted over eight hours before the seas and wind began to slacken. During this difficulty, Harold's eight-year-old son Gary was shouting with glee whenever the waves pounded the ship. He had no understanding or appreciation of the dangerous plight of the ALPHECCA. It was his first fishing trip aboard his father's ship—a summer vacation.

During the struggle, an old-timer shouted a promise to Harold that if he made it home alive, that he would never go back to sea again. Harold recalled: "At the time this desperate promise was made, I did not think we were going to make it either. This was the only storm that gave me this negative feeling, and I've seen a lot of rough weather, but never this rough. Fortunately, the wood-hull ALPHECCA had proven again that, without doubt, it was a good, sea-going vessel."

As the ocean calmed further at sunset, Harold and his crew discovered that the 20-foot "Skiff" had been swept overboard and lost, that the Crow's Nest was blown away and destroyed, that part of the Bridge's railing was washed overboard, and that the deckhouse was severely damaged. The storm had soaked almost every bunk in the crew's section of the deckhouse, forcing the crew to sleep in the engine room. Meanwhile, the cook was found to have slept through the storm, apparently secure and warm in this bunk with his life jacket. The next morning, he greeted his fellow crewmembers, especially "Tiny," in the galley with a smile and a table filled with breakfast offerings.

---

[1] Nathaniel Bowditch (1773-1838), author of the New American Practical Navigator, published in 1802, is generally recognized as the founder of modern maritime navigation.

[2] Brito Bank-by Captain Lou Brito off Central America; NAVIGATOR Bank by Captain Manuel Neves off Cabo Mala, Panama; WHITE STAR Bank, Panama Bight; Cadillac Bank, 175 miles north of the Galapagos Islands by Captain Joe Madruga; PARAMOUNT Bank by Captain George Zeluff, near Cadillac Bank.

[3] "These grounds [off Mexico] were opened in 1922 and produced 100% of the U.S. Tuna Fleet's catch from 1922 to 1930: 1. Ranger Bank; 2. San Benito grounds; 3. Abreojos grounds; 4. Cape Haro grounds; 5. Uncle Sam Bank; 6. Cape Lazaro grounds; 7. Cape Tosco grounds; 8. Ceralbo [sic] grounds; 9. Morgan Bank; 10. Soa [sic] Joa [sic]; 11. Cape San Lucas grounds; 12. Punta Gorda Grounds; 13. Inner San Lucas grounds; 14. San Juanito Island grounds; 15. Tres Marias Bank; 16. Benedicto Island grounds; 17. Roca Partrida [sic] Island grounds; 18. Clarion Island grounds; 19. Socorro Island grounds; 20. Corvetena Rock grounds.

"These grounds [off Costa Rica, Panama, and Ecuador] were opened in 1931. Of total United States catch, they produced 30% in 1931, 40% in 1932, and 50% in 1933. 21. Various banks, Manzanillo to Tequepa Bay; 22. Acapulco grounds; 23. C. Elena grounds; 24. C. Blanco grounds; 25. Quepos Point grounds; 26. Matapalo Point grounds; 27. Hermosa Point grounds; 28. Cocos Island grounds; 29. Negada [sic] Point grounds; 30. Mariato Point grounds; 31. Morro Puercos grounds; 32. C. Mala grounds; 33. Malpelo Island grounds; 34. Galapagos Island [sic] grounds." United States Tariff Commission Report to the United States Senate on Tuna Fish under the general provisions of Section 332, Title III, Part II, Tariff Act of 1930, in compliance with Senate Resolution 159, dated January 30, 1934. Report No. 109 Second Series.(1936): 23.

[4] Names of Tropical storms differ in the world's oceans. They are known as hurricanes in the western North Atlantic, the eastern North Pacific, and the western South Pacific. They are known as cyclones in areas of the Indian Ocean. In the western North Pacific, tropical storms are known as typhoons. Tropical storms are "intense depressions around which the wind circulates anti-clockwise in the northern hemisphere . . . frequently at hurricane strength . . . (causing) very heavy seas, with torrential rain and driven spray reducing the visibility almost to nothing . . . Because of their extreme intensity, with the area of storm concentrated in a small area, they can be immensely destructive." Peter Kemp, ed., *The Oxford Companion to Ships & the Sea*, (London: Oxford University Press, 1976), 892-893.

3

CAPTAIN, F/V **SAN JOAQUIN,** **CONVERTED TUNA SEINER**

Fishing Record

The SAN JOAQUIN started its maiden trip as a converted tuna seiner based in San Diego on February 8, 1961. Harold's father hired Harold as Captain, with the duty of finding schools of tuna. A San Pedro tuna fisherman was hired as "Mastman," whose duty was to make the "sets" of the purse seine on schools of tunas. The vessel completed the trip and returned to San Diego on March 16, 1961. The boat made 27 "sets," 23 of which were made on tuna/porpoise schools. The Mastman hired for the trip made nine consecutive "skunk sets," which failed to encircle the tuna/porpoise schools, so Harold took over the job of "Mastman." On his first "set" on a tuna/porpoise school he was successful, catching about 28 tons of tuna. Within a short time, the vessel had a full load of 205 tons of yellowfin tuna, and Harold had his baptism as Captain and Mastman of a converted tuna seiner.

Harold remembers the exact day in August 1960 when he decided to quit the command of the ALPHECCA. The ALPHECCA and the Converted Tuna Seiner, SOUTHERN PACIFIC, were traveling together off the coast of Mexico, near "Tartar Shoals."[1] Both vessels had just departed the port of San Diego. Lou Brito, Captain of the SOUTHERN PACIFIC, advised Harold during a radio conversation that he planned to search for tunas in the area of the Gulf of Tehuantepec. Harold replied that he was taking his customary voyage to the Galapagos Islands, to catch baitfish and then search for the tunas. After parting company with the SOUTHERN PACIFIC, it took the ALPHECCA three days to get to the Galapagos Islands. On the day that the ALPHECCA commenced its search for live bait, Harold was informed that the SOUTHERN PACIFIC was homeward bound with a full load of yellowfin tuna. That was the moment when Harold decided that he wanted command of a Tuna Seiner, and that he would tell his father that if the ALPHECCA was not converted to a Tuna Seiner, he would quit and seek a command on a Tuna Seiner. After completing his 60-day tuna fishing voyage at the Galapagos Islands, Harold met with his father. Arrangements were made to finance the conversion of the ALPHECCA, estimated at over $150,000.

While considering his decision to quit the ALPHECCA and asking his father to convert it to a Tuna Seiner, he remembered the thoughts of his wife Emily at a particularly frustrating time in his fishing career. In June 1957, the ALPHECCA had grounded off Punta Santo Domingo, Baja California, about 400 miles south of San Diego. At the time, the vessel was loaded with 175 tons of tuna. After the tuna catch was thrown overboard, a salvage tug towed the heavily damaged vessel to San Diego for major repairs. Emily suggested to Harold that he use this opportunity to convert the vessel to a Tuna Seiner. Both knew that the future of the San Diego Tuna Industry was grim; increasing imports of frozen and canned tuna from Japan had shut down four of the six tuna canneries operating in San Diego. Many of their friends in the San Diego Tuna Baitboat Fleet were in serious financial trouble. Trying to be helpful, Emily reminded Harold that nets were used during the times of Jesus Christ to catch fish, and that maybe this was the better way to catch the tunas. Now, four years later, Harold would find out whether Emily's vision was correct.

First Trip Aboard the Converted Tuna Seiner SAN JOAQUIN

While Harold was working to complete his U.S. Coast Guard examinations for an Unlimited Master License, his father requested that he take over command of the SAN JOAQUIN, a converted Tuna Seiner. Harold was told that his boyhood friend, Bill Magellan, had been selected to be the Fish Captain of the SAN JOAQUIN, but that Bill had been persuaded by Lou Brito to take over command of the SOUTHERN

Captain Lou Brito and the SOUTHERN PACIFIC, a converted seiner.
Courtesy of Mrs. Mary Brito;
Vessel photo courtesy of *National Fisherman*
Vessel built by J.M. Martinac Shipbuilding Corporation, Tacoma, Washington

PACIFIC. Captain Brito was completing the construction of his new Tuna Seiner, the ROYAL PACIFIC, in Tacoma, Washington, and needed a new Captain to operate the SOUTHERN PACIFIC. At the time of his father's urgent plea, Harold required time to complete one more written examination to obtain his Unlimited Master's license. Harold, to his everlasting regret, left San Pedro with a Limited (Fishing) Master's License, and took over command of the Converted Tuna Seiner SAN JOAQUIN.

When Harold boarded the SAN JOAQUIN, he found it manned by a crew hired by Bill Magellan. Pete De Luca was hired as the Mastman and Deck Boss. Harold understood that his duty was to navigate the vessel and find the tunas. Mastman/Deck Boss De Luca was hired to capture the tunas with the purse seine (net), and then supervise the crew in transferring the tunas from the net to the vessel's fish wells. Off Acajutla, El Salvador, Harold placed the vessel on tuna/porpoise schools. Following the command of Mastman De Luca, Harold navigated the vessel around and around the mixed school of tuna and porpoise, which allowed Mastman De Luca to observe the reactions of the tuna and porpoise to an encircling maneuver. From his position on the bridge, Harold could do the same thing. Harold's years of tuna baitboat fishing on tuna/porpoise schools, along with his experience of setting a net about schools of baitfish, came into play during this evaluation. In making a "set," or in laying out the tuna purse seine, Mastman De Luca would move the vessel abeam of the leading, leaping porpoise, keeping them in view on the port side of the vessel. Then, he would order an increase in the speed of the SAN JOAQUIN for the purpose of developing a lead over the moving tuna/porpoise school. After deciding that the "lead" was sufficient, De Luca would shout the order of "mola" for the release of the purse seine. This order would be executed by releasing the Net Skiff astern of the SAN JOAQUIN. One end of the rectangular shaped net was aboard the SAN JOAQUIN and the other was secured to the Net Skiff. Mastman De Luca would direct Harold in the vessel's movements around the tuna/porpoise school. When the SAN JOAQUIN and the Net Skiff came "bow to bow" the end of the net held by the Net Skiff would be transferred to the SAN JOAQUIN. Then the "purse line," a steel cable strung through steel rings attached to the bottom of the net, would be retrieved with the winch, closing the bottom of the net and trapping the tunas. If the tunas escape during this operation, which is often the case, the set is called a "skunk set."[2]

After making a number of skunk sets, Harold formed the opinion that Mastman De Luca did not know how to properly encircle a moving tuna/porpoise school. He felt that Mastman De Luca was "leading" the school too much, and that the correct tactic would be to commence the encircling without "leading" the target section of the mixed school. He proposed to Mastman De Luca: that he again try to capture a school, but if skunked, then Harold would make the next set. Mastman De Luca was again skunked on the next set of the net. To retrieve the net after skunking would take the crew at least 60 minutes, provided that nothing went wrong with deck gear or the net retrieval process. When Harold set the net on the next school, he captured 35 tons of tuna. After observing Harold's success, Mastman De Luca went into the Galley and refused to perform his job as Deck Boss. Fortunately, other crewmembers were familiar with the process of "sacking" the net and of "brailing" the tuna aboard.[3] Thereafter, Harold took on the duties of Deck Boss and Mastman aboard the SAN JOAQUIN. Although he recognized that he was on a learning curve regarding purse-seine operations, the successful fishing trip of the SAN JOAQUIN gave Harold a strong dose of confidence in his skill at fishing tuna with purse-seine gear.

On the SAN JOAQUIN, Harold discovered how important the Mastman was to the success of the fishing venture. It was not enough for Harold, as Captain, to find the tuna in making the fishing trip a success. The fishing tool of the SAN JOAQUIN was the purse seine, and its effectiveness in catching the tunas depended wholly on the judgment and skill of the Mastman. The success of a baitboat operation after the Captain placed the vessel on a tuna school depended upon the endurance and skills of the fishermen in the fishing racks and the Chummer. This team of men was the fishing tool of a Tuna Baitboat. From his experience on the SAN JOAQUIN, Harold concluded that it was absolutely necessary for him to become the Mastman, as well as Captain, of the boat.

---

[1] The SOUTHERN PACIFIC was the second Tuna Baitboat to be converted to a purse seiner, commencing its maiden voyage in November 1958. The SAN JOAQUIN was the 51st Tuna Baitboat to be converted; 97 Tuna Baitboats were converted to Tuna Seiners. The ALPHECCA and the SAN JOAQUIN were former USN District Yard Patrol (YP vessels built in 1945, and converted to Tuna Baitboats after World War II.

[2] For a description of a "set" of the Tuna Purse Seiner by a converted tuna purse seiner in 1961: Richard L. McNeely, "Purse Seiner Revolution in Tuna Fishing," *Pacific Fisherman*, June 1961: 50-57.

[3] The term "brailing" means the taking of the fish out of the net into the fishing boat. A long-handled dip net or "brailer" is used to scoop the fish that have been "sacked" in the end part of the net or purse seine bag." "The proper word is bailing but the corrupted form spelled with an "r" is in such common use along the California coast that we accept the 'r.' " W.L. Scofield, "Purse Seines and Other Roundhaul Nets in California," State of California, Department of Fish and Game, Bureau of Marine Fisheries, Fish Bulletin No. 81, (1951): 14, 46. In recent years, significant innovations of the "brailing" operation of tuna seiners have resulted in great efficiency in terms of time and volume of the tunas transferred from the net to the vessel's cargo or fish wells.

4

CAPTAIN, F/V **ALPHECCA,**
CONVERTED TUNA SEINER

Fishing Record

During an 8-year period (April 1961 to September 1968), Harold commanded the ALPHECCA as a converted seiner on 42 fishing trips, recording a catch of 10,351 tons of tuna (25 million cans of tuna) or over 1 million tunas. During 1,599 days at sea, he directed 1,022 sets of the purse seine on tuna schools, including 754 sets on tuna/porpoise schools.

Porpoise Mortality Record

Harold did not record porpoise mortality in the ALPHECCA's logbook. The logbook provided by the Inter-American Tropical Tuna Commission (IATTC) to Harold and other skippers did not allocate space in the forms for this information. The logbook did provide space for the type of school (tuna/porpoise, "log," or unassociated), species of fish in the school (yellowfin, skipjack, or other), the amounts of each species caught, the location, the date, and the times that the set was begun and completed. Also, information such as weather conditions was recorded in blank spaces that were on every page.

For fiscal year 1964, the U.S. Bureau of Commercial Fisheries (BCF), funded a Tuna Behavior Project for its La Jolla, California, laboratory. The objective was "to accumulate basic information on the behavior and responses of tuna to provide fishermen with knowledge which will contribute to improving fishing efficiency and suggest new harvesting techniques." Projects were established for the collection and evaluation of data related to tuna behavior in six areas: tuna schooling, net avoidance, underwater visibility, sharks associated with tuna, porpoise associated with tuna, and logbook analysis. Under the project entitled "Porpoise associated with tuna," which was scheduled for completion in 1968, the data showed an unexpected increasing rate of seiner success in fishing "porpoise-associated schools" compared with success on "all school fish." After noting that this success may be due to the fleet's development of "porpoise herding techniques, using extra speed boats," the Laboratory's December 1966 Monthly Narrative Report advised that "Further studies of trends in efficiencies are planned in collaboration with the IATTC." The policy direction of the Tuna Behavior Project may explain why the BCF did not stress the collection of data on porpoise mortality during the period 1960 to 1970.[1] The four *unofficial* tabulations taken during purse-seine operations used in a government report on porpoise mortalities were based on the four fishing trips mentioned above, two in 1964, one in 1966, and one in 1968.[2]

The First Fishing Trip

In January 1961, Harold took over the newly-converted ALPHECCA for its first trip as a tuna seiner.[3] Harold had worked on the conversion and in the construction and design of the purse seine. He was in complete charge of the purchase of the webbing and its related gear, such as the corkline, purseline, leadline, rings, and ropes. The net was 550 fathoms long and eight "strips" deep. A fathom is 6 feet, and a "strip" is 6 fathoms, or 36 feet, in width. (The net was not exactly 48 fathoms or 288 feet from top to bottom when it was in the water, however, as the meshes of a purse seine are diagonal, permitting the net to stretch from top to bottom or from end to end.) Harold felt confident that he understood how the purse seine should be designed and that he could do it. The ALPHECCA was converted differently from the way tuna baitboats were usually converted to tuna seiners. To enhance seaworthiness, the raised deck of the baitboat design was retained. In contrast to earlier conversions, a "turntable" was not installed. This platform method of stacking the net was known in the fleet as the "Jangaard conversion."[4] The bait tank located in the stern was removed and replaced with two fish wells. These wells, which were installed in the stern area, formed the base of the Net Platform.

On the first "set" of the newly converted ALPHECCA, the vessel was fishing off the Islas Marias, Mexico (known to fishermen as the "Tres Marias"). Harold's mentor, Frank Theodore, was at the "wheel." This set was made on a mixed school of tuna and porpoise, and much "towline" was released. However, wheelman Theodore was unable to navigate the Tuna Seiner so as make a bow to bow contact with the Net Skiff. After watching the failed efforts by the crew to make contact with the Net Skiff, Harold left the Crow's Nest, jumped into ocean from the Bow, rope in hand, and swam to the Net Skiff and then returned with a rope attachment of the net to the ALPHECCA. Because of this long delay in retrieving both ends of the net to the main winch, a "roll-up" occurred. Harold recalled that over 100 fathoms of net was intertwined with the weighted bottom of the net or "chainline" (also called "leadline"). The net was finally stacked onto the ship after 18 hours of non-stop work. This skunk set was the beginning of Harold's education about operating a tuna purse seiner.

After this brutal experience with the first set of the net, Harold moved the vessel to fishing grounds off Champerico, Guatemala. He soon found numerous schools of 18 to 20-pound yellowfin tuna. Harold's favorite fishing grounds for finding schools of tuna and schools of tuna/porpoise were in waters from the Gulf of Tehuantepec to Corinto, Nicaragua. He was not interested in fishing the "cold" area off Baja California, nor within the Gulf of California and central coast of Mexico. He chose to fish south of Mexico, off the coasts of Guatemala, Honduras, El Salvador, and Nicaragua. He knew that the Galapagos Islands were not his best option because when operating the ALPHECCA as a baitboat in this region, most of the tunas were found inshore, close to rocky areas with swift currents.

These conditions were not favorable for purse seining. Also, he was interested in catching yellowfin, rather than skipjack, as higher prices were paid for yellowfin.

On his first set in waters off Guatemala, Harold encircled a large school of breezing tuna (fish that made their presence known by the disturbance that they created at the surface of the water). Long segments of the cork-line sank, which told Harold that there was a large quantity of tuna in the net. This experience was new to Harold, as it had not occurred during his trip aboard the SAN JOAQUIN. As the net came closer and closer to the port side of the vessel, the original circle formed by the cork-line was eliminated, and only lines adjacent to the hull were visible. The result was that less oxygen was available to the crowded tunas, and they were dying. As the dead tunas sank to the bottom of the net, their weight could rip the net, in which case the fish would be lost. With the net and tunas being held secured to the ALPHECCA only by the strength of nylon ropes and by the portion of the net that was secured to the deck, the process of "rolling" or gathering the net onto the net platform was halted. Under these conditions, it was impossible to brail the captured tunas aboard for storage in the fish wells. When the "corks" began to pop to the service, Harold and his crew knew that portions of the net had burst apart, releasing dead tunas to the deep—probably enough for loading the ship. Harold and his Crew were ignorant of the techniques required to avoid this wasteful catastrophe. He and his crew were learning their trade the hard way. Although skilled in encircling and capturing the tunas, Harold had no knowledge of the methods used to manage the retrieval of a net filled with a great quantity of tunas. This frustrating experience of wasting fish occurred to Harold and his crew on three more sets. Meanwhile, member vessels of his Code Group were loading up and heading home fully loaded. A humbled Harold sought advice from more experienced Captains. Within a week after the last "lost" set, Harold successfully brailed aboard a net full of live tunas.

Harold was also forced by his experiences aboard a tuna seiner to recognize the importance of a skilled Deck Boss and Chief Engineer. The job of Deck Boss required that deck equipment related to the net be ready for the net to "pay out" after the Mastman ordered the net released; that the purse-line and towline be correctly released and returned; that the decision to go to the "sack" be correct, and that the tunas in the net be quickly brailed out of the net and efficiently sent to the fish wells. (The fish wells contain brine, ocean water refrigerated at a temperature of about 28°F—above its freezing point of about 25°F. The fish freeze at about 30°F, so when they are placed into a well they quickly become frozen. When a well or, more commonly, a pair of wells are full of fish, the brine is pumped into the ocean. The result of this procedure is to cause a rise in the ship's freeboard, making ship more seaworthy. The Chief Engineer must keep the temperature low enough in the cargo wells to keep the fish frozen. If he makes a mistake, or the generators that keep the refrigerating system running malfunction, the fish will deteriorate and have to be discarded.) The decisions involved in getting to the portion of the net called the "sack" were critical. One could catch a hundred tons of tuna in the net, but it meant nothing if the tunas were not transferred quickly from the net to the deck of the boat and then to the fish wells. The Chief Engineer's job is more critical on the Tuna Seiner than on a

Tuna baitboat. On a baitboat the catches are usually spread out over the day, and the catch on a single day rarely exceeds about 20 or 25 tons, whereas on a purse seiner catches of more than 100 tons in a single set are not uncommon. The Chief Engineer's job was particularly difficult on the vessels that were converted from baitboats to purse seiners, as their refrigeration systems were not as powerful and efficient as those of the purse seiners that were constructed after the early 1960s.

Harold never forgot the lessons learned by trial and error during this trip. To his surprise, the experience had severely tested his patience, perseverance, leadership, and judgment.

The Crew, when using live bait, bamboo poles, and hooks, is the fishing tool aboard a Tuna baitboat. The Captain's job is to bring the baitboat onto schools of tuna, after which the members of the Crew display the skills, strength, and endurance required to bring the fish aboard the vessel. (The chummer must throw the right amount of bait near the fishing racks to keep the fish near the boat. Too little bait would cause the fish to disperse, and too much bait tossed would be wasteful. Ordinarily, a tuna has its head up when it bites the hook. When it first "realizes" that it is hooked, it thrusts its powerful tail, which helps the fisherman bring the fish aboard the boat. However, if a tuna has its head down, it is extremely difficult for the fisherman to bring its head up in order to bring it aboard the vessel. When the tuna in the school weigh more than about 30 pounds, the fishermen employ two or three or four poles attached to a single hook to catch and toss the fish aboard. Teamwork is obviously essential in two-, three-, and four-pole fishing.) As long as the Captain is doing his job, the measure of fishing success is in the hands of the Crew. Necessarily, the Crew had fewer opportunities to be dissatisfied with the Captain's fishing decisions. Harold felt that on a Tuna baitboat, he and his Crew were like a family.

Manual fishing skills are not so essential on a purse seiner, although stacking the net and brailing the fish from the net to the deck of the boat requires strength and endurance. The Mastman usually makes the vital decisions as to whether to deploy the net and, if so, how to deploy it. Sometimes, however, the Bridge provides the best opportunity to see where the tunas are located in a porpoise school. Navigational skills are needed in moving the vessel to the position demanded by the Mastman, but these skills are not used in making the final decision to release the net and, if so, when to release it. Thus, every set of the net gave the members of the Crew the opportunity to be judgmental of the Captain/Mastman's performance. This fact is used to support Harold's opinion that his seiner crews were less loyal to him than his baitboat crews.

Harold recognized that his command of a Converted Tuna Seiner Crew was different than his command of a Tuna Baitboat Crew, and, he readily admits that he became overly sensitive in his relationship with his Seiner Crew. With the growing success of tuna seining, as evidenced by more baitboats being converted and tuna seiners being built, Harold found that his crewmembers would readily leave him to go to work on new tuna seiners or newly-converted tuna seiners. Harold was confronting, for the first time, a high turnover rate in his crew. In contrast to the situation during the baitboat days, Harold found that the Seiner Crew "did not have much, if any, loyalty to the Captain." Harold also regretfully discovered that he made good and bad choices in crew selections for each fishing trip. On some fishing trips he identified certain members of the Crew as "instigators" and others as "followers" of the "instigators." Dissatisfaction by these crewmembers would become particularly high when the Crew saw or heard of other seiners heading home with full loads while the ALPHECCA was experiencing days of not finding fish. Upon completion of the fishing trip, Harold would get rid of "troublemakers." It was difficult for Harold to ignore his Crew's reactions to his decisions as Captain and/or as Mastman. "I could see it in the way they would look at me." Crew hostility was particularly apparent to Harold when he joined the Crew in the ship's Galley. Harold had many more times of lonely anxiety while in command of a Tuna seiner than he had had while in command of a Tuna baitboat. In seining for tunas, there were periods of time when you were working hard, but "you were just in a slump. You couldn't find the correct fishing area, or, after finding a good area for fishing, other vessels found good schools of fish but you were either missing good schools with "skunk sets" or not finding anything to set upon."

---

[1] Tim D. Smith and Nancy C. H. Lo, "Some Data on Dolphin Mortality in the Eastern Tropical Pacific Tuna Purse Seine Fishery Prior to 1970, " NOAA Technical Memorandum NMFS, August 1983. NOAA-TM-NMFS-SWFC-34. U.S. Department of Commerce, NOAA, NMFS, SFC. 26 pp.

[2] "The mortalities of dolphins in this fishery were heavy during the 1960s, but we'll never have a reliable estimate of their magnitude because of the very scanty and biased database available . . . For the 1959-1970 period, there are data for only four fishing trips (out of a total of more than 3500); two from a biologist that was allowed to participate in them (Perrin, 1968, 1969), and two from unsolicited letters from crew members (citation). Of Perrin's two trips, the data for one could not be used because he had recorded mortality data only for the high-mortality sets; the representativeness of the crew members' letters is questionable. . ." pp. 8-9. Martin A. Hall, "An ecological view of the tuna-dolphin problem: impacts and trade-offs," Reviews in Fish Biology and Fisheries, 8: 1-34 (1998).

[3] During 1957-1963, there were 97 tuna baitboats converted to tuna seiners; the ALPHECCA conversion was the 68th.

[4] Sverre Jangaard was of Norwegian descent and had proven his fishing capability in the fisheries of Washington and Alaska. His experimentation with tuna longline gear in the central Pacific proved that this fishing gear alternative was not the answer for the struggling U.S. tuna baitboat fleet. Thereafter, Sverre was invited to visit Australia for the purpose of introducing the American style of fishing for tuna with baitboat gear. He was part owner of the baitboats NORTH AMERICAN and CAPE FALCON. The former was a converted sardine purse seiner; the latter was a converted Navy vessel (YP 645). After ending his fishing career, he and other San Diego-based tuna fishermen purchased Campbell Shipyard. As a supervisor in the repair and conversions of many baitboats, he decided not to install a turntable and remove the raised deck on the CAPE FALCON--the 30th baitboat to be converted. This decision caused considerable controversy in the San Diego Tuna Fleet. The fishing success of this type of conversion proved the foresight and inventiveness of Captain Jangaard. Later, he co-owned and managed the CLIPPERTON, a tuna purse seiner that was a former military hull converted to a tuna seiner at Campbell Machine.

5

CAPTAIN, F/V **KERRI M.,**
NEW TUNA SEINER

Fishing Record

From April 1969 to October 1976, Harold commanded the new seiner KERRI M. on 38 fishing trips, recording a catch of over 20,156 tons of tuna (over 48 million cans of tuna), or over 2 million tunas. During 1,708 days at sea, he directed 1,355 sets of the purse seine on tuna schools, including 911 sets on tuna/porpoise schools.

In 1970, he participated in a successful venture, with the Captains of five other vessels, to search for new tuna fishing grounds in the central and western Pacific Ocean.

In 1971, he developed and tested what is now called the Medina Panel, a panel of smaller mesh in the part of the net in which porpoises were often getting entangled. This experiment was successful, reducing the mortality of porpoises encircled by the net substantially. The U.S. Government confirmed its effectiveness, and installation of the Medina Panel in all tuna purse seines became a regulatory requirement in 1973. Other nations with vessels participating in the tuna fishery soon passed similar laws. Later, Jacques Cousteau visited with Harold on the KERRI M., and filmed Harold's explanation of the Panel and how it works. In 1979, Harold's Panel idea received the annual California Design Award for "environmental design."

In 1972, he commanded an exploratory fishing trip for the U.S. Government in waters around the Marquesas Islands. In 1973, the KERRI M. successfully fished off New Zealand, delivering the tunas to the Star-Kist cannery in American Samoa. During 1974, he explored waters off the east coast of Australia, but found the weather and sea conditions unfavorable for purse seining. He decided to have his sons command the KERRI M. after he was hired to be the Captain of a newly-built Super Tuna Purse seiner during the Fall of 1976.

The Time for a New Vessel

After successfully operating the ALPHECCA as a tuna seiner for eight years, Harold recognized that his aging vessel was no longer competitive. On many more occasions, he was telling his wife Emily that he longed for the day when he could independently control and operate a new tuna seiner. He told her of an offer from Al Brosio to be part of a group of investors and fishermen. The plan was to apply to the U.S. government for support in the construction of one of several new tuna seiners under an arrangement that would use a subsidy to a U.S. shipyard so as to reduce the construction costs and, therefore, the purchase price of the vessels. After understanding that participation in the scheme involved a group ownership and management of the "subsidy" vessels, Harold rejected the offer. Harold was interested in being the controlling owner and operator of the subsidy vessel, rather than just a minority owner.[1]

The "fishing vessel subsidy" building program was temporarily delayed because of opposition by the membership of the American Tunaboat Association (ATA). It was argued during administrative hearings held in 1967 that the vessels built under the subsidy program would cause economic hardship to owners of vessels already operating efficiently in the tuna fishery.[2]

In mid-1967, while at sea aboard the ALPHECCA, Harold received an unexpected radio call from his wife Emily. She told him that he had an opportunity to be an independent vessel owner, and related the results of her meeting that day with Joe Bogdanovich and John Real, President and Vice-President, respectively, of Star-Kist Foods, Inc. The Star-Kist officials had asked her if Harold would be interested in becoming the Captain and Managing Owner of a new tuna seiner. She told Harold that she had responded to the offer enthusiastically, and explained that Joe and John promised to put a "deal" together as soon as possible. Harold told Emily that he was very pleased, supportive, and excited about how she had responded to the offer from Star-Kist. Later, Harold met with John Real to learn more about the "deal" on the new vessel. John explained that Star-Kist was going to be involved in the construction of several "subsidy" seiners. He proposed that Harold would have 70% ownership of the entity owning the vessel, and that Star-Kist would have the other 30%. After a short discussion, Harold and John agreed. John explained that Harold would be working with Edward X. Madruga, a Star-Kist consultant, on the construction and design stages of the new vessel.

> Following this oral agreement, Harold had a conversation with Frank Perry while aboard a new tuna seiner undergoing a trial set of its net in waters off San Diego County. Frank Perry, a consultant to Van Camp Seafood Company ("Chicken of the Sea"), offered Harold 100% ownership interest in a new tuna seiner with a carrying capacity of 1000 tons of tuna, and Harold would not be required to come up with money for his ownership. A condition to the "deal" was that Harold would have to unload its catches exclusively at the Van Camp cannery in Ponce, Puerto Rico. Harold knew that former Captains Joe Soares and Frank Perry had each recently built a new 950-ton tuna seiner (BLUE PACIFIC and JEANETTE C., respectively), that these vessels were fishing for the Van Camp plant at Ponce, and that both had records of operating successfully from Puerto Rico. Frank explained that the new non-subsidy vessel would be built at Tacoma Boat Works, Tacoma, Washington, where the BLUE PACIFIC and JEANETTE C. had been constructed. Harold responded that Frank's offer was "such a good deal that seemingly it could not be refused." Respectfully, and with regret, he explained to Frank that he had to reject the offer because he had just accepted an offer from Star-Kist on the building

of a new "subsidy" vessel, and that it would not be right of him to back-out now on his deal with Star-Kist.

A meeting to finalize the deal with the Government was scheduled at the offices of Star-Kist Foods, Inc., in Terminal Island, California. Prior to that meeting, Harold still understood that Star-Kist was to own 30% and Harold 70%, and that Harold was to transfer 10% of his 70% interest to Ed Madruga. About 10 minutes before the meeting was to begin, Anthony Nizetich, the Star-Kist representative, asked for a private session with Harold. He told Harold that Star-Kist now wanted 50% ownership interest in the corporate entity owning the vessel. Harold objected, and sought a compromise from Star-Kist regarding his promise to Ed Madruga, suggesting that Harold and Star-Kist each own a 45% interest, with the remaining 10% for Ed. Anthony said that Harold would have to take the 10% from his 50% share, since Star-Kist wanted no reduction in its share. A disappointed, but realistic, Harold complied with the demand for the ownership change. As promised, Ed Madruga received his 10% interest from Harold. Without notice to Harold, Ed sold his share to other persons within a year of the KERRI M.'s maiden voyage.

Construction and Design of the KERRI M

The new tuna seiner was named KERRI M., after Emily and Harold's oldest daughter. Harold and Ed worked with the marine architects Rados Engineering of San Pedro, California. For instance, Harold stressed the need for speed—a vessel that could go at least 15 knots. During the speed trials, the vessel traveled at 16 knots. This was quite a change for Harold, as he was used to the 7- to 8-knot "downhill crawl" of the ALPHECCA. The KERRI M. was originally designed with a carrying capacity of 550 tons of frozen tuna. Both Harold and Ed wanted more fish-

KERRI M. speed trail on waters of Puget Sound, Washington
Vessel built by Tacoma Boatbuilding Company, Tacoma, Washington

carrying capacity. To comply with their wishes, the stern fuel tanks were converted to brine fish wells. This design change increased the capacity to over 750 tons. The vessel was designed and built without a double bottom, the customary design feature for steel-hull seiners, which is why the brine fish wells on the KERRI M. were of greater capacity than those of other seiners. Harold was particularly concerned with the design of the fishing and cargo handling winches, and the placement and number of "chaseboats" or speedboats for herding porpoises.

The "Speed" of the KERRI M

On the day the KERRI M. left the shipyard at Tacoma, Harold decided to change course and personally test the vessel's speed. Unknown to him, his cook, Guy Russell, had laboriously set the Galley table for lunch in the belief that the vessel was going to travel smoothly on the quiet waters of Puget Sound. After Harold turned about to start his vessel's unexpected speed trial, the dishes, glasses, and other items on the Galley table were tossed helter-skelter from the table to all parts of the Galley. This unforeseen and abrupt vessel maneuver caught the cook and other crewmembers and guests completely by surprise. The noise of crashing objects and the yelling of the cook reached the Bridge. Later, a contrite Harold, after throwing his hat into the Galley to seek a friendly reaction, confronted his distraught and angry cook and apologized.

During the maiden trip of the KERRI M., which commenced on March 30, 1969, the main winch failed. The trip was aborted, and the vessel returned to San Diego, California. It took a week for repairs to be completed. By this time, the KERRI M.'s sister ship CHERYL MARIE was ready for its maiden departure on April 15, 1969. Together, both vessels left San Diego for the Gulf of Tehuantepec. After reaching this area, Captain John Silveira received reliable reports of good fishing at Finger Bank, which is near Cabo Falso, Baja California, Mexico. Because of the speed of their new vessels, both John and Harold rushed 900 miles to the northwest to Finger Bank. For Captains operating vessels having a top speed of 8 knots, such a decision would be unwise. Fish runs, particularly those occurring off Baja California, do not last longer than a week. The weather is highly volatile in waters of this area, and the risk of the fish runs being over by the time of arrival was too great for a person operating a vessel like the ALPHECCA. Speed gave the KERRI M. and the CHERYL MARIE a competitive advantage in traveling to "hot" fishing spots.

Harold showed off the 16-knot speed of the KERRI

Captain Joe Medina Jr. and the Queen Mary
Courtesy of Mrs. Carolyn Medina
Vessel built by PACECO, Marine Division, Alameda, California

M. on another occasion. His cousin, Joe Medina, Jr., had left San Diego with his new "subsidy" seiner, the QUEEN MARY, at about the same time as the KERRI M. After both vessels left San Diego and were traveling together in waters off Baja California, Harold decided to push the KERRI M. to overtake the QUEEN MARY. After being safely ahead of the QUEEN MARY, Harold navigated the KERRI M. to encircle the QUEEN MARY by making a turn to the starboard, and then he slowed down the KERRI M., to let the QUEEN MARY pass. After encircling the QUEEN MARY, Harold then swiftly passed the slower QUEEN MARY. Clearly, in a race to tuna/porpoise schools, or to a breezing, jumping, traveling school of tuna, or to a school milling about drifting debris, Harold had shown his cousin Joe that the QUEEN MARY could not keep up with the KERRI M. The tuna fleet's customary rule prevailing in a race to the fish is "first come, first served." In a race to a tuna school, the first vessel that navigates in a position to set its net, that is, with the school on its port side, has the right to set its net and the right to insist that other vessels not interfere.

Harold has experienced times when unexpected "luck," rather than vessel speed, determined fishing success. While searching for tunas in the area near 10° North Latitude, 125° West Longitude, Harold recalls running the KERRI M. on a westerly course. He spotted the new tuna seiner LUCKY STRIKE directly ahead, traveling on an easterly course. The vessels were only a few miles apart. Captain Bill Magellan called Harold on the radio, advising him that he was changing to a course due south. Harold thanked Bill, and told him that he was changing to a course due north. Within 20 minutes, Harold found a large school of tuna/porpoise and caught 45 tons of tuna. Captain Magellan did not locate any tunas during the remaining hours of that day.

On another occasion, Harold was running the KERRI M. at full speed toward a school of tuna/porpoise. Harold noticed a vessel heading for the same school. He identified it as the new tuna seiner CAPTAIN FRANK MEDINA, then under the command of his cousin Joe Medina. Harold reasoned that he could not win the race, so he changed course to search for another a tuna/porpoise school. After traveling about three miles on this new course, the KERRI M. spotted and caught a school with over 75 tons of fish. Later, his cousin radioed that the CAPTAIN FRANK MEDINA, which had won the race, had caught only 30 tons of fish. About a month later, the KERRI M. and the CAPTAIN FRANK MEDINA were again engaged in a race for a tuna/porpoise school. Again, Harold decided to give up the race and let his cousin set on the school. Harold initiated a new search, which resulted in the capture of over 80 tons of tuna. Later that day cousin Joe informed Harold that he had caught about 40 tons of tuna on the school that was the original target of the race. He declared that if he were again involved in a race with Harold, he would let Harold win the race and search for another school of tuna/porpoise.

The KERRI M.–a Family Operation

Harold recalls that during a "fishing set," he jokingly told his crew from his location in the Crow's Nest, via the inter-com, "If I had one more crewmember like my four boys, I wouldn't need the rest of you guys!" What prompted this comment was Harold's view of the work of his four sons in stacking the net coming from the power block on the boom. He saw his youngest and strongest son John stacking the cumbersome cork-line, and his sons Gary, Bill, and Harold ("Bomber"), energetically grabbing and stacking almost all of the purse seine's webbing onto the net platform.[3]

When fishing for tuna/porpoise schools, Bill, John, and "Bomber" were operating the three speedboats in response to commands from Harold from the Mast. Speedboats on the KERRI M. were 16 feet in length and powered by 85-h.p. outboard engines. They could reach speeds of about 35 miles per hour. Bill was in the number one position as the leading speedboat. Harold recalled that on one chase of a tuna/porpoise school, he was steadily commanding Bill to continue his course "straight ahead." At the time, the three speedboats were a long distance ahead of the KERRI M. As they traveled ahead, it became more difficult for Harold to see the speedboat drivers. To verify Bill's location, he commanded him to make a circle. When he could not see Bill making a circle, Harold realized that he was looking at John in the second speedboat. When he realized his error, he commanded Bill to run toward the KERRI M. After what Harold considered to be a long time, Bill finally came into view and the fishing operation continued. At the time, Harold recalled the occasion when his cousin Joe Medina on the QUEEN MARY commanded one of his speedboat drivers, after a failed chase of a tuna/porpoise school to "keep going straight for one day, and you will hit the beach."

Harold recalled witnessing the sinking of Bill's speedboat during a chase of a tuna/porpoise school. The seas were rough, as Harold commanded his sons on the three speedboats to follow closely behind the KERRI M. because the sea in this area would be flattened by the movements of the tuna seiner as it ploughed ahead toward the tuna/porpoise school. Another reason for this maneuver was to move the purse seiner in a position to bunch the tuna and porpoises together before sending the speedboats ahead to corral the school. Bill, driving a newly-purchased speedboat, was commanded by Harold to move ahead of the purse seiner, which was traveling at the top speed of 15 knots, and start the chase. As Bill was speeding ahead, Harold saw Bill crash into a large bow wave created by the speeding KERRI M. From his position in the Crow's Nest, Harold saw the bow of the speedboat cut through the curling wave "like a torpedo," causing the speedboat to be completely immersed, and Bill's head was barely visible at the surface of the water. The speedboat sank almost immediately, and Bill was quickly rescued by the other two speedboats and returned to the KERRI M.

During his 25 years of fishing experience aboard tuna purse seiners, Harold recalls seeing the following incident only twice: The leading speedboat was herding a school of tuna/porpoise in very rough seas. A large wave hit the speedboat and sent it high into the air. As it was in the air, the speedboat appeared to be just past being perpendicular to the ocean with the stern area about four feet above the ocean's surface. Because of the speedboat's forward motion while in the air, the back end of the speedboat entered the water first, forcing the hull to right itself as the speedboat fell back into the ocean, allowing it to continue roaring ahead. In Harold's opinion, speedboat drivers "earned their money."

In addition to being loyal and hardworking, Harold's five sons who chose to become tuna fishermen all became accomplished mariners. After satisfying the required years of qualifying time at sea, Gary, Bill, and John became licensed Masters and Harold and Wade became licensed Chief Engineers.

Explorations in the South Pacific by the KERRI M

Explorations by the U.S. Tuna Fleet beyond the traditional fishing grounds in the eastern Pacific Ocean (EPO) were first initiated in 1932 with the maiden trip of what was then the largest Tuna Clipper baitboat in the Fleet, the MAYFLOWER, followed in 1936 on the maiden trip of the newest Tuna Clipper baitboat in the Fleet, the CABRILLO. Harold's uncles, on his father's side, commanded both of these vessels during these ventures.

The 135' MAYFLOWER, under the command of Joaquin Medina and with a crew of 14, left San Diego on March 21, 1932, for the Hawaiian Islands. The trip, 100 miles shorter than a trip to Galapagos Islands, began with catching anchovies for bait off Baja California. The objective of the cruise was to search for Albacore. The vessel carried fuel, 85 tons of crushed ice, and food for a trip of 45 to 60 days. After traveling almost 9,000 miles, the MAYFLOWER returned to San Diego on May 19, 1932. The vessel had spent 17 days in catching about 10 tons of anchovies in Magdalena Bahía, Baja California. It then headed for the Christmas Island. "Capt. Medina reported that at Christmas, Palmyra, Washington and Fanning Islands there were many schools of fish, but they persistently refused to bite. In all, less than 45 tons were caught . . . The object of the trip, a fare of Albacore, failed to materialize, Capt Medina stating that none were seen during the entire voyage." [4]

On August 23, 1935, Mr. H. Rambke, a French biologist, wrote to Fred W. Schellin, Manager of the American Tunaboat Association, advising him that he was departing for the Marquesas Islands "to clarify the bait situation, gather and submit you reliable data on the kind of bait fish, their seasons and best netting locations, also make any other arrangements, you may think necessary to make the fishing adventures less hazardous." Mr. Rambke referred to his 2-year stay at the islands, conducting an investigation of its tuna resources, and the recent article published in the *Pacific Fisherman*. This article is persuasive in claiming that the "Polynesian banks of the Central Pacific" have plentiful tuna and available bait resources, and that they are "not more distant" than the Galapagos Islands.[5] In 1936, Joe Medina, Sr., commanding the San Diego-based tuna baitboat CABRILLO, decided to test the claims of Mr. Rambke. However, this gamble to fish for tuna and bait in waters off the Marquesas was not carried out. Captain Medina aborted the venture after it was discovered that the ship's charts had failed to identify the presence of shoals and reefs seen by the crew in waters near the Marquesas Islands. To salvage the fishing trip, Captain Medina diverted the CABRILLO to the familiar fishing grounds at the Galapagos Islands. Bountiful tunas in these waters made possible a successful 57-day fishing trip. This trip convinced San Diego tuna fishermen that the decision of fishing the tunas around the Galapagos Islands was less of a gamble than exploring South Pacific islands. During World War II many U.S. tuna baitboats were converted to naval vessels, and tuna fishermen served aboard them in the central and western Pacific Ocean, where they saw good signs of tuna. After the war, a few San Diego Tuna Clippers explored the Marquesas Islands, but found the problems of obtaining bait too difficult to justify return trips.

In 1970, Harold followed the footsteps of his uncles, Captain Joaquin O. Medina of the MAYFLOWER and Captain Joe Medina of the CABRILLO, when the KERRI M. joined a group of San Diego Tuna Seiners in an exploration effort of the central and western Pacific Ocean. The other vessels and Captains: CABRILLO (Captain Jose DaLuz); CONQUEST (Captain Richard Madruga); KERRI M., MERMAID (Captain Frank Correia); PACIFIC QUEEN (Captain Frank Paula), and POLARIS (Captain Ollie Virissimo). The adventurers were planning to move westward from the traditional fishing area in the EPO to American Samoa, and then westward to the Palau Islands as the final destination. The objective of this venture was to search for tuna fishing grounds suitable for purse seining in the central and western Pacific Ocean. In fact, the venture found new tuna fishing grounds west of the Commission's Yellowfin Regulatory Area (CYRA), established by the IATTC to limit the catch of Yellowfin Tuna. Four of the six Captains aborted the exploration after San Diego-based Tuna Seiners made successful fishing trips west of the CYRA, later named "the outside area." After refueling in American Samoa, Harold returned to the "outside area" and made a very successful fishing trip on tuna/porpoise schools.

The KERRI M., under Harold's command, explored the Marquesas Islands area during October 15 to November 8, 1972, for purposes of surveying its suitability for American-style tuna purse seining. The venture, supported financially in part by the U.S. Department of Commerce, National Oceanic and Atmospheric Administration (NOAA), National Marine Fisheries Service (NMFS), did not stimulate the development of tuna seining about the Islands.

In 1974-1975, Harold commanded the KERRI M. in exploring skipjack tuna fishing grounds off the east coast of the North Island of New Zealand and the west coast of Australia, near Sydney. This exploration was justified because of the successful 1974 catch of Skipjack by the converted tuna purse seiner PARAMOUNT (Captain Anthony Tipich of San Pedro) in waters off New Zealand. (During 1973, the New Zealand Government and Star-Kist Foods performed an agreement to use a U.S. purse seiner to survey New Zealand's pelagic fish resources.) The KERRI M. was joined by two other U.S. tuna seiners, the SOUTH PACIFIC and the OCEAN QUEEN. Their first port of entry was the city of Nelson. To get acquainted with New Zealanders, the American tuna vessels were opened to the public. Except for a small group of local commercial fishermen who were understandably concerned about foreign competition, the reception was very friendly and cooperative. After a two-day stay in port, the American seiners commenced a search for the tunas in the Bay of Plenty. The first sighting of fish occurred during November just above the Great Barrier Island, off the North Island. Later, fish were found on the west side of North Island, in waters off New Plymouth. Fishing ended by mid-March, and all of the American seiners left for unloading at the cannery in American Samoa.

After this 75-day exploration, the KERRI M. unloaded over 1,000 tons of skipjack tuna. Fishing success, the friendliness of the New Zealand people, and the availability of port facilities, supplies, and skilled shipyard workers, justified plans to return to New Zealand. The KERRI M. returned to New Zealand during the skipjack tuna season, December 1975 to March 1976, December 1976 to March 1977, and finally from December 1977 to March 1978. By then, Harold was convinced that only super seiners with fish-carrying capacities greater than that of the KERRI M. could economically fish for tunas in the central and western Pacific Ocean.

---

[1] During the Spring of 1967, the following five corporate applicants were granted approval by the U.S. Secretary of Interior to build "subsidy" tuna seiners: Marilyn M. Fishing, Inc (QUEEN MARY), Vivian Ann Fishing, Inc. (VIVIAN ANN), Gina Karen Fishing, Inc. (GINA KAREN), Lou Jean II Fishing, Inc. (LOU JEAN II), and Hope Fishing , Inc. (KATHLEEN).

[2] Under the program, the subsidy paid for 40% to 50% of the construction cost of getting the vessel ready for sea, excepting fuel and food. The vessel owner was permitted to borrow 75% of the balance with government mortgage insurance. The result was an initial investment of 12.5 to 15%. The ATA noted that to conserve and manage yellowfin tuna, the fishery was subject to annual quotas enforced by the U.S. Government. The ATA argued that it was harmful and unnecessary for the Government to subsidize additional fishing capacity of questionable "advanced designs" in this highly-regulated fishery. See: BCF-"Fishing Vessel Construction Differential Subsidy", U.S. Fish Wildlife Service, Fishery Leaflet 574, ii + 11 p. Peterson, C.E. "Fishing Vessel Construction Differential Subsidies". *Proc.Gulf Carib.Fish Inst*. 16th Annual Session; 46-50.

[3] At this time, fishermen shared the proceeds of the catch with the vessel owner. Pursuant to a collective-bargaining agreement, agreed trip expenses are first deducted from the proceeds received for the catch accepted by the Cannery. These trip expenses included food, fuel and oil, salt for the brine system, and trip licenses and fees. Per terms of the labor agreement, the money remaining is divided into "Boat Share" and "Crew Share." For the KERRI M, the Crew Share was 37% and Boat Share was 63%. The money remaining in the "Crew Share" is further divided into Shares. Except for apprentices, each crewmember signs on for a "Full Share." All "Bonus Shares" are paid from the Vessel Owner share. This profit-sharing arrangement provided an incentive for the Captain and Crew to work as a team, and for the "Bonus Share" men to work also for the interests of the Vessel Owner.

[4] Anon, "MAYFLOWER" Meets Scant Success on Cruise to Hawaii," *Pacific Fisherman*, June 1932, p. 29

[5] H.Rambke, "Marquesan Banks May Be Next Great Source of Tuna," *Pacific Fisherman*, July 1935, p. 25

6

CAPTAIN, F/V **ZAPATA DISCOVERER**,
"SUPER" TUNA SEINER

The ZAPATA DISCOVERER

With a fish-carrying capacity of 1800 tons, in contrast to the fish-carrying capacity of KERRI M. of only 800 tons, the ZAPATA DISCO-VERER was a good choice for fishing in the western Pacific. Under the command of Harold Medina, with 18 men aboard, including a helicopter pilot and a helicopter mechanic, the ZAPATA DISCOVERER landed over 9,000 tons of tuna, or over 2 million individual tunas. This entire catch, taken during December 1976-April 1979, was converted to products for human and animal consumption. About 24 million cans of tuna for human consumption were produced during a time when the estimated annual per-capita consumption in the United States was about nine cans.

In cooperation with other San Diego-based Tuna Seiners, Harold and his crew aboard the ZAPATA DISCOVERER helped develop new skip-jack tuna fishing grounds in waters off the east coast of North Island, New Zealand, during the summer seasons of 1976-77, 1977-78, and 1978-79.

Harold's fishing operation helped developed a new tuna fishing pattern for the San Diego Tuna Seiner Fleet. He showed that the financial risk of exploration by U.S. Flag Tuna Seiners in the western Pacific could be reduced by including New Zealand as an area of operation. Fishing off New Zealand was a financial stepping-stone to tuna fishing exploration in the Western Pacific. Fishing success off New Zealand allowed him and his fellow Captains to exercise one of two options: the less risky choice of heading east from American Samoa to California for proven good fishing on tuna/porpoise schools in the "outside area" or the high-risk choice of exploring new grounds in the one digit latitudes north and south of the Equator west of American Samoa. After his second season in New Zealand (1975-76), Harold observed that some of his fellow Captains were taking the more risky choice of exploring the western Pacific. Unfortunately, Harold was delayed in joining them in this new adventure by failing to pursue an opportunity to purchase his favorite ship, the ZAPATA DISCOVERER.

In November 1976, Zapata Ocean Resources took delivery of the "Super" Tuna Seiner ZAPATA DISCOVERER from Campbell Industries of San Diego. This vessel was of 272' in length, and had a frozen tuna-carrying capacity of 1800 tons. Its first Captain was Harold Medina. Based upon his 40 years of fishing

ZAPATA DISCOVERER on the high seas of the eastern Pacific Ocean
Vessel built by Campbell Industries, San Diego, California

experience, Harold is of the opinion that the ZAPATA DISCOVERER was the finest Tuna Seiner ever constructed in the United States. Harold still marvels over the seaworthiness of the vessel, the rock-solid state of the vessel as it drifted or sailed in bad weather, the ease with which every part of the fishing operation was implemented, and the comfortable living accommodations aboard the vessel. The stabilizer worked perfectly, making fishing, travel, and drifting comfortable in the worst of seas. He recalls that while drifting one night, he woke up and heard the wind roaring about the vessel, but did not notice any effects on the vessel. He went to the Bridge, looked about fore and aft, and observed great waves breaking over the stern of the vessel. For Harold, the vessel was one of a kind, and he made a special effort to report his praises to the designers and workmen at Campbell Industries. Harold's best fishing voyage aboard the ZAPATA DISCOVERER, lasted only 10 days, during which the vessel caught 1800 tons of skipjack (more than 500,000 fish) off New Zealand.

The Maiden Fishing Voyage to New Zealand

Harold decided to make the maiden voyage of the ZAPATA DISCOVERER off the east coast of North Island, New Zealand, in the company of the KERRI M., then commanded by his son Gary. In 1973, an agreement was reached between Star-Kist Foods and the government of New Zealand for a survey of tuna, mackerel, and other pelagic resources by a California-style purse seiner. During 1974, the PARAMOUNT, a converted tuna seiner commanded by Captain Anthony Tipich of San Pedro, showed that skipjack tuna were available to purse-seine gear. During the following summer (December 1974 to April 1975), Harold was sent by Star-Kist to New Zealand to further test the findings of the PARAMOUNT and to survey the waters off the east coast of Australia, near Sydney, for tuna. The success of this exploration caused Harold to return to New Zealand with the KERRI M. for the1975-1976 skipjack fishing season, and he completed three trips during that period. Harold was confident that the ZAPATA DISCOVERER would also make successful fishing trips. His plan was to unload his New Zealand catches at the Star-Kist cannery in American Samoa, setting the stage for a fishing trip on tuna/porpoise schools in the eastern Pacific Ocean (EPO) outside the CYRA for unloading to canneries in California. Harold was also of the view that this tuna fishing pattern (California to New Zealand to American Samoa to California) could stimulate exploration of tuna fishing grounds in the western Pacific.

During the first trip of the ZAPATA DISCOVERER in New Zealand, Harold found that during the paying out of the net, the problem known in the tuna purse-seine fleet as a "roll-up" occurred during most of the "sets." Observing from the ship's helicopter, Harold found that webbing was wrapped about extensive areas of the "lead-line." On most "sets" about 200 to 250 fathoms of the net would be ripped and heavily damaged. These conditions required immediate repairs so as to be able to continue fishing the next day. Harold and crewmember Nick Marinkovich found that the main cause of the "roll-up" was a twisting condition of the "lead-line." Since it was impractical in New Zealand to replace the nylon rope "lead-line" with the customary "chainline," Harold and his crew adjusted by establishing a unique procedure to quickly repair the net. The usual fishing day would start at sunrise and usually end at midnight. Sunset occurred at about 9:00 pm. In addition to the customary workload involved in making sets, there were additional long hours of labor necessary to repair the net after each "set." By trial and error, Harold and Nick established an approach for them to quickly identify the "key twist" in the nylon-wrapped "leadline" that would permit an unraveling of the "leadline." Harold was of the opinion that the "leadline" was unduly twisted because it was improperly uncoiled from its original package by the individuals who were contracted to make the net.

To illustrate, after a large rip in the net is detected as the net is being hauled aboard, the rip is marked to identify its start and finish. As the net passes through the power block on its way to the net platform, the damaged section of the net is separated and piled on the working deck just forward of the net platform. Two piles of damaged webbing are created for ease of inspection and repair. The undamaged net is piled onto the net platform. After all of the net was aboard, Nick would start the repairs by holding the marker identifying the end of the ripped net. Harold would then proceed to pull each side of the damaged net equally for about twelve feet, whereupon the two damaged sections were tied together. Nick would then hand this tacked section to a crewmember for lacing. Nick would then work on the net to permit Harold to again pull the damaged net into two sections for tacking. This procedure would be followed until the entire damaged area had been tacked and laced. In about one and a half hours, repairs involving 200 fathoms of damaged net would be accomplished; crewmembers were able to lace damaged net as fast as Harold and Nick could tack it. Later, the damaged net would be properly repaired by crewmembers during the slow periods of a fishing day.

Despite the problems created by a poorly-designed and fabricated net, the ZAPATA DISCOVERER captured over 1500 tons of skipjack off New Zealand, and delivered the catch to the Star-Kist cannery in American Samoa. After unloading, the vessel proceeded to a fishing area southeast of Hawaii and captured about 1100 tons of yellowfin on tuna/porpoise schools for delivery to the Star-Kist cannery in San Pedro, California.

In order to fish on tuna/porpoise schools "outside the CYRA," Harold was required to carry a U.S. Government Observer. Having taken a number of government scientists aboard the ALPHECCA and the KERRI M., Harold was experienced in working with Observers. Noting unexpected conduct by an Observer after departing American Samoa, Harold decided to have a private session with him. Harold felt that it was necessary for the Observer to understand that Harold, not the Observer, was in command of the ZAPATA DISCOVERER. During the meeting, Harold and the Observer agreed to the following rules: (1) when Harold was in the Chart Room, the Observer was not permitted to be there; (2) when the Observer needed the vessel's position, he was to obtain it from the Satellite Navigator; (3) the Observer was to record fishing operations only when the vessel was fishing tuna/porpoise schools—not when the vessel was engaged in fishing pure schools of tuna; (4) as much as practicable, the Observer was to be in a location on the vessel where he could not to be seen by Harold while he was on the Bridge or in the Crow's Nest and engaged in a fishing operation. This was the only time that Harold had to work out rules of conduct with an Observer.

ZAPATA DISCOVERER and its helicopter fishing in waters off New Zealand.
Courtesy of Richard Chikami

The experience with a helicopter aboard the ZAPATA DISCOVERER confirmed Harold's opinion that a helicopter was helpful to him in setting on schools of skipjack tuna in waters off New Zealand, but that in fishing tuna/porpoise schools his presence aboard the helicopter was not helpful. Harold felt that he could exercise more control over chase operations on tuna/porpoise schools while aboard the ship than from a helicopter. Harold confirmed that crew observations from his ship guided the helicopter to schools of fish because it was particularly difficult to spot bird activity and tuna/porpoise subsurface movements from a helicopter. Helicopters could be used to reduce fuel costs and fishing time efficiency by checking out signs of fish observed with binoculars on the bridge of the ship to determine if they justified diversion of the tuna seiner.

Upon returning to San Diego, Harold replaced the nylon wrapped "leadline" with a galvanized steel "chainline." After an employee of the ship-owner objected to this proposed expenditure, Harold exercised his written authority to purchase supplies costing up to $30,000. This employee had no appreciation of the fishing difficulties and crew burdens caused by the nylon-wrapped leadline.

Harold completed the 1977 fishing year on a trip begun in August and completed in October. A highlight of the trip was a decision to go to Clipperton Island, based on a report from the Captain of a vessel that was in his Code Group. This Captain reported that he had just passed Clipperton Island, where he had sighted numerous yellowfin tuna schools. He explained to Harold that since his ship was on a "regulated fishing trip," he was unable to catch yellowfin tuna. Harold's ship was not on a "regulated fishing trip," so he decided to take the chance that the speed of the ZAPATA DISCOVERER would justify the three-day diversion to Clipperton Island. Harold found numerous tuna schools, and quickly loaded the boat and returned to San Diego with a catch of over 1600 tons of tuna. During one "set" at Clipperton Island, an incident involving a crewmember still dwells in Harold's mind. While on the working deck, the crewmember fell and exclaimed that he was having a heart attack. Harold went to his aid, and while in Harold's arms, he pleaded, "Please, please, don't let me die." During examination, Harold found that the crewmember had suffered heat stroke, rather than a heart attack.

In less than 12 months, Harold and his crew had captured over 3100 tons of tuna during the maiden fishing season of the ZAPATA DISCOVERER.

Second Fishing Season in New Zealand

On November 30, 1977, the ZAPATA DISCOVERER, commenced its second fishing season when it departed from San Diego for New Zealand. For the first time in their 30 years of marriage, Emily accompanied Harold on a fishing trip. For the Medina Family, it was a perfect venture. It permitted Emily to have the unique experience of observing her husband and sons at work aboard their home away from home. After a particularly long workday, Harold recalls Emily's reaction to what she had seen: "You and your crew earn your money." The vessel was loaded within 10 days. It could be claimed that maybe Emily's presence aboard contributed to this fantastically successful fishing trip. Emily returned to San Diego on a flight from New Zealand, while Harold commanded the vessel during its trip to American Samoa. After arriving on January 23, 1978, the vessel unloaded a record 1800 tons of skipjack tuna.

Early on during that extraordinary fishing trip, Harold observed from the helicopter that the net was not sinking properly after being released. He noted that the "purse seine bridles" were stretched in a manner that caused them to be closely aligned with the "chainline." The problem was corrected by lengthening each of the two lines of every bridle by two feet. The purse rings were now placed at a greater distance from the net's "chainline." This modification by Harold allowed the net to sink freely, and thereby prevent entanglement with the "chainline."

Harold's Lost Opportunity to Buy the ZAPATA DISCOVERER

While in the process of negotiating an arrangement for Harold to again be Captain of the ZAPATA DISCOVERER, an officer of the vessel's owner offered Harold the following opportunity to purchase the vessel. The purchase price of $6 million was to be paid under a financial arrangement provided by the ship-owner, subject to the condition that Harold agree to annually transship one load of tuna from Panama to a cannery in Canada. Harold quickly agreed to this purchase arrangement, and was later told by an employee of the corporate owner that "the vessel was his." In response to what he considered to be a gentlemen's agreement, Harold contacted officials of Star-Kist and obtained their agreement to have Harold fish for Star-Kist, should the purchase be completed. Harold also contacted the insurance broker providing coverage to the ZAPATA DISCOVERER, advising him of the planned ownership change and of Harold's wish to retain the existing coverage as the new owner of the vessel. Later, Harold was informed that while the San Diego employee who made the offer to Harold was on a business trip to Florida, his fellow employee made a trip to the Texas headquarters of the ship-owner and persuaded the ship-owner to change the sale terms of the vessel. Harold was told by employees of the corporate ship owner that the purchase price was now $7 million, rather than the $6 million that had been agreed upon, and that Harold would have to arrange the purchase financing on his own. Harold lost this opportunity because he did not have the personal financial resources to accept this unexpected new offer. Harold regrets to this day his failure to be more aggressive in pursuing this purchase opportunity.

Final Command of the KERRI M

After leaving command of the ZAPATA DISCOVERER, Harold decided to spend more time on shore as the Managing Owner of the KERRI M., and to have his youngest son, John, undertake his first command of a Tuna Seiner. His sons Gary, Bill, and Harold had found positions aboard new, large super seiners. Wade was not interested in continuing a career in the tuna fishery. His son Chris had left San Diego for residence and employment in northern California. Harold had decided that it was time for John to learn how to be a Captain. John's first trip as Captain was not successful. The KERRI M. returned with less than a third of a load after about 90 days at sea. Recalling his first unsuccessful fishing trip as a Captain and of his father's assistance on his second trip, Harold offered to make the next trip with John. After John rejected Harold's offer, Harold took command of the KERRI M. for his final fishing trip aboard that vessel. It was one of those "lucky" trips. As the vessel traveled past Cabo San Lucas, Baja California, and moved east into the Gulf of California, Harold found a compact area with 30- to 50-ton schools of Yellowfin Tuna. He advised his code boats of his find, but they were days away from the area. Fishing alone, he quickly loaded the vessel with over 640 tons of tuna in only 18 days at sea.

Soon thereafter, Harold announced his decision to sell his ownership interest in the KERRI M., as he no longer had the desire to take command. Harold was proud of the fact that, as a result of his fishing success, he had eliminated all debt on the vessel. He was not interested in managing the vessel from shore, knowing that it would be restricted to fishing in the EPO. His experience with the ZAPATA DISCOVERER had convinced him that the KERRI M. would not be competitive in developing the tuna resources of the central and western Pacific. Supportive of his opinion about the future of the KERRI M. were the actions of his fishermen sons, who had secured supervisory positions aboard new super tuna seiners. Also supportive were the opinions prompted during a meeting attended by fellow Tuna Captains. During the meeting, Joe Bogdanovich, President of Star-Kist Foods asked: why had his chief competitor, Van Camp Sea Food, decided to sell its ownership interests in U.S. Flag Tuna Seiners. Harold was impressed by the responses to that question by his fellow Captains. For Harold, the reasons for selling now were compelling. He quickly negotiated with his co-owner, Star-Kist Foods, Inc., and sold his ownership interest in the KERRI M. It was a difficult decision for Harold, especially after his "lucky trip." For the first time in 30 years, Harold was no longer the Captain of a tuna vessel. His hope was that his future in the U.S. tuna fishery was to manage the operations of new super tuna seiners from shore, rather than at sea.

7

CAPTAIN/MANAGER, F/V **OCEAN PEARL,**
"SUPER" TUNA SEINER

In late 1979, Harold was hired by Inter-Oceans Company to manage a new "super" Tuna Seiner, the OCEAN PEARL, under construction at Campbell Industries, Inc., San Diego, California. This opportunity fitted nicely with Harold's plan to continue his involvement with the U.S. Tuna Fleet by becoming a "shoreside" manager. Harold had developed a driving interest in searching for ways to make the existing tuna purse seine more efficient. His success with the KERRI M. in introducing the Medina Panel, satellite navigation, the "Stabilizer," and other technology to the tuna fleet illustrated his willingness to experiment and innovate. His new position would give him the shore time to better implement these interests. Experience in the Fleet had shown that most, if not all, Captains were able to make transitions to new equipment and methods successfully. It was Harold's announced intention to the ship's owner to make two or more "shakedown" trips aboard the new Seiner before John, his youngest son, took command of it.

A Newly-Designed Tuna Purse Seine Net

While the OCEAN PEARL was under construction, Harold persuaded the ship's owner that its purse seine should not be manufactured of the traditional nylon, but of hyper-ester. His belief that hyper-ester netting would sink faster and work deeper than nylon was based upon the following experience with Bill Kirkland, owner of West Coast Netting Company of Cucamonga, California: Kirkland brought one piece of nylon and one piece of hyper-ester netting to Harold; each piece was dry and about three feet square. Kirkland went to the starboard side of a docked seiner and told Harold to watch each piece of netting when they hit the water in the bay. Harold observed that both pieces of netting hit the water at the same time. The hyper-ester netting immediately sank out of sight, while the nylon netting remained at the surface until it had absorbed sufficient water, at which time it slowly sank into the bay. It is Harold's opinion that the hyper-ester webbing placed aboard the OCEAN PEARL was the best netting that he had ever used. The new net was 1000 fathoms (6000 feet) long and 15 strips (540 feet) deep. To minimize the entanglement of porpoises, a "Medina panel" was inserted with a specially-designed "corkline" made with a "hanging ratio" developed by Harold. During the trial set of the new net designed by Harold, the Government Diver who inspected the performance of the net remarked on the uniqueness of its "sail" effect. He told Harold that he was surprised at how the "net just popped open during back-down."

The Stabilizer

A "Stabilizer" is a large tank partially filled with seawater. As the vessel rolls, the water in the tank flows from side to side, causing tons of water to shift and pile up on one side or the other. The purpose of the "Stabilizer" is to neutralize the roll of the vessel, but if not timed correctly it will reinforce it. To time the water flow, baffles are welded into the tank, which restrict the free flow of the water, causing the weight of tank's water to be positioned to offset the roll of the vessel. Commencing with the maiden trip, Harold and his Chief Engineer found that the "Stabilizer" aboard the OCEAN PEARL was not effective, even during flat calm sea conditions.

Fishing was slow, and the helicopter pilot claimed that he was ill and needed to be taken to port.[1] At the time, the vessel was fishing closer to Hawaii than California, so Harold decided to take the pilot to Hawaii and hire a replacement. While in Honolulu, he told the Chief Engineer, Walter Cook, to purchase four steel plates and weld them into the Stabilizer. Chief Engineer Cook was familiar with the Stabilizer aboard the KERRI M., and he agreed with Harold that its design should be followed. The change resulted in marked improvement. After experiencing the improved performance of the modified "Stabilizer," the crew expressed the desire to throw Harold overboard as punishment for making them suffer during the previous fishing trips. (Harold later informed the shipyard of the defects in the design of the original "Stabilizer" and how to make the proper modifications.) From Hawaii, Harold decided to finish the trip by searching for new tuna grounds in the western Pacific. He quickly loaded the OCEAN PEARL by fishing on tuna congregating about floating debris or "logs." Harold completed his third fishing trip aboard the OCEAN PEARL on January 29, 1983, and then handed command to his son John.

A Difficult Decision and a Tragic Loss

During the period in 1983 that John commanded the OCEAN PEARL, the ship's owner and John became more involved in the management of the vessel. After Harold found that his views on managing the vessel differed substantially from those of his son and the owner, he decided to quit his position as shoreside manager of the OCEAN PEARL.

During November 1984, near the South Pacific Island Nation of Tuvalu, John Medina was fatally injured when an explosion occurred in the engine room. During this shipboard incident, his son Wade narrowly escaped death or serious injury.

Other sons of Tuna Captains have died tragically while fishing. The son of Captain Leo Correia, Captain Gregory W. Correia, age 41, in command of the U.S.-Flag tuna seiner TIAFIAMOANA, died in a helicopter crash on June 15, 1998, while fishing in the western Pacific. Nearby vessels failed to find his body. Pilot Todd Lloyd Miller, age 30, died a few hours after rescue.[2] On August 18, 1980, off the coast of Mexico, about 1,200 miles from San Diego, California, crewmember Jerry Correia, age 22, son of Captain Joseph (Joe) Correia, died in his father's arms aboard the U.S. Flag tuna seiner CALYPSO, five hours after being attacked by a shark while removing a live porpoise from a net.[3]

The names of San Diego tuna fishermen who died at sea are listed on the Tunamen's Memorial, located at Shelter Island, San Diego.

---

[1] Captain Harold Medina did not rely on the use of helicopters in fishing tuna/porpoise schools because he felt that he was insufficiently in control of the chase and capture procedures when a helicopter was used. Helicopters were found of value in locating and fishing the tunas in the central and western Pacific, which explains the use of a helicopter on the OCEAN PEARL.

[2] Jack Williams, Obituary, "Gregory Correia, 41; became commercial fisherman at 17," *The San Diego Union-Tribune,* Sec. B-5, June 23, 1998.

[3] Ken Hudson, "Tuna Fisherman Mauled by Shark, Dies Porpoise Rules Blamed," Sec. B-1 and B-8, *The San Diego Union*, August 20, 1980. Vern Griffin, "Tuna Fisherman still close to his beloved sea, even in death," Sec. A-2, *San Diego Evening Tribune*, August 26, 1980.

8

CAPTAIN, F/V **CAROLYN M.**,
"SUPER" TUNA SEINER

THE LAST COMMAND

During 1979-1983, the economic viability of owning and operating a newly-built U.S. Flag Tuna Seiner was being questioned. In addition to problems related to Law of the Sea issues, the yellowfin tuna conservation program of the Inter-American Tropical Tuna Commission (IATTC) and to the administration of the U.S. Marine Mammal Protection Act of 1972, ship operations were adversely impacted by higher expenses, such as the cost of fuel and lubricants, trip supplies, and repairs. Owner costs were also adversely affected by higher interest rates on long-term debt, and by higher premiums for Hull and "Protection & Indemnity" insurance coverage. The ex-vessel prices for frozen tuna delivered to canneries were also low, and no change in this trend was foreseen in the near future, as U.S. Tuna canners were being confronted with competition from tuna canners in Southeast Asia and elsewhere.

CAROLYN M. on trial run, Sturgeon Bay, Wisconsin
Courtesy of Mrs. Carolyn Medina
Vessel built by Peterson Builders, Inc., Sturgeon Bay, Wisconsin

While cruising to or from fishing grounds, most "super" Tuna Seiners would consume, on average, about 3,000 to 5,000 gallons of fuel per day. In an effort to reduce fuel and other trip costs, the owners of the CAROLYN M., a vessel with a carrying capacity of 1100 tons of frozen tuna, chartered it to citizens of Venezuela, making possible the purchase of less expensive diesel fuel and lubricants. For the term of the charter, the name of the vessel was changed to APURE. Harold's first cousin, Joe Medina, Jr., was the managing owner of the APURE, and he asked Harold to take command of the vessel for one trip only and to fish for tuna in the eastern Pacific Ocean (EPO). Harold was permitted to hire only one crewmember, the cook. Since the vessel and crew were located at

Mayagüez, Puerto Rico, Harold expected to immediately take the vessel to Panama for net repairs and installation of a Medina Panel. The latter was necessary because the vessel had been fishing in the western Pacific, where tunas do not school with porpoises. After his arrival in Puerto Rico, Harold was ordered not to depart until the charter agreement had been fully negotiated. About 50 days after taking command, Harold was ordered to take the CAROLYN M. from Puerto Rico to Venezuela to take aboard fuel and lubricants. The vessel was delayed in Venezuela for about a week before its departure to Panama. It took over a week in Panama to repair the net and install the Medina Panel. The vessel commenced its fishing trip on September 14, 1984, and completed it on December 14, 1984.

Most members of the crew had fished only in the western Pacific. The first few weeks at sea were successful, as skipjack were abundant off the coast of Ecuador. However, as ocean conditions changed, fishing for skipjack in unassociated schools became poor. In response, Harold took the CAROLYN M. far offshore, where tuna/porpoise schools were being caught. Harold soon discovered that he and the crewmembers operating the porpoise chaseboats were not working in harmony, and he was not able to quickly teach them how to perform their duties. Harold concluded that he and the chaseboat operators needed a training period to become familiar with his techniques of herding tuna/porpoise schools. In the past, when operating his own vessel during a bad fishing trip, Harold was able to make the necessary adjustments. He had experienced "bad fishing trips" before, but now he was operating a vessel owned by others. For this reason, he felt compelled to gamble on searching for schools of tuna not associated with porpoises. This decision restricted his fishing options, causing the vessel to land only 850 tons of tuna after 90 days at sea. It was his longest and worst fishing trip. It was also his last command. After struggling with his pride and his love with his life's work, he reached the conclusion that after fishing for tuna for over 40 years and spending about 25 years of his life actually at sea and away from his family, it was time to face the reality that his days as Master of a Tuna Clipper had ended. If given the chance to do it again, would Harold take it? "Absolutely; I would do it again in a heartbeat, but with hindsight improvements."

Harold was sad to acknowledge that he was the first and last grandson of patriarch Joaquin Medina to be in command of an American Tuna Clipper.

During his "retirement," Harold continued to be involved in shoreside activities related to the American Tuna Fleet. He served without compensation as President of the American Tunaboat Association, as a member of its Board of Directors for six years, and as a member of its Expert Skipper Panel. This Panel was created to assist Captains in improving their skills in fishing tuna/porpoise schools. He was hired by Campbell Industries of San Diego to undertake "shakedown" cruises of newly-launched "Super" Tuna Seiners before delivery to their owners. He also assisted, without compensation, the IATTC by providing his expertise to its program of improving the design of tuna purse seines so as to minimize the mortality of porpoises. For two years, he served as a member of the U.S. Coast Guard Commercial Fishing Vessel Safety Advisory Committee.

During his "retirement" period, Harold testified as an expert witness in more than 75 lawsuits filed by crewmembers against owners of Tuna Clippers seeking damages for personal injuries. An "epidemic" of crewmember lawsuits was identified by the American Tunaboat Association during the 1980s as threatening the economic viability of the San Diego-based Tuna Fleet. Tort reform in the law governing crewmember injuries and deaths aboard commercial fishing vessels of the United States became the subject of numerous Congressional hearings during the mid-1980s.[1]

In 1989, the National Research Council established the Committee on Reducing Porpoise Mortality from Tuna Fishing.[2] Ten individuals, including Captain Harold Medina, were named to the Committee. The Committee was advised that its report "will be used by the Secretary of Commerce as a basis for a proposed plan for research, development, and implementation of alternative fishing techniques," and that it was charged with the task of identifying "currently available and promising new techniques for reducing the incidental catch of porpoises in tuna fishing." It met on four occasions: 4-5 December 1989, 1-3 February 1990, 21-22 April 1990, and 11-12 June 1990. Its report was reviewed by the Governing Board of the National Research Council, composed of members drawn from the councils of the National Academy of Sciences, the National Academy of Engineering, and the Institute of Medicine. After approval by the Governing Board, the Committee's 176-page report, entitled *Dolphins and the Tuna Industry*, was published in 1992.[3] The Chairman of the Committee, Dr. Robert C. Francis of the University of Washington, in his *Preface* to the Report at page ix, expressed his gratitude to Harold, and noted that Harold had "consistently acted beyond the call of duty." He further wrote that Harold "as the only committee member from the U.S. tuna industry, has consistently provided his unique insight, sometimes in very contentious and uncomfortable situations, in the most distinguished and gentlemanly fashion imaginable."

---

[1] For information on the need for tort reform and the impact on the U.S. Tuna Industry by the filing of crewmember personal injury lawsuits against owners of U.S. Flag tuna vessels:

Hearings before the Subcommittee on Merchant Marine of the Committee on Merchant Marine and Fisheries, House of Representatives, 99th Congress, First and Second Sessions, "Limitation of Shipowner's Liability and Fishing Vessel Insurance and Safety Problems," October 1985, November 1985, April 1986, (Serial No. 99-36).

Hearings before the Subcommittee on Coast Guard and Navigation and the Subcommittee on Fisheries and Wildlife Conservation and the Environment of the Committee on Merchant Marine and Fisheries, House of Representatives, 99th Congress, First Session, "Fishing Vessel Insurance-Part 1," July and October 1985, (Serial No. 99-28).

Hearing before the Subcommittee on Fisheries and Wildlife Conservation and the Environment and the Subcommittee on Coast Guard and Navigation and the Subcommittee on Coast Guard and Navigation and the Subcommittee on Merchant Marine of the Committee on Merchant Marine and Fisheries House of Representatives, 100th Congress, First Session on "Fishing Vessel Compensation and Safety, June 11, 1987, (Serial No. 100-21).

Hearing before the National Ocean Policy Study of the Committee on Commerce, Science, and Transportation United States Senate, 100th Congress, First Session, on "Commercial Fishing Industry Vessel Safety and Compensation Act of 1987," September 16, 1987. (S.Hrg.100-346).

[2] Section 4(e) of the 1988 Amendment of the Marine Mammal Protection Act of 1972, as amended, changed Section 110(a) by adding a new paragraph that required the Secretary of Commerce to establish contract with the National Academy of Sciences (NAS) for conducting an independent review of information pertaining to the identification of "appropriate research into promising new methods of locating and catching yellowfin tuna without the incidental taking of marine mammals." This "independent review" of the NAS had to be submitted to the Secretary by September 8, 1989. Thereafter, the Secretary was required to submit the NAS report and a "proposed plan for research, development, and implementation of alternative fishing techniques, to the Committee on Commerce, Science, and Transportation of the Senate and the Committee on Merchant Marine and Fisheries of the House of Representatives on or before December 5, 1989." The Tuna/Porpoise Enigma was not solved by this Government effort; the fishing of tuna/porpoise schools by Tuna Seiners remains the best option to manage and conserve both the tunas and porpoise populations in the EPO. Public Law 100-711-Nov. 23, 1988, 100th Congress, 102 STAT. 4768-4769; [16 U.S.C.1380 (a)].

[3] Dolphins and the Tuna Industry, Committee on Reducing Porpoise Mortality from Tuna Fishing, Board on Environmental Studies and Toxicology, Commission on Life Sciences, National Research Council. National Academy Press, Washington, D.C. 1992.

PART II

A TUNA FISHERY "ENIGMA"

9

SECRET DISCOVERED

<u>By Author Zane Grey</u>

During 1924, the American author, Zane Grey, fished the waters of the eastern Pacific Ocean (EPO). He wrote about his fishing adventures in waters off Isla Cocos, Costa Rica, the Galapagos Islands, Ecuador, and coastal waters off Costa Rica, El Salvador, and Mexico while fishing on his 190-foot, three-masted schooner FISHERMAN (ex <u>Marshal Foch</u>). A member of his crew was master fisherman, George Takahashi of San Pedro, California. When the FISHERMAN fished off Cabo San Lucas, Baja California, Mexico, Takahashi visited with fellow Japanese immigrants operating California-based baitboats. He probably informed them of his fishing for tuna off Isla Cocas and the Galapagos Islands, and of his sightings of tuna with porpoises.

Zane Grey's book, Tales of Fishing Virgin Seas, contains dramatic photos of tunas and porpoises. While off Cabo San Lucas, Mexico, a crewmember filmed Grey's chase of a herd of porpoises that numbered in the thousands. In addition, Grey authored a beautiful word description of how individuals and ranks of individuals in the porpoise school leaped, dove, splashed, and raced toward the setting sun.

Zane Grey left Balboa, Panama Canal Zone, on January 30, 1924, aboard the FISHERMAN. The vessel first fished off Isla Cocos, and then traveled to the Galapagos Islands. On this trip, Grey provides his readers with the following description of a tuna/porpoise school:

> "When the ship reached a point about two hundred yards behind the porpoises and tuna, and somewhat to their left, they suddenly ceased feeding and began to leap and plunge away from us, charging in almost a solid line, churning the water white. . . . For a few moments tuna showed here and there in that splashing formation; then they vanished the place to porpoises. These kept up the leaping, almost with straight front, for fully a quarter of a mile. Then they slackened their leaps, and slowed down, and sounded. We could only conclude that this mixed school of fishes and porpoises had taken fright at the near approach of the ship."[1]

Thereafter, Zane Grey describes the catching of tuna at the Galapagos Islands, and of sighting schools of porpoises off the coasts of Costa Rica and El Salvador, and of the fishing for tuna by California commercial fishermen on purse seiners and baitboats at Cabo San Lucas, Mexico. Grey gives an excellent account of his speedboat chasing a huge traveling herd of porpoises not associated with tuna off Cabo San Lucas, and a beautifully written record of sights that would become familiar to the future crews of California tuna clippers:[2]

> "One morning as we ran out off the Cape we espied a long dark line of leaping fish on the horizon. . . . When we were within two miles I decided the marching white and black wall was an enormous school of porpoises—by far the greatest number I had ever seen together. The school had fully a mile front. . . ." (p. 198).

> "There were thousands of porpoises, of all sizes, apparently, and all them appeared to be in the air when the other half was down. . . . Chester began to wind his [motion-picture] camera. . . (p. 199).

> "We gave chase . . . . Our boats at top speed made about fourteen miles an hour. Gradually the porpoises slowed down, and we began to gain. . . . Soon they were settling down to their regular gait and their playful water gymnastics. I saw porpoises leap twenty feet into the air, and farther than that on a straightaway forward dive. . . . They drew away from us, and sheering east, headed into the track of the sun. To our right came the other half of the school, soon to join those we had followed . . . . Thus the maelstrom distanced us and swept on into the glare of the sun." (pp. 200-201).

By California Tuna Baitboat Captains

Tuna fishermen are skilled searchers and observers of ocean life, birds, and debris. They scan the ocean for bird activity, floating objects, moving objects, splashes or wind-like turbulence in waves and swells, shades of dark colors mixed with the blues, greens, and grays of an ever-changing ocean hue, bright flashes hinting of life below the surface, anything on, below, or above providing a sign of ocean life. Their livelihood depends upon the success of their searches and observations.

It is not known when California tuna fishermen first discovered the bond between the tropical tunas and porpoises. In fishing off Southern California for Albacore tuna or Bluefin tuna during the early years of the fishery (1903-1917), the California tuna fishermen did not report an association of these two tunas with porpoises. During the period 1918-1927, the California tuna fleet expanded its ventures along the Pacific coast of Baja California and the islands of Guadalupe, San Benito, and Cedros. Mother ships working for California tuna canners were based at Cabo San Lucas, allowing tuna fishermen aboard small baitboats and seiners to fish in this area. In Zane Grey's many descriptions of porpoise herds intercepted in 1924 off Cabo San Lucas, he made little reference to their association with tunas, nor did his descriptions of fishing conducted by California bait and purse-seine fishermen mention their association with porpoises. In the late 1920s, tuna clippers were not dependent upon mother ships as they expanded their search for tunas to the islands of Socorro and Clarion, into the Gulf of California, off Mazatlan and the Islas Tres Marias (Maria Madre, Maria Magdalena, and Maria Cleofas). It is this expansion beyond the fishing areas about Cabo San Lucas that provides our first report of California tuna fishermen fishing for tropical tunas (Yellowfin and Skipjack) associated with porpoises.

Tuna Clipper Baitboat FLYING CLOUD

Based upon co-author Felando's discussion with Captain Joe P. Soares, it is believed that Japanese immigrant fishermen operating tuna clippers from San Diego and San Pedro were the first to fish tuna/porpoise schools. Born in San Diego, California, in 1916, Captain Soares remembered the following fishing experience while aboard the ATLANTIC: The San Diego Baitboats ATLANTIC and FLYING CLOUD were exchanging fishing information after the ATLANTIC intercepted the homeward-bound FLYING CLOUD. The vessels were located in waters off Cabo San Lucas. The captain of the San Diego-based FLYING CLOUD, T. Yamaguchi, told M.O. Medina, captain of the ATLANTIC, that he should go to the Islas Tres Marias and fish the tunas with the "porpoise" schools.[3] Joe clearly recollects that this idea of fishing "porpoise" schools for tuna was not previously known by the captain and crew of the ATLANTIC. Captain Medina followed the surprising advice, and the ATLANTIC loaded up with large yellowfin caught in association with herds of "porpoises." Joe recalled that his partner in the fishing rack for 2-pole fishing was the cook on the vessel, and that this cook was a strong and skilled fisherman. Joe said that he was nine years old when he made his first tuna fishing trip aboard the San Diego-based tuna baitboat VASCO DA GAMA. His best recollection was that he was 13 or 14 at the time of this fishing trip aboard the ATLANTIC. It is very likely that the discovery of tuna/porpoise schools by the California tuna fleet first occurred after tuna clippers became capable of venturing south of Cabo San Lucas in waters about the Islas Tres Marias. Supporting this view are reports made by fishermen, journalists, and biologists concerning fishing on tuna/porpoise schools by California tuna boats prior to World War II. They all state that such fishing occurred "south of Cabo San Lucas."

Tuna Clipper Baitboat HERMOSA[4]

The HERMOSA, formerly a passenger vessel that traveled from the port of Los Angeles to Santa Catalina Island, California, was converted to a tuna baitboat. It was the first U.S.flag tuna baitboat to fish at Isla Cocos, Costa Rica. Captain John Zuanich told a journalist for *Pacific Fisherman*:

> "The banks of Cocos Island are virgin territory for commercial fisheries, and have been fished only by Zane Grey and John Barrymore, on sportfishing expeditions."

The article correctly explained the economic significance of the fishing trip:

> "An interesting long-range exploit was the prospecting trip of W.F. Maggio's 137' bait boat "Hermosa" as far south as Salvador's shores, Cocos Island, tropical spot 2,400 miles south of San Pedro, made famous by legendary pirate Morgan and other freebooters, also was visited by the craft. Both Yellowfin and Albacore [sic.] were reported by Capt. John Zuanich as [sic.] encountered more or less continually in more southerly waters, and he brought back numerous specimens around 300 pounds.

> "Commercially the trip was no outstanding success, as only 30 tons were caught. However, the knowledge gained from actually prospecting and finding fish in these waters may have far-reaching effects, eventually."

This trip by the HERMOSA, made in early 1929, was not successful in terms of catching tuna. However, it did spark the exploratory interests of California tuna fishermen in seeking tuna-fishing grounds south of Mexican waters. By the end of 1929, tuna baitboat fishermen from San Pedro fished for tuna at the Galapagos Islands, Ecuador.

Tuna Clipper Baitboat NAVIGATOR

The tuna baitboat NAVIGATOR explored Isla Cocos in March 1930, and Captain Manuel K. Freitas of San Diego reported [5]

> "A discouraging trip in February brought Capt. Freitas' decision to cruise to Cocos Island, but he said very little about it, and made his preparations by loading his vessel to capacity with extra fuel and supplies.

> "As the "Navigator" approached, Freitas saw a thickly timbered island about 13 miles long and rearing heavenward. Close in-shore he saw a swarm of boobies working the calm surface and edged in until he was over the spot.

> **"He never forgot what he saw. In the transparent deep ocean blue, into which the eye could pierce many feet, he saw tier after tier of porpoises, moving restlessly. When the gliding bodies parted he saw the tuna; great fish, magnified in the water, but which he judged averaged over 100 pounds.** [emphasis added]

> "He set three 4-pole teams on the racks and as the first squids slithered in white lines across the water, the whole ocean around seemed to heave. The huge fish were snapping hungrily at the artificial lures, jumping half out of the water in a mad frenzy to snatch the bait.

> "Freitas, one of the pioneers of this tuna fishing, declares he has never experienced anything like the avidity with which these tuna struck at the lures. Live bait was totally unnecessary—and was not used during the operations.

> "Fish came aboard so quickly that Freitas was at once compelled to call off one team and put them to killing and icing tuna. Hardly a fish was caught that weighed less than 100 pounds—and certainly these Yellowfin had never before been lured by a fisherman's wiles.

> "Capt. Freitas tested the water and it registered over 85 degrees—and at that temperature fish must be stowed almost as quickly as caught. The crew could fish only three hours of each day during the week the "Navigator" lay in this prolific spot. Human endurances could not stand the terrific [sic.] strain longer." The vessel returned to port with 140 tons."

A review of articles in *Pacific Fisherman* during the 1930-1939 period, show that comments on "porpoise fishing" were not reported again until 1936. For example: "The long range boats were concentrated off Costa Rica where, almost without exception, the crews were "porpoise fishing," which means they were working moving schools of tuna in deep water.[6] "In tropical areas the crews relied entirely on moving schools of tuna discovered by the ever-present porpoises, and worked in deep water. The tuna were mostly two and three-pole fish, scaling from 40 to 50 pounds."[7] "While most boats were fishing the banks off Lower California and in the Gulf of California, several of the clippers were engaged in "porpoise" or open seas operations off Costa Rica."[8] "The profitable "porpoise" fishing off Costa Rica and Panama, working moving schools of tuna, had practically ceased at the end of the month in favor of "still" fishing at the Ecuadorian Islands."[9] "It was practically all "porpoise" fishing at the Central American banks, clippers following the schools as the fish swam northward."[10] "A number of the major clippers found profitable schools off Costa Rica, where it was practically all "porpoise" fishing."[11] "There were scattered reports of "porpoise fishing," but it is considered the tuna have not yet begun the annual northern migration."[12] "Schools appear to be definitely on the move after that date (April 15) and "porpoise fishing" becomes general."[13] "Down off Costa Rica schools were said to be prolific, and both types of fishing, "still" and "porpoise" were engaging the tuna crews."[14] "Both "porpoise" and still fishing engaged the crews, with the result several of the major vessels . . . came in with near capacity Yellowfin fares."[15]

In 1938, H.C. Godsil, a highly-respected fishery biologist working for the State of California, described how fishermen use birds and porpoise to find the tunas. It was his opinion-at that time-that the porpoise have reasons to follow the tuna.

> "Tuna (Yellowfin) and skipjack are schooling fish. Their presence may be detected in a number of ways. At times the fish break water, leaping clear. At other times when near but not breaking the surface they cause a dark and ruffled spot, which on a calm day may be seen at a considerable distance. At other times the presence of a school of fish is revealed at great distances by a flock of birds working overhead. It appears that the tuna in pursuit of food will drive their quarry to the surface. Knowing this the sea birds hover overhead following the school, swooping down when the opportunity serves to pounce upon whatsoever food they can secure. Thus to the tuna fisherman the sea birds are a blessing, for "working birds" invariably mean fish.

> "In southern waters from Cabo San Lucas south, tuna are often found with porpoise so that a tuna boat never passes a school of porpoise without investigation. There seems to be a symbiotic relationship between the two. **From observations it appears that the porpoise follow tuna, preying upon whatsoever food the tuna find. This is especially true in the more southern Central American waters where off the mainland tuna is nearly always found with porpoise.**"[16]
> (emphasis added)

Harold Medina has always been convinced that the tunas follow the porpoise, and all tuna captains questioned agree with Harold's opinion. An interest in doing something to temporarily break the tuna-porpoise bond was of no concern to fishermen operating a Tuna Clipper Baitboat. There existed no operational need for fishermen to have the tunas stop following the porpoise; in fact, they benefited from the association. Harold has always believed that the tunas follow the porpoise because the porpoise can more effectively find feed, and that just as tunas find a need to gravitate about floating debris such as logs, so also do they find a need to follow the swift moving "debris" of a porpoise school. Some fishermen have other theories: the excrement flowing from the large porpoise schools being a food source for small fish and the protective canopy that the porpoises provide from sharks and other predators.

In 1949, Harold permitted Giles W. Mead, Jr., a biologist with the U.S. Fish and Wildlife Service, U.S. Department of Interior, to make a fishing trip aboard the tuna baitboat ALPHECCA.[17] Mr. Mead's observations included the following:

"The principal area fished was centered approximately 140 miles off the coast of El Salvador. The catch in this area was composed almost exclusively of two-pole yellowfin, i.e., yellowfin from 30 to 100 pounds. These schools were most often found under porpoise of the type fittingly called "spinners" by the fishermen. The porpoise jumped ten or fifteen feet in the air, spinning as they went. Schools of porpoise and fish were often immense. Birds were usually seen working over the fish, but they were scattered and not numerous.

"Twice the ALPHECCA left this area, proceeding northward to waters forty to sixty miles off central Nicaragua. Here the fish were smaller one-pole yellowfin and oceanic skipjack. Few porpoise were seen in this area, and the schools were located by the presence of birds or by ripples in the water."[18]

Observations of Captain Harold Medina

During the morning, the tunas, porpoises, birds, and "feed" would be individually moving throughout the area. Then, at about noon, significant sea life changes would occur. The porpoises would move as a herd, led by a small group of individuals. When this occurred, Harold would search for the main body of the tunas. (This tactic was used by Harold when operating the ALPHECCA as a baitboat and later as a converted tuna seiner.) The use of Polaroid glasses significantly increased Harold's ability to see the tunas and follow their movements. He first used these glasses to follow a school of porpoises that stretched out for miles in waters off Costa Rica. At about 11:00 a.m., the ALPHECCA moved about the porpoise school while Harold searched for the tunas. None were sighted. Then, Harold put on the Polaroid glasses. The glare of the sun on the smooth, glass-like ocean was removed like magic, and he saw the tunas. In the baitboat operation, bait would be chummed as the main body of the tunas was approached. "Spinner" porpoise would not be attracted to the baitfish, but the "spotter" porpoise would seek the bait, causing the fishermen in the fishing racks to slap the ocean surface with their bamboo poles. This noisy movement would cause the "spotter" porpoise to cease their feeding on the baitfish, leaving the waters about the baitboat to the hungry tunas.[19]

In fishing a mixed school of tuna and porpoises, the captain runs the boat slowly, trying to stay in the middle of the porpoise herd or where he can see the "black spot" or traveling school of tuna. Sometimes, the "black spot" would be centered directly behind the porpoises, and at other times, the "black spot" would be to the right or left of the porpoise herd. After establishing the location of the "black spot," he would position the vessel just ahead of the porpoise herd, and then stop and let the porpoise go by, fishing and chumming as the porpoises went by. Then, he would "kick" the vessel ahead and repeat the above procedure. If and when another tuna clipper joined the original vessel because of the size of the porpoise herd—sometimes consisting of thousands of individuals—the baitboats will duplicate the maneuvers described and overlap each other's last fishing position. (In Harold's experience, conflicts between baitboats fishing the same tuna/porpoise school rarely occurred.)

When bait-fishing a "pure" school of tuna, the captain would position the vessel so that it drifted with the tuna school, with the port side of the vessel, where the fishing racks are located, on the leeward side. If the school of tuna is spread out over a large area and the distance between the vessels exceed about five boat lengths, the vessels do not interfere with one another. However, if the baitboat is fishing a school of tuna and another baitboat begins to fish within a boat length or two, the custom in the fishery would justify action by the original vessel to protect its exclusive interest in fishing the tuna school.

[1] Zane Grey, Tales of Fishing Virgin Seas, (Lanham and New York: The Derrydale Press, Paperback 2000): p. 44.

[2] Zane Grey, Tales of Fishing Virgin Seas, (Lanham and New York: The Derrydale Press, Paperback 2000): pp. 198-201.

[3] The 108' FLYING CLOUD, built in Long Beach, California, for San Diego residents T. Yamaguchi and M. Tomita, was delivered in July 1928. Joe Soares's father was a co-owner of the ATLANTIC. For information on and photographs of the San Diego Tuna Fleet in 1928: Coburn F. Maddox, "San Diego Tuna Industry," California Fish and Game, Vol. 15, No. 1: pp. 34-39.

[4] Anon. "Canned Tuna Catch Continues Light." Pacific Fisherman, May 1929, p. 33. References to this trip in Fish Bulletins published by the California Division of Fish and Game: Geraldine Connor, 1930, "The Five Tunas and Mexico," Fish Bulletin No. 20: pp. 75-89; Geraldine Connor, 1931, "Expansion of Tuna Fishing Areas," Fish Bulletin No. 30: pp. 23-31.

[5] Art Ponsford, "Treasure Island Yields Rich Cargo to the Exploring "NAVIGATOR," Pacific Fisherman, April 1930, p. 38. See also: Geo. Roger Chute, "ADVENTURER Hits Submerged Rock" The West Coast Fisheries, June 1930, pp. 14, 39, 58. "We landed at Cocos. . . The sea was full of porpoise all around the island—thousands and thousands of them—and there were some swordfish, too; big ones."

[6] Pacific Fisherman, July 1936, p. 21.

[7] Pacific Fisherman, August 1936, p. 28.

[8] Pacific Fisherman, September 1936, p. 25.

[9] Pacific Fisherman, December 1936, p. 35.

[10] Pacific Fisherman, August 1938, p. 15.

[11] Pacific Fisherman, October 1938, p. 17.

[12] Pacific Fisherman, March 1939, p. 23.

[13] Pacific Fisherman, May 1939, p. 14.

[14] Pacific Fisherman, September 1939, p.16. Reporters for this fishing trade magazine

described this type of pole-and-line fishing as "still" fishing for purposes of distinguishing it from "porpoise" fishing.

[15] *Pacific Fisherman*, November 1939, p. 19.

[16] H.C. Godsil, 1938. "The High Seas Tuna Fishery of California," Division of Fish and Game of California, *Fish Bulletin No. 51*: pp. 27-28.

[17] Fishery scientists tagged tuna from the ALPHECCA as a tuna clipper baitboat on two trips: March 2 to May 5, 1959, and October 1 to December 23, 1959.

[18] Giles W. Mead, Jr., "Preliminary Report On Tuna Fishing Trip Off Central America, (April 23-June 9, 1949)," *Commercial Fisheries Review,* Vol. 11, No. 8: pp. 20-21.

[19] "During bait-fishing days (jack-pole [sic.] fishing), dolphins would stay near tuna vessels. Bait fish were tossed into the water (chumming) to hold fish near the boat where they could be hooked. If the dolphins remained near the vessel, tuna could be caught, but if the dolphin herd moved away, so did the tuna." Co-author Harold Medina, <u>Dolphins and the Tuna Industry</u>, Committee on Reducing Porpoise Mortality from Tuna Fishing, Board on Environmental Studies and Toxicology, Commission on Life Sciences, National Research Council, National Academy Press, Washington, D.C.: p. 46.

10

SECRET EXPLAINED

After American tuna fishermen discovered nature's working relationship between yellowfin tuna and porpoise, they developed methods to take advantage of this unique association. First, they operated "baitboats," using live bait, and bamboo poles and hooked lines to catch the tunas found with the porpoise. In this fishery, the sighting by fishermen of a herd of porpoises beneath feeding birds regularly resulted in the finding of tuna. Live bait would be skillfully tossed into the part of the porpoise herd where tunas were spotted. In this fishery, there was no need to capture the porpoises to hook the tunas. The "enigma" was not a problem for the baitboat fishermen.

The introduction of the Puretic Power Block (1955) and the availability of nylon webbing (1956) encouraged owners of tuna purse-seine vessels in their belief that they were the most viable alternative to the U.S. tuna baitboat fishery, a fishery struggling to compete economically with Japanese tuna fishermen.[1] Unlike tuna baitboats, tuna seiners did not need to obtain and maintain live bait to capture the tunas. However, tuna seiners had problems fishing tuna/porpoise schools that baitboats did not have. Seiners found it necessary to herd some or all of the traveling porpoises into a relatively compact aggregation and then "set" or encircle them with the net. In seeking ways to capture the tunas in a tuna/porpoise school, seiners found that the tunas shadowed a segment of the porpoise school. If the porpoise leaders moved to the left, so also did the following school of tuna, some of which indicated their presence by "shining." If the porpoises splashed and moved to the right, then so did the deeper–swimming, obedient school of tuna. A "black spot" of these tightly-compacted fish discolored the ocean's blue hues, giving a telltale sign of their presence and movement.

Tuna seiners found that they could not separate the tunas from the porpoises before setting their net. To their distress, the fishermen also discovered that the leaping, acrobatic porpoise would not free themselves as a group from the net, so they had to help them leave the net *en masse* or in small groups. Further, while in the net, the air-dependent porpoise created safety problems for themselves, for the tunas, and for the fishermen. The "good news" is the fact that the "bond" between mammal and fish makes it easier for the fishermen to find and catch the tunas. The "bad news" is the fact that without help from the fishermen, the porpoises suffocate in the net because of entrapment or entanglement with the net's webbing. This fact threatened the loss of the tuna catch because of delays in getting the tuna out of the net and into the wells, where they are frozen, or from ruptures in the net caused by porpoise teeth or by the quantity of captured tuna and porpoises. The replacement of cotton nets with nylon fibers, commencing in 1956, reduced, but did not eliminate, the risk of net damage caused by the quantity of captured tuna and porpoises. (Also, nylon, in contrast to cotton, does not rot, which is particularly important in the warm, humid conditions which prevail in the tropics.) The U.S. tuna seiner fishermen's problem: how to help the porpoise free themselves from the net alive and without injury, and therefore, continue to use the "enigma" in capturing the yellowfin.

The seiner fishermen quickly found that, in most instances, the practice of sending the crew into the net to physically lift individual porpoises over the cork-line, was not the best solution. Too few porpoises were saved, and this practice proved dangerous for the fishermen. Sharks lurking outside the net would attack the porpoises as soon as they were lifted over the cork-line. While the net was being stacked, entangled dead porpoises would slide downward representing a danger to the fishermen who were working below. It was more common for fishermen to be seriously injured by falling porpoises than by shark attacks. Manual release efforts could not effectively solve this problem because many porpoises would become entangled in the webbing of the net many fathoms below the surface areas worked by the rescuing fishermen.

Without porpoises, fishermen knew that they would not be able to economically catch the large yellowfin tuna that associate with them. They knew that they had to find better ways of removing porpoise alive from the purse seine without losing the tunas.

Despite extensive studies, fishery scientists have not discovered the reason for the bond between yellowfin tuna and porpoises in the eastern Pacific Ocean (EPO).[2] There is clear evidence that this "enigma" also prevails in other tropical latitudes in other parts of the world's oceans, such as in the South Atlantic Ocean off West Africa and in the Indian Ocean. The IATTC has written that ". . . judging from its persistence and strength, it is obvious that at least one of these animals obtains some benefit from their close association." For a long period of time, some scientists supported the theory that since the porpoises were more capable of finding prey by echolocation, the yellowfin follow the porpoises. Recent studies found that feeding on shared prey "may not be the primary cause for the association, and that other causes should be explored." These studies hinted, but did not prove, that the bond weakened at night. There exists evidence that San Pedro-based tuna seiners fishing in the vicinity of the Revillagedo Islands, Mexico, experienced successful fishing opportunities arising from a "weakening at night" of this bond.[3]

Do tunas follow porpoise?

In 1941, Captain Guy Silva, a legendary figure in the California tuna fleet, was asked to describe "Porpoise Fishing."[4] At the time of this interview, he was the captain and owner of the 100-foot EMMA R. S., a tuna baitboat built in 1928 that made its first voyage to the Galapagos Islands in 1933.[5] Art Ponsford, the interviewing journalist, sought to provide "interesting sidelights on the little-known 'porpoise fishing' of the Southern California tuna fleet in Central American waters. . . ."

"Porpoise fishing is so called because a moving school of tuna is identified in deep water by its accompanying band of mammals. Actually, it is the other way around, and the tuna are following the porpoises, or at least staying with them, and for a very definite reason.

"Sometimes tuna are discovered ahead of the porpoises; sometimes following just behind, and often mixed up with them. The skipper wishing to fish such a school should be able to slow the pace of his vessel to that of the moving band. This will be as slow as a mile and a half an hour. Many clippers of the fleet cannot achieve this and must act accordingly, by moving through the school until beyond, then stopping to allow it to catch up.

"When porpoise fishing, the skipper maneuvers his vessel to where the tuna are thick and excited and sets his pace to theirs. The pole men then add another to their list of acquired accomplishments that of adjusting themselves to sideways motion as the clipper moves slowly ahead.

As to why tuna follow the porpoise, Captain Silva offered this opinion:

"Captain Silva points out that one of nature's ways of providing bait schools with protection while traveling at sea, is to cause the small fish—and that includes squid—to bunch tightly together. This bunching is referred to as a "ball of bait." Often the center of this compact mass will be raised inches out of water, due to pressure from crowding fish.

"In that condition, the EMMA R.S. owner says, the bait fish are safe from tuna. The big mackerel will not attack a ball of bait, nor seek to break it up. Whales and other mammals, however have no such scruples. Without hesitation, these will charge into the mass, scattering the bait and feeding along."

Journalist Ponsford concluded: "Tuna schools are thus attracted to the scene and use the good offices of porpoises, often seen looping and diving by tens of thousands, to secure food which otherwise would be denied the sharp-tailed fish."

Many fishery biologists have expressed support for the idea that the tunas control their relationship with the porpoise. "In support of the hypothesis that tuna, rather than porpoise, are responsible for the tuna-porpoise association, it was pointed out that tuna have been caught in association with a wide variety of objects such as: a single dead porpoise, whales, basking sharks, logs, oil drums, derelict row boats, etc. It was also noted that bait boat fishermen routinely chum to temporarily "hold" tuna found in association with porpoise, but these tuna cannot be held indefinitely. Eventually, they leave the chumming site, presumably to rejoin the porpoise with which they were originally associated. These observations suggest that visual stimuli may be important for maintaining the bond, but long-distant olfactory or acoustic cues may be more important for the initial establishment of the bond."[6]

What tunas follow porpoises?

For the American tuna fishermen, the term "tuna" is restricted to four species of the genus *Thunnus*. Yellowfin, *T. albacares*, Bigeye, *T. obesus*, Albacore, *T. alalunga*, and Bluefin, *T orientalis*, and skipjack tuna, *Katsuwonus pelamis*.[7] Yellowfin and skipjack have been caught in association with porpoises in the

EPO, although the skipjack, which are caught in only small amounts, may be "innocent bystanders." There have been no reports of bigeye, albacore, or bluefin being caught in association with porpoises, or even having been seen associating with them.

Large yellowfin has always been preferred by U.S. canners because of its high yield (number of cans per ton of tuna) and lower cleaning costs. Also, canners consider the taste of yellowfin to be slightly superior to that of skipjack. Higher prices are paid for large yellowfin (20-150 lbs.) than for large skipjack (7.5-12 lbs.).

The IATTC reports that yellowfin start schooling with porpoises when they reach an age of about 2 years and a weight of about 26 pounds. The average weight of yellowfin caught in schools associated with floating objects and in unassociated schools is only about 8 to 10 pounds. The IATTC further reports that the "critical size" of yellowfin is about 111 cm or 62 lbs. The "maximum sustainable yield" of yellowfin can be obtained if most of the fish weigh about 62 pounds.

Using these facts, Dr. James Joseph, Director of the IATTC, has written:

> "Prohibiting dolphin fishing would eliminate the incidental mortality of dolphins but would probably result in adverse long-term consequences for yellowfin tunas and possible [sic.] harm the ecosystem of the EPO as a whole. Changing from fishing international waters for the large, sexually mature yellowfin usually found associated with dolphins, to fishing on logs and schools for predominantly smaller, sexually immature yellowfin and skipjack tunas closer to shore would, at current levels of effort, lead to overexploitation of the resource and also give rise to political problems over access to areas under national jurisdiction."[8]

If fishing in the EPO for tuna/porpoise schools were prohibited and restricted to "log" and "school" fishing (fishing on schools associated with floating objects and unassociated schools), Dr. Joseph predicted that the net effect of this policy "would be a reduction of between 30 and 60 percent in the catch of yellowfin, from recent levels of 300,000 tons to between 120,000 and 200,000 tons. . . the reduced catches would lead to economic difficulty for many whose livelihoods depend on the fishery, especially since the reduced catches would also be worth less in absolute terms, because smaller fish command a lower price."[9]

Fishery scientists have also declared that a policy of shifting all tuna purse-seine fishing away from tuna/porpoise schools and directing the tuna fishermen to encircle only "pure" schools of yellowfin or "mixed" schools of yellowfin/skipjack or to "log" fishing would also cause an unnecessary loss of juvenile yellowfin and an unacceptable waste of other fish that are caught incidentally in large numbers in sets made on floating objects. Dr. Martín A. Hall, an IATTC fishery biologist, explains:

> "Of the three types of sets, those on floating objects have, by far, the greatest by-catches. As the logs are drifting, fish of all sizes and body configurations, slow or fast-moving, can aggregate under them. On the other hand, groups of tunas and dolphins cruise at high speeds, and prior to setting there is a chase at even higher speed, so that when the group is encircled almost no small or slow-moving spe-

cies of fishes or other animals are encircled. Aside from dolphins, the bycatches of dolphin sets consist of a few sharks and, occasionally, billfishes, mahi-mahi, wahoo, and/or sea turtles. . . . It is clear that dolphin sets are by far the 'cleanest' in this respect. . . ."[10]

Where is the "Enigma" found?

The distribution of the "enigma" within the EPO appears to be limited to the tropical latitudes, north and south of the equator. Insufficient information presently exists about the distribution of the "enigma" in all of the tropical latitudes south of the equator. Prior to the 1960s, the U.S. tuna fishery in the EPO operated within about 250 nautical miles of the mainland and in the vicinity of a few offshore islands and banks. IATTC records show that tuna/porpoise schools occur both within and beyond the 200-mile exclusive economic zones of the coastal States bordering the EPO, and that schools of tuna not associated with porpoises occur more frequently in areas close to shore, well inside of these 200-mile zones. During the late 1960s and 1970s, American fishermen found that adult yellowfin occur far offshore, and that they can be caught when they are associated with porpoises.[11] In 1979, a group of scientists decided that porpoise stocks were distributed in three zones: an "inshore zone" of 1,722,162 square nautical miles; an area called the "calibration zone" of about 800,000 square nautical miles; and, an "offshore zone" of about 4 million square nautical miles.[12]

The regulation of yellowfin fishing by imposing an annual quota required the IATTC to establish a regulatory zone, known as the Commission's Yellowfin Regulatory Area (CYRA). In 1969, the U.S. tuna seiners discovered new tuna/porpoise fishing grounds west of the CYRA, and by 1974, catches were made as far west as 150°W Longitude (near Hawaii). To regulate the fishing of tuna/porpoise schools by the U.S. tuna purse-seine fleet in the Pacific, the National Marine Fisheries Service (NMFS) restricted this method of fishing to the portion of the EPO bounded by 40° South Latitude and 40° North Latitude east of 160° West Longitude. Commencing in 1976, the U.S. Tuna purse-seine fleet was denied permission by NMFS to fish tuna/porpoise schools in any other ocean region of the world. (These regulations did not apply to the increasing number of large foreign-flag tuna seiners operating in the EPO.)

Why tuna fishermen say "porpoise" and not "dolphin"?

American tuna fishermen have given "code names" to certain porpoises. These names are descriptive of a unique behavior or physical characteristic, namely Spotters, Spinners, and Whitebellies.[13] It is not known why the American fishermen adopted the name "porpoise," rather than "dolphin." The word "porpoise" is of Latin origin; a combination of words meaning pig (pocus) and fish (Pisces). (Mammalogists now use the word "porpoise" for members of the family Phocoenidae and the word "dolphin" for members of the family Delphinidae. Porpoises have shorter beaks and flattened, spade-like teeth, whereas dolphins have longer beaks and conical teeth.) When radio operators in the tuna fleet used the word "porpoise" in sending out fishing information in code, the meaning was clear. To fishermen, the word "dolphin" has a dual meaning: a fish (which appears as "mahi mahi" on restaurant menus) and a mammal. Sending coded information using the word "porpoise" avoided error.[14]

"Spotters" and "spinners" are frequently associated with one another." "Spotters" associated with adult yellowfin (>2 years old; >30 lbs) are larger, on average, than spinners and whitebellies, and appear to be more mature and full-grown.[15] The coloration of medium to dark gray is mixed with a pattern of light spots, gives rise to the name "spotters." It is reported that spotters have reached a length of nearly 9 feet and a weight of over 250 pounds. They are found principally far off the coast when associated with large yellowfin, that is, of two-pole fish (30-50 lbs.) or larger. Importantly in terms of tuna conservation and management, female yellowfin are sexually mature and spawn at about age two or about 30 lbs in size. Captain Harold Medina believes that this association of spotters and yellowfin is related to their mutual attraction to the same type of food, namely large sardine-like fish, squid, and flying fish. That belief is based upon his observations that only "spotters" would feed on the baitfish chummed by baitboats; "spinners" were not attracted by chummed baitfish. Baitboat fishermen were compelled to strike the water with their fishing poles in an effort to frighten away the "spotters" from the live bait that was being tossed into the water by the Chummer to induce the tunas in a biting frenzy.

"Spinners" can be distinguished from "spotters" by the shape of their dorsal fin, the posterior edge of which is straight, or nearly so, in contrast to the posterior edge of the dorsal fin of "spotters," which is curved. Some fishermen have described the "flighty" hummingbird-like activity of "spinners" in the net, in contrast to the relatively calm and passive behavior of the "spotters."[16] Captain Harold Medina states that the "spinner" porpoises are associated only with schools of small yellowfin (<30 lbs.) and mixed schools of juvenile yellowfin and skipjack. Again, Harold has observed that "spinners" and small tunas were feeding exclusively on small organisms. Because of their athletic behavior in leaping, twirling, and then splashing, the fishermen named them "spinners." It is reported that some "spinners" have rotated as many as seven times or more in a leap. The color of the "spinners" is more uniformly gray, with white coloration to the underside.

The "whitebelly" porpoises associated with tuna are found mainly off Costa Rica, and far to the west, out to 150°W. They reach a length of about 8 feet.

Dr. Carl L. Hubbs, who had been a member of the staff of Scripps Institution of Oceanography, La Jolla, California, since 1944, testified before the Committee on Commerce, Science, and Transportation, U.S. Senate, on March 9, 1977. The Committee was conducting an oversight hearing on the Marine Mammal Protection Act of 1972 (MMPA). After completing his testimony, Dr. Hubbs was asked if the populations of "porpoise in the Pacific were in danger of extinction." He answered: "I think not. I have had the privilege of discovering two species of marine mammals; they happen to be both fur seals listed as extinct. I found they were still there and they both have increased. Marine mammals have a fantastic ability to recover, just almost seemingly unbelievable. . . . There is something about marine mammals even though they have only one young a year or one young every other or third year, they have a fantastic ability. The probability of the extermination, at least of these marine mammals is to my mind virtually out of the question."[17]

The tuna/porpoise "Enigma" on film

In 1924, the famed author and sportsman, Zane Grey, and his crew used a speedboat to take movies of porpoise schools off Baja California. In 1966, fishery biologist William Perrin filmed the fishing operations of the converted tuna seiner CONTE BIANCO. In addition, he took photos of the method used to help the porpoise leave the purse seine alive. This release method is known as the "Back-down"[18] In November 1972, Richard McNeely, U.S. National Marine Fisheries Service (NMFS) fishery gear specialist, and his assistants were aboard the converted tuna seiner INDEPENDENCE filming the fishing operations for the purpose of documenting the behavior of tuna/porpoise schools.

In January 1973, with the assistance of the American Tunaboat Association (ATA), 10 NMFS porpoise observers were provided with berths aboard 10 San Diego-based tuna seiners.[19] In addition to other gear, each was provided with cameras and instructions to collect data for evaluation of the efficiencies of various rescue techniques such as the "Back-down" and the "Medina Panel." During these early years of cooperation with the NMFS, the Tuna Industry accepted the risk of allowing NMFS personnel to film and photograph how tuna seiners fished tuna/porpoise schools without restriction.

Unfortunately, litigation initiated in 1974 by an environmental group against the NMFS involving the tuna seiner QUEEN MARY, caused captains and crews to assert that their privacy and other rights were being violated by the filming of their activities aboard their "home away from home" without their permission. As a result, restrictions on the use of cameras by NMFS observers aboard tuna seiners were imposed.

The film taken on this experimental charter aboard the QUEEN MARY was used in developing a motion picture to show a collection of severe instances of porpoise mortality events that occurred during various experimental sets of the net supervised by the scientists. The film showed how the vessel encircled the tuna/porpoise school. Underwater footage was taken of the porpoises and tuna within the closed net. Captain Joe Medina, Jr., was ordered to place the porpoise in stressful situations, thereby allowing the scientists to film the reaction of the porpoise to those conditions.

When the scientists first came aboard the vessel with their photographic equipment, Captain Medina advised co-author Felando that he had not been told that his vessel and crew were going to be unwilling actors, and that his vessel was going to be used as a movie set. The officials at the NMFS were asked for an explanation. Felando was assured that the taking of film was part of the scientific study, and that the film would be shown only to scientists for scientific purposes. At the time NMFS asked Felando to arrange the charter of the QUEEN MARY, Felando was not told that a movie would be produced from the footage taken during the trip. After Felando explained the discussion with the NMFS officials, Captain Medina stated that he would cooperate with the scientists after receiving personal assurances from the scientists that the film footage would be used only for, and by, the fishery scientists as part of scientific work.

The existence of this movie of porpoises under stress conditions within the tuna purse seine was first revealed to the ATA and Captain Medina sometime after the filing of a Freedom of Information lawsuit by the organization "Save the Dolphins," located in San Francisco, on January 4, 1974.[20] It is not known how "Save the Dolphins" obtained information that the NMFS Southwest Fisheries Center had produced an 800-foot motion picture from the footage taken during the experimental cruise of the QUEEN MARY.

The chartered fishing cruise commenced on November 17, 1971, and ended on December 16, 1971. The following are statements contained in a ruling made by a United States District Court Judge on November 14, 1975:

> ". . . NMFS chartered the purse seiner, M/V QUEEN MARY, with its captain, Joseph M. Medina, Jr., and its crew, for a research cruise in a part of the EPO closed to tuna fishing during that time of the year. The purpose of the cruise was to conduct experiments relating to the development of equipment and methods designed to improve porpoise rescue operations in tuna fishing. Medina's compensation for the use of his vessel and crew was the right to keep up to 500 tons of tuna caught during the cruise.

> "It appears that neither motion picture films nor photographs had been mentioned either in negotiations or in the actual charter agreement. On or about November 18, 1971, Medina expressed to Dr. William Evans, the government research team leader, his concern about the motion picture equipment which had been loaded onto the vessel, Medina sought assurances that first, the filming would not interfere with the operating of the vessel, and second, the films would not be shown to anyone but those involved in the research, since the scenes therein would depict fishing trade secrets and commercial information used by Medina's crew. Evans assured Medina that the films would be used only for research purposes and would not be made available to the public. Medina asserts that he would not have permitted filming but for the promise of confidentiality given by Evans. . . . (The Evan's film was later edited from) approximately 5,000 feet of film to produce an 800-foot motion picture film, which has not been released to the public.

> "The present controversy began when plaintiff (Save The Dolphins) requested that defendant (United States Department of Commerce) make the motion picture film available under the Freedom of Information Act. Defendant agreed to comply with the request on the condition that plaintiff obtain the consent of Medina, owner of the M/V QUEEN MARY. Medina denied consent.

> "A primary reason for the intervener's (Joseph M. Medina, Jr.) opposition . . . had been to the inclusion of tuna fishing trade secrets in the motion picture film. Accordingly, after several viewings both in camera and among the parties and their representatives, the film was jointly re-edited on two separate occasions to eliminate any trade secrets that may have been contained therein . . . . "

On September 22, 1975, the Court had previously ordered that any showing or reproduction of any frame of the government's motion picture film be accompanied by the following disclaimer:

> "The following scenes depicted in this film were obtained during government con-
> trolled situations in which experiments were conducted and do not necessarily re-
> flect commercial fishing operations."

Judge Charles B. Renfrew concluded: "It would appear appropriate to release the film accompanied by a disclaimer informing viewers that the scenes therein were taken during the course of experiments and do not necessarily depict occurrences in normal fishing operations . . . the disclaimer would not withhold or limit the release of information. To the contrary, it would provide the public with additional information in regard to the source of the scenes in the film. The disclaimer would aid viewers in forming more objective opinions as to the contents of the film and would thus be consistent with the purposes of the Freedom of Information Act." The Court ordered that plaintiff's motion for summary judgment be granted, and that "the motion picture be released forthwith to plaintiff, provided that the film will be displayed with a disclaimer pursuant to the order of this Court dated September 22, 1975."

Ironically, when the QUEEN MARY was chartered for a government/tuna industry "cooperative dedicated vessel research program," on the fifth and final experimental cruise (11 November to 9 December 1978), 7,000 feet of 16-mm movie film was shot of fishing sets made on tuna/porpoise schools.[21] This film footage was later used in a training movie for tuna captains, crews, and NMFS observers; it was also shown to members of Congress and their staffs.

---

[1] "Boom-Point Power Offers New Angle for Seine Fishing," *Pacific Fisherman*, May 1955: pp. 26-27. In 1954, working models of the Puretic Power Block were used aboard the San Pedro-based purse seiners ANTHONY M. (Captain Anton Misetich) and COURAGEOUS (Captain Andrew Kuljis). In 1955, the Puretic Power Block was successfully introduced to the Salmon Purse Seine Fleets of Washington and Alaska. Mario Puretic, a San Pedro commercial fisherman, invented the Power Block; an idea that changed the efficiency of commercial fishermen throughout the world. In commenting on the importance of the Puretic Power Block and the Nylon tuna purse seine, Captain Misetich stated that these two innovations represented the "salvation of the tuna purse seine fishery." "ANTHONY M. Pioneers All-Nylon Tuna Seine," *Pacific Fisherman*, April 1956: pp. 38-43.

[2] The IATTC has defined the "Eastern Tropical Pacific Ocean" (ETPO) as the area between 30° N and 40° S east of 150° W. The term used in the IATTC Convention of 1950 referred to the "Eastern Pacific (EPO)." During 1999, the IATTC adopted a resolution defining the EPO as the portion of the Pacific Ocean east of 150° W between 40° N and 40° S. Bayliff, William H. 2001, Organization, Functions, and Achievements of the Inter-American Tropical Tuna Commission, Inter-Amer. Trop. Tuna Comm., Spec. Rep., 13: p. 11.

[3] San Pedro-based tuna purse-seiner fishermen were expert at fishing tuna at night; San Diego-based tuna purse seiners did not favor night fishing for yellowfin. San Pedro fishermen, seeing tuna/porpoise schools about islands during the day would later successfully search for, and capture pure schools of tuna at night. Personal conversations of co-author Felando with Captain Nick Mosich (converted seiner MAURITANIA), and Captain Philip Felando (converted seiner ELSINORE), circa 2005 and 2006.

[4] " Porpoise Fishing' Described by Capt. Guy Silva," *Pacific Fisherman*, February 1941: p. 36.

[5] Edward M. Ries, "Guy Silva, San Diego Fisherman," *Mains'l Haul*, Vol. 29, No. 3: pp. 10-14, A Journal of Maritime History, Maritime Museum Association of San Diego.

[6] Final Report of the Marine Mammal Commission (MMC) Workshop held on 8 and 9 December 1975, at the University of California, Santa Cruz, Summary of Preliminary Discussions Section. See copy of final report, see: Hearings before the Subcommittee on Fisheries and Wildlife Conservation and the Environment of the Committee on Merchant Marine and Fisheries, House of Representatives, 94th Congress, 2nd Session on Save the Gray Whale Study—H.R. 15445-A Bill to Save the Grey Whale –Sept.10, 1976—Oversight of the Tuna-Porpoise Problem Sept 27-30, 1976--(Serial No. 94-45). (Cited herein: Sep 1976 House Subcommittee Hearings -SN-94-45): p. 198.

During a House hearing conducted by Rep. John Murphy, Chairman of the House Merchant Marine and Fisheries Committee—the first Congressman to observe the fishing of tuna/porpoise schools aboard a U.S. tuna seiner—Dr. William Fox, NMFS marine biologist was asked: "Do you have any explanation for the affinity which tuna may have for porpoise?" Dr. Fox answered: "No; we do not know whether it is tuna affinity for porpoise or the reverse, although we suspect it is the former case. We do not really know, but we have hypotheses. Tuna, porpoise, birds, it is a moving ecosystem that travels around together and may exist to optimize foraging for each of the members." Chairman Murphy responded: "Many of the crews have spent their lives in this industry, and yet they do not have a definitive reason as to why yellowfin follow dolphins." Hearings before the Committee on Merchant Marine and Fisheries, House of Representatives 95th Congress, First Session on Reducing Porpoise Mortality, May 13 and 16, 1977; Tuna-Porpoise Oversight, August 1, 1977 (Serial No. 95-3 (cited herein: May 1977 House Committee Hearings -SN 95-3): 458

[7] ". . . the process by which the word "tuna" gained entry into American usage is unknown. . . The principal species, all seven species of the genus *Thunnus* and the skipjack tuna, *Katsuwonus pelamis*, are the ones which [sic.] most sought for canning purposes" W. L. Klawe, "What is a Tuna?" *Marine Fisheries Review*, Vol. 39, No. 11, November 1977, pp. 1-5. This helpful and learned article provides the reader with the scientific and vernacular nomenclature of the tunas as defined by the U.S. Food and Drug Administration

[8] Joseph, James 1994. "The Tuna-Dolphin Controversy in the Eastern Pacific: Biological, Economic, and Political Impacts," *Ocean Development and International Law*, Vol. 25, pp. 1-30: p. 10.

[9] Joseph, James 1994. "The Tuna-Dolphin Controversy in the Eastern Pacific: Biological, Economic, and Political Impacts," *Ocean Development and International Law*, Vol. 25, pp. 1-30: p. 20.

[10] Hall, Martin A. 1998. "An ecological view of the tuna-dolphin problem: impacts and trade-offs," Reviews in Fish Biology and Fisheries 8, pp. 1-34, p. 21.

[11] See: Watters, George M. 1999, IATTC Data Report 10, "Geographical Distributions of Effort and Catches of Tunas By Purse-Seine Vessels in the Eastern Pacific During 1965-1998. Inter-Amer. Trop. Tuna Comm., Data Report 10.

[12] U.S. Department of Commerce, Office of the Secretary, Washington, D.C. 20230. In the Matter of Proposed Regulations to Govern the Taking of Marine Mammals Incidental to Commercial Fishing Operations, Docket No. MMPAH 1980-1, Recommended Decision of ALJ Hugh J. Dolan dated 18 July 1980. (Cited herein: "1980 ALJ Decision"): Finding 101, p. 42.

[13] Fishermen also fish for tunas associated with porpoises named by the NMFS as "Common Dolphin." At some unknown date, the NMFS dropped the use of "Porpoise" and substituted the word "Dolphin." In 1977, the NMFS identified the following species of cetaceans as being involved in the EPO tuna purse-seine fishery: two stocks of the Spotted porpoise, coastal and offshore; three stocks of the Spinner species, Costa Rican, Eastern, and Whitebelly; three stocks of Common porpoise, northern, central, and southern, and two stocks of Striped porpoise, northern and north-equatorial. Also identified as minimally involved in the tuna fishery were the following porpoise and whale species: bottlenose, rough-toothed, Fraser's, Risso's, Pacific white-sided, short-finned pilot whale, Melon-headed whale, and Pygmy killer whale. 42 FR 64550 (December 23, 1977)

[14] In 1975, the NMFS notified the public that "the terms porpoise and dolphin shall be interchangeable." 40 FR 41531 (September 8, 1975).

[15] Fishermen were able to reduce their traveling costs (time and fuel) by using helicopters to determine whether a porpoise herd was associated with tunas. Not all porpoise herds carry tunas, only Spotted, Spinner, and Common porpoise species are primarily associated with the tunas captured in the EPO fishing grounds. "Only about 25 percent of the porpoise schools encountered (by fishermen) are associated with yellowfin tuna. However, about one-half the yellowfin catch and 92% of the yellowfin taken on porpoise are taken in association with spotted porpoise." See: Finding 94, 1980 ALJ Decision: 41. Based upon 1988 data from the IATTC, 81.6% of all sets made catching tuna were on Tuna/Northern Offshore Spotted porpoise.

During the House Floor Debate on H.R. 6970, June 1, 1977, the following exchange between two Representatives occurred: "**Mr. Carter**: Through this discussion the gentleman from New York has referred to dolphins. Of course porpoise are sometimes called dolphin, but there is a fish which is a dolphin, also. I trust that the gentleman is aware of that. **Mr. Murphy** of New York: Yes. Many environmentalists feel that to refer to such a noble mammal as a dolphin by using the name porpoise is a disservice to it. **Mr. Carter**: Mr. Chairman, if the gentleman will yield further, I am one of the people who think that calling a porpoise by the name dolphin renders a disservice to the porpoise, because that is a general name. Porpoise is what it is called almost always. It is not known as a dolphin, as the gentleman has stated but more generally as a porpoise." *Congressional Record-House*, June 1, 1977, pp. 17154-17155.

[16] For a description on how behavior of "spotters" differ from "spinners," see the written testimony of William A. Walker, an NMFS observer aboard a tuna seiner (Cruise 113-January 2-March 12, 1975), Hearings before the Subcommittee on Fisheries and Wildlife Conservation and the Environment of the Committee on Merchant Marine and Fisheries House of Representatives, 94th Congress 1st Session on Oversight of the Marine Mammal Protection Act of 1972; To Review the Implementation, Administration, and Enforcement of the Act, October 21, 29, 30, December 9, 1975, (Serial No. 94-16). (cited hereinafter: "1975 House Subcommittee Hearings -SN-94-16"): 65-66.

For a report of porpoise behavior observations during the fishing of tuna/porpoise schools, See: Bratten, David; W. Ikehara, K. Pryor, P. Vergne, and J. DeBeer, 1979, Summary of Research Results from the Second Leg of the Third Cruise of the Dedicated Voyage, 20 July to 17 August 1978). SWFC Admin. Rep. LJ-79-13: 39 pp.

[17] Hearings before the Committee on Commerce, Science, and Transportation United States Senate, 95th Congress, 1st Session on Oversight into the Marine Mammal Protection Act, February [sic] 9 and 11, 1977, Serial No. 95-12, (cited herein "1977 Senate Committee Hearings -SN-95-12"): 117

[18] This film was shown to members of Congress and the public during a House Oversight Hearing on the MMPA: 1975 House Subcommittee Hearings-SN-94-16, pp. 60-61.

[19] The American Tunaboat Association is a non-profit cooperative association, formed without shares of stock, and incorporated under provisions of "The Fish Marketing Act of the State of California" Its principal place of business is at One Tuna Lane, San Diego, California. Its membership is comprised exclusively of persons who own or operate commercial tuna fishing vessels documented as vessels of the United States. The original name of the Association at the time of its incorporation on October 10, 1951, was "California Tuna Clipper Cooperative." On November 20, 1952, the name was changed to "American Tunaboat Association". In 1917, a group of San Diego fishermen owning 15 fishing boats organized a group named "American Fishermen's Protective Association" (AFPA). In 1930, the AFPA was divided into two organizations: "American Fishermen's Tunaboat Association" (AFTA) and "Pacific Coast Fishermen's Association (PCFA)." At that time, the membership of the AFTA was comprised of 30 tuna vessels. The AFTA continued into existence until the incorporation of the "California Tuna Clipper Cooperative."

[20] *Save The Dolphins* v. United States Dept. Of Com., 404 F.Supp. 407 (1975). This matter concerned the interpretation of the Freedom of Information Act, [5 U.S.C. § 552 (b)(4)]. No appeal to the decision was filed and the case was dismissed 2 December 22 1975. See: Report of Secretary of Commerce: 41 FR 50152 (22 July 22, 1976) at 50157.

[21] Holts, D. R. McLain, F. G. Alverson, and J.DeBeer, 1979. Summary of research results from the fifth cruise of the dedicated vessel, November 11 to December 9, 1978, SWFC Admin. Rep, LJ-79-20: 60 pp.

11

TUNA SEINER CAPTAINS DISCOVER

THE "ENIGMA"
AND PORPOISE MORTALITY

Early Tuna Purse Seine History

On September 29, 1914, *The San Pedro Daily Pilot* reported that, for the first time, a commercial fishermen's purse seine was successfully used to catch tuna off Southern California:

> "That tuna can be caught with a net has been demonstrated by Andrew Petrich. Yesterday, a second trial was made with a big purse seine and so many fish caught that they broke the net and escaped. A few days ago Petrich demonstrated that tuna can be caught in a set when he landed twelve. Had the net been strong enough to hold the fish there would have been a supply for the Van Camp cannery today. The net used was a barracuda net 300 fathoms long and 24 fathoms deep. It cost $1,800." (p. 1)

In this same article, it was reported that Frank Van Camp, an officer of the Van Camp cannery in San Pedro, advised that the cannery expected to receive delivery of a special net for experimental use in catching tuna "when they will not bite a hook." Mr. Van Camp explained: "I have learned that tuna weighing 250 pounds are caught in Japan and the Mediterranean Sea by nets and I am going to get the nets to catch them here . . . A friend of mine in the Pathe service . . . had a film showing the tuna industry in the Mediterranean." The experimental heavy twine net was 400 fathoms long and about 35 fathoms deep, with a mesh size of 4 inches, costing $2,500.[1] (Mesh is measured from one corner to the opposite corner, with the two corners pulled as far apart as possible ("stretched measure"). Thus each edge of a square of 4-inch mesh is about 2 inches long.) This effort was intended to test the capacity of a purse seine to capture Albacore tuna and solve the problem of fish shortage. The idea was "to use live bait to get the fish to the surface and then surround them drawing in the purse when the net is full." During one experiment, a tug was used to set and retrieve the net and the few captured tuna. By December 1914, it was reported that the experiment was unsuccessful, "owing to its [the net's] enormous weight and length, together with lack of proper gear to handle it . . . Other canneries are working along the same lines, as it is a well known fact that the tuna frequent these waters long after they refuse to take the hook."[2] Experimentation with the net was also unsuccessful during the 1915 fishing season.[3] Experimentation with a purse seine by Halfhill Tuna Packing Company was unsuccessful in 1916.[4] With the assistance of a Japanese fishing expert, experimental nets to catch tuna were financed by Long Beach Tuna Packing Company in 1917. One of the three nets was 1 mile in length, 15 fathoms in depth, with a mesh size of 8 inches.[5]

On August 19, 1917, the largest catch of Bluefin tuna (about 75 tons) "ever recorded" was taken in nets off Point Dume, near San Pedro. It was not realized that the tuna captured were Bluefin until they were brought aboard the boat. The catch was packed for the Italian trade, using double the usual quantity of olive oil.[6] Between June 25 and July 18, 1918, "ten purse seine vessels caught upwards of 1,000 tons of bluefin off Los Angeles Harbor.[7] This experience in 1918 proved that the purse seines could consistently capture large quantities of Bluefin tuna, but not Albacore tuna. It was also demonstrated that purse seining was more efficient than bait fishing for catching Bluefin tuna.

This new development caused the San Pedro seiners to concentrate on Bluefin tuna found seasonally off Southern California. In addition, purse seiners that had formerly fished for salmon in Puget Sound, Washington, transferred to San Pedro, California, to participate in this fishery. It was soon found that purse seining was also an effective method to capture barracuda, sea bass, bonito, and skipjack south of San Diego. Small purse seiners then moved to Cabo San Lucas, where they caught tropical tunas (Yellowfin and Skipjack) found close to shore near Cabo San Lucas and along the coastline of Baja California within the Gulf of California. During 1928, Bluefin tuna were caught by San Pedro purse seiners off Mexico, and by 1930, these seiners were catching Bluefin tuna off Isla Guadalupe, Mexico. During the fall of 1933, the 105' seiner MUSKETEER (later renamed SEA TERN) successfully completed the first trip by a California-based tuna seiner to and from Galapagos Islands. In 1936, the steel-hulled purse seiner PARAMOUNT was built for the purpose of fishing exclusively for tuna. The failure of this venture—it was sold to San Diego fishermen and converted to a baitboat in 1939—slowed down the development of purse seining as a "year-round" method for fishing for tuna.

During World War II, the San Pedro-based purse seiner SPARTAN was very successful in fishing for tuna off the coast of Mexico, particularly in waters within the Gulf of California and on fishing banks south of Cabo San Lucas. A bold effort by Captain Nick Dragich, owner of the new purse seiner PLOVER, and a proven tuna purse-seine fisherman, to fish in waters off Costa Rica in 1945 was prevented by unexplained political actions taken by the government of Costa Rica.

In all of the above written reports about the expansion of California tuna purse seining in waters south of California prior to World War II, no written government report of fishing tuna/porpoise schools has been found. The explanation may be that most California purse seiners were not large enough to fish south of Cabo San Lucas during the 1916-1930 period. For the few purse seiners that were capable of fishing alongside Tuna Clippers during the period 1931-1941, namely the SEA TERN, BREMEN, PARAMOUNT, FALCON, and VINDICATOR, perhaps they were compelled by the limitations of purse-seine technology to restrict their fishing to areas where "pure" tropical tuna schools were known to occur.[8]

Tuna Seining in Pacific Waters off Central America

In March 1947, a group of San Pedro seiners was based in the port of Puntarenas, Costa Rica, where they unloaded their catches to an anchored cannery-freezer ship, carried its cargo, canned and frozen tuna, to canneries in Oregon and Washington. This operation of freezer ships servicing California tunaboats gave rise to memories of mothership operations first established by California canners off Cabo San Lucas, Mexico, in 1917.[9] This group of purse seiners made sets with their cotton nets on tuna/porpoise schools, and may have been the first California tuna purse-seine fishermen to encircle tuna/porpoise schools after World War II.

Some of the unintended consequences of this purse-seine expansion in Costa Rica included the first post-World War II tuna fishery negotiations by the Department of State with the governments of Mexico and Costa Rica, and the commencement of serious investment activity by American tuna firms in shore facilities in Colombia, Ecuador, Peru, and Chile.

Tuna Seining in Pacific Waters off Mexico

In April 1947, San Pedro seiners first fished tuna/porpoise schools off the coast of Mexico, just south of Manzanillo. In April 1947, co-author Felando was a crew member aboard the purse seiner WESTERN SKY. "My father, August Felando, Sr., was captain and co-owner of this vessel. While drifting off the coast of Mexico, south of Manzanillo, we observed three other seiners set on tuna/porpoise schools scattered in an area of at least one mile square. I was in the net skiff waiting

Circa 1956, fleet of Tuna Purse Seiners located in San Pedro, California

for a signal from the mastman to another crew member to release the net. Instead, we drifted about, watching how the other seiners were setting their nets. My father had commanded and co-owned two baitboats during the 1928-1936 period, and was familiar with fishing tuna/porpoise schools. On this maiden voyage of the WESTERN SKY, he had decided to leave the fishing grounds off the Islas Tres Marias and fish in the waters south of Manzanillo, Mexico. The other three seiners followed us to this area. We observed that the porpoises were not leaping or escaping from the nets of the other three vessels. Later, we watched the three seiners leave us and head for the nearest anchorage on the coast. Radio reports explained that their nets had been heavily damaged and needed extensive repair. We did not make a set that day.

"The next day, the WESTERN SKY was alone in the area, as the other seiners had not returned. Rather than trying to encircle an entire tuna/porpoise school or large sections of it, we 'worked the school' by seeking to discover what part of the porpoise herd was being followed by the tuna. While patiently following and scouting the tuna/porpoise school, we found that the tunas would follow a portion of the school of porpoise. This fact gave us the impression that a select group of porpoises were the 'leaders.' The tunas would faithfully follow these porpoises, moving deep and behind the 'leading' porpoises as though they were a shadow of the surfacing porpoises. In this way, we surmised that we did not have to encircle the entire herd of porpoises to catch the tuna. Again, we saw some porpoises coming alongside, as though greeting us. Again, we saw birds diving and tuna scattering their prey. We patiently and quietly followed the moving tuna/porpoise school.

"At about noon we set our net. Only a very few porpoises were in the net. After I had come aboard from the net skiff, my father ordered me to take the small skiff, row to the cork line, and start freeing porpoises by pulling them over the cork-line. I went to the cork-line, where it was stretched out off the seiner's port side and straddled the skiff over the cork-line, submerging a small portion of the cork-line. Bending over from the skiff, I pulled a nearby porpoise over the cork-line. Quickly, another porpoise came into position for me to help it out of the net. Within a short time, the porpoises had created a line-up, waiting for me to pull them over the net. They were big and heavy, but manageable. I still recall the stale smell coming from their spouts as I grabbed their snouts and dorsal fins. While working the line-up, a juvenile porpoise tried to cut ahead of the others. I whacked him on the snout, and he went back to the end of the line, making a whimpering sound as he did so. My impression now is that they were 'spotters,' not 'spinners.' After working about 20 minutes, I was called back to the vessel to help finish the set. My recollection of this incident and later sets on tuna/porpoise schools is that the numbers of porpoises dead or severely injured when they were removed from the net were small in number. At that time, we were very careful in sacking the net, concerned that the sharp-toothed porpoises could cut the webbing and cause the loss of the captured tuna.

"In 1948, I was aboard the WESTERN SKY, from about February to August. We successfully made sets on tuna/porpoise schools off Cabo Blanco, Costa Rica, and off the coast of Mexico. We noticed that the behavior of the porpoises off Mexico in 1948 was different than it had been in 1947: in 1948 we had to increase our speed in order to come alongside the schools, as they were no longer seeking our presence, as they had in 1947. I believe that manual release was the only effective procedure used by purse-seine fishermen to remove porpoises alive from the net during 1947-48."

It is believed that purse seiners based in San Pedro set their nets on tuna/porpoise schools for the first time off southern Mexico in April 1947. The fishermen found that the encircled porpoises would not move as a group and leap over the cork line; instead they tried to swim under the cork-line, and became entangled in the webbing. Once in the net, they could not go into reverse and away from the net. The result was mortality of the porpoises and severe damage to the net, forcing the vessels to leave the fishing grounds to anchorages where they could repair their nets, which was costly in terms of both materials and lost fishing time. (Prior to 1956, a tuna purse seine was made of cotton. The webbing was tarred to increase its strength, weight, and resistance to rotting and the effects of exposure to the sun and seawater.) Tunas and porpoises in the net attracted sharks; the sharks would damage the net with their sharp teeth when seeking their prey.

Tuna purse seine fishermen realized that it would be highly beneficial to them if they could find a way to temporarily break the tuna-porpoise bond. Could it be done before initiating a set? Could it be done after starting a set? Because they soon discovered that it was impractical to encircle an entire herd of porpoises, the fishermen sought a way to encircle the part of the herd in which the tunas were concentrated. By patiently observing the behavior of the herds, they discovered that the tuna-porpoise bond existed between a key group of porpoises—the "leaders"—and the tuna school, and that it was not necessary to encircle all of the porpoises to catch the tuna.

To avoid possible crew injury, waste of tunas, mortality of porpoises, and damage to the net, the few San Pedro seiners that fished tuna/porpoise schools developed various fishing procedures and gear to reduce the number of porpoises captured with the tunas. This innovative effort accelerated after the fleet-wide use of the Puretic power block and nylon webbing. The principal tactic discovered to be effective was to patiently navigate the seiner so as to limit the number of porpoise targeted for encirclement. Fishermen described this maneuver as "cutting out the porpoise" or "working the school." The fishermen observed that during select times of the day, the main body of the tunas followed a small number of leader-like porpoises. To make a successful and trouble-free set, the mastman had to be patient as to when to set and to exercise good judgment as to how to set. The objective was to keep the net "open" as long as possible after the purse line had been winched aboard and the tuna captured. This "open" net would allow time to manually release many of the porpoises over the cork-line.

These fishermen had many reasons to minimize the mortality of porpoises. Experience had proven that the tunas could not be captured without capturing porpoise. By saving the porpoise, the opportunity to capture the tunas was assured. Also, the sighting of a surface-traveling porpoise school was easier than the sighting of a subsurface tuna school. Also, the removal of numerous porpoise from the net was time-consuming and dangerous, especially when the porpoise could not be released alive over the cork-line. The risk of fishermen of being severely injured by entangled dead porpoises piercing the net or by dead porpoises sliding and ripping the net was high. This risk usually occurs while the net is being lifted aboard by the power block for placement or "stacking" by the fishermen on the net platform. Delays caused by efforts to avoid this type of incident by removing the dead porpoise entangled in the net aboard the ship increases the time of transferring the tunas from the net to the vessel, thereby increasing the risk of fish spoilage due to the failure to freeze them promptly. After capturing a tuna/porpoise school, the ship's company fully recognized that time was of the essence in removing live porpoise from the net and in transferring the tunas from the net to the vessel's fish wells.

During the years prior to the introduction of nylon nets and the Puretic Power Block, only a few San Pedro tuna seiner captains consistently risked fishing tuna/porpoise schools. Most San Pedro captains concentrated their fishing effort in the traditional areas where tuna schools did not associate with porpoises, *i.e.* the Gulf of California, Uncle Sam Bank, Morgan Bank, Lusitania Bank, Golden Gate Bank, Isla Guadalupe, Rocas Alijos, and the nearshore waters of the Revillagigedo Islands.

Porpoise Mortality, 1947 to 1959

The porpoise mortality due to fishing that occurred during the 1947-1958 period was caused almost exclusively by the operations of a relatively small number of vessels known as the "San Pedro regular purse seiners." During this period, these seiners fished regularly along the Mexican coast from the Islas Tres Marias to Puerto Angeles, off Central America, and in the Panama Bight. During the 1950s, some of these seiners would venture to the waters off the coast and islands off Ecuador and northern Peru.

In 1947, the year believed to be the first in which seiners encircled tuna/porpoise schools off Mexico and Central America, a fleet of 84 San Pedro-based seiners landed 24,311 short tons of tunas (12,686 yellowfin, 7,637 bluefin, and 3,988 skipjack). The lack of logbook data and scientific reports makes it impossible to determine with reasonable accuracy what percentage of that fleet's yellowfin catch in 1947 was taken in tuna/porpoise schools.

For a variety of practical reasons, only a few seiners in this fleet regularly fished tuna/porpoise schools. The high risk of losses in catch and damage to nets in fishing these schools with cotton nets, along with the risk of personal injury or death to crewmembers, were major factors in limiting this fishing effort. However, a small number of these seiners mitigated these risks by developing skills and tactics in fishing tuna/porpoise schools. By trial and error, certain captains became specialists in this method of fishing. With the introduction of the Puretic Power Block and the all-nylon net, more captains found it practical to fish tuna/porpoise schools during 1956-1958. By the end of 1958, this purse-seine fleet had declined to 44 vessels, but the 1958 annual catch of 32,584 tons (20,088 yellowfin; 10,352 bluefin, 2,144 skipjack) was the greatest on record.[10] Again, the data recorded in logbooks by the vessels in this fleet makes it extremely difficult to estimate its total of yellowfin caught on fishing tuna/porpoise schools. Some San Pedro fishermen estimate that this catch did not exceed 10 percent of the fleet's annual landings of yellowfin.

---

[1] *San Pedro Daily Pilot*, October 17, 1914, front page, "Will Try Out New Tuna Net Next Week-Big Purse Net 400 x 35 Fathoms Arrives and Is Being Made Ready-Boats Loaded with Fish this Morning-Canneries Running Part of Time with Good Outlook for Next Week."

[2] *Pacific Fisherman*, December 1914, p. 22.

[3] *Pacific Fisherman*, August 1915, p. 31, and July 1915, p. 29.

[4] *Pacific Fisherman*, November 1916, p. 16; August 1916, p. 34; April 1916, p. 21. In 1917, an order was placed for a net 1,400 fathoms long by 50 fathoms deep, made of manila hemp and 2-inch mesh. Two 80' tugs and a fleet of smaller boats would be used to catch tuna on a large scale. *Pacific Fisherman*, March 1917, p. 21.

[5] *Pacific Fisherman*, October 1917, p. 37.

[6] *Pacific Fisherman*, October 1917, p. 40.

[7] *Pacific Fisherman*, September 1918, p. 50. "Pete Dragich, well known as the high man on Puget Sound for a number of years, also took the lead in this phenomenal run with 137 tons in his new boat GOOD-PARTNER." His biggest haul was 32 tons. The MARY-LAND was next with a total of 120 tons; MINNIE F., 110 tons; CALIFORNIA, 110 tons; SAN JUANA, 100 tons; JUPITER, 70 tons; TWO BROTHERS, 70 tons; PETER PAN, 80 tons; SUPREME, 80 tons; VERIBUS UNITAS, 60 tons. Taken altogether, this was the greatest catch of fish ever known in Southern California waters. The fish was sold for $90 per ton, and went, principally, to the South Coast Canning Company of Long Beach, who put up some 18,000 cases of this fish in the month of July." See also: *Pacific Fisherman*, November 1918, p. 52.

[8] For a more detailed description of the early development of a tuna purse seine, see: R.E. Green, W. F. Perrin, and B. P. Petrich, "The American Tuna Purse Seine Fishery," pp.182-183 in H.Kristjonsson (ed), Modern Fishing Gear of the World: 3. Fish Finding, Purse Seining, Aimed Trawling. Fishing News (Books) Ltd. This article states that Captain Nick Dragich of the tuna seiner SEA TERN (ex baitboat MUSKETEER) was "the first to set on porpoise schools for the tuna found with them." Co-author Borti Petrich was an experienced and respected captain of purse-seine vessels operating from San Pedro. He was also an expert in designing and making tuna and sardine purse seines. Knowing Borti personally, co-author Felando believes that the comments in this article about Captain Dragich and of his fishing tuna/porpoise schools while in command of the SEA TERN during the early 1930s are accurate.

[9] In 1916, the schooner JOHN G. NORTH was converted as a floating tuna cannery for operation off Southern California during the Albacore summer fishery. It was not very successful. In 1917, the schooner was towed to Bahía Magdalena and Cabo San Lucas, and tropical tunas were canned. The exploratory trip was considered moderately successful because tunas other than Albacore were found. During May 1918, the schooner again recorded a moderately successful season off Cabo San Lucas. It was again sent to Cabo San Lucas for the Spring season of 1919; unfortunately; the vessel was totally destroyed by fire on May 14, 1919.

[10] Craig J. Orange and Gordon C. Broadhead, "1958-1959-A Turning Point For Tuna Purse Seine Fishing?" *Pacific Fisherman,* (June 1959): 57 (7): pp. 20-27. The authors were members of the scientific staff of the IATTC, and, as tuna scientists, they had made trips aboard U.S. baitboats and purse seiners. Photos of the SUN KING in a fishing set is on the front cover of the magazine and on page 20. The SUN KING, converted from a baitboat to a seiner in the fall of 1957, was operating from Coischo, Peru, at the time of the article.

PART III

TUNA SEINER CAPTAINS ADAPT TO THE "ENIGMA"

12

SOUND AND PORPOISE BEHAVIOR

By using a fathometer to separate porpoise from the tunas before setting

Prior to 1968, no report describing the tactics used by American fishermen to encircle tuna/porpoise schools was published by any periodical in the United States. Some of the procedures used to encircle tuna/porpoise schools were not circulated freely by tuna captains for competitive reasons. One example is the technique developed by the captain and crew of the San Pedro "regular seiner" DEFENSE.

John (Blackie) Zorotovich, captain and part owner of the tuna seiner DEFENSE, was recognized in the San Pedro "regular seiner" fleet as an expert in fishing tuna/porpoise schools. In April and May 1948, Blackie and co-author Felando had high-seas radio conversations concerning the locations of porpoise schools sighted by the WESTERN SKY off Mexico. Blackie had a reputation in the

Captain John Zorotovich and the DEFENSE, a regular San Pedro seiner
Courtesy of Mrs. John Burich
Vessel photo courtesy of Richard Chikami
Vessel built by Western Boat Building Company, Tacoma, Washington

San Pedro fleet of being "a loner." He searched for tuna/porpoise schools in fishing areas where few, if any, other vessels would be fishing. To have his unique fishing technique and equipment be successful in fishing a tuna/porpoise school, he required isolation from other tuna vessels.

During the first six months of 1960, Philip Felando, brother of co-author Felando, was at the "wheel" of the DEFENSE, and recalls that the vessel fished mainly off Mexico from Manzanillo to Puerto Angeles, and that the crew searched for spotted porpoise because Blackie was more successful in controlling them with sound than he was with spinner porpoise. As Blackie directed Philip's steering of the vessel about the tuna/porpoise school from the crow's nest, he would relay orders on the intercom system to a person on the bridge (usually the cook), who could control the fathometer. When the underwater sound of this fathometer was on, the portion of the porpoise targeted by Blackie would react by rapidly moving away from the boat and the tunas. This procedure required not only skill, but also patience, which is why he avoided other fishing vessels as much as possible. The result of this carefully-performed tactic was that there would be only a few porpoise leading the tuna before Blackie ordered the release of the net. Philip estimated that only about 2 to 10 porpoise were encircled by the net, and these were quickly and easily released alive.[1] Philip considered Blackie to be the best of the few captains in the San Pedro fleet who exercised the option of fishing tuna/porpoise schools, in addition to "log" fishing and "tuna school" fishing. During the late 1940s and the 1950s, most of the San Pedro seiners concentrated their fishing in traditional areas along the Mexican coast and offshore islands, where tuna did not associate with porpoise.[2]

By using speedboats to herd the tuna/porpoise school before setting

The first reference by the Bureau of Commercial Fisheries Fishery-Oceanography Center in La Jolla, California, to the use of speedboats by American tuna fishermen to herd tuna/porpoise schools appeared in the December 1966 issue of its monthly publication. The report noted: "In previous years, there has been little or no difference in rates of success between these two categories. It is probable that the late development of the fishing fleet, of porpoise herding techniques, using extra speed boats, is responsible for this increased success."[3] Only a few of these reports made comments on the Center's Tuna Behavior Program, and the project entitled "Porpoise Associated with Tuna," and none contained reports on the problem of porpoise mortality associated with the fishing of tuna/porpoise schools by purse seines.

It is believed that the first use of a speedboat by a U.S. flag tuna seiner to herd a tuna/porpoise school occurred during the summer of 1960.[4] At this time, Joseph Scafidi, captain of the converted tuna seiner LIBERTY BELL, was fishing off the northern coast of Nicaragua, near the Golfo de Fonseca, in the company of the converted tuna seiner HISTORIC. The views of Captain Scafidi on the subject of using speedboats to herd tuna/porpoise schools are important because of his legendary success in using this technique during the 1960 to 1976 period. Captain Scafidi remembers watching the converted seiner HISTORIC maneuver about a tuna/porpoise school in a manner customarily practiced by Captain Scafidi with little success. He saw the crew of the HISTORIC place a one-man speedboat, powered by an outboard engine, in the water, and then he observed how the speedboat would first chase the school and then move to gather the leading porpoise so as to temporarily stop the entire tuna/porpoise school. He observed the HISTORIC move toward the school and then set its net about the school as the porpoises were being driven closer together and slowed by the movements of the speedboat. Later, Captain Scafidi was informed by the captain of the HISTORIC, Richard ("Cookie") Virissimo, that the successful set had produced a catch of 20 tons of Yellowfin. In explaining the use of the speedboat to chase the tuna/porpoise school, Captain Virissimo advised that the speedboat was owned by a crewmember, and that the speedboat was aboard the HISTORIC because the crewmember was repairing it during his free time. Captain Virissimo further explained that he had no idea before the trip started that a speedboat could be used to help catch tuna/porpoise schools. This incident convinced Captain Scafidi that the use of a speedboat would help to catch tuna/porpoise schools.

Prior to his witnessing the success of the HISTORIC, Captain Scafidi had experienced various tactics used by the porpoise to evade his capture of tuna/porpoise schools. Following these failures, his crewmembers were insisting that he would never be able to catch a tuna/porpoise school. Scafidi had been fishing tuna aboard tuna baitboats operating from San

Captain Joseph Scafidi and the LIBERTY BELL, a converted seiner
Courtesy of son Gregory Scafidi
Vessel built by Hodgeson-Greene-Halderman Shipbuilders, Long Beach, California

Diego since his immigration from Sicily in 1950, progressing in status from crewmember to captain. Necessarily, he was experienced and successful in fishing tuna/porpoise schools with a baitboat. He was also experienced in purse seining, having fished for sardines aboard a small seiner operating from San Pedro.

Upon his return to San Diego, Captain Scafidi asked Managing Owner Frank Gonsalves to purchase a speedboat, explaining his observation of the fishing set by the HISTORIC. Gonsalves told Scafidi to purchase two speedboats, rather than one, so as to have a back-up. Each of the speedboats was equipped with a 45-H.P. outboard engine.

On the second trip of the converted seiner, Captain Scafidi drove the 10-knot LI-BERTY BELL, to fishing grounds where tuna/porpoise schools were located off-shore in an area along the Mexican coast between Manzanillo and Acapulco. Recognizing the need for communication between him and the speedboat driver, Captain Scafidi worked out hand signals with his speedboat driver. Captain Scafidi believed that radio communication devices were not necessary at this stage of his experiment. On the first set, Scafidi signaled for the speedboat driver to move forward to "out-race" the tuna/porpoise school, and then herd the porpoise together in the same manner as a sheepdog would herd sheep together. When the tuna/porpoise school was in position, Captain Scafidi ordered the release of the net skiff and the seine. His first set using a speedboat to encircle and capture a tuna/porpoise school was successful.

Within a short time, Captain Scafidi found it necessary to use two speedboats to encircle tuna/porpoise schools in this familiar fishing area, as the porpoise were reacting to the use of one speedboat and moving so as to out-race the LIBERTY BELL before it was able to close both ends of its net by meeting with the drifting net skiff. To offset this evading tactic, Captain Scafidi directed his second speedboat to move about in this open area, that is, between the circle-closing LIBERTY BELL and the drifting net skiff.

The next thing that the porpoise did to avoid capture was to dive below the bottom of the net before it was pursed. The porpoise would dive deep below the surface and then rush underneath the slow-sinking net as the purse-line was winched aboard and before the purse-rings were drawn together. In all of these evasive tactics, the tunas would shadow the porpoise, seemingly an inseparable companion. To offset this new tactic, Captain Scafidi found it necessary to use three speedboats. The third speedboat patrolled outside the net, creating powerful sound waves in the area of the net where the porpoise could dive to the bottom of the net. By this time, radio communication between Captain Scafidi and the speedboat drivers had been introduced. The distances involved between the seiner and the speedboats, plus the new tactics adopted by the speedboats, made the use of hand-signals impractical.

When Captain Scafidi commanded large, new "super" tuna seiners, he used up to five speedboats, each equipped with a 65-HP outboard engine, in fishing tuna/porpoise schools.[5] In time, he discovered that five speedboats were helpful in offsetting another new evasive tactic developed by "spotter" porpoises. He recalls the first time that he experienced this new tactic: as his boat approached the slow-moving tuna/porpoise school, he reduced the vessel's speed so that the speedboats could be lowered into the water. As this process was underway, he noticed that this seemed to send a signal to the tuna/porpoise school causing it to suddenly pick up speed and then, like a burst of fireworks, the porpoise scattered in all directions, with the tuna following them, away from the school's original track. In response, Captain Scafidi decided to direct all of his speedboats to create a giant circle that would encompass as many individual porpoise as possible. Then, he patiently directed the speedboats so as to gradually reduce the area of this circle, sometimes working as long as 60 to 90 minutes in herding the porpoise and tuna together. At the appropriate time, Captain Scafidi would then release the net, encircling the part of the restructured school that included the tuna.

This "game" of capture and release by the tuna fishermen and the tuna/porpoise schools was developed over a period of about ten years during the 1960s. For a short period of time, many fishermen thought that the porpoise were winning the game; new evasive tactics by the porpoise forced some captains to forsake fishing in areas where tuna/porpoise fishing prevailed. The necessity of using many speedboats to herd the tuna/porpoise schools made it virtually impossible for the San Pedro "regular seiners" to compete, as they were too small to carry four or five speedboats and enough crew members to man them.[6]

The area off Mexico, roughly from the Islas Tres Marias to the Golfo de Techuantepec, soon became one of the most frequented areas of tuna/porpoise fishing, followed closely by areas off Central America. The fishermen who were skilled in capturing tuna/ porpoise schools found that it was easier to fish the spotted porpoise in these two areas. The "spotters" reacted more favorably to the efforts of the fishermen to implement the "Back-down" procedure, during which the porpoise were induced to swim over the submerged cork-line of the net, than did the spinner porpoise. Within the fleet, the phrase "Sea World porpoise" was being used by fishermen to describe those "spotter" schools that seemed to be well trained in helping the fishermen's rescue effort following their capture. (Actually, the animals exhibited at Sea World and other amusement parks are bottlenose dolphins, *Tursiops truncatus*, which are rarely encircled by purse seines.) Fishermen found that the "spinners" did not react in the net in the same manner as the more docile "spotters." As a result, it was harder to herd and encircle the "spinners," and, if they were encircled, it was more difficult to release them from the net unharmed.

Observations of Captain Harold Medina

When fishing on his first tuna/porpoise school with the converted tuna seiner ALPHECCA, Captain Harold Medina observed that his vessel's sound and movement were apparent attractions to the porpoise. Individual porpoise would play about his vessel as he navigated about the traveling school of porpoise. There was no need to chase the porpoise, only the need to identify the location of the main body of the tunas—to the rear of the porpoise, or to the left or right. At that time, the vessel was equipped with a small skiff powered by an 18-HP outboard engine. This boat was on the large net skiff and was used for traveling to and from the net skiff, but not to herd porpoises. Harold recalls—just as he experienced aboard the tuna seiner SAN JOAQUIN—that the tuna/porpoise schools acted as they did when the ALPHECCA was a baitboat. This behavior suggested to Harold that the porpoise schools in the Central American area had very little, if any, exposure to fishing by purse seiners.

During the 1930-1960 period, U.S. baitboats operated in areas of the eastern Pacific Ocean (EPO) where tuna/porpoise schools were abundant. This type of fishing became more popular during the late 1930s as more large tuna baitboats entered the U.S. fleet. During World War II, there was less fishing effort directed at tuna/porpoise schools off Central America and more directed at such schools off the Mexican coast. As the U.S. fleet expanded after World War II and until the mid-1950s, the baitboat effort directed at tuna/porpoise schools off Mexico and Central America increased significantly. During that period, baitboats were providing live sardines and anchovies not only to the tunas, but also to the porpoise. Harold noted that in his experience, the "spotters" were attracted to the same live bait as the tunas, but that the "spinners" rejected the baitfish. Harold noted that the fishermen would have to take action by using their fishing poles to splash water about their fishing racks in order to move the "spotters" from their fishing positions. When the tunas were in a feeding frenzy, this act would cause the "spotters" to move away from the live bait. Harold believes that the friendly behavior of the "spotter" porpoise toward the baitboats may be explained by the years that baitboats chummed live bait at and about the tuna/porpoise schools.

Harold discovered, as captain of a tuna seiner, that the porpoise were learning ways to avoid the "unfriendly" vessels that no longer tossed out live-bait, so he had to chase the schools. He accomplished this by directing his small skiff, powered by an 18-HP outboard engine, about the tuna/porpoise school in order to prevent it from evading the encircling purse seine. This tactic complemented the sounds made on the seiner to scare the school away from the opening of the net under the vessel while the purse line was being winched aboard. This small skiff was not used to chase the porpoise school, but rather to herd it into a tightening circle within the encircling net and to restrict its movement within the net.

During subsequent fishing trips, Harold regularly observed porpoise schools moving away from the sound and movements of the tracking ALPHECCA. As soon as his two speedboats were placed in the water, the tuna/porpoise school would quickly move away from the seiner. This second change in porpoise behavior required the ALPHECCA to adjust its methods by chasing the school with the speedboats before encircling it, and then using speedboats to reduce the chances that the fish could escape from the net. Soon, it was necessary for Harold to add more speedboats with more powerful outboard engines. By this time it was no longer practical for him to use hand signals to direct his speedboat operators. Harold found that other captains were also experiencing the new evasive tactics of tuna/porpoise schools. The contest between the fishermen and the porpoise was becoming more difficult for the captains whose vessels were not properly equipped, especially in areas where the tuna/porpoise schools had years of experience in dealing with purse seines. Off Costa Rica, for example, tuna/porpoise schools had been fished by tuna seiners since 1946. Some of these schools were called "the untouchables." Despite numerous efforts by highly-skilled captains, these porpoise always escaped their nets.

---

[1] The use of the underwater sound of a certain make of fathometer to cause porpoise movement was accidentally discovered by Joe Medina, Sr., captain of the San Diego tuna clipper baitboat QUEEN MARY. While the crew was in the fishing racks pulling aboard tuna associated with porpoise, teenager Joe Medina, Jr., was exercising his curiosity with various objects on the bridge. When Joe, Jr., turned on the fathometer, the

porpoise reacted by leaping and swimming away from the QUEEN MARY. The tunas followed the porpoise, and the crew of the QUEEN MARY lost a day of good fishing. This discovery was later used as a weapon in fishing disputes between two vessels fishing the same tuna/porpoise school (personal conversation with Joe Medina, Jr, 2000).

[2] During 1970-1981, U.S. government researchers experimented with acoustical signals, such as killer whale sounds, for the purpose of achieving increased release efficiency of live porpoises from the net during the "Back-down," but no success was recorded. Experimenters also failed when they used visual stimuli, such as chunks of dry ice to create a bubble screen, dyed rocks to create a screen, underwater strobe lights, and magnesium flares. They could not get either the tunas or the porpoise to move in a desired direction by using these devices. They also failed to attract the tunas to olfactory stimuli; the theory being that the tunas would stay in one spot in the net while the net was opened for release of the encircled porpoise.

[3] Monthly Narrative Report, December 1966 (5 pages), U.S. Department of the Interior, Fish and Wildlife Service, Bureau of Commercial Fisheries, Tuna Resources Laboratory, La Jolla, CA 92037. See section entitled: "Operations Research" at p.3. The two categories referred to in this internal report: "school" fishing and "porpoise-associated fish."

[4] In 1924, author Zane Grey reported on his use of a speedboat to film a porpoise school off Cabo San Lucas, Baja California, Mexico. See: written description of this porpoise school: pages 198-201, and four pages of eight photos of "leaping" porpoise, inserted between p.192 and p.193. Zane Grey, "Tales of Fishing Virgin Seas," The Derrydale Press, (Lanham and New York. Paperback. (2000)

[5] The LIBERTY BELL was built as a tuna baitboat in 1944, and converted to a tuna seiner in 1960. It had a wooden hull, its registered length was 105.1 feet, and its gross tonnage was 282 tons. In 1970-71, Captain Scafidi commanded the NAUTILUS, ex-military mine-layer built in 1944 and converted to a tuna purse seiner in 1962. It had a steel hull, its registered length was 172.9 feet, and its gross tonnage was 811 tons. Later, he successfully commanded the new seiner J.M. MARTINAC (1972-1974), and super seiners FINISTERRE (1975-1976), SOUTH PACIFIC (1977), and MARGARET L. (1978-1979). His last command occurred in 1980, when he completed a very successful tuna/porpoise fishing trip aboard the new seiner ANTONINA C.

[6] A report on a workshop sponsored by the Marine Mammal Commission (MMC) held on December 8-9, 1975, at the University of California, Santa Cruz, presented documentation of "untouchable" behavior of tuna/porpoise schools, as follows: "Reports from fishermen and NMFS observers as well as set log data collected in 1972-1974 (see NMFS progress report of 1974), indicate increasing set-avoidance behavior by porpoises. Indices of this behavior are: (1) ignoring the chaser speedboats and refusing to be herded into directions and densities favorable for a set; (2) breaking-up into small groups and scattering in all directions at the approach of a purse seiner; and, (3) heading into the set and immediately diving down and under it, or passing through the towline gap between the tuna boat and the end of the purse net. Fishermen claim that such behavior is more prevalent in in-shore areas where setting on porpoise has been done for the longest time . . . . " Sep 1976 House Subcommittee Hearings-SN-94-45: 198.

13

"BACK DOWN"

A MANEUVER THAT SEPARATES TUNAS FROM PORPOISE IN THE NET

Prior to 1970, American tuna purse-seine fishermen were trying to solve the problem of porpoise mortality, through trial and error, on their own. On shore, representatives of three segments of the American tuna industry—canners, vessel owners' associations, and unions—were struggling with international problems that threatened the industry's capacity as a supplier of tunas to the American consumer. They were not focused as a unified industry on the problems confronted by fishermen in fishing tuna/porpoise schools. Entanglement of porpoise in nets was considered to be a problem that individual captains would have to solve, rather than as an industry problem.

Tuna scientists had not publicly identified porpoise mortality as a problem of concern, although they had developed data showing the growing efficiency of fishing tuna/porpoise schools relative to fishing for tunas associated with floating objects or in unassociated schools. Nor had anyone—fishermen, tuna scientists, or interested public—suggested that the design and construction of the purse-seine nets was the cause of excessive porpoise mortality. Customarily, these activities were wholly within the purview of the captain and crew. If confronted by the existence of porpoise mortality problems, it would have been perceived that if poorly-designed nets were causing the entanglement of porpoise, it would have to be solved by the fishermen who had the problem. Tuna nets were not standardized; each net was generally a unique product of the captain and crew or of individuals and firms offering their services to build tuna nets. Each captain was in a position to use his net as he saw fit. The industry, as a unified group, had never focused on ways captains were to avoid "net collapse" or with the way a tuna net was to be set on a tuna/porpoise school. There was no perception by anyone in the industry or anyone regulating the fishery that porpoise mortality was a problem requiring an industry-wide solution.

During this period, the American tuna industry was being forced to confront threats to the fleet's access to traditional tuna fishing grounds. In response to the Japanese tuna import challenge, it was a time when former tuna baitboat fishermen were still learning how to be successful tuna purse-seine fishermen. It was a time when regulations to conserve yellowfin tuna in the eastern Pacific Ocean (EPO) were being developed, implemented, and enforced. In response to this regulatory action, tuna clippers were developing new fishing grounds off West Africa, and west of the Inter-American Tropical Tuna Commission (IATTC) Yellowfin Regulatory Area (CYRA). It was a period when U.S. tuna clippers were being seized and harassed on the high seas by naval forces of Latin American governments, claiming they could deny or control the fishing of tuna within 200-miles of their coasts and offshore islands. It was a period when government and industry energies were focused almost entirely on tuna conservation and management, rather than on porpoise mortality, and how the U.S. tuna fleet could economically adjust to these new challenges.

A successful, impulsive response to a fishing crisis by Captain Anton Misetich, 1959

During these early years of development (1947-1958), various captains of San Pedro seiners experimented with many methods to reduce the total number of porpoise captured, and in seeking means to induce the porpoise to leave the net alive. Although tuna seining benefited from significant fishing gear developments in the mid-1950s, such as the introduction of nylon webbing and the Puretic Power Block, it was not until 1959 that a breakthrough occurred in inducing porpoise to leave the net alive without fishermen having to manually pull them over the cork-line of the net. This new fishing procedure, called the "Back-down" by fishermen, was implemented first by Captain Anton Misetich of San Pedro. This unexpected discovery occurred during the first set on the maiden voyage in 1959 of the converted tuna seiner PARAMOUNT.

Captain Misetich was on the bridge, observing a set that involved large quantities of tuna and porpoise. He saw that large numbers of the porpoise remained in the net and became entangled in it, despite the efforts of the crew to pull them over the cork-line. These events caused him to fear that his decision to set on a particularly large

Captain Anton Misetich and the PARAMOUNT, a converted seiner
Courtesy of sons Ronnie and Anthony Misetich
Photo courtesy of *National Fisherman*
Vessel built by Avondale Marine Ways. Inc., Avondale, Louisiana

tuna/porpoise school would cause the loss of tuna, high mortalities of porpoise, injuries to his crew, and heavy damage to his net. In an effort to mitigate the problem, when about two-thirds of the net had been retrieved and the rest was in the water off the port side of the vessel, Captain Misetich drove his vessel into reverse. As the vessel moved slowly backward, he observed numerous porpoise moving toward the sunken portion of the cork-line and leaping or swimming over it to freedom outside the net. Excitedly, he asked his sons and others to come to the bridge to observe the reactions of the porpoise and the tunas as he repeated the "Back-down" maneuver. This previously-unplanned procedure of the moment eventually removed most of the porpoise alive from the net. After the successful set, Captain Misetich was on the radio, happily explaining to his peers the results of his saving of the porpoise and explaining the procedure he called "Back-down" to his fellow fishermen.[1]

Years later, Captain Misetich could not explain why he decided to drive his vessel in reverse in response to the conditions that he was observing. He admitted that the procedure of putting the vessel in reverse was a maneuver that he and other San Pedro seiner fishermen used when fishing sardines close to shore as a way of avoiding stranding of the seiner and the loss of the purse seine. This maneuver resulted in the loss of the sardines from the net, but not the loss of the seiner or the net or injury to the crew. Captain Misetich did not confirm or deny whether this prior experience contributed to the discovery of the "Back-down" in the tuna fishery. He just "didn't know."[2]

The leadership of Captain Manuel Neves, 1961

In early 1961, Captain Manuel Neves, operating the converted tuna seiner CONSTITUTION, based in San Diego, had a radio conversation with Captain Anton Misetich, during which Anton explained the "Back-down" procedure.[3] Following this talk, Manuel called his crew for a meeting in the vessel's galley. He explained the "Back-down" procedure used by Anton, and told them that he was

going to try it during the next set. Some members of the crew objected that such a tactic was useless, arguing that both tuna and porpoise would leave the net alive during the "Back-down." During the next set, as promised, Manuel employed the "Back-down" procedure, and, as

Captain Manuel Neves and the CONSTITUTION, a converted seiner
Photos courtesy of *National Fisherman*
Vessel built by Campbell Industries, San Diego, California

predicted by some members of the crew, both tunas and porpoise left the net alive as Manuel put the CONSTITUTION in reverse. Shortly thereafter, another meeting was held in the galley, and Manuel announced that he would again use the "Back-down" procedure. On this occasion, the tuna remained in the net and the porpoise left the net alive. Over 75 tons of tuna were captured. Pleased with the effectiveness and safety of the "Back-down" procedure and confident that it would work again, Manuel made a third set. Again, over 75 tons of tuna were captured, with the porpoise safely leaving the net alive. Manuel held his third meeting with a happy crew, exclaiming over how exceptional it was for a boat to make three sets on tuna/porpoise schools during a single day. Usually, a successful set on a large tuna/porpoise school would take most of the day to complete, leaving it unlikely that a second set could be made.[4]

When Captain Neves, respected by fellow captains and crews of the San Diego tuna fleet, told his peers about his success with the "Back-down" procedure as a way to remove the porpoise from the net alive, they believed him and followed his leadership. Because of its simplicity and practicality, captains of the tuna fleet quickly accepted the idea of the "Back-down."

Why was Captain Neves so persistent in trying to make the "Back-down" work? When porpoise become entrapped in the net, their weight and that of the tuna can cause the net to split, resulting in a failed set, lost catch, and lost fishing time while the net is being repaired. When porpoise become entrapped, the process of retrieving the net and brailing the tuna aboard into the wells where they are stored is slowed down considerably. The longer the dead tunas remain in the warm tropical waters (usually 80°F or greater in areas where tunas associate with porpoise), the greater the risk of their becoming unacceptable to the canners. When porpoise are in the net, the only option other than the "Back-down" is for the crew to enter the net and manually remove the porpoise from the net by pulling them over the cork-line, which is dangerous, particularly when there are sharks in and about the net. Also, if unseen porpoise entrapped in the webbing are pulled up through the Puretic Power Block at the end of the boom and fall about 30 feet toward the crew stacking the net on the net platform, these crew-members are likely to be injured. The removal of these porpoise from the webbing on the net platform created further delays to the retrieval of the net and in commencing the brailing of the tuna from net into the wells. By using the "Back-down" to remove live porpoise from the net as quickly as possible, the CONSTITUTION proved that this procedure saves the tunas from spoilage. Importantly, it also proved that more fishing sets per day were possible.

After the successful trial of the CONSTITUTION, the idea of the "Back-down" was quickly spread throughout the San Diego tuna fleet by "word of mouth." Captain Harold Medina had heard the story of Captain Manuel Neves and the success of the CONSTITUTION. Harold was not given special instruction on how to "Back-down," but he was able to do it effectively on his first try. He explained that it was just a question of finding the best time to go into reverse to let the porpoise escape alive from the net. Also, the Captain must remember that sea conditions, weather, and human activity make every set different from previous ones.

Art and Skill of Captain George Sousa and his Crew, 1971-1972

To better understand the methods and skills developed to make the "Back-down" more effective in saving porpoise after 1961-1971, we are fortunate in having a description of the gear and methods used by the Captain and crew of the new tuna seiner JOHN F. KENNEDY during its fishing trip of January 1- February 9, 1972. The vessel was commanded by George Sousa, a highly-respected San Diego tuna captain. We believe that the techniques and gear used to save porpoise aboard the JOHN F. KENNEDY were regularly used by those captains and crews who were recognized in the fleet as highly competitive in fishing tuna/porpoise schools: skills in using wind, currents, and other ocean conditions to keep the net open as long as possible, in using the net skiff to tow the seiner to prevent it from drifting over the net prior to and during the "Back-down," and the use of a speedboat to guide porpoise movements prior to and during the "Back-down."

Captain George Sousa and the JOHN F. KENNEDY
Vessel photo courtesy of J.M. Martinac Shipbuilding Corporation, Tacoma, Washington

The net of the JOHN F. KENNEDY was 540 fathoms (3,240 feet) long and 48 fathoms (288 feet) deep. This report of the vessel's 40-day fishing trip illustrates the state of the art practiced by this captain and crew in ensuring that the net was kept open, giving the tunas and porpoise a spacious enclosure for as long as possible, and how important it was for the net to be gathered aboard the vessel as quickly as possible. The description also shows how the "Back-down" stretches and squeezes the webbing of the net so as to minimize entanglement of porpoise.[5] The methods and procedures that were developed by Captain Sousa and his crew were brought to the attention of other captains and crews during meetings and workshop sessions sponsored by the American Tunaboat Association (ATA) during 1971 and 1972.[6]

---

[1] Telephone conversation with Ronnie Misetich, 2003

[2] Telephone conversation with Captain Anton Misetich, 1975

[3] Personal conversations with Captain Manuel Neves.1980

[4] Personal conversation with Captain Manuel Neves.1989

[5] James Coe and George Sousa, "Removing Porpoise from a Tuna Purse Seine," *Marine Fisheries Review* (1972) 34 (11-12): pages 15-19. The fishing trip observed by NMFS Observer James Coe was aboard the San Diego-based tuna seiner JOHN F. KENNEDY, commanded by Captain George Sousa. At the time the article was published, Captain Sousa was in command of the new "Super Seiner" RAFFAELLO. Captain Sousa praised the work ethic and dedication of James Coe during this fishing trip (personal conversation with Captain George Sousa, May 1, 2006). In addition to having been an NMFS Observer, James Coe had worked with fishing gear specialist, Richard McNeely. Because of his dedication and skills, he became extremely well qualified in the work of developing and explaining the gear and methods to reduce porpoise mortality to tuna captains and crews. The article was prepared while Congress was considering the MMPA in 1972. Importantly, it illustrates the skills of a tuna captain who was recognized in the fleet as an expert in using the "Back-down" technique and other methods to reduce porpoise mortality.

See photo and comments of Captain George Sousa about seven years later regarding the behavior of porpoise during the "Back-down" and about the tactics porpoise used to avoid encirclement by the fishermen. Also see photos of porpoise in a tuna net awaiting the "Back-down" and a drawing and a photo of the "Back-down" procedure. Edward J. Linehan, "The Trouble With Dolphins," *National Geographic*, (1979), 155 (4): pages 506-541, 532, 522-523.

[6] "The American Tunaboat Association (ATA) conducted tuna/porpoise workshops for skippers and other key vessel personnel between [sic] 1972-1975. At these meetings, ad hoc groups of the most experienced and successful skippers were formed and paneldiscussions were held in order to seek solutions to the porpoise problem. These panels were an effective means of exchanging knowledge among the participants. In 1976, the NMFS took over the tuna-porpoise workshops . . . .

"Base [sic] on the favorable history of the tuna/porpoise workshops, Porpoise Rescue Foundation (PRF) cooperated in forming a successor to the workshop, a group known as the "Captain's Panel." The panel was organized to serve principally as a peer review group to assist those skippers having problems with the release of porpoise. Additionally, it serves as a 'sounding board' for new gear and operating techniques which may enhance porpoise rescue." F. M. Ralston (editor),1977, "A workshop to assess research related to the porpoise/tuna problem February 28 and March 1-2, 1977, SWFC, Admin.Rep. LJ-77-15, NOAA, NMFS, pp 34-35, (cited herein as "March 1977 SWFC Workshop").

14

"MEDINA PANEL"

A NET DESIGN THAT ENHANCES THE "BACK DOWN"

Because they were unable to separate the porpoise from the tunas prior to encir-clement, the fishermen needed to develop gear and procedures to remove the porpoise from the net. The "Back-down" procedure, which was developed in 1959 and quickly adopted by the fleet, freed most of the porpoise, but not all of them. Hand release procedures to remove the porpoise that failed to leave dur-ing "Back-down" appeared to be the only feasible option. Porpoise mortality con-tinued to occur, but the magnitude of this mortality was unknown. There were many ways in which porpoise mortality could occur prior to, and during, "Back-down." Procedures using speedboats were developed by some captains to re-duce entanglement prior to "Back-down." Other methods and gear were devel-oped to speed up the retrieval of the net so as to proceed to the "Back-down" procedure as quickly as possible. The focus of some fishermen's efforts to more effectively remove the live porpoise from the net was on ways to avoid delays in proceeding to the "Back-down" procedure, rather than on changing the configura-tion of the net. As was the custom in the fleet, searches by some tuna captains and crews for new ideas were underway individually, but not in a concerted or industry-organized fashion prior to 1970.

The Search of Captain Harold Medina

An eight-year (1961-1968) learning experience of seining on the ALPHECCA aided efforts by Harold to make improvements in the design of his net, with em-phasis on its effectiveness in capturing tuna and minimizing porpoise entangle-ment. During this period, he had directed 1,022 sets of his purse seine from the crow's nest, of which 754 sets were made on tuna/porpoise schools. He was al-so helped by the steady transfer of new ideas and improvements in tuna fishing gear and fishing techniques communicated by the fleet's captains and crew-members. To Harold, this continuing contribution of ideas, original or borrowed, from crewmembers on his vessel was extremely important to his successful fish-ing operation. Commencing in mid 1961 and ending in December 1970, 22 new seiners made maiden voyages, resulting in transfers of highly-skilled and expe-rienced fishermen from older, smaller vessels to newer, larger ones. Necessari-ly, vessels like the converted ALPHECCA experienced continuing crew turnover. In most cases, the new crewmembers brought with them ideas on gear, equip-ment, and techniques that had been proven by trial and error on other vessels. Anything related to fishing success was not a secret very long on the San Diego waterfront, and the captain and crew of every new tuna seiner benefited from this "transfer of technology." Fishermen, driven by self-interest, brought with them proven ideas on how the tuna net could be improved, on how the net skiff and speedboats could be better worked, and how their "new home" could be more competitive and productive.

In his position as Mastman, Harold was able to evaluate how his net was working in the water as it was paid out, as the circle was being completed, and as the purse line was being pulled and the net closed. Captains, such as Harold, who fished primarily tuna/porpoise schools for most of the year, classified the various options of fishing tuna in the following way: if given a choice, he would prefer setting on a school of tuna milling about floating debris ("log fishing"). His next preference would be setting on a pure school of yellowfin or skipjack or on a mixed school of yellowfin and skipjack. His last choice would be setting on a tuna/porpoise school. Fortunately, these types of schools are scattered over most of the traditional fishing grounds during most of the year. It also explains why fishing skills and experiences of captains were so variable. If your niche was night fishing on pure schools of tuna in waters close to islands, why go to areas where you would be required to fish tuna/porpoise schools? If you and your crew were not experienced in fishing schools at night near islands, you wouldn't gamble on fishing tuna in that circumstance; you would leave it to others.

Individuals in the tuna purse-seine fleet performing the unique task of a mastman knew that they were an important key to fishing success, and that the vessel owner and crew constantly demanded fishing success. As in baseball, where the pitcher must perform successfully if the team is to stay in the game; so also must the mastman on a tuna seiner. The quality of the competition for the mastman who focused on tuna/porpoise schools made success especially difficult. The newest, largest, and fastest vessels with the best captains and crews tended to fish mostly on tuna/porpoise schools. Such being the case, only the most skilled mastmen could get positions on such vessels. These individuals had learned much about the behavior of tuna/porpoise schools from observing their behavior before and during hundreds of sets. From the mast, these fortunate few observed the behavior of the tunas as they followed the leaping porpoise. They saw the black "spot" of the tunas moving and circling deep within the net and the "shiners" flashing their presence nearer the surface. They saw the spotter porpoises at the surface slowly swimming next to the cork-line, seemingly knowing that the opportunity to leave the net would come soon. They observed the tunas wheeling quietly in the net, away from the swishing sound of the surface-swimming spotters and their muffled blowing of air and the spinner porpoises, more excitable and seemingly more emotional than the spotters, acting less at home than the well-adjusted and mature spotters.

Because of his skill in fishing tuna/porpoise schools, Harold and his crew had more fishing options than the captains and crews of some other tuna seiners. Not all seiners were equipped with the speedboats required to set on tuna/porpoise schools; these vessels, usually the small seiners based in San Pedro, found their niche in fishing areas where pure schools of tuna occurred. By having crewmembers use speedboats to chase and herd the tuna/porpoise school, the behavior of the porpoise and their tuna followers reduced the number of tuna seiners fishing for tuna/porpoise schools. Porpoise were no longer swimming toward the tuna seiners, making it easy for the fishermen to spot and encircle the porpoise and associated tunas in their nets.

The persistent problem confronted by Harold during the first two years of commanding his new vessel, the KERRI M., was entanglement of the porpoise in the net just before and during the "Back-down." During 1969-1970, Harold had directed 299 sets of the purse seine, of which 215 were on tuna/porpoise schools. He had thought that the entanglement problem could be reduced, or even eliminated, by a longer and deeper net and by the use of new and powerful tools that could reduce the time that it took to commence the "Back-down." These included new equipment, such as a powerful main winch to quickly pull the towline and purse-line; a unique flume stabilizer system that reduced the roll of the vessel during the set by 70%, thereby making work by the crew on the deck safer, speedier, and more productive; and, a larger and more powerful net skiff so as to quickly tow the seiner in positions that would keep the net open. Also, his three speedboats could be better deployed, because the operator of each was equipped with a radio head receiver with which he received instructions as to how to herd the porpoise to the middle of the ever-decreasing perimeter of the net. Furthermore, a more powerful Puretic Power Block helped the crew to quickly pull the net aboard and stack it on the net platform. Finally, the 3600-HP main engine of the KERRI M.—more than five times as powerful as the 550-HP main engine of the ALPHECCA—enabled it to accomplish the "Back-down" more effectively.

All of these innovations in gear and equipment addressed the following realities: The less time the porpoise remain in the net, the less risk of their entanglement. The sooner the "Back-down" is implemented, the greater chance for success in releasing the porpoise alive from the net. And, yet, Harold still observed porpoise entanglement during "Back-down." This entanglement was costly, because it delayed the process of freezing captured tunas and commencement of another search for tuna/porpoise schools. If these entanglements could be minimized, the "Back-down" would become more efficient. Less time in a set means more time available to search for another school of fish. Thus it made economic sense to solve this problem. In addition, the fishermen perceived the porpoise as playful, harmless creatures, and they disliked seeing them die. Also, many of them realized that if large numbers of porpoise died in their nets, the populations of porpoise could decrease, which would have a negative effect on their fishing success.

Harold was convinced that a deeper net that sinks more rapidly would be substantially more effective in dealing with tuna/porpoise schools than the smaller net used aboard the ALPHECCA. He designed, and, with his crew, constructed a net that was 750 fathoms (4,500 feet) long and 12 strips or (72 fathoms or 482 feet) deep. Changes to the "chainline" and "rings" were used to make the net sink more quickly. The "towline" was 300 fathoms (3,600 feet) long. In comparison, the net aboard the ALPHECCA was 550 fathoms (3,300 feet) long and 8 strips (48 fathoms or 288 feet) deep, and the "towline" was 200 fathoms (1,200 feet) long.

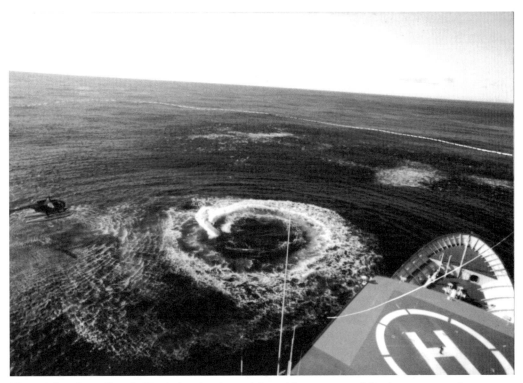

Photo taken from Crow's Nest showing in part the wide expanse of the tuna purse seine operation during the early period of a "set". The encirclement stage has been completed, with the vessel's main winch engaged in pursing or closing the net. Speedboats and helicopter are in action to keep the tuna from escaping the net.

Harold's two years of fishing experience on the KERRI M. proved that the greater volume of the ocean available for the encircled tunas and porpoise provided by the longer, deeper net gave them the opportunity to behave more naturally within the net. The porpoise tended to swim near the surface and the tunas below them in the deeper portion of the net. To a certain extent, the "enigma" was being mitigated, as the greater expanse enclosed by the net gave the fishermen the opportunity to control the movements of the porpoise in preparation for release during the "Back-down." The sound and movement of the three speedboats kept the porpoise milling in the middle of the net and away from the area where the net was being pulled aboard by the Power Block and stacked by the crew on the net platform.

The new innovations of the KERRI M. gave Harold an edge in his competition with other captains by making him more successful in fishing tuna/porpoise schools. He had available a powerful main engine to push the sleek hull forward at a speed of 15 or more knots, which enabled him to search more ocean area for tuna/porpoise schools. He had a variety of innovations in fishing gear and equipment that would speed his crew in the race to conduct the "Back-down," after which most of the rest of the net could be brought aboard, and the tunas could be removed from the "pocket" that remained and stored in the wells. And, yes, by reducing the time that the porpoise were in the net, the opportunity for their entanglement and entrapment was reduced. Nevertheless, he became convinced that his net had to be changed in a way that would enhance the proven benefits of the "Back-down."

During the "Back-down," the hope is that the porpoise will leave the net quickly and steadily as a group without entanglement and without being physically assisted by the fishermen. If porpoise become entangled in the net just before or during "Back-down," then manual removal by the fishermen is required. This increases the time of the fishing operation, thereby increasing risks of loss of tunas, damage to the net and other gear, and injury to crewmembers. Completing a set more quickly than a competing vessel on the fishing grounds gives the vessel more time to find another school of tuna/porpoise and set the net around it. Tuna/porpoise schools are not uniformly distributed in the ocean; the fishermen have to find them, and when they find them they can disappear after a few days. Therefore, the fishermen must make as many sets as possible during the periods when fishing conditions are favorable. Also, rough weather restricts fishing opportunities for purse-seine fishermen. With its flume stabilizer system, the KERRI M. was capable of fishing in winds up to 18 knots and wave heights up to about 5 feet, but the wind speeds and/or wave heights often exceed those limits. The traditional fishing grounds for tuna/porpoise schools are subject to many tropical storms, particularly during June through October. These are the realities and economic imperatives that push tuna fishermen to complete a set on tuna/porpoise as quickly and safely as possible.

Understandably, for the first two years operating his new tuna seiner, Captain Harold Medina, was particularly concerned about this unique operating problem with fishing tuna/porpoise schools. During the same period, the issue of porpoise mortality in tuna seiner fishing operations also became the obsession of, William F. Perrin, a young marine mammalogist working for the U.S. Bureau of Commercial Fisheries (BCF), Department of Interior.

The Search of William F. Perrin

During 1966, Gerald V. Howard, BCF, asked for the assistance of co-author August Felando (hereinafter cited as "Felando") in making arrangements for a government employee to go on a tuna fishing trip aboard a converted tuna seiner. He explained that the BCF was collecting data for use in an economic study, and made reference to its studies on the fishing fleet based in San Pedro.[1] In the capacity as the General Manager of the American Tunaboat Association (ATA), Felando asked Louis Castagnola, Captain and Managing Owner of the CONTE BIANCO, to take the government employee aboard the vessel's next fishing trip.[2]

After much discussion about the purpose of Mr. Howard's request, Captain Castagnola agreed to the arrangement. The government employee who was making his first trip aboard a converted tuna seiner was William F. Perrin. The fishing trip commenced on July 10, 1966, and was completed on August 11, 1966. Based upon "rough" observations of porpoise mortality, Perrin prepared a two-page memorandum dated September 8, 1966, and submitted it to the Acting Laboratory Director, Tuna Resources Laboratory, La Jolla, California. The ATA and the Captain Castagnola were not provided with a copy of this report[3] or even in-formed by personnel of the Tuna Resources Laboratory about its contents. Thereafter, a number of reports prepared by the BCF during 1966-1968 made refer-ences to the collection of data on the fishing of tuna/porpoise schools, but not to the problem of porpoise mortality. The BCF December 1966 report of the Tuna Resources Laboratory noted that its work with the Inter-American Tropical Tuna Commission (IATTC) revealed that an "interesting side line as a result of examin-ing these data is the comparison of rates of success on school [unassociated] and porpoise-associated fish: 67.8% on all porpoise schools, and 48.0% on all school fish. . . . Further studies of trends in efficiencies are planned in collabora-tion with the IATTC." This report made no reference to any porpoise mortality problem associated with the purse-seine fishery.

BCF regulations to implement the IATTC recommendations to conserve and manage the yellowfin tuna fishery in the EPO were promulgated for the first time in 1966. A group of newer and larger U.S. purse seiners adjusted to these measures by developing new tuna fishing grounds in the South Atlantic off West Africa. In 1967, a BCF scientist aboard the new U.S. tuna seiner CARIB-BEAN recorded the fishing of tuna/porpoise schools in these waters.[4] This pub-lic report made no reference to any porpoise mortality problem associated with this fishing trip.

The BCF Monthly Report for March 1968 notes the following: "Cost and earnings data collection for the San Diego seiners has slowed down during the month. . . . During the lull, Mr. William Perrin has gone out on the tunaboat CAROL VIRGIN-IA to continue our at-sea monitoring of tuna seiner operations. He also expects to collect a series of porpoise (Stenellus [sic.]) for population studies in coopera-tion with Mr. Andrew Vrooman."

The BCF Monthly Report for June 1968 includes reference to work by Mr. William Perrin, on the completion of financial and operations data for 10 boats for the pe-riod January 1, 1963, to April 30, 1968, to be used in an economic study of the wetfish seine fishery. This report also referred to the work of Perrin on porpoise, namely an investigation of the morphometry of two species of porpoise associa-tion with the tropical tuna fishery based on measurements of 143 specimens of *Stenella graffmani* from four schools and 95 specimens of *S. longirostris* from three schools. It also refers to the tuna/porpoise article by Mr. Perrin published during 1968 in *Sea Frontiers,* "The Porpoise and the Tuna."

In 1968, Perrin made his second fishing trip aboard the converted seiner CAROL VIRGINIA. The fishing trip commenced on April 1, and was completed on April 29. Based upon "rather precise counts" and observations of porpoise mortality, Perrin prepared a three-page memorandum to the Director, Fishery-Oceanography Center, La Jolla, dated May 13, 1968. This memorandum was not brought to the attention of the ATA. Thereafter, a second Perrin article, en-titled "Using Porpoise to Catch Tuna" was published in a fishing trade magazine, *World Fishing*.[5]

At the Sixth Annual Conference on Biological Sonar and Diving Mammals, held at the Stanford Research Institute, Menlo Park, California, William Perrin presented a paper entitled, "The Problem of Porpoise Mortality in the U.S. Tropical Tuna Fishery." During the presentation, Perrin showed his film of a set of purse seine by the CONTE BIANCO on a tuna/porpoise school. Perrin reported to the gathering that: **"The fishermen know that they are dependent on the porpoise, and they are receptive in conservation ideas. They have put a lot of effort in developing the backing-down method (described in the film), and they have tried other things that did not work. If somebody could devise something that looks as if it might work, they will try it."** (emphasis added) His presentation was published by the Stanford Research Institute in 1970 as a part of the Proceedings of the Sixth Annual Conference on Biological Sonar and Diving Mammals, edited by M. W. Odemar and K. C. Wilson.

Significantly, Perrin's Conference paper, on page 48, reported: "In one set (No. 9 in Table 1) we got almost all the porpoise out which were visible at the surface during backing-down and yet we came up with 185 dead animals in the sack. Almost all of these must have died before the backing-down operation . . ." Perrin concluded that the "problem" has three parts: "(1) finding a way of getting the porpoise to come to a particular point on the cork-line, which is 1/2 mile long; (2) devising a gate which can be rapidly opened and closed; and, (3) finding a way to induce the animals to pass through the gate."[6]

After hearing informal reports about Perrin's presentation at the Stanford Research Institute, the ATA asked the BCF to provide whatever information it had on the issue of porpoise mortality in the U.S. tuna purse-seine fishery.

Dr. Alan R. Longhurst, Director, BCF Fishery-Oceanography Center, La Jolla, California, responded to the ATA in writing. Dr. Longhurst's letter, dated January 21, 1970, explained the Center's "view of the porpoise situation." The ATA staff and officers reacted with concern and surprise about the letter's porpoise mortality estimates, and to the following statement:

> "If the information that we have on the mortality rate of porpoise in the fishing operation is valid, large numbers of porpoises are killed annually, and there is a strong possibility that the stocks of the animals may be in danger. We must stress the word 'if' because the data we have thus far are very meager. They are, however, the only data available at present."

Dr. Longhurst recited the findings of Mr. Perrin aboard the tuna seiners CONTE BIANCO in 1966 and CAROL VIRGINIA in 1968. He stressed that Perrin's trip aboard the CAROL VIRGINIA was "with the express purpose of studying porpoise biology," and he attached a table compiled by Perrin showing the porpoise mortality estimated on 15 sets made in April 1968. He also attached a table compiled by an observer during a trip in November/December 1969 aboard a U.S. tuna seiner operating under a charter with the IATTC. Dr. Longhurst commented:

> "For all three sets of data, two of which consist of estimates and one of careful counts, the figure for average mortality falls around five or six porpoise per ton of fish. Let us use the figure of 5 per ton; if we multiply this figure times the total ton-

nage of yellowfin taken on porpoise (50,000 tons), we arrive at a figure of 250,000 porpoise killed per year."

"The crucial question, of course, is, if we assume the estimated level of mortality to be the actual one, is there any reason to think that the level of mortality would be harmful to the porpoise population? As it turns out, there are reasons for concern . . ."

The concern expressed in this letter was that Perrin's counts aboard the CAROL VIRGINIA showed a 20% mortality rate, which was higher than the then-estimated porpoise reproductive rate of 15%. Longhurst referred to the concerns arising from a former Russian fishery for whitebelly porpoise in the Black Sea. (The Russians used the porpoise for animal food, fertilizer, oil, and leather.) Dr. Longhurst claimed that "there is enough of a parallel here to the Russian situation to make us nervous."

Dr. Longhurst expressed the BCF's need for help in: (1) obtaining actual counts, rather than estimates, of porpoise mortality "gathered by biologists riding on tunaboats;" and, (2) "a concentrated effort by all concerned to reduce porpoise mortality," explaining:

"We have heard that there is a great variation in the success of backing down as practiced by different boats. Some of this is no doubt due to differences in techniques. Perhaps information on improvements in techniques could be given freer circulation in the fleet. Such an exchange of information would be very much to the common good. On our part, we intend to work on the development of existing and/or new techniques and gear for rescuing porpoise, possibly using chartered tunaboats for some of the fieldwork.

"Any and all cooperation and suggestions will be greatly welcomed . . . ."

The Staff and Officers of the ATA could not accept Perrin's estimate that for every ton of yellowfin landed, over 5 porpoise had died, and of his computation that if 45,000 tons of yellowfin was caught on porpoise during 1966, then over 244,000 porpoise died in the fishery during that year. ATA knew that the logbook records maintained by the fleet customarily recorded the catch of tuna taken with porpoise, and that the entries were reasonably accurate. However, ATA also knew that the logbooks did not request that the captain record the estimate of porpoise mortality. Therefore, ATA had no way of evaluating Perrin's estimates by using the IATTC records of fishing activity. The question was whether the porpoise mortality experience aboard the CONTE BIANCO in 1966 and on the CAROL VIRGINA in 1968 could be used to estimate the porpoise mortality experience for the entire fleet in 1970.[7] Felando advised Captain Castagnola of Perrin's rough counts of porpoise mortality during his 1966 trip aboard the CONTE BIANCO, namely that about 2,000 porpoise had died while catching about 300 tons of yellowfin. Captain Castagnola admitted that numerous porpoise had died during the sets made on tuna/porpoise schools, but that he had no recorded data to refute the Perrin estimate.

Thereafter, Felando contacted Franklin (Frank) G. Alverson, Living Marine Resources, Inc. (LMR), and asked him to quickly develop some data on porpoise mortality experienced in the U.S. tuna fleet. Frank asked captains known in the fleet for their skill in fishing tuna/porpoise schools to undertake a confidential per-sonal count of porpoise mortality during their next fishing trip. After analyzing the data, Frank reported that some of the captains found that the total mortality dur-ing the trip was greater than they had expected. Frank advised that it was impor-tant for the ATA to cooperate with the BCF to obtain as much observer data on porpoise mortality as possible. LMR and the ATA understood the importance of keeping the U.S. tuna seiner fleet competitive and how much the fleet depended upon its ability to successfully fish tuna/porpoise schools.

During the 1960s, the U.S. tuna seiner fleet had proven that it could compete with Japanese imports of frozen yellowfin tuna. By fishing the large, adult yellow-fin tuna found in association with porpoise, the US tuna fishermen were landing tuna comparable to the yellowfin caught by the "Longline" gear used by the Jap-anese, not only in quality, but also in price. The U.S. converted seiner fleet found that the fishing of "pure" yellowfin schools on the high seas, far offshore, to be virtually impossible. In these clear blue waters, these yellowfin tuna schools were too speedy and elusive. When the tuna schooled with porpoise in these waters, the fishermen discovered that when their nets encircled the porpoise leading the tunas, they also caught the tunas. As they developed the speedboat herding method, their fishing success on tuna/porpoise schools increased. In contrast to the situation during the 1950s, the U.S. tuna fleet was benefiting from the growth in the domestic canned tuna market. By seining tuna/porpoise schools, the U.S. tuna fishermen had developed new fishing grounds that made them uniquely competitive. For instance, the IATTC reported that during 1966-1971, a period when yellowfin tuna conservation regulations were in force, the portion of seine-caught yellowfin tuna taken from tuna/porpoise schools averaged 62.4% (with a low of 46.8% in 1968 and a high of 86.4% in 1969). Since most tuna/porpoise schools were found far offshore, U.S. tuna seiners avoided sei-zures by foreign governments claiming sovereignty of 200-mile maritime zones.[8] Since the fishing of tuna/porpoise schools involves the taking of sexually-mature yellowfin, rather than juveniles, their fishing of tuna/porpoise schools by the U.S. tuna seiner fleet lessened any adverse impact on recruitment. For these and other reasons, the U.S. tuna industry reacted seriously and quickly to Dr. Long-hurst's letter to the ATA, and to Perrin's report submitted to the meeting at the Stanford Research Institute. At the ATA, the members agreed that the fleet should take all necessary steps to reduce porpoise mortality to its lowest practic-al level. It was to the interest of the fishermen to accomplish this goal, and it was agreed at the ATA that it was a fishermen's problem that would have to be solved by the fishermen.

In February 1970, Dr. Longhurst established a program of research to develop methods for reducing porpoise mortality. "Perhaps the most sensitive issue I had to deal with in the scientific programme was Bill Perrin's exposure of porpoise mortality in the tuna fishery. He asked my advice about publishing an account of the techniques of 'setting' on porpoise schools and I remember telling him to go ahead . . . . I can't think of any scientific paper in the marine sciences that had greater political and economic consequences. It was a whistle-blower that I'm glad I didn't have the good sense to veto."[9]

While at sea during 1970, Captain Harold Medina had concluded that the porpoise entanglement problem could be solved by changing the web size of the purse seine in the "Back-down" area.[10] Smaller-size mesh would prevent the snouts of the porpoise from becoming entangled in the net. Harold had observed that the porpoise could swim only ahead, and not in reverse, thereby making it virtually impossible for a porpoise to extricate its snout from the 4 1/4-inch webbing. (Mesh is measured between opposite corners, with those two corners stretched apart, so a square of 4 1/4-inch webbing has four sides, each about 2 1/8 inch long.) Unlike William Perrin, Harold had the singular experience of observing the behavior of spotters and spinners as a mastman during over 1,000 purse-seine sets on tuna/porpoise schools.

> "While watching porpoise behavior during the "Back-down," I would see them maneuver trying to escape, but in doing this, they would get their noses stuck through the 4 1/4-inch netting and try to swim through the net while their nose was still stuck in the net. Porpoise cannot swim in reverse. Seeing this behavior, I thought that if smaller size webbing was used in the "Back-down" area, this would allow the porpoise to escape from the netting. They would be able to use the netting to slide over the sunken floats, clear and free. I felt that the 2-inch mesh would not unduly obstruct the effectiveness of the "Back-down" by reducing the water flow passing through the net."

> Another important event related to porpoise mortality occurred in 1970. Congress approved President Nixon's plan to reorganize the nation's oceanic and atmospheric research organizations into a single part of the Department of Commerce—the National Oceanic and Atmospheric Administration (NOAA). The result was a transfer of the Bureau of Commercial Fisheries (BCF) and the marine sport fishing activities of the Bureau of Sport Fisheries and Wildlife (BSFW) from the Department of Interior to the newly-created National Marine Fisheries Service (NMFS) in NOAA. The ATA expressed concern that the U.S. commercial fishing industry had lost an advocate within the government when the BCF disappeared, and that this re-organization could adversely affect the government's policy of working with the tuna fleet in solving the technological problem of fishing tuna/porpoise schools.[11]

On October 22, 1970, in response to a request by Dr. Longhurst, a meeting was held in ATA's boardroom. Felando's recollection of this meeting is that he, Dr. Longhurst, William Perrin, Captain Harold Medina, Captain Edward X. Madruga, and Captain Frank Gonsalves were active participants. The meeting commenced with Mr. Perrin's report on his memorandum to Dr. Longhurst dated October 29, 1970.[11] He explained the various ideas of experimental porpoise rescue gear, and in particular his "hydraulic gate" idea.[12] During the meeting, Captain Medina talked about his idea of having small mesh inserted in the net to reduce porpoise entanglement. Most of the discussion focused on arranging a field trial of various experimental gears by using a converted seiner to encircle porpoise in waters off San Diego. The ATA agreed to contact vessel owners and arrange for a converted seiner to test the government gear.

After the meeting, Harold told Felando privately that he was going to work on his small mesh idea independent of any government help. At the time, Felando did not realize the merit of Harold's view on the porpoise entanglement problem that existed before and during the "Back-down," as he had had no first-hand experience with the workings of the "Back-down." This explains his interest in testing sound devices to herd some of the porpoise away from the tunas before commencing the "set," and in using these new devices to help move the captured porpoise out of the net during "Back-down." If successful, these devices would reduce the number of porpoises encircled, and help those encircled to escape during the "Back-down." Felando thought that the entanglement and entrapment problems would be reduced or eliminated by effective herding of the porpoise. Time would prove the wisdom of Harold's opinions about modifying the webbing of the net and in developing a system to better identify and standardize the configuration of the net area utilized by the "Back-down."

Pursuant to the request of Longhurst and Perrin, the ATA arranged to have a tuna seiner available for testing Perrin's idea. The seiner CONQUEST left San Diego for coastal waters on December 22, 1970, equipped with the government's experimental rescue gear. Captain Richard Madruga and his brother, Captain Joseph Madruga, because of their excellent reputations in the tuna fleet, were selected to test the government-designed gear. At the ATA, we knew that if the Madruga brothers found the experimental gear successful, the rest of the fleet would quickly accept it.

The result of the trial trip is described in a Perrin memorandum to the Director, National Marine Fisheries Service (NFMS), Fishery-Oceanography Center, La Jolla, dated December 31, 1970.[13] Following experimental efforts, the captains involved advised the ATA that they disliked the complexity of the "gate" idea, but showed considerable interest in the use of sound devices to herd porpoises. Although offered the government equipment for use on their next fishing trip, the Madruga brothers refused to further test the "gate." They did agree, however. to further test the deep sound emitter. The following excerpt from the December 31 trial trip report describes the entanglement problem observed during the trial trip by Perrin. This description by Perrin is important because it effectively describes the problem raised by Captain Medina during the ATA/NMFS October meeting:

> "All but seven of the porpoise escaped through the gate during backing down. The seven remaining animals . . . headed into the webbing to the right of the gate, becoming entangled. Of these, one was later extricated and released alive, and the other six died . . . The skiff operators and I observed that the porpoise apparently did not dive to the bottom of the net but made only short, shallow dives of 10-15 feet and a few seconds duration. This is in contrast to previous observations I made aboard tunaboats of porpoise in the net making prolonged, apparently very deep dives (in very clear water). Also, in this set the only animals to entangle themselves in the webbing were those that became confused during the backing down operation, while in my experience, at least several porpoise usually perish in this manner before backing down begins. The fishermen on the Conquest said that porpoise often behave as they did during the test set but conceded that the deep transducer may have contributed to the phenomenon."

Meanwhile, Captain Harold Medina was taking action on his own to test his idea. In December 1970, Harold ordered 2-inch mesh netting from a San Pedro supplier for delivery in Panama in early 1971.

The KERRI M. departed San Diego on January 2, 1971, and subsequently delivered its catch to the Star-Kist cannery in Mayaquez, Puerto Rico. In April 1971, Harold told me that the small-mesh panel system, which he had used on his second trip of 1971, was a success, as it had virtually eliminated porpoise entanglement before and during "Back-down." During that 37-day trip, Harold made 42 sets on tuna schools, of which 41 were on tuna/porpoise schools. He explained that while the KERRI M. was docked at the port of Balboa, Panama Canal Zone, he and his crew inserted the small-mesh panel in the purse seine, as follows:

> "Before starting my second trip of 1971, I replaced the netting in the "Back-down" area from 4 1/4 inch to 2 inch mesh size netting. The netting replaced was 100 fathoms (600 feet) in length and 6 fathoms (36 feet) in depth. The replaced netting was located just below the floats on the cork line. The entire ""Back-down" area" was now covered by 2 inch netting."

I asked Harold to diagram the new panel system and provide information on how he inserted it into the net so that I could circulate the information to the ATA membership as soon as possible. I asked him why he decided on 2-inch mesh, and he said that he didn't want to try a smaller size at that time because he didn't want to create problems that would reduce the effectiveness of the "Back-down." Harold reasoned that if the net mesh was too small, it could reduce the water flow as he performed the "Back-down," and he didn't want this small-mesh section of the net to act like a "bucket" that would cause the net to sink too fast. Also, based upon his measurements, most porpoise snouts would not get caught in the 2-inch mesh. Harold provided the document as requested, and it was circulated to the membership, as promised. We called the new idea the "Medina Panel."[14] NMFS officials were quickly informed of Harold's report on the success of his small-mesh panel system.

The next vessel to order and insert the "Medina Panel" was the QUEEN MARY, managed and operated by Captain Joe M. Medina, Jr., first cousin of Captain Harold Medina. By the fall of 1971, ten vessels had inserted the "Medina Panel" or ordered the small-mesh webbing.

1971 Congressional Hearings

Meanwhile, hearings were being held by Congressional Committees in Washington, D.C., on legislation for the preservation and protection of marine mammals. On September 13, 1971, the "Medina Panel" was described with drawings and comments to members of the House Subcommittee on Fisheries and Wildlife Conservation by Howard W. Pollock, Deputy Administrator, NOAA.[15]

Also testifying about the Medina Panel, was Joseph (Joe) Medina, Jr., Captain and Managing Owner of the QUEEN MARY. He described the at-sea incident that convinced him to inset a Medina Panel in his vessel's purse seine, as follows:

> "We compared the QUEEN MARY together and we had the old netting and he [Harold] had the new and we both made sets on schools of porpoise and tuna at the same time. He [Harold] was through an hour before we were . . . . (p.348)

"Let me say not only for saving the porpoise, but when I am out there and I make a set and I finish an hour before my competitor, I guarantee you he is going to put that webbing on. He will have to, to compete. We do not have enough data, but we are really happy with result, I think it is a fantastic thing. (p.350)

"Yes, when we [QUEEN MARY] "Back-down," this is the first thing that really saves the porpoise, when we "Back-down" we may have 1,500 or 2,000 porpoise. This is a large school. Sometimes we may make a set on 40 or 50 porpoise and have no trouble getting them out. When we "Back-down" out of that 1,500 porpoise, maybe 40 to 50 porpoise will get tangled in the net. The rest of them slide out over the top of the net and get out alive. This is the problem we have with the 40 or 50 porpoise and we get in [the net] and [manually] save them, the ones that get tangled up. With this new webbing and smaller [mesh] net, and we are not having the problem, these porpoises are sliding right out of the net and getting out alive." (p.354)

During his testimony, Captain Joe Medina, Jr., additionally stated the following:

"I talked to my vessel this past Wednesday. They have the webbing on this trip and they say it is like the difference between day and night. It has been a real help. We have the problem licked. I say this is one thing the fishermen always try to do is save the porpoise caught because without them we would not be in business. (p.348)

"Well, to answer your question, we still see as much porpoise as we ever did. We have this problem licked with this net of mine. I wish it could be a year later so we could have a little more data for you. Within a year, everybody will have this net." (p.353)[16]

By February 1972, about 40 vessels had ordered or inserted the webbing required for the "Medina Panel." On February 16, 1972, before a U.S. Senate Subcommittee, William Perrin provided the following testimony on the effectiveness of the Medina Panel, as follows:

"In the last year, there has been a major technological development that bears on the problem. Last spring, a captain named Harold Medina developed a net modification. He replaced a large section of the net in the backing down area with smaller-than-usual mesh webbing—2 inch-mesh instead of 4 1/4-inch mesh. The idea is that the porpoise are less likely to become entangled when they hit the net if the mesh openings are smaller. (p.402)

"This modification is rapidly being adopted by the entire fleet and is a definite improvement. From the data available to us now from four cruises with the new net we estimate that it has cut porpoise mortality by as much as 75 percent. On the average, about 90 percent of the encircled porpoise are saved by using the modified net." (emphasis added) (p. 402)

"This year . . . we will have enough data for the modified net to allow us to evaluate the contribution of the modification. As I said earlier, the preliminary results are quite encouraging. (p. 405)

After the "Medina Panel" idea became known and practiced by many tuna captains in the fleet during 1971 and 1972, a number of tuna captains decided to add two "Medina Panels" to their net, explaining that by having a deeper panel, even less risk of entanglement would occur. The "Medina Panel" was nurturing new ideas to reduce porpoise mortality.[17]

It is very important to acknowledge that William Perrin was the first federal government employee to direct efforts on reducing porpoise mortality by seeking improvements to the "Back-down" idea developed by fishermen. However, he was not a fishing gear specialist, nor did he have sufficient experience in observing the behavior of tuna/porpoise schools during a variety of fishing operations. These two facts explain why his "hydraulic gate" idea was a failure.[18]

It is also important to acknowledge the contributions of Franklin (Frank) G. Alverson and Gordon Broadhead, of Living Marine Resources, Inc., (LMR) of San Diego, California, in assisting the ATA and other segments of the tuna industry in working more effectively with appropriate federal agencies (BCF and NMFS) and the IATTC in reducing porpoise mortality during the period prior to and after the enactment of the Marine Mammal Protection Act of 1972.

In early 1971, the ATA hired LMR to provide data and recommendations after studying the porpoise mortality problem.[19] This was done for two main reasons: (1) concerns about various bills introduced in Congress to protect marine mammals by prohibiting tuna purse seining on tuna/porpoise schools; and; (2) the fleet's need to work with the scientists of the IATTC and the NMFS in seeking solutions to the porpoise mortality problem.[20] To have an effective industry interaction with the IATTC and the NMFS, the ATA needed the scientific expertise and credibility of Gordon Broadhead and Frank Alverson. Both were biologists who had previously been employed by the IATTC. Each of them had participated in scientific studies aboard U.S. tuna baitboats and each had published scientific papers on the EPO tuna fishery. The IATTC, the NMFS, and all segments of the U.S. tuna industry recognized these two founders of LMR and their employees, as dedicated, honest, and experienced tuna scientists.

Major contributions were made by Frank Alverson during that period in developing a research program by the U.S. tuna industry to reduce the fleet's porpoise mortality. Frank had served the United States as a paratrooper during World War II, and during the years he worked with the ATA staff, his performance was consistently honest, industrious, and passionate. As a scientist and consultant, he was persistent and thorough in developing data and recommendations regarding the tuna/porpoise problem. His friends would fondly describe Frank's verbal approach as one that would sound aggressive and confrontational while saying the Lord's Prayer. Frank spent years observing American tuna fishermen as they worked aboard baitboats and while they made the transition to purse seining. He had great communication skills in obtaining confidential fishing information from tuna fishermen because they knew he could be trusted with this information. Much of LMR's early work for the ATA on the tuna-porpoise problem during 1971-1973 is described by Alverson's testimony before Congress.[21]

First, Frank developed data in early 1971 showing that there existed a wide range of skills shown by the captains and mastmen in capturing tuna/porpoise schools, and in using the "Back-down" to release live porpoise. His studies confirmed the understanding in the fleet that tuna captains considered their methods of fishing tuna/porpoise schools and in releasing porpoise alive from the net as trade secrets that should not be freely exchanged with competitors.

An important meeting was held exclusively with a key group of tuna captains in 1971. During this meeting, various bills introduced in Congress were reviewed, and Frank explained his confidential study on porpoise mortality in the U.S. tuna fleet. It showed that there existed a wide range of individual skills in capturing tuna/porpoise schools and in using the "Back-down" method to release porpoise alive from the net. During the meeting, the Captains were told that it was absolutely necessary for them to start exchanging their "trade secrets" in the fishing of tuna/porpoise schools. These captains were also told that many of them had developed gear other than the Medina Panel that had reduced porpoise mortality, and that they had to start transferring their secrets and technology to other captains. Thereafter, the captains were left alone to discuss their reactions to the ATA/LMR presentations. Later, the captains reported that they had agreed among themselves to "spread the word" to other captains and crews in the fleet.

Importantly, Frank was successful with the ATA and other segments of the tuna industry in arranging for tuna seiners to voluntarily carry U.S. government observers.[22] The importance of this effort to work with the NMFS was noted on February 16, 1972, by William Perrin during his testimony before Congress. His testimony was concerned with the history of the tuna/porpoise problem, biological information on the porpoise involved in the problem, and the status of the research effort being conducted by NOAA/NMFS on the problem, as follows:

> [The Federal Government has] "been doing some work on the natural history of the porpoises since 1962, but the formal program of research on the problem of mortality, per se, began in February 1970. . . . In assessing the problem, . . . we are collecting data on mortality by sending observers out on commercial seiners. When the program began in 1970 . . . we did not get any observers out in 1970. . . . In 1971, we had one person on each of five vessels. This year (1972) so far, we have 10 observer trips and expect to arrange more. . . . I should add here that all cooperation by participating members of the tuna fleet has been entirely voluntary. We would not have known the magnitude of the problem if we had not initially been allowed to ride along commercial cruises . . . ."

In 1972, ATA/LMR commenced a series of formal workshops on the tuna-porpoise problem. These sessions were also for the benefit of the shoreside members of the U.S. tuna industry. For instance, in May 1972, an ATA porpoise workshop was held in San Diego for captains and others in the tuna industry to discuss the following subjects: (1) techniques that yield the lowest incidence of porpoise mortality; (2) possible modifications in gear; (3) new equipment that might contribute to reduction of porpoise mortality; (4) results of recent NMFS gear research; and, (5) items of general interest concerning the porpoise mortality problem.[23]

Observations of Captain Harold Medina: the "Back-down" with the Medina Panel

> "After a set has been made and the rings are up, the net is now closed and the tuna/porpoise school is milling around the interior of the closed net. Now, the process to release the porpoise safely and keep the tunas is started. The after-end of the

net is hauled through the Puretic Power Block and the net haul-in is started. A speedboat is circling on the outside of the net, where the net leaves the water, keeping the porpoise clear of the net while the net is being hauled aboard. The net skiff is hooked to the vessel via a bridle and a 40-fathom line. The operator of the net skiff is making sure that the net is kept open and the vessel is moving slowly backward in the direction of the floats that are part of the net circle still in the water. As the net is being hauled aboard, one crewmember will pull three bunches on the bow (about 90 fathoms in length) before the 'Back-down' can be started. A large red float is secured to the float line showing the starting location of the Medina Panel. When the red float has been placed in the proper location, the 'Back-down' is now started. The net below the Puretic Power Block is now secured to the vessel by a strong line, keeping this net from being pulled back into the water. The vessel now starts the 'Back-down'—slowly until the total net is stretched out as the vessel is moving slowly astern. The key to a good "Back-down" is how and when the vessel will use its speed to release the porpoise safely and still hold the tunas in the net.

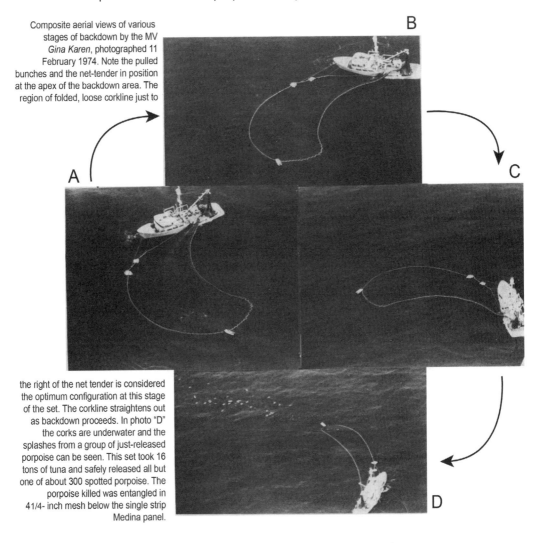

Composite aerial views of various stages of backdown by the MV *Gina Karen*, photographed 11 February 1974. Note the pulled bunches and the net-tender in position at the apex of the backdown area. The region of folded, loose corkline just to the right of the net tender is considered the optimum configuration at this stage of the set. The corkline straightens out as backdown proceeds. In photo "D" the corks are underwater and the splashes from a group of just-released porpoise can be seen. This set took 16 tons of tuna and safely released all but one of about 300 spotted porpoise. The porpoise killed was entangled in 4 1/4- inch mesh below the single strip Medina panel.

Photo courtesy of National Marine Fisheries Service

"As the vessel is going slowly astern, the porpoise are milling around on the surface and being guided toward the Medina Panel and the tunas are now feeling the net start closing around them, causing the tunas to panic and move back and forth, looking for a way out. As the tunas are looking for the way out, they will charge toward the net area used by the 'Back-down,' creating a surface boiling action. Then, the tuna mass will charge toward the vessel and again come to a surface boil next to the port side of vessel. I use this tuna behavior to help me during the 'Back-down.' While the tunas are boiling on the surface next to the Medina Panel and starting back toward the vessel, I would then speed up the astern maneuver of the vessel. This action causes the porpoise to roll over the floats and be clear of the net. I hold this speed until the tunas turn around from their location near the vessel and commence their charge toward the Medina Panel. As the tunas near the Medina Panel, I would again slow the speed astern until the current tuna charge ceases. Then, I return to the maneuver of speeding up the vessel astern for a 'Back-down.' This procedure would be repeated until almost all of the porpoise are released alive from the net.

"If a few porpoise are still left behind in the net, the speedboat driver and his helper hand release them from the net. During the 'Back-down' procedure, the speedboat is stationed just outside the location of the Medina Panel.

"If the captain pushes his vessel astern too fast and too long during 'Back-down', then the floats on the cork line of the Medina Panel will sink too deep below the surface. Under this condition, all of the porpoises and tunas will escape the net free and clear. This is why the maneuver must be a patient and careful 'start and stop' method of releasing the porpoise and retaining the tunas. This technique varies with each captain. Maybe a slightly different style may be used than described above but the objective is the same: Release the porpoise alive from the net and keep the tunas."

---

[1] "San Pedro Fleet's Financial Condition Studied," *Commercial Fisheries Review*, 1970, Vol. 32, No. 4: 6.

[2] The CONTE BIANCO was a very successful converted tuna seiner. It was built in San Diego during 1951 as a tuna baitboat. It had a steel hull, 116.8' registered length, 361 gross tons, 600 HP diesel engine. It was converted to a tuna seiner in September 1959, the 12th of the 97 seiners converted.

[3] Based upon this report, Mr. Perrin wrote an article about his trip aboard the CONTE BIANCO. See: William F. Perrin, "The Porpoise and the Tuna," *Sea Frontiers*, 1968, Vol 14, No. 3, pp. 166-174. This article contains photos taken by Mr. Perrin while aboard the CONTE BIANCO, showing the use of large binoculars to search for tuna/porpoise schools, photos of the CONTE BIANCO, and of its chase boat, and photos of sets of the net with porpoise and tuna in the net. A copy of Perrin's report to the acting director of the laboratory on his trip aboard the CONTE BIANCO appears in Smith, Tim D. and Lo, Nancy H., 1983, "Some Data on Dolphin Mortality in the Eastern Tropical Pacific Tuna Purse Seine Fishery Prior to 1970," NOAA Technical Memorandum NMFS, MPAA-TM-NMFS-SWFC-34. pp. 19-22.

[4] Simmons, D.C. "Purse Seining off Africa's West Coast" *Commercial Fisheries Review*, 1968, Vol. 30, No. 3: 21-22. "Ten sets were made from Nov.17 to Nov. 21 (8 were on porpoise-common dolphin, *Delphinus delphis* schools) and caught 89 tons of yellowfin tuna. The water off Cape Palmas was generally blue and clear. The yellowfin tuna

swam beneath the porpoise schools (this could be seen from the helicopter) and made it difficult to determine the tonnage before the sets were made. The two speed boats and helicopter were used to herd the porpoise and thus the tuna into the net. Some sets were made without seeing any tuna with the porpoise. . . . The yellowfin were all of the larger size (950mm fork length and above). No skipjack tuna or bigeye tuna were captured in this area." The report makes no mention of porpoise mortality.

[5] Perrin, W. F., 1969, "Using Porpoise to Catch Tuna," *World Fishing* 18 (6): 42-45. See" Anon. "Recipe For Success with Yellowfin Tuna: FIRST TAKE A PORPOISE," *The Fish Boat*, 1970, Vol. 15, No. 1: 19, 36-37. The photo of swimming tuna and porpoise in the purse seine on the cover of the trade magazine and the photos shown on page 19 were provided to *The Fish Boat* by William F. Perrin.

[6] Perrin, W.F., 1969 "The Problem of Porpoise Mortality in the U.S. Tropical Tuna Fishery." Proceedings of the Sixth Annual Conference on Biological Sonar and Diving Mammals, Stanford Research Institute, Menlo Park, California: 45-48. During the 1969 "Proceedings of the Sixth Annual Conference on Biological Sonar and Diving Mammals," Perrin presented a paper to describe "a problem" of porpoise mortality in tuna seiner fishing operations and to "stimulate interest in the problem and to obtain constructive feedback from you." He also showed a short film of tuna seiner fishing operations, and referred to his 1969 article on how porpoise are used to catch tuna in *World Fishing*, 18 (6); 42-45. In a paper published by the Stanford Research Institute in 1970, on page 45, Perrin reported: "In 1966, the boat I was on took approximately 300 tons of yellowfin tuna. I made rough counts of the number (of) porpoise killed and arrived at an estimate of about 2,000. Last year I went out again, on a different boat. This time I made rather precise counts. We took 312 tons of yellowfin tuna and accounted for 1,359 spotters and 338 spinners (Table 1) . . . 5.44 porpoise per ton of tuna."

[7] IATTC data showed that in 1966, 5,443 sets were identified as involving porpoise; 896 sets were unidentified but estimated to have involved porpoise, and 529 unlogged sets were estimated to be porpoise sets. In 1968, the numbers were 3,833, 175, and 150 respectively. Data from a total of 36 sets were used in Longhurst's letter of January 21, 1970, to the ATA.

[8] IATTC identification of areas of tuna/porpoise school fishing during the 1960-1969: 110°W to 95°W, and 20°N to 10°N (Northern Area), and 95°W to 80°W and 15°N to 5°N. (Southern Area) During the 1960s, seizures of U.S. tuna vessels occurred primarily on the high seas off the coasts of Peru, Ecuador, and Colombia.

[9] Vlymen, Lillian L. "The First 25 Years." NOAA Technical Memorandum NMFS (September 1989). NOAA-TM-NMFS-SWFC-134, p. 29. "It was in February, 1970 that Longhurst made what later proved to be a fateful decision when he started a program of research to develop methods for reducing the mortality of porpoise involved in the tropical tuna purse seine fishery. As he later wrote: 'Perhaps the most sensitive issue I had to deal with in the scientific programme was Bill Perrin's exposure of porpoise mortality in the tuna fishery. He asked my advice about publishing an account of the techniques of "setting" on porpoise schools and I remember telling him to go ahead. I think neither Bill nor I expected anything like the full consequences to flow from his paper—the Marine Mammal Act, the observer programme, the new seine-net technology, and perhaps even the departure of U.S. flag vessels to foreign registration. I can't think of any scientific paper in the marine sciences that had greater political and economic consequences. It was a whistle-blower that I'm glad I didn't have the good sense to veto.'"

[10] Prior to having the Medina Panel identify the "Back-down" area, each captain and his crew marked their net by using a float to identify the start of the "Back-down" area. Not every set on a tuna/porpoise school required a "Back-down" to have the porpoise escape the net alive. This was especially true when a very small number of porpoise were associated with the tuna. Customarily, the "Back-down" area involved about a 100 fathoms of cork-line.

[11] "Nixon Proposes National Oceanic and Atmospheric Administration," *Commercial Fisheries Review*, 1970, Vol. 32, No. 7: 1-4.

[12] "Gate Designed to Release Porpoise from Purse Seines," *Commercial Fisheries Review*, 1970, Vol. 32, No. 4: 7.

[13] The Memo is dated December 31, 1970, to "Director, NMFS, FOC," signed by "Bill Perrin," "Fishery Biologist," with the subject" "Porpoise rescue gear." "Reply to Fishery Biologist through: Leader, Operations Research Group."

[14] Thinking that the original drawing provided by Harold was important historically, it was placed in the ATA safe shortly after receiving it from Harold. Years later, the safe was searched but the original drawing was not found.

[15] Hearings before the Subcommittee on Fisheries and Wildlife Conservation of the Committee on Merchant Marine and Fisheries, House of Representatives, 92nd Cong., 1st Session, on Legislation for the Preservation and Protection of Marine Mammals September 9, 13, 17, 23, 1971, (Serial No. 92-10). (cited hereinafter, "1971 House Subcommittee Hearings-SN-92-10"): See Drawings at pp. 214-215; Testimony at pp.210-220, and pp. 229-233; Perrin testimony, pp. 255-256. August Felando and Joe Medina testified on September 17, 1971, See: pp. 344-355.

[16] The testimony of Captain Joe Medina, Jr., was used by some persons to unfairly claim that the tuna industry had assured Congress that the introduction of the "Medina Panel" to the tuna fleet in 1971 was the solution to eliminate porpoise mortality. Hearings before the Subcommittee on Fisheries and Wildilife Conservation and the Environment of the Committee on Merchant Marine and Fisheries House of representatives, 94th Congress 2d Session on Marine Mammal Amendments, April 30, May 4, May 20,21,24, 1976, (Serial No. 94-29), (cited hereinafter "May 1976 House Subcommittee Hearings-SN-94-29"): pp. 306-307, pp. 374-375, and the decision of District Court Judge Charles R. Richey, footnote 8, filed May 11, 1976, in *Committee For Humane Legislation, Inc. v. Richardson,* 414 F. Supp 297 (D. D.C.1976).

The testimony of the ATA before the House Subcommittee in 1971, clearly shows that the ATA was not making such a claim:

> "In the past two years, we have been working with the National Marine Fisheries Service (NMFS) in attempting to work out more information about the porpoise and in developing new ideas concerning the assistance to be given porpoise to leave the captured tuna. Necessarily, insufficient data has been developed in this period of time by the fleet concerning the impact of their using porpoise to capture tunas on the porpoise population.

> "Recently, the American Tunaboat Association (ATA), along with other organizations of the tuna industry, have worked out a program with the (NMFS). **Under this pro-**

gram, we hope to gather specific information on the success of the techniques developed by the fishermen to assist the porpoise in helping themselves to escape from the captured tuna. (emphasis added)

"Under this program, Government scientists will be aboard the vessels for the purpose of observing the techniques used by the fishermen. In addition, the fishermen will provide porpoise specimens to the fishery service. Plans are also being developed to have special charter trips, wherein a set number of days will be devoted exclusively to porpoise research. Preliminary views seem to indicate that this program will be substantially completed by the end of 1972. **It is our opinion that upon the completion of this program, the industry and the Government will be in a better position to evaluate the apparent problem associated with porpoise and tuna fishing.**" (emphasis added) 1971 House Subcommittee Hearings-SN-92-10, pp. 346-347.

[17] Memorandum dated June 17, 1971, by William Perrin to Director, Fishery Oceanography Center (FOC). "Results of trials with small-mesh webbing on schools of whitebelly porpoise by M/V SAN JUAN." (2 p). Cruise Report dated September 25, 1971, M/V WESTPORT, September 7 and 8, 1971, NMFS, SFC, (6 p).

[18] See: "Porpoises Saved from Tuna Seine by Underwater Sounds," *Commercial Fisheries Review*, 1971, Vol. 33, No. 10: 23-24 (Photo). "Several innovations such as hydraulic gates, skimmer nets, and various kinds of acoustic signals had previously been tried by Southwest Fisheries Center personnel. None had shown real promise." Eric G. Barham, Warren K.Taguchi, and Stephen B. Reilly, "Porpoise Rescue Methods in the Yellowfin Purse Seine Fishery and the Importance of Medina Panel Mesh Size," *Marine Fisheries Review*, 1977, Vol. 39, No. 5: 2.

Dr. Eric G. Barham, as Manager of the Porpoise/Tuna Interaction Program, Oceanic Fisheries Resources Division, was always welcomed at the ATA because he was considered a positive force in working with the tuna captains, crews, and others in the tuna industry. He exercised prudent leadership in seeking improvements in gear and methods to reduce porpoise mortality. His earlier San Diego employers included the Naval Electronics Laboratory and the Naval Underseas Warfare Center, where he participated in projects involving experimental dives with the bathyscaphes TRIESTE and ARCHIMEDE.

[19] LMR, formed in 1969, was an internationally-known fishery research and consulting firm based in San Diego, California, owned and controlled by its employees. LMR claimed expertise in marine biology, fishery population dynamics and resource assessment, operations research and computer model building, economics and marketing, vessel and gear operations, and seafood processing.

[20] Howard W. Pollack, Deputy Administrator of NOAA , testified before Congress that the tuna industry, "has recently agreed with NMFS to engage in a cooperative research program. Among other things, this program will include the use by the Service (NMFS) of tuna purse seining vessels for a total of 60 ship days, and will permit the Service observers to accompany commercial tuna operations on 20 fishing trips." 1971 House Subcommittee Hearings-SN-92-10: p. 216. See also, testimony of August Felando, General Manager, American Tunaboat Association (ATA), pp. 346-347.

[21] Hearings Before the Subcommittee on Oceans and Atmosphere of the Committee on Commerce, United States Senate, 92nd Congress, 2d Session, on Ocean Mammal Leg-

islation, February 15, 16, 23, and March 7, 1972. (Serial No. 92-56), Part 1, (Cited herei-nafter: "1972 Senate Subcommittee Hearings-SN-92-56"): pp. 479-482, pp.490-492, pp.831-835. pp. 475-492.

For comments negative to the tuna industry in this hearing: pp. 56-57, Herrington, pp. 89-90, p. 100; pp. 125-126; Cong. Obey, p. 327; Cong. Ryan, p. 340; pp.386-388, p. 391; p.402; Dr. Ken Norris at pp. 404-407, 410-413, p. 422, p. 437); Others: p.430, p. 439, p.441, p. 466. Mrs. Stevens: pp.489-492, 499-500; Others: p. 505, p. 521, p. 524, p. 529-530; p.532, p.533, p. 535, p. 540 (use "porpoise" instead of dolphin).

See: Testimony of August Felando (ATA) and Franklin Alverson (LMR), pp.2-32, pp. 37-42. Hearings before the Subcommittee on Fisheries and Wildlife Conservation and the Environment of the Committee on Merchant Marine and Fisheries, 93rd Congress, on Oversight of the Marine Mammal Protection Act of 1972, La Jolla, Cal-ifornia, August 21, 1973; Anchorage, Alaska, August 31, 1973, and Washington, D.C., January 16, 17, 1974, (Serial No, 93-24), (Cited hereafter: "1973 House Sub-committee Hearings-SN-93-24").

[22] In 1966, ATA arranged for William Perrin to observe the fishing operations of the CONTE BIANCO. In 1967, National Marine Terminals (NMT), the operator of the con-verted seiner INDEPENDENCE, arranged a two week trip for William Perrin. In 1968, NMT granted permission to NMFS to place William Perrin aboard the CAROL VIRGINIA. In 1971, NMFS observers were allowed by NMT to make fishing trips aboard their three converted seiners: LARRY ROE, SAN JUAN, and CONCHO. Also during 1971, with the consent of the owners, NMFS observers made fishing trips aboard the following three ATA member vessels: military hull converted new seiner NAUTILUS, new seiner KERRI M, and new seiner QUEEN MARY.

[23] The success of these workshops prompted their continuation after the Marine Mammal Protection Act (MMPA) was enacted. During the ATA Workshop held in San Diego on July 26, 1973, the speakers included William Evans, of the Naval Undersea Research and Development Center, who lectured the group on the general biology and behavior of porpoise, Eric Barham, Manager of the NMFS Tuna-Porpoise Program, who informed the group on the proposed 1974 Porpoise Observer Program, and Richard McNeely, NMFS Fishery Gear Specialist, who reported on the results of the recent Experimental Gear Cruise in waters off San Diego aboard the tuna seiner JOHN F. KENNEDY, and of his plans for testing experimental gear during a fishing trip that was going to depart in October 1973. In the afternoon session, different work groups of captains were formed to discuss the techniques that have been shown to reduce porpoise mortality.

"The two workshops this year (1974) attracted 70 skippers, mates and vessel operators, including some people attending both sessions. To date, 117 different industry people have attended these workshops. Inasmuch as the fleet is comprised of approximately 130 seiners, we feel that our coverage has been satisfactory." Hearings before the Sub-committee on Fisheries and Wildlife Conservation and the Environment of the Committee on Merchant Marine and Fisheries, 93rd Congress, 2nd Session on Import Restrictions, June 10, 1974, Endangered Species Act Amendment, July 29, 1974, and Incidental Tak-ing of Marine Mammals, H.R. 15273, H.R. 15459, H.R. 15549, H.R. 15810, H.R. 15967, H.R. 16043, H.R. 16777, August 8, 9, 1974, (Serial No. 93-36), (Cited hereinafter: "1974 House Subcommittee Hearings-SN-93-36"), p. 195.

15

PUBLIC AWARENESS OF PORPOISE MORTALITY

Tuna scientists first began to accompany U.S. tuna vessels on fishing trips in significant numbers during 1953, but only a few of those trips were made aboard tuna seiners. Data compiled by the scientific staff of the Inter-American Tropical Tuna Commission (IATTC) show that scientists employed by the IATTC, the California Department of Fish and Game (CDFG), and the U.S. Bureau of Commercial Fisheries (BCF) have tagged tens of thousands of tropical tunas (Yellowfin, Skipjack, and Bigeye) and about 3,500 Bluefin Tuna. (Most of the Bluefin were tagged by a joint program of the CDFG and the BCF during 1962-1968.). During 1953-1959, IATTC and CDFG scientists made 74 trips aboard U.S. baitboats based in California and Peru, but only 12 trips aboard U.S. purse seiners.[1] During those 12 purse-seine trips, 940 yellowfin, 9 skipjack , and 130 bluefin were tagged. It is not known whether the seiners set on tuna/porpoise schools during these tagging cruises or whether the reports filed by the scientists on the following trips contained entries on the fishing of tuna/porpoise schools. This preference of baitboat trips over purse-seine trips by tuna scientists during this time period was justified because baitboats fished all over the eastern Pacific Ocean (EPO) throughout the year, whereas purse seiners did not. Furthermore, it was believed that baitboat-caught tunas would be more likely to survive after tagging than would purse seine-caught fish, as the baitboat-caught fish are out of their element for only a few seconds, whereas the purse seine caught fish are confined in the net for about half an hour to an hour, during which time they are fatigued by struggling against confinement and perhaps harmed by rubbing against the net and other fish.

It is understandable that there existed a low level of scientific discussion and public reporting about seining tuna/porpoise schools prior to 1959. But, as the San Diego tuna fishermen were rapidly converting to purse seining during 1959 and 1960, reports were being circulated on the waterfront that the porpoise had developed new evasive tactics to avoid encirclement. In addition, there were reports of serious ship-board accidents during efforts to remove porpoise from the net.

Prior to 1959, most of the public information about the operations of the San Pedro tuna purse-seine fleet was found only in trade magazines, almost exclusively *Pacific Fisherman*. During the 1960s, more scientists and other interested invitees were making trips aboard U.S. tuna seiners to observe their operations. During that period there were three categories of U.S. tuna seiners: San Pedro regular seiners, seiners that had been converted from baitboats, and newly-built seiners.[2] During 1960-1969, 41 tropical tuna tagging trips were made by tuna scientists aboard 35 U.S. tuna baitboats, and 6 tropical tuna tagging trips were made aboard one converted and three new U.S. tuna purse seiners.[3] Nevertheless, very little information concerning the fishing of tuna/porpoise schools by U.S. tuna seiners was published. The increased operating efficiency of the tuna seiners in catching Yellowfin during the late 1950s became a subject of interest to scientists of the IATTC:

> "Purse-seine fishing was not particularly successful during the early years of the fishery and the small fleet of these vessels produced during the period 1931 to 1956, on the average, less than 15 percent of the yellowfin and about 13 per cent of the skipjack catch made by U.S.-based vessels. However, [in] about 1957, and before any major technological changes occurred within the purse-seine fleet, the catch-per-day's-fishing began to increase substantially . . . .

> "By 1959, the operations of the modernized and expanded purse-seine fleet were extended south of areas off the coasts of southern Mexico and Central America, as the vessels began to catch substantial quantities of yellowfin tuna associated with schools of spotted and spinner porpoise. Fishing was also extended to include the offshore grounds fished in earlier years mainly by the baitboats, and, by the end of 1960, the purse-seine fleet was operating throughout the entire range of the fishery from California to Peru."[4]

Commencing in the early 1960s, the IATTC was collecting data on the ratio of successful sets to total sets for different types of sets to determine whether the successful-set ratios differed among types of sets and whether the differences, if they existed, were related to fishing techniques or to some behavioral characteristic of the fish. The data seemed to show that the increase in the successful-set ratios was due to improved techniques in fishing tuna/porpoise schools. Logbook data for 1962-1966 were collected and analyzed by the IATTC staff; data were not available for 1961 on the total number of sets. A report based upon this study found that during this five-year period, the following types of purse seine sets were made in one area of the EPO: 6,772 tuna/porpoise school sets, with an average catch per set of 4.2 tons; 1,856 "school-fish" sets (sets on free-swimming schools of tuna), with an average catch per set of 4.3 tons; 1,658 "night sets," with an average catch per set of 6.4 tons; and, 34 sets on "floating objects," with an average catch per set of 3.8 tons.[5]

In early 1959, Raul Rodriguez, associate editor of *Pacific Fisherman*, accompanied the newly-converted tuna seiner SUN JASON to Paita, Peru, where its purse seine was ready for pick up.[6] The July 1960 issue of *Pacific Fisherman* noted on page 5: "[The] commanding fact in American fisheries today is the revolution in tuna fishing." It also published one of the first public reports on the existence of "porpoise mortality" associated with the U.S. tuna purse-seine fishery in the EPO. The article was entitled "How Do Tuna Fishermen Find Fish? . . . Mostly by Looking for Them," stating in part:

> "To find the exact spot where the fish are, the skipper makes use of birds more than any other single evidence. Tuna fishermen recognize two kinds of fish—bird fish and porpoise fish. Schools of tuna are usually accompanied either by flocks of birds in the air above them or by schools of porpoise frolicking in the water with them.

> "Once a vessel is in the vicinity of a school of fish, he can make close contact with the school by following the birds or the porpoises.

"Getting rid of the porpoises without killing them needlessly is often a great problem with conscientious skippers. Many skippers have strong feelings about killing porpoises, and go to great lengths to avoid catching them in their nets or, having caught them, they often show great skill and patience in trying to ease them out again—an almost impossible feat, because a porpoise hasn't sense enough to jump over the edge of a net even when it easily could do."[7]

During 1961, more items and articles concerning the fishing on tuna/porpoise schools appeared in *Pacific Fisherman*. In 1960, Richard McNeely, fishing gear specialist of the Bureau of Commercial Fisheries (BCF), Department of the Interior, made a fishing trip aboard the converted tuna seiner DETERMINED, then under command of Captain John J. Cvitanich. This trip was part of his lengthy study of the American style of tuna purse seining. McNeely's article, "Purse Seine Revolution In Tuna Fishing" printed in the June 1961 issue of *Pacific Fisherman*, was recognized by the trade as "A Contribution of the Highest Order." McNeely's report makes the following brief reference to the fishing of tuna/porpoise schools in the section of the article entitled: "Problem No. 1-Finding the Fish":

"In tropical waters, schools of Yellowfin tuna are sometimes mixed with porpoise schools. When porpoise are sighted, the vessel circles the area to determine if tuna are present. If no sightings of fish are made after several passes, the vessel continues its search in other areas. When sets are made on mixed schools (porpoise and Yellowfin) considerable care is exercised to avoid capture of porpoises."[8]

In a section of his article entitled, "Setting the Tuna Purse Seine," McNeely does not describe methods used aboard the DETERMINED to set the net on a tuna/porpoise school. Co-author Felando's personal conversation with McNeely confirmed that only one set was made on a tuna/porpoise school during the fishing trip; it was also the last fishing set of the trip because enough tuna was caught to finish off the load.[9] McNeely explained how sets are made on pure schools of tuna ("breezers," "boilers," "jumpers," "black spots," "shiners," *etc.*), but he did not explain the techniques used aboard the DETERMINED to remove porpoise from the net, nor did he discuss the problem of "porpoise mortality." In the same issue of *Pacific Fisherman*, there is a two-page advertisement with photographs in which Captain Anton Misetich, captain and part-owner of the converted seiner PARAMOUNT, is quoted, as follows:

"The TRILOCK net works better-no friction. It's lightweight, works better in the equipment. **Porpoises do not seem to get tangled up in it, but roll freely.** We had less shark problem with our TRILOCK."[10] (emphasis added)

The October 1961 issue of *Pacific Fisherman*, published an article on the first new U.S.-flag tuna seiner since "nets displaced live bait as the primary source of American-caught tuna." The article has a photo of the "Shark-Dumper" built on the ROYAL PACIFIC. This innovation was to be used to dump dead porpoise and sharks over the starboard rail mechanically, thereby reducing the manual labor and risk of injury to crewmembers:

"It is a wire mesh belt conveyor built almost flush with the deck in the way of the brailer discharge point and running to the starboard rail, where it terminates in a gate which can be opened in the bulwark."

"What is it? It's a shark-and-porpoise dumper. In brailing tuna unwanted sharks frequently come aboard. They're apt to be big, truculent devils, weighing 100 to 500 lbs . . . a dead enemy weighing 400 lbs is hard to heave overboard, unless you have a handy sharkveyor on which to drag him. . .

"Porpoise are returned to the sea unharmed, a process facilitated by the 'sharkveyor'."[11]

In early 1959, Gerald V. Howard, a veteran tuna scientist, was appointed head of the EPO tuna research program that had been recently established by the Bureau of Commercial Fisheries, Department of Interior. Prior to the government appointment, he had been a senior scientist with the IATTC since 1951. From 1941 to 1948, Howard had been employed by the International Pacific Salmon Fisheries Commission and, briefly, by the United Nations Food & Agriculture Organization. At the time of the announcement of the appointment, Donald R. Johnson, California Area Director, BCF, stated that the purpose of the new eastern Pacific Ocean tuna research program was "to gather information concerning the behavior of tuna, the best strategy for catching them, and the ocean conditions under which tuna can be caught most efficiently and quickly."[12] Hence its functions did not overlap with those of the staff of the IATTC, which made investigations appropriate for assessing the conditions of the various stocks of tunas and other fishes caught by tuna vessels and advised the Commissioners of the results of those investigations. One of the projects of the BCF program was entitled: "Porpoise Associated with Tuna."

An article published in the November 1961 issue of the *Pacific Fisherman* reported on a "fishing-scientific" cruise (June 24 to August 28, 1961) aboard the converted seiner WEST POINT. Aboard were two BCF scientists, Dr. Richard J. Whitney, leader of the tuna behavioral research program, and Frank J. Hester. During the cruise they worked with two Simrad sonar units, along with Ralph Eide, chief engineer of Simonsen Radio, A.S., and maker of the Simrad. The article notes how tuna/porpoise schools were impacted by the use of the sonar units, as follows:

"One of the riddles the scientists sought to solve was how to avoid scaring away porpoise when the sonar is tuned on to try to locate a school of tuna associated with the porps [sic]. It had been previously found that certain sound frequencies sent out by the sonar scared away the porpoise and, presumably, the tuna along with them. Dr. Whitney and Mr. Hester worked to discover what ranges of sound frequencies scared the porps [sic], with the view to recommending frequencies that did not have an adverse effect.

"According to Dr. Whitney, experience on the cruise seemed to indicate that no particular range of sound is offensive to a porpoise once he gets used to it. Within an hour, it was found, porpoise seemed to lose their fear of any sonar sound, even though they been startled and driven off by it at first.

"Mr. Eide, taking another approach, found that by graduating the power of the Simrad impulses from mild to strong, the sonar could be used without affecting the porpoise. These observations, while not final, seem to show that sonar will be more effective in commercial fishing when the sound range and the power output can be graduated. When the impulses were turned on suddenly, the porpoise was found to scare away, the reaction being manifest over a wide range of sound frequencies."[13]

The above article suggests that the BCF fishery scientists were unaware of the use of a fathometer in fishing tuna/porpoise schools by John Zorotovich, Captain of the San Pedro "Regular Seiner" DEFENSE.

An article entitled, "Porpoise Tagging Program To Aid Tuna Fishermen," published in the September 1963 issue of the *Pacific Fisherman* described a BCF expedition to tag porpoises "in an attempt to find out as much as possible about their migrations."[14] This effort, which was part of the Tuna Behavior Program, was under the direction of Dr. Richard R. Whitney of BCF's San Diego Laboratory. The article explained, in part, the following:

> "The porpoise tagging is part of a program to solve the very practical problems of how tuna escape nets, as well as other mysteries of the behavior of tuna. The overall purpose, the Bureau explains, is to inform fishermen of how they can cut down losses, increase efficiency and catch more fish with the same amount of effort.

> "Every tuna fisherman knows the importance of porpoise in fishing tuna. Porpoise jumping out of the water are an almost sure sign of schools of tuna unseen beneath the surface, and one of the concerns of a really conscientious fisherman is how to take tuna without hurting the porpoise swimming with them."

No records of the program entitled "Porpoise Associated with Tuna" showing that Dr. Whitney and his staff were working on ways to improve the purse-seine gear so as to reduce porpoise mortality, such as improving the "Back-down" procedure or modifying the purse seine to make the "Back-down" procedure more effective have been uncovered. Reports pertaining to tuna/porpoise fishing were part of the Third Annual Government-Industry Tuna Meeting at La Jolla, California, on January 9, 1962. They were presented by two members of the BCF Biological Laboratory, San Diego, California: Gerald V. Howard, Laboratory Director and Dr. Richard R. Whitney, Chief, Tuna Behavior Investigations.

The report by Director Howard was silent on the issue of fishing tuna/porpoise schools. His report was an update on the work of the Laboratory in providing "the specific application of oceanographic and biological findings to the problems of the west coast tuna fishing industry." In the section of the report entitled "Behavior," Mr. Howard stated:

> "I have pointed out at previous meetings that learning about the behavior of tunas will be tremendously difficult and obtaining results which are applicable to the improvement of fishing techniques will be slow in coming to light. Nevertheless, during the course of making observations for this program of basic research, our scientists will be continually aware of the industry's needs. . . . The observations we are making on the depth to which tuna seines sink and the time they take to sink is an example of what I have in mind in this regard . . . Also, we know that sharks are becoming more and more of a problem in seining operations, particularly off Central America. We have decided, therefore, to initiate studies on shark behavior and to look into the possibility of a shark control program which we could recommend to the seine fleet."

Dr. Whitney's report, "Tuna Behavior Research In the Eastern Pacific," contained a section entitled, "Porpoise and Tuna." This report commented upon observations taken by BCF scientists aboard the U.S. converted tuna seiner WEST POINT during August 1961, as follows:

> "We need to investigate the nature of the relationship of porpoise and tuna. If we knew more about this we might be able to suggest a way to avoid taking so many porpoise in the net and still take the tuna.

> "Our preliminary tests with sonar brought out the fact that schools of porpoise were frightened by the high frequency sound of the sonar. The sound caused them to stampede away faster than the boat could follow. Not all porpoises were frightened, but the spinner porpoise and spotted porpoise, which are the species most often associated with tuna were frightened by the sound of our sonar unit. By waiting for them to calm and approaching them again with sounds of different frequencies and volumes, we discovered that within about an hour they would adapt to the sounds and would no longer be stampeded by them.

> "We attempted to take advantage of this fright reaction of porpoise to induce them to jump over the cork line after a set was made around them, but we were not successful. After they are enclosed in the net porpoise seem to stay under the surface as much as possible and only rarely escape over the cork line. They do not react to sounds when enclosed in the net either."

During this period, only the tuna fishermen were seeking ways of improving their fishing gear and procedures to reduce porpoise mortality. On the matter of operations research, the BCF Laboratory was giving attention to working with the IATTC on ways of "determining the average size of Yellowfin in schools prior to setting the seine" because "it will be to the fishermen's advantage eventually, in order to obtain the maximum harvest of Yellowfin from the eastern Pacific, to reduce the fishing effort on small fish. If the fishing intensity on small Yellowfin could be reduced, the added growth would, according to the IATTC, exceed natural mortality losses and the maximum sustainable catch from the eastern Pacific could be raised." Within a few years, tuna scientists would confirm that the fishermen, in fishing tuna/porpoise schools, were catching large, sexually-mature yellowfin, an optimum size tuna in terms of yield per recruit.

---

[1] Data provided by William H. Bayliff, IATTC, personal communication. A trip commencing on May 1 and ending June 30, 1953, with CDFG scientists aboard the San Pedro regular seiner WESTERN MONARCH, 18 Yellowfin and 2 Skipjack were tagged. During September 1955, CDFG scientists tagged 50 Bluefin aboard the San Pedro regular seiner STELLA MARIS. During the period February 21 to March 17, 1956, IATTC scientists tagged 234 Yellowfin and 5 Skipjack while aboard the San Pedro regular seiners SEA KING and WESTERN FISHER. Commencing January 24 and ending February 28, 1958, IATTC scientists tagged 122 Bluefin aboard the San Pedro regular seiner COLUMBIA. During February 21 to April 6, 1959, aboard San Pedro regular seiners JO ANN, WESTERN FISHER, RONNIE M., and converted seiners DETERMINED and SANTA HELENA, IATTC scientists tagged 414 Yellowfin and 2 Skipjack. IATTC scientists aboard the converted seiners JEANNE LYNN and DETERMINED tagged 274 Yellowfin during February 20-March 15, 1959.

[2] The classification of the tuna purse seine fleet into three groups was developed by V. J. Samson, Supervisory Market News Reporter, San Pedro Fishery Market News Service, U.S. Department of the Interior, Bureau of Commercial Fisheries, Division of Resource Development, San Pedro, California Mr. Samson identified seiners as "Regular San Pedro Tuna Seiners," and "Other" (New and Converted).

[3] The converted seiner SANTA HELENA (2 trips; 708 Yellowfin and 8 Skipjack tagged); new seiner PACIFIC QUEEN (2 trips; 994 Yellowfin and 35 Skipjack tagged); new seiner MARIETTA (1 trip; 30 Yellowfin and 304 Skipjack tagged), and new seiner CONNIE JEAN (1 trip, 8,523 Yellowfin and 232 Skipjack tagged) During the summers of 1962, 1963, and 1964, CDFG and ELSINORE to tag 2,285 Bluefin tunas . On July 24, 1968, CDFG scientists tagged 1 Bluefin aboard the San Pedro regular seiner SEA SCOUT.

[4] Broadhead, Gordon C. 1962, Recent Changes in the Efficiency of Vessels Fishing for Yellowfin Tuna in the Eastern Pacific, Inter-Amer. Trop. Tuna Comm. Bulletin, Vol. 6, No. 7, pp. 283-284.

[5] Bayliff, William H. and Craig J. Orange, 1967, Observations on the Purse Seine Fishery for Tropical Tunas in the Eastern Pacific, Inter-Amer. Trop. Tuna Comm. Internal Report No. 4, p. 69.

[6] "The Gigantic Purse Seiner Enters the Tuna Fisheries of Peru." *Pacific Fisherman* (May 1959) 57 (6): 14-17. Journalist Raul Rodriguez reported on his trip aboard the converted seiner SUN JASON, traveling from San Diego, California, to Paita, Peru, where the all-nylon purse seine awaited pick-up. Mr. Rodriquez took photos of the converted seiner SUN KING bringing in a tuna catch at a location some 35 miles off the coast of Peru. He also reported on the at-sea visit to the seiner by the captain of the baitboat MARY LOU and of two IATTC tuna scientists. The captain of the SUN JASON, Jack Borcich, was an experienced tuna and sardine purse-seine fisherman from San Pedro, California For years, he was in command of the San Pedro regular purse seiner, MARSHA ANN, when it fished off Central America, the Galapagos Islands, and off the coasts of Colombia, Ecuador, and Peru. During 1957, he commanded the purse seiner SUN STAR from Ilo, Peru, fishing for bonito and tuna. In 1958, he commanded seiners operating from Coishco, Peru.

[7] "How Do Tuna Fishermen Find Fish? . . . Mostly by Looking For Them." *Pacific Fisherman,* July 1960 58 (8): 10. Note: Another article reported on the actions by captains of tuna seiners to introduce new gear to encircle tuna/porpoise schools: "'Fish Chaser' Is New Aid In Tuna Seining," *Pacific Fisherman,* August 1960, 58 (9): 19. This article reported that the captain and co-owner of the converted seiner SANTA HELENA, Frank Gargas, had introduced a "fish chaser" boat that could reach speeds of 25 to 27 knots for use in driving "tuna into the net while a set is being made." Captain Gargas started tuna seining in 1946 aboard his father's vessel, the COLUMBIA. He was well experienced in seining tuna/porpoise schools. Captain Gargas advised Co-author Felando that this speedboat was not used to herd porpoise so as to encircle a tuna/porpoise school. Personal conversation with Frank Gargas, March 2006.

[8] Mc Neely, Richard L., "Purse Seine Revolution In Tuna Fishing," *Pacific Fisherman* (June 1961) 59 (7): 50.

[9] Personal conversation with Richard McNeely: 10 March 2006. He explained that this last set of the purse seine caught enough tuna to load the vessel, estimating the catch of

tuna at about 40 tons. With respect to the porpoise that were captured and not released alive by the fishermen, he recalled watching how the manually-removed dead porpoise were floating vertically and moving away from the tuna seiner, with only their snouts showing above the ocean's surface. He also observed a band of sharks attacking only one or two of these dead porpoise, causing him to wonder why the sharks were ignoring the other dead, floating porpoise.

[10] *Pacific Fisherman* (June 1961) 59 (7): 20-21.

[11] Anon. "ROYAL PACIFIC First of the New Fleet," Pacific Fisherman (October 1961) 59 (11): 13, 19

[12] The announcement of the appointment was published in *Pacific Fisherman,* (April 1959) 57 (5): 52.

[13] Anon. "Sonar Spies on Reactions of Tuna To Fishing, Sound and Temperature." *Pacific Fisherman*, (November 1961) 59 (12): 21-22. See the companion article: Frank J. Hester. "Tuna Seines: How Deep." *Pacific Fisherman* (November 1961) 59 (12): 19-20. The article notes that the WEST POINT fished normally until her holds were filled. Meantime, the scientists had a contracted right to 20 additional days of the vessel's time, which they took whenever conditions were convenient to all concerned and when there was likelihood of benefit from the scientific observations." In 1971, Captain Harold Medina purchased a Simrad sonar for the operation aboard the KERRI M for approximately $100,000. Unfortunately, he found that the gear was not able to consistently track the tunas, and after much trial and error decided that the gear was useless in fishing tuna. He reported that while the tuna school was traveling parallel with his vessel, the target was visible for tracking purposes. When the tuna school veered away from the vessel at an angle to the vessel, the target could no longer be seen. He speculates that perhaps the configuration of the school at the time of such movement made it a "stealth" target, that is, invisible to the Simrad perhaps, just as the design of "stealth" aircraft are invisible to radar.

[14] Anon. "Porpoise Tagging Program to Aid Tuna Fisherman," *Pacific Fisherman* (September 1963) 61 (10): 45.

PART IV

THE "ENIGMA" AND THE UNITED STATES GOVERNMENT

16

MARINE MAMMAL PROTECTION ACT OF 1972

1972 Report of the Tuna/Porpoise Review Committee

In May 1972, the U.S. Department of Commerce (DOC) and the National Oceanic and Atmospheric Administration (NOAA) established an *ad hoc* review and advisory committee called the "1972 Tuna-Porpoise Review Committee." This committee was "given the mandate to: (1) assess present state of knowledge of the relation among the various porpoise populations and the tuna seine fishery; and, (2) determine the path of future research and the relative importance of various aspects of research proposed."[1]

Another duty of this committee was to determine the scope, direction, and priority of future research on the problem of reducing porpoise mortality in the tuna purse-seine fishery. The committee's report of September 1972 concluded that the most significant new development was the Medina Panel. In Appendix IV of the report, the Medina Panel evaluation stated: "for smoothly running sets . . . the panel was associated with 36% lower mortality . . . [but] was not associated with a significant lower mortality in the problem sets." The committee urged the use of the Medina Panel by the fleet as soon as practicable because the Medina Panel was clearly causing a substantial reduction of porpoise mortality when the fishing operation was proceeding to the "Back-down" in a normal manner.

The committee also recommended that the program of research be conducted at the National Marine Fisheries Service (NMFS) Southwest Fisheries Center (SWFC) in La Jolla, California. At the SWFC, the research program was organized into two major efforts: gear dynamics and development, and biology and stock assessment. Initially, the program's staff included four biologists concerned with Porpoise Life Studies, eight biologists dealing with population assessments, and seven specialists handling the Gear Program. An Observer Program, involving large numbers of specialized temporary employees was organized to assist in the collection of data at sea aboard tuna seiners. The gear dynamics program was staffed primarily with personnel from the NMFS Northwest Fisheries Center (NWFC) in Seattle, Washington.

As the NMFS was developing data on porpoise mortality and its causes during 1971-72, more information was being developed on how and why the fleet was experiencing "problem sets." Only one thing was certain about a "problem set;" it was an event that could happen to the best of captains. To reduce annual porpoise mortality, the industry and the NMFS recognized the need to reduce the number of "problem sets" experienced during the fishing season. The porpoise mortality associated with "problem sets" could not be reduced by deploying a "Back-down" enhanced by the use of a Medina Panel, as they occurred before the captain could use the "Back-down." Perhaps, "problem sets" could never be eliminated as long as sets were made on tuna/porpoise schools, but maybe the porpoise mortality involved in "problem sets" could be substantially reduced by improved practices and performances resulting from the captains and crews working with NMFS fishing gear experts.

In 1972, the NMFS selected Richard L. McNeely, Supervisory Electrical Engineer of the Northwest Fisheries Center, as chairman of the NOAA Porpoise-Tuna Mortality Reduction Subcommittee, and then assigned him to the SWFC in San Diego to conduct research in methods of reducing porpoise mortality in the U.S. tuna purse-seine fishery in the eastern Pacific Ocean (EPO). McNeely and his assistants, NMFS observers James M. Coe and David Holts, were aboard the converted tuna seiner INDEPENDENCE tagging porpoise and conducting behavior and fishing gear studies when he was informed by ship-to-shore radio that the Marine Mammal Protection Act (MMPA) had become law.[2]

Legislative History

The Subcommittee on Oceans and Atmosphere of the Committee on Commerce, United States Senate, 92nd Congress, Second Session, conducted legislative hearings on ocean mammal legislation during February 1972. Written and oral testimony was provided by Co-author August Felando, General Manager of the American Tunaboat Association (ATA), accompanied by Franklin G. Alverson, Living Marine Resources (LMR).[3] The ATA argued that because the United States had recognized that tunas cannot be conserved unilaterally; so also should the United States recognize that it cannot successfully unilaterally regulate fishing on porpoise associated with tunas. Further, since the Secretary of Commerce already had been delegated regulatory power over the U.S. tuna fleet operating in the EPO under the Tuna Conventions Act of 1950, as amended, any government action concerning the U.S. tuna fishery should be limited to that of providing funds for research to solve a "technological problem."[4]

Frank Alverson testified that the only practical solution to the tuna/porpoise fishing problem "is a joint effort by industry and the various governments whose nationals participate in this fishery." He testified that legislation denying the use of purse-seine gear to the U.S. fleet "would destroy the U.S. tuna fishery as we know it today."[5] The Chairman of the Subcommittee, Senator Ernest F. Hollings, South Carolina, reacted to Frank's testimony, as follows:

> "You have made a very valuable contribution because there is one point that some of our friends have not discussed and that is the capacity of the United States to

regulate effectively, unilaterally, an international problem."[6]

The MMPA (Public Law 92-522, 92nd Congress, H.R. 10420) was the result of an agreement by a Committee of Conference composed of five House Managers and seven Senate Managers. The Conference Report (H. Rept. No. 92-1488) was filed on October 2, 1972.[7] The portion of the report entitled "Joint Explanation Statement of the Committee of Conference" provides insight on the intended effect of the action agreed upon and recommended by the conferees. Essentially, the Senate struck out the House bill after the enacting clause and inserted a substitute amendment. The MMPA was enacted on October 21, 1972.

Unlike the House bill, the Senate amendment provided a permanent moratorium in the "taking" of marine mammals, rather than a five-year moratorium. Exceptions to this moratorium were made for scientific research and commercial fishing. The House bill required individual and general permits covering commercial fishing operations during the moratorium. During the hearings and floor debate, supporters of the bill attested that most fisheries would justify the issuance of general permits.[8] The Senate bill, S. 2871, also followed this approach; however, it established taking by commercial fishing without permits during a two-year period that started on the date of the Act's enactment. In addition, the Senate's bill "expressed a general goal that damage to marine mammals shall be reduced to insignificant levels approaching a zero mortality and serious injury rate." The Conference Report noted further that the objective of regulation by the Secretary during and after the two-year period stated in the Senate bill "would be to approach as closely as is feasible the goal of zero mortality and injury to marine mammals. The conferees agreed to the Senate approach, explaining: **It may never be possible to achieve this goal, human fallibility being what it is, but the objective remains clear.**" (emphasis added)[9]

Section 102 (c) (3) provided that it was unlawful to import into the United States "any fish, whether fresh, frozen, or otherwise prepared, if such fish was caught in a manner which the Secretary has proscribed for persons subject to the jurisdiction of the United States whether or not any marine mammals were in fact taken incident to the catching of the fish."

Section 111 of the Senate bill authorized and directed the Secretary to immediately undertake a program of research and development for the purpose of devising improved fishing methods and gear so as to reduce to the maximum extent practicable the incidental taking of marine mammals in connection with commercial fishing. For the fiscal year ending June 30, 1973, $1 million was authorized to be appropriated; the same amount was authorized for the next fiscal year. During this 2-year period, the Secretary was expressly authorized to regulate commercial fishing operations, to have agents board fishing vessels and observe fishing operations, to enter into negotiations with the Inter-American Tropical Tuna Commission (IATTC), and to guarantee private loans to fishermen for the purchase of equipment to meet the requirements of the Act. Comparable provisions were not included in the House bill.[10] The Senate Report of its bill makes the following comments about the 2-year research program:

" . . . It is the committee's intent that regulations be imposed as soon as practicable to minimize marine mammal fatalities through the use of currently available technology, which might include the Medina net with escape panel. Results of research in the yellowfin tuna fishery in 1972 show that with careful utilization of known technology, porpoise mortality can be significantly reduced. The committee is convinced that the industry will comply with strong federal regulation and will cooperate with scientific research to find the safest practicable tuna fishing methods.

"After the 2-year research period, permits are required and are authorized to be issued in accordance with the Act. While it should be the goal of Congress and the Executive eventually to eliminate totally the killing of porpoises, present technology is not adequate to the task. Imposing a ban on incidental taking of porpoises would require the American tuna industry to scrap hundreds of millions of dollars of investment in purse-seining tuna clippers to return to uncompetitive labor-intensive bait boat and long-line fishing. Since this is completely unrealistic, the industry, we are convinced, would shift from the American flag to a flag of convenience and simply avoid the regulations. Tuna is now a worldwide commodity. Loss of the American market would be a severe blow, but one which would not decrease fishing in the Southwest [sic.] Pacific, and certainly more dolphins will be killed as more nations compete for fish."[11]

Section 111(c) directed the Secretary of Commerce and the Secretary of State to commence negotiations with the IATTC "in order to effect essential compliance with the regulatory provisions" of the Act "so as to reduce to the maximum extent feasible, the incidental taking of marine mammals by vessels involved in the tuna fishery. The Secretary [of Commerce] and Secretary of State are further directed to request the Director of Investigations of the [IATTC] to make recommendations to all member nations of the Commission as soon as is practicable as to the utilization of methods and gear devised under subsection (a) of this section."

During the House floor debate, Representative Tom Pelly of Washington recognized the nation's treaty obligations respecting the tuna fishery, stating:

"In short, unilateral action on the part of the United States, in the adoption of the proposed amendment, [by Rep. Mario Biaggi] will not remove the biological fact that porpoises are associated with tunas, and that a law cannot create a technology to eliminate completely the accidental capturing of porpoises in order to capture tuna. Under the Tuna Convention Act of 1950, this country has a firm international commitment and duty to regulate the tuna industry in order to properly protect and conserve this valuable natural resource. Adoption of this amendment would destroy my and this country's firm belief that government action with respect to the problems associated with porpoises and tunas be complementary to an existing regime of management concerning both species."

The conference bill adopted the Senate version, but eliminated the loan-guarantee program after finding that it duplicated existing law. The Senate debates of S. 2871 included no discussion on the provisions of Section 111. Senator Hollings of South Carolina was the manager of the bill, and in his opening remarks he explained the need for the two-year research program, and noted the following:

"The American tuna industry today is providing the leadership in developing

on its own, new methods of fishing to eliminate porpoise mortality. (emphasis added) This legislation will greatly expand these efforts through federal funding of research and mandatory application of new methods..... It is the goal of this legislation—and it should be the goal of this Nation as well as the goal of all nations—to reduce and eventually totally eliminate the taking of porpoises in tuna fishing. We recognize that tuna is now a worldwide commodity. Acting alone, the United States cannot control other nations. **We have determined that the better course is to work with the American tuna industry, utilizing their vessels as our labs, applying the best American technology to solve this problem. We have also empowered our Government to induce other nations to use these methods through import restrictions. We believe this is the way to protect porpoises. By placing an unrealistic deadline on the U.S. tuna fleet, we shall be participating still further in chasing away from our shores the remnants of the one great American fishing industry . . ."**[12] (emphasis added)

On October 31, 1972, the MMPA was signed into law, but it did not become effective until December 21, 1972. The Administrator of NOAA was delegated the authority of the Secretary of Commerce to carry out the functions of the MMPA on November 30, 1972. NOAA's final regulations to implement Section 101 (a) (2) of the MMPA stated: "Until October 21, 1974, marine mammals may be taken incidental to the course of commercial fishing operations, and no permit shall be required as long as the taking constitutes an incidental catch." NOAA's interim regulations to implement Section 111 of the MMPA provided that when the Secretary determines that space is available on regular fishing operations, then his "duly authorized agents" could "accompany commercial fishing vessels documented under the laws of the United States . . . for the purpose of conducting research and observation operations."[13]

---

[1] NOAA Tuna-Porpoise Committee. 1972 Report of the NOAA Tuna-Porpoise Review Committee September 8, 1972. U.S. Dept. Commerce, NOAA, Washington, D.C., (63 pp). Four Appendices were also attached to this report, 24 pp. (cited hereinafter: "1972 NOAA Porpoise Committee Report"). It was a seven-member committee: Dr. Dayton L. Alverson, NWFS (Chairman), Mr. William Perrin, SWFC, Mr. Richard McNeely, NWFC, Dr. William Fox, SWFC, Dr. Kenneth Norris, University of California, Santa Cruz, Dr. Douglas Chapman, University of Washington, and Dr. William Aron, NOAA Headquarters. Dr. Dayton L. Alverson is the younger brother of Franklin G. Alverson (deceased).

A press conference was held at Marineland, California, on October 18, 1972, by Secretary of Commerce Peter G. Peterson for the purpose of receiving the report of the NOAA Tuna-Porpoise Committee. The report's recommendations, endorsed by the Secretary during the press conference, included the following: that all tuna seiners use the Medina Panel, that government-industry programs be developed to teach tuna fishermen ways to improve their "Back-down" technique and to improve fishing techniques and gear to reduce porpoise mortalities, in general, and that NOAA work to develop porpoise population assessments. On June 19, 1972, Secretary Peterson's announcement of a $250,000 program to reduce porpoise mortality in the tuna purse-seine fishery was made part of the Senate debate on S. 2871, a bill to protect marine mammals. See: 118 *Congressional Record--Senate*, (No. 116. July 15, 1972): S.11765.

[2] Prior to passage of the MMPA, "NOAA had already recognized a need for studies on the problem of porpoise mortalities in the Eastern Tropical Pacific Ocean tuna purse seine fishery and had made $250,000 and personnel available to commence work during late summer, 1972." After passage of the MMPA, and during early 1973, "$300,000 and four positions were allocated to a porpoise-tuna research program. . . ." See: 38 FR 20564 (August 1, 1973).

[3] Report No. 92-863, 92d Congress, 2d Session, Marine Mammal Protection Act of 1972, Report of the Senate Committee on Commerce on S. 2871, June 15, 1972. See: Hearings before the Subcommittee on Oceans and Atmosphere of the Committee on Commerce, United States Senate, 92nd Congress Second Session on ocean mammal protection, February 15, 16, 23, and March 7, 1972 (Serial No. 92-56) Part 1 (hereinafter cited as "1972 Senate Subcommittee Hearings-SN-92-56"): Oral testimony, pp 475-484; written testimony, pp 484-492, and pp. 831-835,

[4] "It is generally accepted that the ultimate solution of the tuna-porpoise problem is a technological one." Report of the Secretary of Commerce dated June 21, 1976, 41 FR 30152, 50160 (July 22, 1976). The American Tunaboat Association position was noted by Senator Harrison Williams, Jr., of New Jersey during the Senate Debate on the MMPA (S. 2871) on July 26, 1972, when he offered an amendment that was rejected. Senator Williams was wrong in claiming that the Convention for the Establishment of an Inter-American Tropical Tuna Commission [1 UST 230; TIAS 2044] and Tuna Conventions Act of 1950, as Amended [16 U.S.C. 951 et. seq.] did not apply to the fishing of tuna/porpoise schools. 118 *Congressional Record--Senate*, (No. 116, July 25, 1972): S 11799-11801.

[5] Franklin Alverson's written testimony noted that, "Nationals of the United States are not the only fishermen engaged in purse seining for tunas in the eastern tropical Pacific Ocean. At the present time, 12 nations are actively fishing tunas in the area . . . . The nationals of a number of other countries are expected to join this fishery over the course of the next several years. During 1971, United States flag vessels captured 111,000 tons or 82 percent of the 135,000 tons of yellowfin taken in the eastern Pacific fishery. This share will drop as the foreign fleets expand." 1972 Senate Subcommittee Hearings-SN-92-56: 479-482, 481.

[6] 1972 Senate Subcommittee Hearings-SN-92-56: 482.

[7] Conference Report on H.R. 10420, Marine Mammal Protection Act of 1972: 118 *Congressional Record--House*, (No. 156, October 2, 1972): H 8980-8997.

[8] During the debate on the House bill, Congressman John Dingell explained how the Secretary of Commerce is to use his power of discretion in issuing permits, as follows: "Before issuing any permit for the taking of a marine mammal, the Secretary must first have it proven to his satisfaction that any taking is consistent with the purposes and policies of the Act, that is, to say, that taking will not be to the disadvantage of the animals concerned. If he cannot make that finding, he cannot issue a permit. It is that simple." 118 *Congressional Record--House*, (No. 36, March 9, 1972): H 1900, H 1901.

[9] 118 *Congressional Record*, (No. 156, October 2, 1972): H 8986.

[10] During the debate on the House bill, a complex amendment by Representative Mario Biaggi of New York was offered in part that the Secretary "shall, in cooperation with other federal agencies, undertake to assist in the development of new technological means of

capturing fish in such a way as to eliminate injury or death to porpoises and dolphins. Federal inspectors shall be appointed to periodically accompany vessels engaged in commercial fishing operations before and after the expiration of the two year period to assure compliance with the provisions of this subsection and the regulations issued pursuant thereto. Separate funds sufficient for the study, under the supervision of the Marine Mammal Commission . . . of alternative commercial fishing methods in order to aid in steadily reducing such injury and killing and to achieving complete reduction by the expiration of the two-year period." After making certain findings by the Secretary, three one-year extensions beyond the two-year period were permitted. The proposal was rejected because of its complexity and absence of prior review by members and Staff of the Committee. 118 *Congressional Record--House*, (No. 36, March 9, 1972): H 1923-H 1925.

[11] Report No. 92-863, 92d Congress, 2d Session, Marine Mammal Protection Act of 1972, Report of the Senate Committee on Commerce on S. 2871, June 15, 1972: 6-7.

[12] The Senate debate on S. 2871 started on July 25, 1972, and final passage occurred on July 26, 1972. The vote was 88 for, 2 against, and 10 not voting. 118 *Congressional Record-Senate*, (No. 117, July 26, 1972): S 11902. See: 118 *Congressional Record*-Senate, (No. 116, July 25, 1972): S 11758-S 11813. Senator Hollings' remarks, see: S 11765.

[13] 37 FR 25731-25746, at 25733-25735 (December 2, 1972); 37 FR 28177-28185, at p. 28181 (December 21, 1972). 50 Code Federal Regulations (CFR) § 216.10 (a) provided that no permit was necessary to take marine mammals incidental to commercial fishing operations until October 24, 1974, and that these mammals may be processed and transported, but not sold or offered for sale. 50 CFR § 216.10 (b) also provided that "research and observation operations shall be carried out in a manner as to minimize interference with commercial fishing operations," that no master, charterer, operator, or owner of the vessel "shall impair or in any way interfere with the research or observations being carried out," and that "the Secretary shall provide for the payment of all reasonable costs directly related to the quartering and maintaining of such agents aboard such vessel." In the proposed regulations published on December 2, 1974, the provisions of 50 CFR §216.10 (b) applied only to tuna and salmon commercial fishing operations. This limitation was not included in the interim regulations published on December 21, 1972.

17

EVOLUTION OF THE MEDINA PANEL

Before Passage of the Marine Mammal Protection Act of 1972

During 1971, some captains of tuna seiners, on their own, modified the Medina Panel design by adding an additional strip of small-mesh webbing, so as to double the depth of the panel. They found that this modification reduced porpoise mortality even more because it provided greater protection to the porpoise from entanglement. In 1972, other captains were making the Medina Panel longer, as well as deeper. Some tuna boat captains were using 1 7/8-inch mesh, rather than 2-inch mesh, in the Medina Panel.[1] These individual innovations were the norm for the U.S. tuna fleet for introducing new fishing gear and tactics. Successful ideas, especially those of highly-respected captains, were quickly adopted. The American Tunaboat Association (ATA) and Living Marine Resources (LMR) encouraged the fleet to experiment with the concept of the Medina Panel as a way to make the "Back-down" more effective in saving porpoises, as they strongly believed that "multiple-experimentation" would lead to a more effective tuna purse-seine net and further reduction in porpoise mortality.

After Passage of the Marine Mammal Protection Act of 1972

During the 24-month period of the National Marine Fisheries Service (NMFS) research and development program mandated by Section 111 of the Marine Mammal Protection Act (MMPA) of 1972, "the philosophy of the program was to work with the existing purse seining system and to help perfect those rescue procedures that the fishermen had developed, that they believed in, and that many of them were already using, to rapidly effect as great a reduction in porpoise mortality as possible."[2] The NMFS later found the value of working with the U.S. tuna fleet on a "multiple-experimentation" approach in testing new concepts to reduce porpoise mortality.

In March 1973, Dr. Eric Barham, formerly the head of the Marine Biology Branch of the Ocean Sciences Department at the Naval Undersea Center in San Diego, commenced work as Manager of the Porpoise/Tuna Program at the Southwest Fisheries Center (SWFC) of the NMFS.[3] With the assistance of Dr. Barham, the ATA conducted six workshops in 1973 that included interaction between NMFS gear experts and captains, vessel owners, and fishermen. During these meetings, the NMFS gear experts would present their opinions on rescue methods and the results of recent experimental studies, and then receive reactions from the fishermen. These discussions were helpful in developing a better understanding by both parties as to how cooperation could develop successful rescue methods and techniques to reduce porpoise mortality.

By the summer of 1973, NMFS fishing gear specialists were convinced that three of the four ideas considered to be feasible by a report of the 1972 NOAA Porpoise Committee should be put to rest. To achieve the goal of short-term and immediate reduction in porpoise mortality, the NMFS gear specialists decided to focus on experiments to improve the Medina Panel and the "Back-down."[4] The staff of the NMFS Porpoise/Tuna Interaction Program described this activity as work on "Phase One" or "research concentrated on mechanisms for reducing mortality if and when porpoise contact the net, and reducing the probability of contact, through minor changes in gear and procedures, as opposed to more sophisticated electronic, chemical, or biological mechanisms which might prevent contact with the net ("Phase Two" activities)."[5]

In 1973, the NMFS gear specialists chartered three new tuna seiners for the testing of new ideas to reduce porpoise mortality, and in 1974, the chartering of a new "super seiner" for two trips, and for one trip of a new tuna seiner.[6] These specialists were focusing on ideas to prevent the development of conditions that would prevent a smooth movement of pursing the net, retrieving it, and then proceeding with the "Back-down." This was called a "normal" set. A "problem set" can quickly develop if the net is not set properly, so as to cause the boat and the net to be forced together by wind and sea. In this circumstance, the volume of the ocean encompassed by the net and the circumference of the net's circle are drastically reduced. This gives the captured porpoise less room to maneuver away from folds of the net, which is contrary to the fishermen's objective of keeping the net open as long as possible. In cases in which the captain does set the net properly in relation to wind and sea conditions, undetected adverse currents, unexpected gear malfunctions, and human errors can cause net retrieval delays. In these cases, the net gets configured in forms that are hazardous to porpoise. To deal with this problem, NMFS gear specialists experimented with the use of speedboats and with the idea of a "large volume net" that included changes in the Medina Panel, modifications to the purse-line cable (torque-balanced), and the use of ribbon current indicators.[7]

Final NMFS regulations required that all tuna purse-seine vessels install a Medina Panel in their nets for fishing trips commencing after April 1, 1974.[8] The dimensions of the Medina Panel were set forth in 50 CFR §216.24(b) (1)-(5), including the requirement that the small-mesh webbing not exceed 2-inch stretch mesh pre-shrunk, either knotted or knotless. The regulations set forth in 50 CFR §216.24(d) required a certification by masters or owners of tuna seiners to be filed by April 1, 1974, that the Medina Panel had been installed in accordance with the regulations, and that the net "will be maintained in good repair" and in accordance with the regulations. The time limit for installing the Medina Panel was extended to June 1, 1974, by the NMFS because of limited supplies of nylon webbing resulting from a petroleum shortage (Middle East Oil Embargo) and impacts of the proposed regulations on normal net stock. Later, authority to waive the rule under certain conditions regarding availability of nylon netting was provided to the Southwest Regional Director of the NMFS.

The provisions of Section 111 of the MMPA required that the Secretary of Commerce deliver a written report to Congress "with respect to the results" of the Department's two-year program of research and development.[9] The purpose of this program was to devise "improved fishing methods and gear so as to reduce to the maximum extent practicable the incidental taking of marine mammals in connection with commercial fishing." This report was delivered to Congress on October 21, 1974.[10] In Appendix B of this report, an example list of 18 methods offered to solve the porpoise mortality is provided. Ten ideas were considered and rejected; the remaining eight were temporarily postponed for reasons that were explained in the report.

As more NMFS observer data on porpoise mortality were collected and analyzed, the gear experts focused primarily on ways to enhance the effectiveness of the Medina Panel in reducing porpoise entanglement and entrapment, on ways to improve the "Back-down," and on methods to prevent the problem of "net collapse."[11] Data showed that about 95% of the porpoise encircled were released by the "Back-down," that about 2% died, mainly because of entanglement and entrapment, and that the remainder were manually rescued or saved when the porpoise managed to jump out of the net.

Experimentation with Webbing of Less than 2-inch Mesh In the Medina Panel

The NMFS conducted a study in 1974 that showed that up to 30% of the porpoise mortality was still occurring during the "Back-down" procedure with nets equipped with a Medina Panel having 2-inch mesh. Seven porpoise specimens returned to shore were used to take measurements of porpoise snouts and flippers through four different mesh sizes: 2-inch, 1 7/8-inch, 1 ½-inch, and 1-inch. "It should be noted, however, that even the 1-inch mesh would not totally exclude the tip of the jaws when they were agape. Clearly, however, the test results strongly indicate the potential reduction in entanglement that can be gained through the application of small mesh netting."[12]

The NMFS gear specialists recognized that the insertion of small-mesh webbing into the huge nets used by the newer tuna seiners had to be approached with the same care and thought exercised by Captain Harold Medina in 1971 with his new tuna seiner KERRI M. "Because of its added weight, drag, and tendency to clog, addition of large amounts of small-mesh webbing to a net of this size (600-700 fathoms in length and 60 to 84 fathoms deep) must be approached with caution, for the buoyancy of the net can be lessened to the point that once the floats or "corks" go under and are squeezed by increasing water pressure they will not rise to the surface. In such a situation, the net can sink to the point where it, and even the vessel, are in jeopardy."[13]

The efforts of the U.S. fleet in 1976 to quickly change the "Medina Panel" from 2-inch to 1 1/4-inch mesh was delayed for a variety of reasons. American manufacturers advised that they would not start the production of 1 1/4-inch webbing until 1977. Further, domestic suppliers were not producing the net floats required to meet the specifications to hold the added weight caused by an installation of small-mesh webbing. In addition, only about four firms in Japan were able to manufacture the proper floats. An order for 10,000 floats had been placed during 1976, but delivery took 120 days. By late 1976, about 91 of the 96 large tuna seiners had placed orders for the smaller-mesh webbing. An NMFS witness tes- tified at an administrative law judge hearing held in late 1976 that the small-mesh webbing would be delivered sometime in December 1976, and that it would "probably take a few more months to get all the webbing that had been ordered, and that an additional three or four days will be required for installation on the respective vessels."[14]

The tuna industry was encouraged by the results of the 2-year "joint venture" with the NMFS in seeking ways to reduce porpoise mortality. The ATA voiced the opinion that if this "joint venture" could continue on course, dramatic reductions in porpoise mortality would result, and that this would occur before reliable porpoise population assessments could be obtained by the NMFS. Further, the ATA was of the opinion that the combination of charters of tuna seiners funded by alloca- tions of yellowfin tuna by the Inter-American Tropical Tuna Commission (IATTC) during the "Closed Season" in the Commission's Yellowfin Regulatory Area (CY- RA) plus "multiple-experimentation" at sea by many tuna captains of promising ideas should be given a higher priority by the NMFS over behavioral studies de- signed to solve the tuna/porpoise enigma. A government report recommended a continuation of the "Joint venture" approach: "The large-scale joint NMFS/Industry approach to research on the problem of incidental porpoise mor- tality is a logical and productive way to combine the resources and ideas of both communities. It should be continued as long as advancements in mortality- reduction technology can be realized . . . ."[15]

As the 2-year research and development program was coming to a close, along with the 2-year permit exemption period for the commercial fishing operations, some "protectionist" groups were lobbying the NMFS, with the help of members of Congress, to adopt conditions to any General Permit issued to the ATA that included a "porpoise mortality quota" that would be ratcheted downward annually, plus the use of National Oceanic and Atmospheric Administration (NOAA) agents or observers for strict shipboard enforcement of NMFS regulations. Some in Congress were aware that these groups were also working to file a lawsuit against the Secretary of Commerce, NOAA/NMFS, to void any issuance of a General Permit to the tuna industry.[16]

Experimentation with Attachment of Appendages to the Medina Panel

During 1974-1976, a series of experiments concerning modifications to the Medi- na Panel were conducted jointly by the fleet and NMFS gear specialists. Various designs, *e.g.* the "porpoise apron," the "chute," and the "super apron," were tested to improve the dynamics and shape of the "Backdown area." The technic- al nature of these designs makes their discussed more appropriate in Appendix A. During 1976, an at-sea experiment involving 10 tuna seiners using the NMFS effort called the *BOLD CONTENDER system* and 10 tuna seiners using a mod- ified Medina Panel system was temporarily interrupted by federal judicial action.

The nature of this experiment and of its organization and performance is also discussed in Appendix A.

1976 Scientific Voyage of the ELIZABETH C. J.[17]

An outstanding record was achieved by the Captain Manuel Jorge and the crew of the "Super" tuna seiner ELIZABETH C. J. during a charter of that vessel by the NMFS. The ship's net was use to encircle an estimated 30,233 porpoise and land over 915 short tons of yellowfin during 45 sets on tuna/porpoise schools. The two-month voyage (October 7 to December 9, 1976) occurred off Mexico and Central America. Five of these 45 sets on tuna/porpoise schools resulted in a total of 16 porpoise deaths. However, 12 of the 16 deaths occurred in sets during which members of the scientific party aboard the vessel conducted activities in the net during "Back-down" that "hampered porpoise release ... The remaining four deaths occurred during "Back-down" in two experimental sets that had no operational malfunctions. The animals became folded into the side of the "Back-down" channel at a depth that precluded hand rescue." (p. 3)[18] The report of this cruise further explains:

> "The extremely low porpoise mortality rate experienced during this cruise was the result of the care and efficiency of the fishing captain and crew members in setting and hauling their net, using speedboats to adjust the cork line (18 sets), and in backing down until all live porpoise were released (42 of 45 sets). These efforts, in conjunction with the "super apron" and double-depth (Medina) safety panel of 1 1/4" stretch mesh webbing allowed this vessel to achieve a record low kill rate. ... (p. 3)

> "The record low mortality rate experienced on the charter cruise is the result of concurrent evolution of improved fishing techniques and gear modifications developed by NMFS and the tuna industry and increased awareness of the captain and crew of the necessity to reduce incidental porpoise mortality ..." (p. 4)

The gear research on that cruise was conducted by James M. Coe, Chief Scientist of Gear Research, SWFC-NMFS, and Philippe Vergne, Porpoise Rescue Foundation. The main objective of their work was to test a modification of the *Bold Contender System*.[19] This change was the placement of an appendage in the shape of a triangle attached to the apron. The length of the base for this appendage, 26 fathoms, was not changed. The top of the appendage did represent a change from the flat top of the "chute" appendage used in the *Bold Contender System*. This new triangular-shaped appendage was called the "Super Apron." The removal of extra webbing in the "Chute" appendage "eliminated the two-step shelf (formation) ... Thus, as 'Back-down' proceeded with the 'super apron,' the channel became progressively shallower and ramp-like, raising the 'passive' spotters up and flushing them out of the net. This reduced the necessity for hand rescue considerably."

To obtain further information on the tuna/porpoise enigma, some 8,000 feet of film was taken on the cruise for later analysis.[20] The cameraman was Joe Thompson, founder of Seavision Productions of San Diego and a recognized expert in underwater filming. He had worked with Jacques Cousteau for 14 years, making many underwater filming trips aboard the famed CALYPSO. After the

experimental cruise aboard the ELIZABETH C. J., filmmaker Thompson persuaded the ATA and some vessel owners to produce an hour-long documentary
on the fishing of tuna/porpoise schools. The film, "Voyage of a Yankee Tuna
Clipper," received the Golden Eagle award. It was shown extensively overseas,
but was not distributed successfully for showing on TV in the United States. In
addition, Thompson produced a 15-minute documentary on the U.S. tuna fleet for
use by the the ATA at public and governmental forums. Experience with these
two films proved once again the old adage that a few pictures are worth a thou-
sand words. Both films illustrated the effectiveness of the "Back-down" and other
porpoise rescue methods used by the fishermen. The aerial and underwater footage used in the hour-long documentary was taken during a regular fishing trip

LENGTH: 252' 4"
BEAM: 43' 0"
DRAFT: 21' 8"
DISPLACEMENT: 3,595 long tons
FROZEN FISH PAYLOAD: 1,700 short tons

MAIN ENGINES: 2 EMD 16-cylinder
turbocharged diesels
TOTAL HORSEPOWER: 5,750 BHP at 900RPM
PROPELLERS: 2 Coolidge 5-blade 126" stainless steel
SPEED: 18 knots
AUXILIARY POWER: 2 Caterepillar D379 diesels with
400kw Kato generators and 1
Caterpillar D353 diesel with
300kw Kato generator

FUEL OIL CAPACITY: 138,000 gallons
LUBE OIL CAPACITY: 14,700 gallons
CREW: 16-20
CONSTRUCTION: Welded steel; aluminum pilot
house, stack, and crow's nest
DESIGNED AND BUILT BY: Campbell Industries,
San Diego, California

Captain Manuel Jorge and the ELIZABETH C.J.
Vessel built by Campbell Industries, San Diego, California

aboard the ELIZABETH C. J. when under the command of Captain Joe Jorge.
The 15-minute film used footage taken aboard tuna vessels, including the ELIZ-
ABETH C. J. when under the command of Captain Manuel Jorge.

Another objective of the experimental cruise, unrelated to the net, was the further
testing of the "use of a small, one-man inflatable raft to assist in porpoise removal
during and after "Back-down." A mask and snorkel were used in this operation.
Coe and Vergne found that the raft was successful in herding the porpoise to the
release area, provided that the raft stayed more than 10 meters (33 feet) away
from the nearest porpoise. When the raft was first used during the fall 1975 charter of the BOLD CONTENDER, NMFS gear technicians found "that spotted porpoise sometimes become passive and pile up on the bottom of the "Back-down"

channel where they can be mistaken for dead." It was found that the raft-man "could hear vocalizations of porpoise that were still in the net but could not be seen. This final listening check became common practice, and several animals were saved as a result."

Much has been reported about the ELIZABETH C.J. charter cruise. To the surprise of many scientists aboard the vessel, and also other individuals and organizations having an interest in the "tuna-porpoise problem," the cruise confirmed the fact that there were captains and crews in the U.S. tuna fleet who were highly skilled and dedicated in using gear and procedures to save porpoise.[21]

The decisions by the McNeely (NMFS) Gear Team during fiscal years (FYs) 1975 (July 1, 1974-June 30, 1975) and 1976 (July 1, 1975-June 30, 1976) to develop and test changes in the configuration of the net and mesh size of the "Medina Panel" in the "Back-down" area, and to require greater use of speedboats to reduce net collapses prior to "Back-down" were later proven justified and wise. Analysis of data developed for the NMFS fiscal year 1976 Progress Report showed that 92.8% of the porpoise encircled by the net were released alive by the "Back-down" in FY1975, and 97.0% in FY1976. The recorded increased use of speedboats to prevent "net collapse" in FY1976 reduced reports of these incidents by about half.[22]

> "The improved fishing gear and new methods tested and demonstrated during 1976 represent a culmination of approximately 6 years of research directed towards the development of practical and economically feasible methods to reduce incidental porpoise mortalities. Many of the alternatives which were investigated during this period proved to be economically unsound, impractical, or ineffective. . . . [23]

The results of the 1976 charter cruise of the ELIZABETH C. J. were used by some in the tuna Industry to support a declaration by Richard L. McNeely that the "fine-tuning" of existing gear and procedures was the future for gear research and development by the NMFS in the U.S. purse-seine fishery directed at tuna associated with porpoise.[24]

---

[1] Why the use of 2-inch mesh? "There are several cogent reasons for using this dimension mesh: it is regularly hung in the large dip nets or brailers used to scoop tuna out of the sacked-up bunt end of the purse seine, and is therefore usually available; the 4 ¼-inch webbing shrinks to approximately 4 inches after moderate usage and the 2-inch mesh can be easily laced in two meshes to one and even though the small mesh will suffer shrinkage after use, the lines of strain work well in the net with the larger mesh." Barham, Eric G., Warren K. Taguchi, and Stephen B. Reilly, "Porpoise Rescue Methods in the Yellowfin Purse Seine Fishery and the Importance of Medina Panel Mesh Size," MFR Paper1246, *Marine Fisheries Review*, 39 (5): 1, 4. (cited hereinafter: "Barham 1977 MFR Paper")

[2] Barham 1977 MFR Paper: 2.

[3] The name of the program was changed to "Porpoise/Tuna Interaction Program, Oceanic Fisheries Resources Division."

[4] The ideas rejected: mid-depth dual purse line; mini-purse seine or a lampara skimmer net; porpoise gate. 1972 NOAA Porpoise Committee Report: 51-53.

[5] Staff, Porpoise/Tuna Interaction Program Oceanic Fisheries Resources Division, NOAA, NMFS, SWFC, La Jolla, California, "Progress of Research on Porpoise Mortality Incidental to Tuna Purse-Seine Fishing for Fiscal Year 1975," August 8, 1975, SWFC Administrative Report No. LJ-75-68 (cited hereinafter: SWFC-1975"), at p. 9. See also: Staff, Porpoise/Tuna Interaction Program Oceanic Fisheries Resources Division, NOAA, NMFS, SWFC, La Jolla, California, "Progress of Research on Porpoise Mortality Incidental to Tuna Purse Seine-Seine Fishing for Fiscal Year 1976," dated September 7, 1976, SWFC Administrative Report No. LJ-76-17 (cited hereinafter, "SWFC-1976"), at p. 42.

[6] For 1973: (1) trip aboard the converted seiner INDEPENDENCE (January 1-February 13), to observe and photograph porpoise and tuna in the net during the Yellowfin Open Season; (2) non-fishing charter trip in waters off San Diego (May 21-June 5) aboard the new tuna seiner JOHN F. KENNEDY, to study net dynamics, test torque-balanced cable, and experiment with the use of speedboats to prevent "net collapse"; (3) charter fishing trip (October 16-November 11) aboard the new tuna seiner TRINIDAD during a period when purse seiners were not permitted to fish for yellowfin in the Commission's Yellowfin Regulatory Area (Closed Season), to test the NMFS innovations relating to the purse-line cable, current indicators, and the keeping of the net open when threatened by collapse by using speedboats; (4) charter fishing trip (November 10-December 15) aboard the new tuna seiner JOHN F. KENNEDY during the Closed Season to test an experimental large-volume net and acoustic devices, and the tagging of porpoise. For 1974: the "Super Seiner" SOUTH PACIFIC, June 25-September 14 and October 28-December 1; the new seiner J.M. MARTINAC, November-December.

[7] The modification to the Medina Panelwas the use of 1 ½-inch mesh, rather than 2-inch mesh, and the "webbing was extended in depth to the equivalent of three strips deep (about 30.2 m) so that the small mesh extended down to reach the floor of the channel where porpoise frequently dive during Backdown." Barham 1977 MFR Paper: 4.

[8] 39 FR 2181 (January 22, 1974). Proposed regulations: 38 FR 31180 (November 12, 1973).

[9] The MMPA limited the "responsibility of the Department of Commerce to those mammals which are members of the order *Cetacea* (whales and porpoises) and members other than walruses, of the order *Pinnipedia* (seals and sea lions) ... On November 30, 1972, the Secretary of Commerce delegated authority for the functions prescribed by the MMPA to the Administrator of the National Oceanic and Atmospheric Administration (NOAA). On February 9, 1973, the Administrator of NOAA delegated this authority to the Director, National Marine Fisheries Service (NMFS). ... "Administration of the Marine Mammal Protection Act of 1972, December 21, 1972 to June 21, 1973. Report of the Secretary of Commerce. 38 FR 20564 (August 1, 1973)

The MMPA also required the Secretary of Commerce to report to the public through publication in the Federal Register and to Congress on a variety of matters concerning his administration of the MMPA. Included in these reports are summaries of activities entitled: "Tuna-Porpoise Research and Development" and on "International Program—Inter-American Tropical Tuna Commission (IATTC)" See: Administration of the Marine Mammal Protection Act of 1972, June 1974, Report of the Secretary of Commerce: 39 FR 23896 (June 24, 1974).

[10] The Secretary's report, which includes six appendices, is entitled: "Administration of the Marine Mammal Protection Act of 1972. Report to the Congress on the Research and Development Program to Reduce the Incidental Take of Marine Mammals October 21, 1972 through October 20, 1974."

[11] When the cork-lines or float-lines of the net come together and form canopies of webbing, a "net collapse" occurs. This action causes a steady reduction of the volume of the net and its circumference, thereby reducing the open area of the net for use by the tunas and porpoises. A gear malfunction most often causes a net collapse. So also do adverse sea and current conditions. A "net collapse" often occurs because of the quantity of tunas and porpoises captured.

[12] Barham 1977 MFR Paper, p. 8.

[13] Barham 1977 MFR Paper, p. 5.

[14] January 1977 ALJ Decision: 33.

[15] SWFC-1976: 69-70

[16] "I take it that the effective bar to the issuance of permits is likely, if it occurs at all, to come in the form of litigation. I do not wish in any way to comment upon what may be the merits of any such lawsuit. The function of this hearing is not to make that kind of inquiry. At the same time, it seems certain that the outcome of such a suit might be to stifle or even to force the American tuna fleet to move out of the country and to sail under foreign flags. This would appear to be a result which no one wishes ..." August 8, 1974, statement of John Dingell, Chairman, Subcommittee on Fisheries and Wildlife Conservation and the Environment, Committee on Merchant Marine and Fisheries, House of Representatives. 1974 House Hearings-SN-93-36: 143.

[17] The ELIZABETH C. J was built in San Diego by Campbell Industries. In 1926, this shipyard built the ATLANTIC, the first documented U.S.-Flag tuna clipper greater than 100 gross tons.

[18] James M. Coe and Philippe J. Vergne, "Modified Tuna Purse Seine Net Achieves Record Low Porpoise Kill Rate," MFR Paper 1251, *Marine Fisheries Review*, 39 (6): 1, 3-4. The ZAPATA DISCOVERER, operated by Captain Harold Medina in 1976, was a sister ship of the ELIZABETH C. J

[19] Karen Pryor, a marine biologist who had considerable experience with captive Hawaiian spinner and spotted porpoise behavior, was aboard the ELIZABETH C. J as a researcher for the University of California at Santa Cruz. She reported: "During last fall's behavioral cruise, we found that porpoises in the net can easily be guided. They can be herded. ..." See: Hearings before the Committee on Merchant Marine and Fisheries, House of Representatives, 95th Congress, 1st Session on Reducing Porpoise Mortality, H.R. 6146, H.R. 6409, H. R. 6729, H.R. 6807, H.R. 6907, H.R. 6928, and H.R. 6970, May 13 and 16, 1977; Tuna-Porpoise Oversight, August 1, 1977 (Serial No. 95-3). (Cited herein: "May/August 1977 House Hearings-SN-95-3): 299. The chairman of the MMC, Dr. Douglas G. Chapman, reported: "It became more generally known that some porpoises exhibit so-called sleeper behavior. They sink down and rest for a while before rising back up to the surface. The research cruise demonstrated that continuing the "Back-down" operation, until these sleeper animals come to the surface and pass out of the net, allows these animals which would otherwise probably die to be rescued." Hearings before the Subcommittee on Fisheries and Wildlife Conservation and the Environment of the Committee on Merchant Marine and Fisheries, House of Representatives, 95th Congress, 1st Session, on Marine Mammal Oversight, February 17, 1977; Tuna-Porpoise Regulations, March 2, 1977, Marine Mammal Authorization-H.R. 4740, March 15, 1977. (cited hereinafter: "February 1977 House Hearings-SN-95-8"): p. 31.

[20] The ATA made a condition to the charter of the vessel, as follows: "... we would pay for the film, we would pay for the processing of the film, we would pay for the photographing (approximately $22,000). ... we want title, we want control. We promise and we agree to provide the film data to the researchers for research purposes. September 1976 House Hearings-SN-94-45: 118-121 By having the ATA, rather than the Government, hold title to the film, the ATA believed that the Freedom of Information Act would not be applicable to non-government organizations in an effort to obtain the film. The MMC strongly objected, arguing that the ruling in the QUEEN MARY would apply and that unnecessary litigation would result from such condition. September 1976 House Hearings-SN-94-45: 118-121. For these and other reasons, MMC insisted on title and control of the film, and offered to caption the film in the way ordered by the Federal Judge in the QUEEN MARY litigation. The ATA backed off from insisting on its condition.

[21] "Report on the Tuna-Porpoise Cruise to the Marine Mammal Commission" by Warren E. Stuntz. A copy of this report is in the following record: February 1977 House Subcommittee Oversight Hearing-SN-95-8: 33-37. See: Copy of Cruise Report (Gear Research) U.S. Department of Commerce, NOAA, NMFS: February 1977 House Hearings-SN-95-8: 38-42. A better copy for viewing, see: *1977 Senate Hearings-SN-95-12*:179-184. Note: These hearings were held in March, not in February as printed. See: February 1977 House Hearings-SN-95-8: 65-90, for information about the ELIZABETH C. J charter cruise: comments by industry representatives and February 1977 House Hearings-SN-95-8: 88-89, for remarks of the captain of the vessel, Manuel Jorge. Copy of article: Roy J. Harris, *Wall Street Journal,* March 4, 1977, "Must Porpoise Die for a Tuna on Rye? Maybe Not After All": 1977 Senate Hearings-SN-95-12:.118-121. Copy of the article in the *Smithsonian Magazine* published in its February 1977 issue about the results of the 1976 experimental cruise of the ELIZABETH C. J. It was written by Dr. Kenneth S. Norris, and entitled: "Tuna Sandwiches Cost at Least 78,000 Porpoise Lives a Year, but There is Hope." Senator Edwin J. Garn, Utah, obtained consent to have a copy of the article, without photos, printed in the *Congressional Record—Senate*, at pp. S 4690-4692, March 23, 1977.

[22] SWFC-1976, pp. 40-41.

[23] F. M. Ralston (editor), 1977. A workshop to assess research related to the porpoise/tuna problem, February 12, March 1-2, SWFC Administrative Report. LJ-77-15: 119 pp.. See statement on page 8, part of a report presented by Richard McNeely and James Coe. They reported on porpoise mortality occurring after backdown, the large-volume seine experimentation in 1975, and the pre-backdown release of porpoise experience associated with the net modification to the "chute" aboard the tuna seiner EVELYN DA ROSA by Captain Cristiano DaRosa in 1976. Appendix V (12 pp.) of this report is a glossary of 49 tuna seining terms, arranged alphabetically from "Apron" to "Zipper."

[24] For a summary of the work done to reduce porpoise mortality by the Industry/NMFS gear efforts in 1975 and 1976 prior to the experimental voyage of the ELIZABETH C.J, see the testimony of Dr. William Fox, Chief, Oceanic Fisheries Resources Division, SWFC-NMFS. Hearings before the Subcommittee on Fisheries and Wildlife Conservation and the Environment of the Committee on Merchant Marine and Fisheries, House of Representatives, 94th Congress, Second Session on Tuna-Porpoise, September 27-30, 1976, (Serial No. 94-45). (Cited herein: "September 1976 House Hearings-SN-94-45"): 151-158.

18

GOVERNMENT TUNA/PORPOISE RESEARCH DECISIONS

The U.S. National Marine Fisheries Service (NMFS) decision to initiate "Phase Two" research and development, establishing a priority on porpoise behavioral research, was announced in 1975. The NMFS expressed hope that it would be able "to execute longer-term sophisticated projects of the "Phase Two" type with base funding in fiscal year (FY) 1976.[1] In its FY1976 report, the NMFS announced that it was working with the Marine Mammal Commission (MMC) and others to develop baseline knowledge of porpoise behavior during tuna-fishing operations."[2]

A recital of this conflict of views between the NMFS and the MMC on what porpoise research activities should be implemented to solve the tuna/porpoise problem was presented during a September 1976 House Oversight Hearing. Dr. Kenneth S. Norris, member of the MMC Committee of Scientific Advisors, Chairman of the MMC's Subcommittee on the Porpoise-Tuna Problem, and appointee to the 1972 NOAA (U.S. National Oceanic and Atmospheric Administration) Tuna-Porpoise Review Committee, stated as follows: [3]

> "... the priorities established by the original NOAA committee have been shifted. Most expenditure has been on status work-population estimation, reproduction and growth—and gear research. The latter category, which I have always regarded as crucial, has at times been inadequately supported. The effort to investigate behavior of fish and porpoises, as a means of trying to find ways of separating the two and releasing the porpoise unharmed, has lagged very badly. Meaningful behavior studies on the tuna grounds have not been carried out to date ..."

During the informal hearing conducted by the NMFS, held in Washington, D.C., on October 9, 1975, the American Tunaboat Association (ATA) and Living Marine Resources, Inc. (LMR) submitted written statements and participated in the informal discussions. The ATA written statement noted:

> "Although the 'Apron' device is not considered by our captains an automatic success, we are encouraged by the results so far. More importantly, we are enthusiastic about the fact that testing new ideas developed during a charter cruise can be quickly and effectively field tested by a group of tuna vessels in a coordinated, well-planned, experimental program. We believe this1975 at-sea experiment towards developing porpoise rescue technology can be used to test a variety of other ideas. We have a new idea ready for such a test."

The ATA proposed that its general permit be valid for three years, and that it be modified by the NMFS so as to allow a one-year test during 1976 of a porpoise radio-tracking system. This was necessary because an existing regulation adopted in 1973 prohibited its use by tuna seiners.[4] The technology to be tested in fishing tuna/porpoise schools, developed by the San Diego firm, Ocean Applied Research Corporation, was known as O.A.R. Porpoise Tracking System. The system was first used in 1971 during normal commercial fishing operation aboard the tuna seiner QUEEN MARY, which had been chartered for conducting studies on porpoise behavior, by a naval marine mammal scientist. Joe Medina, Jr., captain of the QUEEN MARY during the 1971 NMFS charter, later used the system in 1972. Captain Medina explained why he believed that the ATA proposal would result in a reduction of porpoise mortality and the development of new porpoise rescue technology. The ATA advised participants at the hearing that 20 tuna seiners were available for at-sea testing of the O.A.R. Porpoise Tracking System during 1976, and that more information about this proposal would be presented during the informal hearing to be conducted in San Diego on October 24, 1975.[5] In justifying the proposal, the ATA argued: "Besides the expectancy of reduced incidental mortality, we at the ATA are of the opinion that [the proposal] will result in the development of new porpoise rescue technology ... We also believe that such system will help the tuna industry, the government and the concerned public to learn more about porpoise behavior, the relationship between feeding behavior of porpoises and herd structure, and the relationship between porpoise herd movements and oceanographic conditions ... The need to develop more behavioral information about the porpoise/tuna relationship is essential. ..." (ATA Statement, October 9, 1975: p. 13.)

On the first day of the House Oversight Hearings, October 21, 1975, the subcommittee listened to testimony from the Chairman, Executive Director, General Counsel, and Research Program Director of the MMC (pp. 2-31, 69). The MMC provided the subcommittee with documentation (pp. 275-304) that explains in part the interest of the NMFS in working with the MMC during 1976 to develop a behavioral research program.[6] This documentation suggests that the MMC was of the view that the gear research effort termed "Phase One" was history, and that the highest priority for research should be exclusively in efforts involving "Phase Two." In its letter to the NMFS dated July 30, 1974 (Appendix A), the MMC and its committee of scientific advisors stated their view that the methods and gear developed jointly by the tuna industry and the NMFS fishing gear specialists "will not, in themselves, produce an acceptably low rate of incidental kill and injury." At this time, the MMC was pushing the NMFS to agree with its views on solving the tuna/porpoise problem.[7] After noting that the NMFS wanted to work with the MMC, and that the NMFS now "intends to vigorously pursue behavioral investigations," the Executive Director of the MMC advised the Director of the NMFS as follows:

> "The Commission feels that highest priority should be assigned to those research efforts which will concentrate on solutions to the problem rather than assessment. The importance of quickly starting a really strong behavioral program cannot be over emphasized. ... I reiterate that the Commission does not wish to separately pursue the behavioral research work in a fashion that might prove wasteful and duplicative. We are, therefore, very pleased at your expressions of real interest and intent to do something promptly about the situation. We are anxious to cooperate and assist in any way possible."

A workshop,[8] sponsored by the MMC, was held at the University of California,

Santa Cruz, on December 8-9, 1975. In attendance were 12 participants from the MMC, the NMFS Southwest and Northwest Fisheries Centers, LMR, the Naval Undersea Center, the University of Hawaii, the National Science Foundation, and the Coastal Marine Laboratory, University of California, Santa Cruz.

The participants found a "critical need for innovative research that might suggest new approaches to the problem of incidental porpoise mortality," because even a "mandatory fleet-wide use of (the *Bold Contender System*) is unlikely to entirely eliminate the incidental kill"; therefore, the need "to develop technology that effectively separates tuna and porpoise prior to complete encirclement by the purse seine."

A suggested research program was presented that would document the "untouchable" behavior of porpoises experienced by tuna fishermen, the time-sequence (ethological)[9] description of events occurring during porpoise sets, the characterization of the acoustic environment, the characteristics of the tuna-porpoise bond, and the social structure and behavior of free-ranging porpoise schools."

In the report's "conclusions and recommendations," the NMFS was asked to immediately" plan and organize a research cruise to take place as soon as possible, and stating the following requirements: (1) the tuna seiner should have helicopter capability and operate on a 90-day charter "without the *need* to fish in order to pay for the vessel charter"; (2) a support ship, either a U.S. Coast Guard vessel or a NMFS research vessel, should accompany the tuna seiner; and, (3) the highest priority should be given to the study of the time sequence of events that occur during a set on a tuna/porpoise school. The report concluded:

> "It was noted that the ultimate goal was truly to achieve zero incidental mortality, and that this goal probably could be achieved only if tuna and porpoise could be separated prior to complete encirclement. The development of a 'super stimulus' seems to be the only hope for separating tuna and porpoises prior to encirclement; therefore, most participants felt that it would be desirable to initiate studies with captive animals as soon as possible."

In December 1975, a draft document entitled "Cooperative Agreement among the National Oceanic and Atmospheric Administration, Department of Commerce, the Marine Mammal Commission, Representatives of the Tuna Industry, Representatives of Conservation Organizations," was circulated and discussed by representatives of the parties. The final Memorandum of Agreement was signed on January 2, 1976, by representatives of the Tuna Research Foundation, the MMC, the ATA, the Fishermen's Union of America, Pacific & Caribbean Area (AFL-CIO), United Cannery and Industrial Workers of the Pacific, and NOAA, acting through the NMFS. The words "Representatives of Conservation Organizations" were deleted in the final, executed Agreement. The objective of the Memorandum Agreement was to have the parties conduct their affairs so as to avoid unproductive and duplicative research efforts. To implement this goal, the parties agreed to "1. exchange and evaluate relevant data; 2. discuss, develop, and coordinate current and future research and development projects; and 3. exchange any other relevant information and views." Other provisions dealt with the right to modify, supplement, add additional parties, and to permit any party to withdraw upon 30 days notification.[10]

Prior to the negotiation of the Memorandum of Agreement, the ATA proposal regarding the porpoise radio-tracking project was rejected by the NMFS.

---

[1] SWFC-1975, p. 9. The title of this Report: "Progress of Research on Porpoise Mortality Incidental To Tuna Purse-Seine Fishing For Fiscal Year 1975" by Staff, Porpoise/Tuna Interaction Program Oceanic Fisheries Resources Division, NOAA, NMFS, SFC, La Jolla, California 92038, August 8, 1975. Southwest Fisheries Center Administrative report NO. LJ-75-68.

[2] SWFC-1976, p. 9. The title of this Report: "Progress of Research on Porpoise Mortality Incidental to Tuna Purse-Seine Fishing For Fiscal Year 1976" by Staff, Porpoise/Tuna Interaction Program Oceanic Fisheries Resources Division, NOAA, NMFS, SFC, La Jolla, California 92038, September 7, 1976, Southwest Fisheries Center Administrative Report NO. LJ-76-17.

[3] September 1976 House Hearings-SN-94-45: pp.112, 114-115. See: MMC Supplemental Material Relating to Research on Incidental Injury to Porpoises in the Course of the Yellowfin Tuna Fishery; Statement of Dr. Kenneth S. Norris, and Supplemental Statements of Committee on the Porpoise Tuna Problem of the Committee of Scientific Advisors on Marine Mammals. 1975 House Hearings-SN-94-16: pp. 284-291.

[4] 38 FR 7987 (March 27, 1973): "... that the taking of a marine mammal which otherwise meets the requirement of this definition shall not be considered an incidental catch of that mammal if it is used subsequently to assist in commercial fishing operations."

[5] A Notice was published in the Federal Register by the NMFS advising that additional informal public hearings would be held on the reissuance of the ATA General Permit on October 24, 1975, in San Diego, California 40 FR 45213 (October 1, 1975)

[6] The letter of John R. Twiss, Executive Director, MMC, to the Chairman of the House Subcommittee on Fisheries and Wildlife Conservation and the Environment, dated December 11, 1975, details the actions taken by the MMC to fulfill its duty to provide "considered recommendations on actions necessary to reach a solution to the tuna-porpoise problem." Attached to this letter are five appendices. In Appendix A, a letter from the MMC to the NMFS dated July 30, 1974, made 11 recommendations, and asked the "NMFS to promptly join with it in exploring with the fleet the feasibility of industry dedication of a tuna purse seiner and crew to conduct relevant research and testing at sea ..." Recommendation (4) called for research efforts on obtaining a better understanding of "the tuna-porpoise bond, and a detailed behavioral analysis ... utilizing such means as underwater films of the entire process (pursuit and capture) and the placement of behavioral scientists as observers on experimental and regular fishing cruises." The MMC estimated that the "dedicated vessel" might be required for as long as "two years or more." In addition to the cost of the vessel and crew, the MMC proposed a program estimated to cost $1.25 million. 1975 House Hearings-SN-94-16: pp. 273-293.

[7] The letter of John R. Twiss, Executive Director, MMC, to the Chairman of the House Subcommittee on Fisheries and Wildlife Conservation and the Environment, dated

November 11, 1975. "During late 1974 and until July 1975, the [NMFS], on a number of occasions, thwarted Commission efforts to gain access to data relevant to the tuna-porpoise situation. Furthermore, access of Commission contractors to key Service personnel was not granted. In early July, disturbed by the Service's flagrant disregard for the requirements of the Act, I informed them that the Commission intended to immediately file with the Congress a statement to the effect that the Commission was unable to fulfill its responsibilities under the (MMPA) because of a lack of cooperation on the part of the Service ..." 1975 House Hearings-SN-94-16: pp.273-293, at p. 274.

[8] To read the Final Report on this Workshop: September 1976 House Hearings-SN-94-45: pp. 196-205. For information on the details of research cruise, *Id.*, pp. 112-114

[9] The Report at page 199 defines the term "ethogram" as a description of the form and functional relationship of an animal's behavior patterns.

[10] See testimony of John Hodges: February 1977 House Hearings-SN 95-8": p. 108.

19

THE "MMPA JOINT VENTURE" AND RELATED EVENTS

The economic survival of the U.S. tuna fleet was being challenged both at sea and on shore during 1970-1976. At sea, the U.S. tuna fleet achieved spectacular success in developing improved gear and methods to reduce porpoise mortality. These developments took place even though the U.S. fleet was burdened with two domestic regulatory systems on the fishing of yellowfin tuna and by the threat of being seized by Latin American nations on what the U.S. government consi-dered to be the high seas. Ashore, representatives of all segments of the U.S. tuna industry were dealing with complex Law of the Sea problems—domestic and international—in Congress and the United Nations.

Law of the Sea Issues: Congress and the United Nations

For the U.S. tuna industry, the decade of the 1970s was overflowing with serious international and domestic Law of the Sea challenges, During 1970, the unex-pected collapse of the Second Buenos Aires tuna fishery negotiations convened by governments of the United States, Chile, Ecuador, and Peru, caused con-cerns to the captains and crews that they would again face the risk of being seized by the navies of these countries.[1] Those fears were justified: during the 1971-1973 period. Latin American nations seized 111 U.S. tuna seiners (53 in 1971, 30 in 1972, and 28 in 1973).[2]

In preparation for the convening of a United Nations (UN) conference on the Law of the Sea in 1973, the work sessions of the UN Committee on the Peaceful Uses of the Sea-Bed and the Ocean Floor beyond the Limits of National Jurisdic-tion began in March 1971 and were completed in August 1973.[3] By monitoring these meetings and by participating as advisors to the U.S. Delegation, repre-sentatives of the U.S. tuna industry assisted its delegation in taking the position before this UN Committee that tuna be managed by international organizations, rather than by individual coastal states.[4] This position persisted during the Third United Nations Conference on the Law of the Sea.

The first session of the conference was held in New York on December 3-15, 1973, the second in Caracas, Venezuela, on June 20-August 29, 1974, and the third in Geneva, Switzerland, on March 17-May 9, 1975. The eleventh, and final, session was held in New York in March-April, 1982, and a draft convention on the Law of the Sea and Resolutions 1-IV were adopted on April 30, 1982. A deli-berately ambiguous provision regarding the conservation and fishing of tuna ("highly migratory species") was a result of the conference.[5] Representatives of the U.S. tuna industry, acting as expert advisors to the U.S. delegation, attended all eleven sessions. The negotiations among governments during these sessions may explain why Latin American seizures were much reduced during the period of 1974-1977.

During the period that the UN Committee was preparing for the Third UN Law of the Sea Conference, the U.S. Congress was conducting hearings on how to re- duce or eliminate the presence of large Russian, Japanese, and other foreign fishing fleets harvesting groundfish, coastal pelagic species, and other fish in wa- ters off the coasts of New England and Alaska. The legislative device favored by many key legislators in Congress was to establish a 200-mile fishery manage- ment zone off the coasts of the United States. Numerous Congressional hear- ings conducted throughout the country during the period 1973-1975 reflected the extent of the divide between the nation's coastal and high-seas fisheries.[6]

On April 13, 1976, President Gerald R. Ford signed H.R. 200, accompanied by the following written statement: "The extension of our jurisdiction to 200 miles will enable us to protect and conserve the valuable fisheries off our coasts. It is in- deed unfortunate that the slow pace of the negotiations of the United Nations Law of the Sea Conference has mandated our course of action here today. However, the foreign overfishing off our coasts cannot be allowed to continue without resolution."[7] Congress fashioned the 200-mile bill in a manner that pro- tected the interests of the U.S. tuna industry by declaring that the United States was not asserting exclusive fishery management jurisdiction over the tunas oc- curring off its coasts.[8]

The Yellowfin Tuna Conservation Program of the Inter-American Tropical Tuna Commission

Conservation and management measures on the fishing of yellowfin in the east- ern Pacific Ocean (EPO) were first proposed at a meeting of the Inter-American Tropical Tuna Commission (IATTC) held on September 14, 1961. The scientific staff of the IATTC recommended a yellowfin catch quota for 1962 applicable to all countries on a first-come, first served basis. This recommendation was adopted by the IATTC commissioners following approval by the U.S. Department of State. However, the Tuna Conventions Act of 1950, as amended, requires a condition precedent to the promulgation of domestic regulations to implement recommendations of the IATTC. This condition precedent is an "agreed date" that results from negotiations between the United States and certain other major tuna fishing nations. Negotiations between the United States and these other governments on the "agreed date" were not successful until 1966,[9] which ex- plains why the U. S. tuna fleet was not federally regulated to comply with the yel- lowfin catch quota and the "closed season" measure of the IATTC yellowfin con- servation program until 1967.

Efforts to reach political agreement on matters pertaining to quotas, enforcement, special coastal State allocations, *etc.*, were conducted during intergovernmental meetings held apart from the IATTC sessions. These government-to- government meetings would include representatives of both member and non- member nations concerned with the fishery. At these meetings, attempts were made to reach agreement as to whether to accept the recommendations of the IATTC scientific staff on an overall quota for yellowfin and as to whether special allocations of this quota should be established. The principal point of contention was the issue of special allocations for various coastal states. Many of the nations bordering the EPO wanted to base these allocations on criteria such as coastal adjacency to the resource, level of economic development, *etc.*, whereas some of the other nations were opposed to these criteria for special allocations.[10]

As indication of the difficulties experienced in negotiating with "countries whose vessels engaged in fishing (yellowfin) in the regulatory area on a meaningful scale," ten inter-governmental meetings with considerable industry participation were held during the period of 1971-1974. Why the difficulties? The IATTC yellowfin tuna conservation regime and the trends of negotiations in the United Nations Law of the Sea meetings provided incentives for coastal states, such as Mexico, Ecuador, Peru, Costa Rica, Nicaragua, Honduras, and El Salvador, to make investments in tuna vessels and shoreside tuna facilities. The coastal states' share of fleet fish-carrying capacity jumped from 9% in 1969 to 26% by 1979. More importantly, non-coastal States, including Bermuda, the Congo, Netherlands Antilles, New Zealand, the Republic of Korea, Senegal, Spain, and Venezuela, were also entering the fishery in 1972-1973.[11] In addition, some U.S. citizens had shifted to the ownership and operation of foreign-flag tuna seiners. These "flags of convenience" operations benefited from little or no at-sea enforcement activity, and from special allocations of the yellowfin quota agreed to by the U.S. government at the inter-governmental meetings.

The following explanation of the workings of the IATTC Yellowfin tuna quota system illustrate other concerns that caused problems for participants in the inter-government negotiations during IATTC meetings:

> "... The fishing season in the region starts about January 1 and closes when the IATTC determines that the cumulative catch plus the projected catch of vessels at sea and the quantities of special allocations equal the quota. ... At the close of the season, the U.S. tuna fleet is given generally an average of seven days notice. If a vessel returns to port before the closure date, it is given 30 days to unload its fish and is then eligible for one "free trip" inside the CYRA [Commission's Yellowfin Regulatory Area]. ... When the season is closed, fishing for tuna within the CYRA may continue, but no more than 15 percent of the landed fish can be yellowfin. Vessels then either fish for skipjack tuna within the area or fish outside the CYRA. Those vessels which exceed the 15 percent quota must discard the excess catch. **Of the international fleet within the CYRA only the U.S. observes and enforces the IATTC edict closing the season and the 15 percent rule. Many foreign boats are not equipped to fish west of the CYRA and remain within the area after closing with some evidence of poaching of yellowfin in excess of the 15 percent ceiling.**"[12] (emphasis added)

Commencing in 1973, U.S. tuna fishermen became subject to a second system of NMFS regulations on the fishing of tunas in the EPO, namely the taking of tunas in tuna/porpoise schools. These regulations were promulgated by the Secretary of Commerce, NOAA/NMFS, under the authority of the Marine Mammal Protection Act (MMPA). Under this law, there existed no "condition precedent" to the enforcement of federal regulations applicable to the U.S. tuna purse-seine fishery. Under the Tuna Conventions Act of 1950, as amended, unilateral regulation of the U.S. tuna purse-seine fishery by the U.S. Department of Commerce, NOAA/NMFS, for the purpose of implementing recommendations of the IATTC could not be enforced in the absence of an international agreement. In the opinion of the co-authors, these legislative facts explain why foreign-flag tuna purse seiners operating within the EPO during the 1970s and 1980s could not be regulated by their flag governments in a manner comparable to the federal regulatory regimes imposed on the U.S. flag tuna seiner fleet. In an effort to seek regulatory enforcement fairness, the U.S. tuna industry supported the U.S. Department of Commerce's action in 1973 to halt efforts by some U.S. citizens to avoid yellowfin tuna regulation by operating foreign-flag tuna seiners.[13]

Under Section 111(c) of the MMPA, the Secretary of Commerce and the Secretary of State were "directed to commence negotiations within the Inter-American Tropical Tuna Commission (IATTC) in order to effect essential compliance with the regulatory provisions of this Act so as to reduce, to the maximum extent feasible, the incidental taking of marine mammals by vessels involved in the tuna fishery. The Secretary and the Secretary of State were further directed to request the Director of Investigations of the [IATTC] to make "recommendations to all member nations of the commission as soon as practicable as to the utilization of methods and gear devised under subsection (a) of this section." Reports to Congress by the Secretary of Commerce required by Section 103(f) of the MMPA show that no significant progress was made in negotiations within the IATTC until 1976.[14]

Morris D. Busby, Director, Office of Ocean Affairs, Department of State, testified during oversight hearings conducted by the Subcommittee on Fisheries and Wildlife, Conservation and the Environment of the House Committee on Merchant Marine and Fisheries, on September 30, 1976. In the course of his testimony, he provided an assessment of the efforts by the Secretary of State to comply with the direction of the MMPA to negotiate within the IATTC, as follows:

> "It is fair to say that at the first, the response of the foreign governments to our proposals was not terribly encouraging. However, in the last two years the commission has made available to the United States a 1,000 ton allocation out of the overall IATTC quota for gear research. And, at the 1976 annual meeting, the commission passed a resolution supporting arrangements with the commission by any country which can provide assistance with the tuna/porpoise problem. Thus, we have been able to keep the issue alive among the nations involved, and have done so in a positive way. We believe we have moved toward creating an atmosphere that will allow the affected nations to consider in a serious and thoughtful way, implementation of measures designed to solve this serious problem ..."[15]

During the 33rd Annual Meeting of the IATTC, held in Managua, Nicaragua, on October 11-14, 1976, the commission agreed "that the Commission staff undertake a comprehensive technical review of all existing information pertaining to the tuna-porpoise problem, and prepare a detailed proposal for porpoise research by the commission," that the commission would "convene a special meeting at a time and place to be determined, in order to review the commission's proposal for porpoise research," and permit 1,000 short tons of yellowfin tuna to be taken during the closed season by a vessel or vessels of the United States of America for continued research on the reduction of accidental porpoise mortality."[16] It was also agreed by the commissioners that the IATTC "should strive to maintain a high level of tuna production and also to maintain porpoise stocks at or above levels that assure their survival in perpetuity, with every reasonable effort being made to avoid needless or careless killing of porpoise."[17] While at this meeting of the IATTC, representatives of the tuna industry first learned, to their surprise, that the NMFS had taken action to formally announce a prohibition of fishing on tuna/porpoise schools by the U.S. Fleet. 41 FR 45569 (October 15, 1976).

STATUS OF THE TUNA INDUSTRY: DECEMBER 31, 1976

World Consumption of Canned Tuna Increasing

During the 1970s, consumers in Europe, South America, and parts of Asia were acquiring a taste for canned tuna, resulting in its eventual classification as a world commodity, rather than just a product for U.S. consumers. Commencing in the mid-1960s, the "Fishing World of Tuna" was also learning about the productive power of purse seining for tuna by U.S.-style tuna seiners. By 1976, a crew of 15 to 18 men aboard a U.S "Super" tuna" seiner operating in the EPO had the equipment and skills to annually land over 4,000 tons of brine-frozen tuna. The tuna canners would process this catch into 14 million standard cans of tuna and into byproducts such as pet food, fish oil, and animal feed. Assuming an annual per capita consumption of about 9 standard cans for U.S consumers, the crew of one "Super" tuna seiner was providing enough canned tuna for over 1.5 million fellow citizens.

For California, 1976 was a record year for the landing of tuna and the canning of lightmeat tuna (all species except albacore, which are canned as white meat tuna). This record still stands. In 1976, over 1.4 billion cans, valued at about $854 million, were packed by canneries in California, Hawaii, Oregon, Washington, Puerto Rico, and American Samoa. Landings of the U.S. tuna fleet represented 44.1 percent of this total pack. U.S. residents were consuming half of the world's catch of tuna. The annual per capita consumption of canned fishery products in the United States for 1976 was 4.3 pounds, of which 2.9 pounds was tuna.[18] To meet a growing market demand, major U.S. tuna canneries were operating in Latin America, West Africa, South Pacific Island Nations, and in the U.N. Trust Territory of the Pacific Islands.[19] U. S. tuna seiners were exploring tuna grounds off New Zealand and other islands in the central and western Pacific Ocean.

On May 15, 1976, a new $23 million tuna cannery was dedicated in San Diego, California, by Van Camp Sea Food, a division of Ralston Purina Company. It was recognized then, and until its closure in 1984, as the most modern tuna cannery in existence. The plant housed 640,000 square feet of work space under three roofs or enough working space as eleven football fields. In response to public concerns, fish-smell areas were sealed from the outside by an inverted atmosphere system that prevented air from escaping when the doors were open.

It had an 8,000-ton cold storage room and a thawing area that could daily handle 200 tons of tuna. The 1,900 cannery workers produced an average of 1,200,000 cans of tuna a day. In addition to the cannery, Van Camp Sea Food ("Chicken of the Sea" brand) had a can-manufacturing plant and headquarters in other areas of the city of San Diego.[20]

Changes in the U.S. Tuna Purse-Seine Fleet Operating in the EPO

The U.S. fleet operating within the EPO had changed substantially between June 30, 1972, and December 31, 1976. During this period the number of seiners with not more than 400 short tons of carrying capacity declined from 46 to 28 and the total capacity of those vessels declined from 11,917 to 6,789 tons. During the same period the number of seiners with more than 400 tons of capacity increased from 80 to 113, and the total capacity of those vessels increased from 68,095 short tons to 111,708 short tons.[21]

> "These new, modern, long-range purse seiners, sometimes called "super seiners" cost about $4.5 million dollars to construct, plus another $600,000 for outfitting. **They are built particularly to fish on porpoise.** In the last three years the price of a 1,000 ton plus capacity seiner has increased about $1.2 million ... (p.114) ... Until recently, these large seiners caught approximately 2,000 to 4,000 tons of tuna per year worth $1.2 million ..." (p.115) (emphasis added)

> "There exists on about 104 seiners mortgages, liens, or other encumbrances of nearly $204 million and for 21 purse seiners converted from bait boats this figure is over $9 million for a total of over $215 million, which encumbrances are held by banks and insurance companies. ... (p.117)

> "The total replacement value, which today would probably exceed market value (the former is a more reliable figure) of the entire U.S tuna fleet operating presently in the ETP [eastern tropical Pacific], is approximately $562.5 million. For vessels operating under the ATA [American Tunaboat Association] general permit, the value of such seiners is about $526.5 million." (p.118)[22]

From 1971 to 1975, the frozen tuna-carrying capacity increased by 113 percent for the foreign tuna seiner fleet and 60 percent for the U.S. fleet. "While the actual tonnage increase of the U.S. fleet was greater than the foreign growth, it is estimated that the foreign fleet fishing the ETP increased to around 60,000 short tons carrying capacity during 1976. If this estimate is correct, foreign flag vessels would represent more than 30 percent of the carrying capacity of the vessels fishing in the ETP. Most new vessels built under foreign flag are in the large seiner category capable of fishing porpoise." (p. 118)[23]

These changes in the U.S. tuna seiner fleet occurring during 1971-1976, also involved significant changes in composition of their crews. Tuna captains and crews experienced in both the baitboat and purse-seine tuna fisheries, were being replaced with young, aggressive second-generation fishermen who had little or no tuna baitboat experience. Customarily, these "older" captains moved to shoreside positions as managing owners making the critical decisions in selecting the Captains, Chief Engineers, and key crewmembers. Being a successful tuna captain has always been a young man's game; very few captains remain competitive after about 45 years of age. In addition, more U.S. captains and "key" crewmembers were beginning to accept opportunities to operate foreign-flag seiners based in Latin American countries. To adjust to this rapid change in number and size of tuna seiners, the industry was moderately successful in training new fishermen to operate and maintain the complex deck machinery, engines, and hydraulic, electronic, and refrigeration systems aboard "super seiners." For instance, the operation/maintenance of helicopters aboard "super seiners" was aided greatly by the availability of former military personnel who had operated or maintained aircraft in Vietnam.

There had been a few U.S. vessels based in Puerto Rico since the 1950s, and many members of the crews of these vessels were citizens of various Latin American countries. When a Puerto Rico-based vessel got a full load of fish in the EPO, the crew members of countries other than the United States would leave the vessel in Panama before it transited the Panama Canal on the way to Puerto Rico to unload. These crewmembers would board the vessel when it stopped in Panama after transiting the Canal on the way back to the fishing grounds in the EPO. During the 1970s the numbers of vessels based in Puerto Rico increased, and hence there were more Latin American crew members on U.S. vessels than there had been during the earlier years.

During the 1973-1976 period, a "Joint Venture" between the industry and the NMFS had developed the following ideas to make the "Back-down" and the "Medina Panel Concept" more effective in releasing porpoise alive from the net by creating the following systems: (1) "Double-Depth, Small-Mesh Medina Panel System;" (2) the "Porpoise Apron/Chute" or "Bold Contender System;" and, (3) the "Elizabeth C.J. System" or the "Super Apron System." In the opinion of the ATA, the results of the ELIZABETH C.J. cruise also showed that the "Joint Venture" approach had reached a high level of success and that this was time to place the highest priority on increasing efforts to improve the skills of the captains and crews who needed extra guidance and assistance. It was not the time to give higher priorities to projects designed to unravel the behavioral secrets of the "enigma" or to collect and analyze data about the ocean distribution and biology of porpoise populations throughout the vast area of the EPO. Now, was the time for the government to upscale its participation in the "joint venture" with the fleet by assisting the fishermen to help themselves. This could be done by continuing to work constructively with the fishermen at sea and on shore to use proven gear and methods that would reduce or eliminate porpoise mortality, and by encouraging fishermen to continue being inventive and innovative in using their experiences and skills to save porpoise.[24]

Administrative Law Judge Frank W. Vanderheyden, in his January 1977 Recommended Decision, stated: "Improvements in fishing techniques that reduce porpoise mortality is in reality and in the long run the solution to porpoise mortality."[25] He noted that the data from observer trips had shown "vast improvement over a span of 5 years in mortality to the porpoise ... The 1976 statistics show increases in the average size of porpoise school set on, the percentage of the school captured, and the number captured. ... Compared to 1975, the 1976 kill per set is 25 percent lower, the kill per ton is 31 percent lower, the kill per porpoise captured is 48 percent lower, the percent of sets with zero kill is 31 percent higher, and the percent of captured porpoise that are released has risen to 98.7 percent."[26]

Unfortunately, the "joint venture" died quietly in early 1977, the victim of judicial rulings interpreting the MMPA in mid-1976. Commencing in 1976, the other two branches of the federal government would act in ways that adversely affected the U.S. tuna fleet during 1976-1980. Congress would fail to amend the MMPA. The Department of Commerce (NOAA/NMFS) would promulgate burdensome and punitive regulations, and then, in hearings conducted by the Department's administrative law judges, use the testimony and reports of NMFS observers as evidence in proving violations by captains and vessel owners.

---

[1] The Conference was in session until it was officially announced that candidate Salvador Allende had been elected as the new president of Chile. Co-author Felando recalls seeing the entire delegation of Chile leave their desks and walk out of the meeting, followed shortly thereafter with an announcement that the negotiations were over.

[2] During a 15-year period (1961-1975), the ATA records show that 211 U.S. tuna vessels were seized on the basis of claims of coastal state sovereignty or jurisdiction not recognized by the United States. About $7.9 million was paid by vessel owners to obtain the release of the vessels and crews; the total costs were estimated to be over $11.2 million. For the 111 tuna seiners seized during 1971-1973, the total paid to obtain the release of crews was over $5.3 million; the total costs were over $ 6.1 million. After payment by the vessel owners, claims for recovering the fines were filed under a federal statute to obtain partial recovery of their losses (the amounts paid in fines and other costs paid to the foreign governments to obtain the release of the vessels and crews, but not the costs of lost fishing time).

[3] In 1971, the Committee met twice, from 12-16 March, and 19-27 August. In 1972, the Committee met twice, from 29 February to 23 March, and from 19 July to 15 August. In 1973, the Committee met twice, from 7 March to 5 April, and from 3 July to 17 August. As members of the United States Delegation, representatives of the U.S. tuna fleet and of U.S tuna canners attended all six sessions of the Committee. The work of Subcommittee II was of critical importance to the U.S tuna industry, because it was responsible for "preparing a comprehensive list of subjects and issues relating to the law of the sea, including those concerning the regime of the high seas, the continental shelf, the territorial sea (including the question of its breadth and the question of international straits), and contiguous zone, fishing and conservation of the living resources of the high seas (including the question of the preferential rights of coastal states) and to prepare draft treaty articles thereon."

[4] See: Testimony of Ambassador John R. Stevenson, Legal Advisor of the Department of State on the Law of the Sea, in response to a question by Senator Stevens of Alaska: "... we recognize broad coastal state management jurisdiction, and a preference with respect to both the coastal species and the salmon throughout their migratory range, whereas in the case of the tuna, we favor international management. So we continue to adhere to the three-tier program as you characterize it." Hearing before the Subcommittee on Oceans and Atmosphere of the Committee on Commerce, United States Senate, 92nd Congress, 2nd session on the Law of the Sea, October 3, 1972, (Serial No. 92-79), p.6.

[5] The Draft Convention, "Article 64, Highly migratory species" is comprised of two para-

graphs, as follows:

"1. The coastal State and other States whose nationals fish in the region for the highly migratory species listed in Annex I shall co-operate directly through appropriate international organizations with a view to ensure conservation and promoting the objective of optimum utilization of such species throughout the region, both within and beyond the exclusive economic zone. In regions for which no appropriate international organization exists, the coastal State and other States whose nationals harvest these species in the region shall cooperate to establish such an organization and participate in its work.

"2. The provisions of paragraph 1 apply in addition to the other provisions of this Part."

[6] Nine Congressional Hearings were conducted on this law of the sea issue: **(1)** Hearings before the Subcommittee on Fisheries and Wildlife Conservation and the Environment of the Committee on Merchant Marine and Fisheries House of Representatives, 93rd Congress, 2nd Session on Extending the jurisdiction of the United States beyond the present 12-mile fishery zone, June 11, 1974-Serial No. 93-37; **(2)** Hearings before the Subcommittee on Fisheries and Wildlife Conservation and the Environment of the Committee on Merchant Marine and Fisheries House of Representatives 94th Congress, 1st Session on Extending the jurisdiction of the United States beyond the present 12-mile fishery zone, March 10-14, 18-20, 27, 1975-Serial No. 94-4; **(3)** Hearings before the Subcommittee on Oceans and Atmosphere of the Committee on Commerce United States Senate 93rd Congress 1st Session, on the Interim Fisheries Zone Extension and Management Act of 1973, December 6 and 7, 1973, Part 1-Serial No. 93-51; **(4)** Hearings before the Subcommittee on Oceans and Atmosphere of the Committee on Commerce United States Senate 93rd Congress 2nd[t] Session, on the Interim Fisheries Zone Extension and Management Act of 1973, February 11, 14. March 29-31. April 1, 1974- Part 2-Serial No. 93-54; **(5)** Hearings before the Subcommittee on Oceans and Atmosphere of the Committee on Commerce United States Senate 93rd Congress 2nd[t] Session, on the Interim Fisheries Zone Extension and Management Act of 1973, April 18-20, May 3,13-14; and June 14, 1974- Part 3-Serial No. 93-54; **(6)** Hearing before the Committee on Commerce United States Senate 94th Congress 1st Session on S.961-Emergency Marine Fisheries Protection Act of 1975, June 6, 1975, Part 1-Serial No. 94-27; **(7)** Special Oversight Hearing before the Committee on International Relations House of Representatives 94th Congress 1st Session on H.R. 200-The Marine Fisheries Conservation Act of 1975-September 24, 1975-Hearing held pursuant to Rule X, Clause 3(d) of the Rules of the House of Representatives; **(8)** Hearing before the Subcommittee on Oceans and International Environment of the Committee on Foreign Relations United States Senate 94th Congress 1st Session on S. 961-Two-Hundred Mile Fishing Zone-October 31, 1975, **and (9)** Hearing before the Committee on Armed Services United States Senate 94th Congress 1st Session on 961, Emergency Marine Fisheries Protection Act of 1975-November 19, 1975.

[7] Public Law 94-265, 94th Congress H.R. 200, April 13, 1976, "Fishery Conservation and Management Act of 1976." See: Committee Print: A Legislative History of the Fishery Conservation and Management Act of 1976, For the Use of the Senate Committee on Commerce and the National Ocean Policy Study (October 1976) at p.34. Section 103 of this Act provided: "**The exclusive fishery management authority of the United States shall not include, nor shall it be construed to extend to, highly migratory species of fish.**" Section 3 (14) of the Act states: " **The term 'highly migratory species' means species of tuna which, in the course of their life cycle, spawn and migrate over great distances in waters of the ocean.**" The Act in Section 403 amended the Fishermen's Protective Act (22 U.S.C. 1971-1980) so as to protect the U.S. tuna fleet from seizures by countries that did claim exclusive management authority over tuna. (emphasis added)

[8] In 1990, Congress deleted this provision, causing great economic injury to the U.S. Tuna Purse-Seine fishery operating within the EPO

[9] In 1967, to adjust to the "closed season" measure of the IATTC yellowfin conservation program, a significant number of U.S. tuna seiners commenced fishing for yellowfin and skipjack tunas in the Atlantic Ocean, mainly off West Africa. By the early 1970s, new fishing grounds for skipjack had been discovered off the coast of Angola by U.S. seiners, allowing this seasonal fishery to expand. Unfortunately, the 1973-1974 Middle-East Oil Crisis forced the return of these tuna seiners to their traditional grounds in the EPO. The "oil crisis" increased the existing burdens and risks of developing the fishery off West Africa by creating new economic and political uncertainties. Within a few years, this new South Atlantic tuna fishery for the U.S. tuna seiner fleet disappeared. In addition, disappointing explorations in the Caribbean area and problems in the seasonal bluefin fishery off New England provided little or no incentive for Puerto Rico-based tuna seiners to develop fisheries in these areas. In the western Pacific, in waters off Papua New Guinea, Japanese tuna seiners were beginning to fish successfully. By 1976, some of the U.S. tuna seiners that had fished seasonally in the South Atlantic were sent by two major tuna canners to expand explorations for tuna seining in waters off New Zealand and other South Pacific Island Nations.

The removal of the U.S. tuna seiner fleet from the waters of the South Atlantic provided an opportunity for the development of Spanish and French tuna seiner fleets. With the assistance of major U.S. tuna canners, these fleets expanded their traditional tuna grounds off the coast of West Africa and developed new tuna fishing grounds in the Indian Ocean, particularly about the Seychelles Islands.

[10] During the 1977 through 1979 period, the United States was given a special allocation for U.S. seiners chartered by the U.S. Government for gear research to reduce porpoise mortality. U.S. flag seiners were allowed to catch a total of up to 1,000 tons of yellowfin tuna during the closed season. For details of the complicated history of IATTC special allocations to the tuna fleets of coastal states during the period 1969-1978: See: Bayliff, William H. 2001, Organization, Functions, and Achievements of the Inter-American Tropical Tuna Commission, Inter-Amer. Trop. Tuna Comm. Spec., Rep. 13, pp. 36-37, 58, Table 4

[11] Hearings before the Subcommittee on Fisheries and Wildlife Conservation and the Environment of the Committee on Merchant Marine and Fisheries House of Representatives on Tuna Oversight (May 16, 1973) Serial No. 93-17, (cited hereinafter: " May 1973 House Subcommittee Hearings-SN-93-17"):1-126. See: Documentation at pp. 16-23, 62-66, and pp. 95-99; Affidavits of Tuna Captains, pp. 116-126.

[12] In the Matter of Proposed Regulations to Govern the Taking of Marine Mammals Incidental to Commercial Fishing Operations for the Year 1977. Docket Number MMPAH NO. 2-1976, Frank W. Vanderheyden, ALJ, Recommended Decision, served on NMFS on January 17, 1977, (cited hereinafter: "January 1977 ALJ Decision"):102-103.

[13] May 1973 House Subcommittee Hearings-SN-93-17: 48-49.

[14] For responses by NOAA/NMFS confirming this conclusion: 1975 House Subcommittee Hearings-SN-94-16: 263-264, 272-273.

[15] September 1976 House Subcommittee Hearings-SN-94-45: 382. See also: "U.S. Efforts Regarding International Aspects of the Tuna/Porpoise Problem," a document sub-

mitted by Mr. Busby at the request of the chairman of the House Subcommittee during the hearing on September 30, 1976.384-386.

[16] Annual Report of the IATTC 1976: 8, 12. See also: Report of the Secretary of Commerce Juanita M. Krebs dated June 20, 1977: 42 FR 38982 (August 1, 1977): 39989-38990.

[17] Bayliff, William H. 2001, Organization, Functions, and Achievements of the Inter-American Tropical Tuna Commission, Inter-Amer.Trop.Tuna Comm. Spec. Rep., 13: pp. 18-19, 28.

[18] Sources: M.S. Oliphant, Marine Resources Region, Circular No. 51, State of California, The Resources Agency, Department of Fish and Game, Statistical Report of Fresh, Canned, Cured, and Manufactured Fishery Products for 1976, Table 1, p. 4, Table 7, p.14. Current Fishery Statistics No. 7200, Fisheries of the United States, 1976, April 1977. DOC, NOAA, NMFS, p. 24. Current Fishery Statistics No. 8000, Fisheries of the United States, 1979, April 1980, DOC, NOAA, NMFS, p. 77.

[19] In 1956, Van Camp Seafood Company had facilities in American Samoa, Manta, Ecuador, Tema, Ghana, Palau, U.S. Trust Territories, and Agana, Guam. More detailed data on the value of the U.S. pack of canned tuna, number of workers in tuna canning, and annual payroll for the years 1971-1975, Low and High Ranges: Pack Value: $413 million to $823 million; 9,321 to14,065 workers, and payroll $52 million to $99 million. See: Jerome R. Gulan, Vice-President, Legislative Affairs, National Canners Association, May 1977 House Subcommittee Hearings-SN-95-3: 400-401.

[20] For reasons of economic consolidation, on May 28, 1959, Van Camp Sea Food closed its plants in San Diego after a stay of 33 years. All canning operations were moved to Terminal Island, Los Angeles Harbor. After the Port of Los Angeles was unable to locate a suitable site for a new plant to replace the 60 year old cannery on Terminal Island, the decision was made to re-locate to San Diego.

[21] January 1977 ALJ Decision: 115. At this time, the U.S. Tuna Seiner Fleet was categorized by the NMFS as follows: Class I, vessels with 400 tons or less carrying capacity; Class II, vessels of more than 400 tons capacity constructed before 1961, and Class III, vessels of more than 400 short tons capacity, constructed after 1960.

[22] January 1977 ALJ Decision: 114-118.

[23] January 1977 ALJ Decision: 118. On December 31, 1957, there were 57 vessels of 7,125 tons capacity in the San Pedro Regular Seiner Fleet and 1 Converted Tuna Seiner of 255 tons capacity. By December 31, 1976, the San Pedro Regular Seiner Fleet was reduced to 9 vessels of 1,538 tons capacity. The Converted Seiner fleet would rise to a high of 97 vessels of about 25,000 tons capacity, and then decline by December 31, 1976, to 26 vessels of 9,409 ton capacity. These two segments of the U.S. Tuna Seiner Fleet would virtually disappear as a result of the changes in the tuna fishery of the EPO during 1977-1980.

[24] This approach of working constructively and positively with the captains and crews of non-U.S. flag tuna seiners operating in the eastern Pacific in reducing porpoise mortality was successfully implemented by the IATTC staff during the 1980s.

[25] January 1977 ALJ Decision: 47.

[26] January 1977 ALJ Decision: 29.

"There comes a point when the industry has been flogged enough.
That point has been reached."

Representative John Murphy, State of New York, Chairman, Committee on Merchant Marine and Fisheries, during House floor debate on H.R. 6970, a bill amending the Marine Mammal Protection Act of 1972 (MMPA) on the "tuna-porpoise problem," June 1, 1977, *Congressional Record-House*, page 17164.

PART V

FLOGGING THE TUNA INDUSTRY

20

FAILED 1977 U.S. SENATE MMPA OVERSIGHT HEARING

After completing his written statement before the U.S. Senate Committee on Commerce, Science, and Transportation, held on March 9 and 11, 1977, on the background of the tuna-porpoise problem, Dr. Robert White, Administrator, NOAA, stated: "It appears that we have two options. The first is to proceed with the implementation of our regulations and not seek any amendments to the Act, or seek an amendment to the Act, which would permit a modification of the regulations. The administration is considering these options actively."[1]

At the close of his testimony, Dr. White offered "a drafting service if the members of the committee would indicate to us the kinds of things they would like to have in such amendments." When asked by the Chairman for recommended amendments, Dr. White responded:

> "I would like to comment on the question of amendments. ... the views which I have expressed, except those dealing with the need for increased authorization under the Act, are my personal views. The administration at this point has not taken a position on whether it wants to amend the Act or not, or in what ways it wishes to amend the Act. That is now under consideration, so I have given you my personal views. I have expressed those views before."[2]

The first witness for the tuna industry was Harry Bridges, International President, International Longshoremen's and Warehousemen's Union of the West Coast of America, Alaska (ILWU). He expressed "grave concern" over the "stringent application of the (MMPA) by the courts and the regulatory agencies." He advised the committee to address ways of extending the Act so as to enable the tuna fleet to fish, and urged that "you give this your highest priority so that the tuna boats now in port in San Diego and elsewhere may get to sea again soon, to fish on porpoise, and on mixed species of porpoise ..."[3]

Mr. Bridges was followed by John Royal, Secretary-Treasurer, Fishermen's Union of San Diego and Southern California, affiliated with the ILWU, who, as a former tuna fisherman, gave an eloquent description of the past and current problems faced by his membership and other segments of the tuna industry. Mr. Royal told the Committee: "... you know it is in your hands. The government says to us, Go to the agency involved. Change the regulations. We go to the agency, it says, Well, go to the government, change the law. The court in Washington (D.C.) says, You cannot do this. You go to [court in] California, You can do it ... We are confused and frustrated. Somebody has to tell us what to do ... You have to because we have nobody else to turn to."[4]

Douglas G. Chapman, Chairman of the Marine Mammal Commission, and Carl L. Hubbs, Scripps Institution of Oceanography, La Jolla, California, provided oral and written testimony. Chairman Chapman offered assistance to the committee's staff in resolving the issues raised by NMFS proposed regulations to prohibit the taking of eastern spinners, and that the MMC has not as yet decided whether legislation to amend the MMPA was needed. Dr. Hubbs testified that he did not think that the present populations of porpoise in the Pacific were in danger of extinction, that recent reports of experimental tuna purse-seine fishing operations makes " it clear that netting of a combined schools of tuna and porpoise can be effected with wholly negligible loss of porpoise—by taking advantage of modified nets and newly-derived methods of fishing," and that he was "convinced that the innovative industry can indeed, if given the chance, devise gear and methods that will allow tuna fishing with negligible harm to the porpoise population."[5]

During the second day of the Oversight Hearing, oral and written testimony was given by Pete Wilson, Mayor of San Diego, and written submissions were placed in the record from Tom Bradley, Mayor of Los Angeles, and Baltasar Corrada, Resident Commissioner, Commonwealth of Puerto Rico.

Thereafter, testimony and written submissions were received from a panel composed of a former NMFS observer who made one fishing trip aboard a tuna seiner, and individuals representing a consortium of 23 animal protection and welfare groups, the Animal Welfare Science Institute, the Humane Society of the United States, the Environmental Defense Fund, and the Friends of the Earth. Essentially, this panel argued that the economic problems affecting the tuna industry could be cured without amending the MMPA.

This panel was followed by testimony from representatives of the Committee for Humane Legislation, Inc. (CHL), which advised the committee: "We have been in litigation on this matter since 1974 and it is far from resolved at this time."[6] CHL representatives then provided for the record a copy of legal documents filed to attack the validity of the NMFS final regulations pertaining to the taking of marine mammals in the course of commercial fishing operations.

A panel of tuna captains from San Diego appeared to testify: Andrew Castagnola, Thomas A. Crivello, Manuel Silva, Manuel Vargas, Oliver Virissimo, and Julius Zolezzi. They explained how the four-month prohibition on the fishing of tuna/porpoise schools, along with implementation of the enforcement orders of the

U.S. Court of Appeals for the District of Columbia had caused severe economic impacts on their operations. The members of the panel chose Captain Manuel Silva to make the initial presentation to the committee, who stated:

"Our fishing fleet cannot survive the recent (NMFS final regulations) ... We must be allowed to fish, to set on tuna in association with the eastern spinner and whitebelly spinner ... The agency totally ignored an administrative law judge ... recommendation [on mortality quotas, optimum sustainable population, and take of eastern spinners]. He had a 3-week hearing, 60 people testified, 90 exhibits, 3,400 pages of transcript, several months of deliberation ... Our desires are a realistic quota in line with the [administrative law judge's] recommendation and an allowable take of porpoise at the lowest practical level and eliminate the confusing issue of zero. Eliminate the permit proceedings. As it stands, though, we can fish only if the Secretary of Commerce wants us to. We welcome constructive presence and scientific and gear research ..." [7]

During the remainder of the hearing, the committee heard from other groups, including a panel composed of union leaders representing the Executive Board, Maritime Trades Department, AFL-CIO, Steve Edney, President, United Cannery & Industrial Workers of the Pacific, Affiliated with the Seafarers International Union of North America, AFL-CIO; Jack Tarantino, President, Tuna Fishermen of North America, Affiliated with the Seafarers International Union of North America, AFL-CIO, and seven women cannery workers.

Steve Edney, who first started working in the California tuna canning industry in 1945, testified that his union had a membership of 9,000 cannery workers employed in plants in the United States, Puerto Rico, and American Samoa, and that the need to amend the MMPA and the NMFS regulations "sensibly" was the "most critical issue facing our industry ..." He noted that some argue that the threat of tuna vessels going foreign "is just crying wolf. **That is not true. I think there is a real danger of going foreign-flag. There is a bigger danger. Multinational corporations exporting the tuna industry to other countries."** [8] (emphasis added) He concluded by expressing the hope to the committee that "I have conveyed to you in short time the urgency of this problem ...." Jack Tarantino expressed the concern that his membership would lose their jobs, medical insurance coverage, and pensions, should the tuna fleet go foreign.

In his written submission to the Senate Committee, Baltarsar Corrada, Resident Commissioner, Commonwealth of Puerto Rico, provided economic data on how NMFS regulatory inaction and its restrictive 1977 regulations adversely impacted the island's five tuna canners and its fleet of U.S. tuna seiners:

"... [employment in the five tuna canning plants] represents 5% of all manufacturing employment in Ponce and Mayaguez, the second and third largest cities in Puerto Rico.

"I have been informed that of the (48) vessels registered in Puerto Rico, 32 have returned to various ports with 16,210 tons of fish representing only 42% of their 38,055 ton carrying capacity because they insist they cannot fish economically under the 1977 regulation prohibiting sets on mixed porpoise schools containing eastern spinners. I am told that fourteen vessels are still at sea but have caught only 40% of their 14,950 ton capacity based on each vessel catching a daily average of 13.25 tons. ... I am also informed that the loss from the 32 vessels not fishing is 424 tons of tuna per day worth $275,000 and 12,700 tons per month worth $8,268,000 or $258,375 per vessel. To the estimated 833 crewmembers, their families and communities the loss in pay is about $30,000 per day, $902,000 per month, and $10,839,000 per year.

"The monthly loss of 12,720 tons represents a loss of 585,120 cases of canned tuna worth $14,628,000 and a loss of $6,368,000 in value added by canning. If the Puerto Rico plants were forced to close, the loss in payroll alone would be $2,833,000 per month or $665,380 per week plus unemployment compensation and welfare payments."[9]

Seven of eight women cannery workers, presented short, but informative, oral statements that included expressions of concerns about losing their jobs and health and pension benefits. A panel, composed of six tuna fishermen's wives and a tuna fisherman's daughter, also provided short oral statements.[10] The testimonies of these fourteen women were particularly powerful, dramatic, and concise. Senator Daniel Inouye, Hawaii, advised the women:

"You have done very well ... your statements have been most helpful ... I have only one regret. I am certain all of you realize I do not constitute the committee. In fact, I am not the chairman of the committee. I would like to read the names of the Senators who have not been able to be with us, so you can convey your message to them because the decision has to be made not by me alone, but also by many others. I regret they were not here to listen to all of the statements today and two days ago ..."[11]

In a submission to the Senate Committee after the Hearing, Thomas A. Crivello, a member of the Tuna Captain Panel that appeared before the Senate Committee but who did not orally testify, wrote:

"The prohibition of fishing mixed schools of porpoise might as well be a prohibition to fishing porpoise period because 80-90% of the porpoise I have seen thru [sic] my life as a tuna fisherman have been mixed schools of porpoise." He then noted the civil and criminal penalties provided in the MMPA, including "confiscation of all fish aboard the vessel, $25,000 fine for the master of the vessel and a possible two year sentence in a federal penitentiary and all of this to be inflicted on persons trying to earn a living."

"My fellow fishermen and I will not be subject to such injustices. Our boats will not leave port and run the risk of the economical pressures of breaking this law. In effect, if we are going to go broke, we are going to do it at home."[12]

On April 15, 1977, a general permit was issued to the ATA, and made available for public inspection by the NMFS.[13]

---

[1] Hearings before the Committee on Commerce, Science, and Transportation, U.S. Senate, 95th Congress, 1st Session on Oversight into the Marine Mammal Protection Act, March 9 and 11, 1977, (Serial No. 95-12). (cited herein, "1977 Senate Committee Hearings-SN-95-12"): p. 5. Also read pp. 2-18, To view previously-expressed views of Dr. White: Sep 1976 House Subcommittee Hearings-SN-94-45: 207-211.

[2] 1977 Senate Committee Hearing-SN-95-12:19.

[3] 1977 Senate Committee Hearing-SN-95-12: 90-91.

[4] 1977 Senate Committee Hearing-SN-95-12: 95.

[5] 1977 Senate Committee Hearing-SN-95-12: 117.

[6] 1977 Senate Committee Hearing-SN-95-12: 197.

[7] 1977 Senate Committee Hearing-SN-95-12: 212.

[8] 1977 Senate Committee Hearing-SN-95-12: 219.

[9] 1977 Senate Committee Hearing-SN-95-12: 132.

[10] See: *Congressional Record—House*, pp. H 4693-4694, May 18, 1977, remarks of Representative Lionel Van Deerlin, San Diego, California, entitled, "Environmentalist Casts Unwarranted Slur." He said that an article of the *Washington Post*, printed on May 18, 1977, reported on the "ugly side of the environmental lobby." This article quoted an evaluation by a representative of the Defenders of Wildlife on the Congressional lobbying effort of the eight California women tuna cannery workers and seven tuna fishermen's wives during March1977. The quote confirmed as "essentially correct" by the representative of the Defenders of Wildlife: "They came across like upper middle income hussies with their spangled jewelry—not like poor fishermen's wives." The Record of the Hearing lists the following panel of women cannery workers: Beatrice Aviño, Mrs. Baquino, Mrs. Belstay, Ella Mae Fair, Tami Malicary, Raquel Moreno, Margie Richardson, and Christine Shaw. The Record of the Hearing lists the following panel of fishermen's wives that testified: Mrs. Dela Balelo, Mrs. Brenha, Mrs. Phil Gavin, Mrs. Nino La Coco, Mrs. Mary Alice Rosa Gonsalves, Mrs. Carolyn Medina (Spokesperson), and Mrs. Roland Virissimo.

The panel of fishermen's wives included officers of the Women's Organization for the Tuna Industry (WOTI): Mrs Carolyn Medina, President, and Mary Alice Rosa Gonsalves, First Vice President. Other WOTI officers: Jeanette Finete, Second Vice President, Eva Archuleto, Recording Secretary, Donna Shanski, Corresponding Secretary, and Tina De Falco Johnson, Treasurer.

[11] 1977 Senate Committee Hearing-SN-95-12: 228.

[12] 1977 Senate Committee Hearing-SN-95-12: 281-282.

[13] Notice of General Permit Issuance: 42 FR 20484 (April 20, 1977).

21

FAILED 1977 HOUSE AMENDMENT OF THE MMPA

The House Merchant Marine and Fisheries Committee conducted Marine Mammal Protection Act (MMPA) legislative hearings on May 13 and 16, 1977, followed by a lengthy House floor debate and then passage of H.R. 6970, as amended on June 1, 1977.[1]

The following are excerpts from the opening remarks of the Chairman of the Committee, John M. Murphy, New York, as he addressed members of the committee:

> "Today ... begins consideration of a variety of proposals to resolve the tuna-porpoise controversy. ... The U.S. tuna fleet has been tied to the dock for months.[2] Thousands of cannery workers in California and Puerto Rico have been thrown out of work. It is these innocent, hardworking individuals who have suffered most in this crisis, and who can least afford to wait several months—perhaps longer—for the industry and the environmental community to reach a compromise. ...

> "The Subcommittee on Fisheries, Wildlife Conservation and the Environment has held 9 days of hearings on this issue in the last 2 years, without resolution. For months now, I have been told that the administration would have a bill on this issue. To date, no bill has been forthcoming.[3] The Senate Commerce Committee sponsored extensive negotiations between industry and environmentalists—again without success. Senator Cranston has conducted personal negotiations, and still there has been no compromise. Senator Inouye and Senator Hayakawa have held hearings, with still no promise of a solution. In light of this background, I decided to introduce legislation and hold hearings so that we can provide for the continued conservation of marine mammals, get the fleet back to sea, and cannery workers out of the unemployment lines.

> "I personally flew to San Diego this past week (May 9) to make an assessment of the situation. I spoke to every facet of the tuna industry—boat owners, captains, crewman [sic.], yard workers, canners, cannery employees, and a whole host of people related to the industry.

> "I saw people who have not had a paycheck since October 1976.

> "I saw an entire fleet of vessels tied up to the docks, empty.

> "And, I inspected two canneries that were also empty. ...

> "The long-term solution to this problem is not possible in 1977. ... There is a short-term solution which I believe is represented in my bill, H.R. 6970. ..." (pp. 1-2)

During the first day of the hearing, a member of the committee asked the Chairman about his visit to San Diego on May 9, 1977, and of his evaluation of the relationship between management and employees. Chairman Murphy answered:

> "The last group to vote to go out was the seamen. They did not want to go out, have

a set and have an observer find an eastern spinner in the catch and have the catch forfeited. It would be just more of an exercise in frustration. It was the last and hardest group that the industry had to manage in order to go out to set." (p. 101)

The NMFS published an "Enforcement Policy" regarding the fishing of tuna/porpoise schools by tuna seiners: 42 FR 22575 (May 4, 1977). The statement of enforcement policy stated that if at the time the net skiff is released, no eastern spinners are sighted the fact that eastern spinners were later found to have been encircled or dead "will not be the cause for issuance of a notice of violation or assessment of penalty ..."

The need for this change was first stimulated by the immediate refusal of numerous crews of San Diego-based tuna seiners to go to sea when they heard that the NMFS was persisting in not recognizing the difficulty of identifying the different species and stocks, and the problems of having observers deciding identification.[4] This resistance to the position taken by the NMFS on the encirclement of mixed schools was at times violent on the San Diego waterfront. Crews aboard tuna seiners at the dock were told that if they did not leave the vessels and participate in the boycott, they would be attacked physically.

The NMFS, in explaining this change of policy, noted that both the Marine Mammal Commission and the Environmental Defense Fund had proposed an accidental take of up to 6500 eastern spinners—a level that would permit the stock to increase with virtual certainty. Further, at the administrative law judge hearings, "it was established that there are circumstances where an unintentional and accidental mortality would occur. Moreover, there is evidence that once a set involving porpoise has begun, aborting the set is extremely difficult, if not impossible, and that there may be more harm done to porpoises by attempting to abort the set than by continuing it."[5] This change of policy was helpful in having union leaders, tuna captains, and others convince the tuna fishermen to stop their resistance and go fishing. The appearance and statements made to them by the Chairman of the House Committee on Merchant Marine and Fisheries, Congressman John M. Murphy, on May 9, 1977, were also very persuasive in getting the fleet out to sea.

A number of San Diego tuna seiners left port for the fishing grounds on May 13, 1977. Within a week, many tuna seiners departed port. Captains and fishermen were convinced by the statements of Congressman Murphy and others that Congress was going to quickly enact legislation to solve the eastern spinner prohibition and other problems caused by the recent court interpretations of the MMPA and by the 1977 NMFS regulations. This visit by Congressman Murphy to San Diego and the action by him as Chairman of the Committee on Merchant Marine and Fisheries to immediately conduct hearings on legislation to amend the MMPA to resolve the tuna/porpoise controversy were strongly opposed by the editors of the New York Times and other members of the media.[6]

On May 20, 1977, a report, together with separate and dissenting views to accompany H.R. 6970, as amended, was submitted to the Committee of the Whole House on the State of the Union and ordered to be printed.[7] In preparation for the debate on the floor, many remarks were published in the *Congressional Record* about the need to amend the MMPA to resolve the tuna/porpoise controversy.[8]

Nine California congressmen were involved in the House Floor debate of H.R. 6970.[9] Rep. Bob Wilson, representing a district in the city of San Diego very much involved in the tuna industry, advised his fellow members:

"The argument has been made that this is a fishermen's strike, they have purposely imposed the economic hardship on themselves to force the Congress to bend the law to their advantage. Nothing could be further from the truth. The fact of the matter is that, in addition to the legal confusion of last year, they were forbidden to fish at all this year until mid-April, when the National Marine Fisheries Service issued its fishing permit for 1977. Prior to that time, no permit, no fishing. Then, when the permit was finally issued, the regulations it contained made conditions so restrictive that not only did fishing become uneconomic, but that disobedience to the regulations—even though accidental—was punishable by criminal penalties and jail sentences. Therefore, to avoid these penalties, not to mention incurring extra expenses by going to sea when the prospect of even a break-even trip was small, the fishing boats remained in port.

"What the situation boils down to is this: From the conflicting court orders of last year, the withholding of the permit by the government and the excessive regulations that accompanied it when it was ultimately issued, most of our fishermen have not drawn a paycheck in something like seven months.

"This enforced killing of our tuna fleet has resulted in a ripple effect that has, is, and will continue to be felt for months to come. Of course, the first to feel the crunch were the fishermen themselves. Next came the cannery workers, for without fish to can, plants were forced to shut down and employees either laid off or placed on shortened work weeks.

"This effect is spreading throughout all of the business whether closely or peripherally associated with the tuna fishing industry—the contractors, investors, shipbuilders, warehousemen, engineers, scientists, net weavers, soybean oil suppliers, steel and paper workers, wholesalers, retailers—workers across our entire nation. The final ripple will hit the already suffering consumer ..."[10]

The Resident Commissioner of the Commonwealth of Puerto Rico, Baltasar Corrada, made the following remarks during the debate in support of H.R. 6970:

"The importance of tuna fishing to the area I represent is tremendous. In Puerto Rico, the tuna industry directly employs 6,630 canning workers, with an annual payroll of $34.6 million. Another 12,800 workers are indirectly employed. The reports from individual tuna canning plants in Puerto Rico are frightening. In Ponce, the National Packing Co. has laid off 2,000 of its employees. In Mayaguez, Starkist has laid off 250 workers and the remaining 1,000 workers have been employed on a reduced work-day basis in the month of May. I have been informed that the Neptune Packing Co. had sufficient supplies to employ its 500-person workforce for only one more week, after which 75 percent of the workers would be laid off. Bumble Bee, another tuna plant in Puerto Rico, has sufficient supplies to keep less than 400 of its 1,346 employees at work in the coming months. The combined layoffs and reduced working hours represent a 47 percent reduction in tuna industry employment in Puerto Rico.

"... For mainland United States, the closing of Puerto Rico's tuna plants would mean [a loss of] 41 percent of the entire U.S. production, with a value of $226 million. Such a decrease in supply will result in sharply increased prices for consumers.

"... I have just described the impact of the overly restrictive 1977 regulations on Puerto Rico, similar impacts will be felt up and down the west coast of the United States."[11]

Captain Julius Zolezzi and the JEANNINE
Photo courtesy of Captain Julius Zolezzi
Vessel built by J.M. Martinac Shipbuilding Corporation, Tacoma, Washington

While in Washington, D.C., during May 1977, co-author Felando was told by the Office of Congressman Murphy that the Congressman wanted to go aboard a tuna seiner and view its fishing of tuna/porpoise schools. Felando was asked to make the arrangements for the Congressman and his aide. He called his assistant in San Diego, Michael Zolezzi, and asked him to make a radio call to the tuna seiner JEANNINE and ask his brother, Julius, Captain and Managing Owner of the vessel, if he would be willing to take aboard Congressman Murphy and his assistant. Michael called back and said that Julius gave the okay. The Office of Congressman Murphy was informed of the decision by Captain Julius Zolezzi, and arrangements were made by that office to connect with the vessel in the Mexican port city of Acapulco. Later, Captain Zolezzi informed me that the total time from departure to return to Acapulco was four days, that the water temperature on the fishing grounds was about 81°F, and that the Congressman wanted to swim outside the net, as well as inside the net. Captain Zolezzi stated further that he instructed Congressman Murphy not to swim outside the net because of dangers from sharks, explaining: "I want to return you to Washington, D.C., alive!" Captain Zolezzi explained to the Congressman that the fishermen had discovered that sharks are not aggressive inside the net, but very aggressive and dangerous outside the net. To provide him with some protection, Congressman Murphy was given a protective jacket for swimming and mingling with the tunas and porpoises.

On the fourth and final day of the trip, Congressman Murphy asked Captain Zolezzi for permission to have a private meeting with his crew in the galley. Afterward, Congressman Murphy told Captain Zolezzi that he was surprised to learn that 90 percent of the crew had served in the U.S. armed services. To our knowledge,

Congressman Murphy is the only member of Congress to board a U.S.-flag tuna seiner and observe the fishing of tuna/porpoise schools, let alone swim within a tuna purse seine to watch the movements of tuna and porpoise.

During the House floor debate of June 1, 1977, Congressman Murphy made references to his trip aboard the JEANNINE:

> "We have heard so much about physical injury of dolphin. I observed two settings on dolphins, of 1,000 in one instance, and of 1,500 dolphin [sic.] in the second instance. In neither instance was there any serious injury. There were two drownings [sic.][12] in just one of the sets. So in the setting on 2,500 animals, there were two kills, both of which resulted from drownings [sic.]. In my conversations with the captains in this fleet, I was told the serious injury factor is virtually a fraction of a percent."[13]

> "I did not give up the Memorial Day weekend to go away from my district for no reason. One of the interesting statistics of the American tuna fleet is the very high number of American veterans who are skippers, ex-Navy men who have fought in World War II, the Korean war, and in Vietnam. On the vessel I was on, there were three ocean masters as part of the crew. Most of the crew were veterans, with the exception of the young men. The fact that I was associating with veterans on a Memorial Day weekend in a fact-finding expedition is proof of the fact that the veracity of those men cannot be questioned."[14]

H.R. 6970, as amended in Committee, passed the House with floor amendments on June 1, 1977.[15] On May 18, 1977, Senator Hayakawa introduced Senate Bill 1552 to amend the MMPA, a bill identical to Congressman Murphy's original H.R. 6970.[16] Since no action was taken by the U.S. Senate on S.1552 and H.R. 6970, as amended, Congress did not amend the MMPA during the remainder of the 95th Congress.

---

[1] During 1977, the Committee on Merchant Marine and Fisheries, House of Representatives, held one hearing on legislation to amend the MMPA, and one hearing on tuna/porpoise oversight: Hearings before the Committee on Merchant Marine and Fisheries, House of Representatives, 95th Congress, First Session on Reducing Porpoise Mortality H.R. 6146, H.R. 6409, H.R. 6729, H.R. 6807, H.R. 6907, H.R. 6928, and H.R. 6970. These bills amend the MMPA of 1972 with respect to the taking of marine mammals incidental to the course of commercial fishing operations, May 13 and 16, 1977. Tuna-Porpoise Oversight, August 1, 1977. (Serial No. 95-3). (cited hereinafter, "May 1977 House Committee Hearings-SN-95-3)

[2] Comments by Congressmen following the hearing about the serious problems of the tuna industry: **Rep. Glenn M. Anderson, California**, "Tuna-Porpoise Solution Sought," *Congressional Record—Extensions of Remarks*, E **--n/a--**, March 16, 1977; **Rep. Bob Wilson, California**, "Government Regulations Are Strangling the Tuna Industry," *Congressional Record—House*, pp. H 2584-2585, March 24, 1977; **Rep. Bob Wilson, California**, " Tuna Industry," *Congressional Record—Extension of Remarks*, E 1936, March 30, 1977.; **Rep. Paul N. McClosky, California**, "Tuna and Porpoise Controversy," *Congressional Record—Extension of Remarks*, E 2170-2171, April 7, 1977; **Rep. Daniel K. Akaka, Hawaii**, "Porpoises and Tuna Fish," *Congressional Record—Extensions of Remarks*, E 2162, April 7, 1977; **Rep. Glenn M. Anderson, California**, "Tuna-Porpoise

Controversy Causing Loss of Jobs," *Congressional Record—Extension of Remarks*, E 2226, April 18, 1977. **Rep. Clair W. Burgener, California**, "U.S. Tuna Industry Shut Down," *Congressional Record—Extensions of Remarks*, E -- n/a--, April 18, 1977. Legislation to amend the MMPA was introduced by **Rep. Bob Wilson, California**, "Legislation Offered to Resolve Tuna-Porpoise Dispute," *Congressional Record—Extensions of Remarks*, E 2762, May 4, 1977, and by **Rep. Lionel Van Deerlin, California**, "Legislation Offered to Resolve Tuna-Porpoise Dispute," *Congressional Record—House*, H 4032, May 4, 1977. See: **Rep. John M. Murphy, New York**, "Purpose and Need for a Bill to Amend the [MMPA] with Respect to the Taking of Marine Mammals Incidental to the Course of Commercial Fishing Operations," *Congressional Record—Extensions of Remarks*, pp. E 2806-2807, May 5, 1977.

[3] The Administration submitted its proposal to amend the MMPA to the Committee on May 16, 1977.

[4] This matter was discussed during the administrative law judge (ALJ) Hearings conducted in San Diego. The ALJ recommended that an unintentional incidental take to be permitted only in mixed schools of eastern spinners until the quota is met. The NMFS rejected this recommendation, explaining that enforcement guidelines would be developed for accidental taking. See: Mar 1977 House Subcommittee Hearings-95-8: 23.

[5] The NMFS published regulatory changes: 42 FR 41128 (August 15, 1977). The quota on the take of spinner porpoise (whitebelly) for 1977 was increased to 2,120,000 taken, 1,403,000 encircled, and 11,219 killed. Also, the rule granting limited time extensions for installation of fine mesh webbing was finalized. This interim rule on the fine-mesh extension problem was published on May 16, 1977 (42 FR 24742).

[6] See two remarks of **Rep. Edward I. Koch, New York**, "Slaughtering Porpoises Is Not Defensible," *Congressional Record—House*, H 4432-4433, May 13, 1977; "More on Porpoise." *Congressional Record—Extensions of Remarks*, E 5080-5081, August 3, 1977.

[7] MMPA Amendments, Report together with Separate and Dissenting Views," to accompany H.R. 6970, May 20, 1977, 95th Congress, First Session, Report No. 95-355 (54 pages)

[8] **Representative Bob Wilson, California**, "Tuna/Porpoise Controversy" inserting a reply by **Rep. John M. Murphy** to an editorial in the Washington Post, *Congressional Record—Extensions of Remarks*, p. E 3262-3263, May 26, 1977; **Rep. Helen S. Meyer, New Jersey**, "The Great Tuna-Porpoise War," Congressional Record—Extension of Remarks, p. E 3344, May 26, 1977. **Rep. Stewart B. McKinney, Connecticut**, "Et Tu Thunnus?" *Congressional Record—Extensions of Remarks*, E 3375, May 26, 1977. **Rep. Paul N. McClosky, Jr., California**, "Dissenting Views on H.R. 6970," Congressional Record—Extensions of Remarks," pp. E 3191-3193, May 23, 1977. **Rep. Tim Lee Carter, Kentucky**, "Save the Porpoises," *Congressional Record—Extensions of Remarks*," p. E 3012, May 15, 1977.

[9] There were 27 Congressmen and the Resident Commissioner of Puerto Rico who are recorded as participants in the debate by the *Congressional Record*. The three amendments proposed by **Congressman McCloskey of California** and the one by **Congressman Joel Pritchard of Washington** faced opposition in the debate by the eight California members (**Glenn M. Anderson, Clair Burgener, Barry M. Goldwater, Jr., Robert L. Leggett, John H, Rousselot, Lionel Van Deerlin, Bob Wilson, and Charles H. Wilson**).

[10] *Congressional Record-House*, June 1, 1977, p. 17151.

[11] Congressional Record-House, June 1, 1977, p. 17147.

[12] It is a common misconception that porpoise can drown if not permitted to breathe for an extended period, but actually they suffocate, rather than drown. The difference is that when an animal drowns its lungs fill with water, whereas when a porpoise suffocates no water enters its lungs.

[13] *Congressional Record-House*, June 1, 1977, p. 17144. Congressman Murphy made additional comments about his experience aboard the tuna seiner JEANNINE on this point during an oversight hearing on Tuna/Porpoise held on August 1, 1977. After a NMFS scientists (Dr. William Fox) responded to Chairman Murphy's question about whether the porpoise that die in the net are healthy or ill, by saying that a current study may provide information, Chairman Murphy stated: "Well, the reason I asked that question is that the crewmen seem to have the opinion that the dolphin stocks were pretty healthy animals, and that many of the animals, not all of them, that became casualties in the nets were not healthy, but were old and/or diseased animals." May 1977 House Committee Hearings-SN-95-3: 459. Chairman Murphy also reported: "In each of the sets I have observed, there were billows in the net. The dolphin—of course, you notice their high IQ, as one of my colleagues noted before the debate, still did not know that they should dive to get out of it. That could be difficult to do with marine life around them and with the currents and bad weather that could affect those billows. And that is a difficult problem, I think, with the net experimentation. ... There was a speedboat at the end of the net during the "Back-down," trying to keep it back and open and—of course, to pull animals out, but that still did not prevent the billow from developing." May 1977 House Committee Hearings-SN-95-3: 457

[14] *Congressional Record-House*, June 1, 1977, p. 17160. This remark was prompted by a question posed by **Rep. Bob Wilson of San Diego, California:** "Does the gentleman think that all the tuna skippers are liars, untrustworthy individuals who just completely lie on every occasion?" This exchange in turn was prompted by an earlier question posed by **Rep. McCloskey, of California**, to **Rep. Leggett, of California**, and recorded who noted that a provision in HR. 6970 required a temporary 100-percent observer program, on page 17157, as follows: "**Mr. McCloskey**: Is that not because we cannot believe the tuna skippers? **Mr. Leggett**: The gentleman knows very well that we have no way of verifying their figures. A 100-percent observer program, would help in that regard. **Mr. Murphy**: I would like to speak to a point that I do not think is relevant in the debate, and that is the veracity of the count and numbers about which we are speaking. We all know that we are in a numbers game, but the tuna skippers are under surveillance. They do maintain with the U.S. Coast Guard their exact positions. They have been forced to give away most of their trade secrets from the records that are carefully examined by the (NMFS). I feel that the records that I have examined are correct and that they are viable. Also, the limited observers that have been out confirm the veracity of the tuna captains. I think it is a disservice to them and to the industry to imply that there is impropriety in their normal reporting procedures."

"**Bob Wilson, of San Diego, California,** I commend the chairman of this committee, the gentleman from New York ... He does not have any tuna fishing around Staten Island. Instead he took the time to go out to San Diego. ... He did so in order to try to understand this problem, and to really find out the truth about it. That is because we are getting so many conflicting arguments. Not only that, as he told us, the gentleman just returned from actually going out on a fishing boat and watching them set a net on porpoises and to see the remarkable techniques they are using. I commend the gentleman from New York for doing that. I believe there are very few chairman [sic.] in the history of this Congress who have gone as far as he has to try to observe and understand the problem before this committee. ..." *Congressional Record*, June 1, 1977, p. 17158.

[15] Statement urging opposition to H.R. 6970, **Rep. Abner J. Mikva, of Illinois**, "H.R. 6970", *Congressional Record—Extensions of Remarks*, E 3469, June 2, 1977; Statement in Support: **Rep. Benjamin A. Gilman, of New York**, *Congressional Record— Extensions of Remarks*, p. E 3589, June 8, 1977; **Rep. Don Bonker, of Washington,** "Explanation of Bonker Amendment on Porpoise Issue," *Congressional Record— Extension of Remarks*, p. E 3624, June 8, 1977. See: Elizabeth Wehr, "House Passes Bill To Ease Tuna-Dolphin Controversy." *Congressional Quarterly Weekly Report*, Vol. XXXV, No. 23, June 4, 1977, pp. 1101-1102.

[16] *Congressional Record—Senate*, May 18, 1977, p. S 7842,

22

WHY CONGRESS AND NOAA SOUGHT AMENDMENT TO THE MMPA IN 1977

Judicial Decisions of 1976

On August 6, 1976, the U.S. Court of Appeals for the District of Columbia Circuit affirmed the judgment of the U.S. District Court[1] that the National Marine Fisheries Service (NMFS) should not have issued a general permit authorized by the Marine Mammal Protection Act (MMPA) to the American Tunaboat Association (ATA) because it "was not issued in compliance with the requirements of the Act." The Court noted that its stay of the District Court Order was granted effective June 1, 1976, and explained that this action was taken:

> "... in the belief that compliance with the Act could be effected **within a short time and invalidation of the American Tunaboat Association's general permit thereby averted.**" (emphasis added)

The Court noted that the request by the NMFS for a stay of the Court Order

> "**was founded in part on the assertion that if ongoing research being conducted with the tuna fleet were permitted to continue, figures could be obtained by autumn of this year. The court is now informed that '[I]t will take three to seven years for a scientifically valid figure' ... We cannot, however, approve the suggestion of NMFS that it might not be in compliance with the Act as much as a decade after enactment** ... The court is aware, however, that the immediate impact of this decision would be disastrous to commercial fishermen operating under the general permit.[2] In further consideration of the efforts by the government to achieve good faith compliance with the requirements of the Act, and of the need to conduct ongoing gear studies throughout the entire fishing season, we find it appropriate to continue our stay of the District Court order until January 1, 1977." (emphasis added)

In the "Argument" part of the decision of the U.S. Court of Appeals for the District of Columbia Circuit ("Circuit Court"), agreement was declared "with the District Court's conclusion that the Act was to be administered for the benefit of the protected species rather than for the benefit of commercial exploitation." The Circuit Court also stated: "It is clear that Congress did not intend that the [MMPA] would force American fishermen to cease operations; the Act does not prohibit purse-seine fishing on porpoise. It is equally clear, however, that Congress intended that the requirements of the Act be complied with."[3]

In examining the requirements that the MMPA imposes upon the Secretary of Commerce when he determines the need to regulate the taking of marine mammals, the Circuit Court noted that the "Act was deliberately designed to permit takings of marine mammals when it was **known** that that taking would not be to the disadvantage of the species ..." The Circuit Court found that such knowledge was not evidenced by the Secretary, finding (emphasis added):

> "In promulgating the instant regulations in both 1974[4] and 1975[5], the NMFS did not fulfill the requirement that it determine the impact of the takings on the optimum sustainable populations of the species of porpoise involved. **The statement that "[t]here is no evidence that the porpoise populations would substantially increase or decrease as a result of the regulations and re-issuance of the general permit' is not at all responsive**; the fact that actual stocks may be stable may supply little or nothing to the determination of effect on optimum sustainable populations. We therefore affirm the judgment of the District Court on this issue." (emphasis added)

Government Agency (NOAA/NMFS) Reactions

The Circuit Court's finding on the failure of the NMFS to show evidence of knowledge that the taking would not adversely impact "optimum sustainable populations" dramatically changed the administration of the MMPA by the Secretary of Commerce, National Oceanic Atmospheric Administration (NOAA), and NMFS. The immediate reaction by NOAA/NMFS to this finding was to invite 12 experts in population analysis to conduct a workshop on porpoise stock assessment. This "OSP [optimum sustainable population] Workshop" was held at the SWFC-NMFS, La Jolla, California, during July 27-31, 1976.[6] Dr. William W. Fox, Jr., Chief, Oceanic Resources Division, SWFC-NMFS, provided a written statement and testimony on the report of the workshop, which produced "estimates of existing porpoise population levels, optimum sustainable population (OSP) levels, and the impact of incidental taking on those levels for each and every species or population stock of small cetaceans involved in the U.S. yellowfin tuna purse seine fishery."[7]

> Thereafter, the agency made its determinations based upon its analysis of the report of the OSP Workshop and outlined its course of action with respect to the regulation of the U.S. tuna purse-seine fishery. This was first announced publicly by Dr. Robert M. White, Administrator, NOAA, on September 29, 1976, in his testimony before the House Subcommittee on Fisheries and Wildlife Conservation and the Environment.[8] The following are excerpts of this testimony:

> "What I would like to do is describe the difficult situation in which we find ourselves (p. 208).

> "Our assessment of the status of porpoise stocks ... is based on the advice of scientists ... There is no doubt that we have sought the best advice possible, but it should be kept in mind that even with all this available expertise, we are still acting on what in many cases can be described only as informed approximations. (p. 209)

> "In attempting to meet the court's requirements and to develop and refine population and (OSP) estimates, we organized a workshop of internationally renowned senior scientists in July of this year; to make these determinations using the best information available ... Unfortunately, the report of the scientists introduces a new and even more serious problem. Under the Act, if a species is depleted except for scientific research, no fishing for or incidental taking of that species is allowed. A species becomes depleted when, as a practical matter, it falls below optimum sustainable population (OSP) ... (pp.209-210)

"I have judged this stock (Eastern Spinner porpoise) to be below the (OSP)[9] ... to prevent this stock (Whitebelly Spinner porpoise) from dropping below (OSP), we will propose to allow little or no take ... If the incidental taking of these two major stocks is not allowed, then setting on mixed schools of porpoise will not be possible ... 54 percent of the sets on porpoises by the U.S. fleet over the past 4 years have been associated with mixed schools of porpoises involving these two stocks ... we must reduce the kill (of the other major stock, the Offshore Spotted porpoise) ... In our proposal for 1977, the approximate total take of Offshore Spotted porpoise, foreign and domestic, allowed, will be 48,000, compared to an average of 90,000 in 1974 and 1976. This will further reduce the tuna available to the fleet ... There must be some allowance for foreign fleets, which, according to our best information, have a kill rate 2.5 times that of the U.S. fleet ... therefore, it would be prudent to propose that the U.S. fleet be allowed to take under an (OSP) regime in 1977 no more than 30,000 of all species. The quota for all species in 1976 was 78,000. Quotas in 1977 will be by separate stock even though this will complicate the administration and monitoring of the regime. We believe separate stock quotas are required by the court." (pp. 210-211)

Dr. White made it clear that the court had required the agency to administer the MMPA under what he called an "Optimum Sustainable Population Regime." He also made it clear that this means that the regulations planned by the NMFS to administer the MMPA would have a **Draconian** impact on the U.S. tuna seiner fleet.

> **"Accordingly, in order to comply with the Act as interpreted by the court, we plan to propose a very strict regulatory regime for 1977, which may make the operation of U.S. vessels uneconomical.** In this matter we have no choice. I find, Mr. Chairman, it the height of irony that this strict regime which will so adversely affect the tuna fishing industry is unlikely to yield a solution to our porpoise mortality problem; but is likely to make matters worse ... "Foreign-flag vessels involved in this fishery do not have to meet the requirements of the Act. They will be able to set on porpoises while our flag vessels will not be permitted to do so.[10] (p. 211) (emphasis added)

> "As I indicated, I think the course we are following may result in larger porpoise kills. That is a very deep concern to all of us."[11] (p. 269)

Dr. White's testimony is a near repeat of the testimony of Robert W. Schoning, Director, NMFS, before the same House Subcommittee in October 1975.[12] Director Schoning commented that Congress must amend the MMPA because the "law is not that clear and the goals are not that readily obtainable." He also explained why his agency needed time to develop more creditable objective data on porpoise population levels in the vast eastern Pacific Ocean (EPO), as follows:

> " ... We are talking about roughly 5 million square miles of fishing area associated with the tuna-porpoise problem. A ball park population estimate right now for the two major species of porpoise involved is that there are about 5 million animals in that area where they are harvesting, on a sustained basis, approximately 35 million yellowfin tuna annually.

> "Our porpoise estimate relates to just the specific population of spinners or spotters. There are other kinds out there in other numbers. We have been working on the

problem of tuna porpoise since the late sixties, and beginning in 1973 we got more deeply into it when the problem we identified resulted in the (MMPA).

"We have spent about $2 million on tuna porpoise activity … We are trying to find out how many porpoise there are. It is not a simple task … And, in that big an area, although our procedures are being refined, there are specific areas which resist estimates, and so we are trying to get figures for these populations."

Dr. White reaffirmed the current need of the NMFS for more time to collect data at sea by referring to his reliance on just "informed approximations."[13]

Under questioning by the Chairman of the House Subcommittee, Dr. White advised that "our most optimistic date for the granting of a new permit conforming to the court's ruling is February 7, 1977, and this date may slip.[14] There will be no setting on porpoise between January 1, 1977, and February 7, 1977, or later, unless we are successful in obtaining a continuance of the stay during this period. We will ask to obtain such a stay." (p. 212)

Unexpected Fishing Closure During 1976

The NMFS published an amendment to 50 Code of Federal Regulations (CFR) §216.24 (d) (3) (i) (A) that was effective immediately on June 8, 1976. The NMFS explained that: "Since this amendment is prescribed under sanction of a court of the United States, it is effective immediately, in accordance with the provisions of 5 U.S.C. § 553 (d)." 41 FR 23680 (June 11, 1976). This amendment stated in part: "The number of all other stocks or species of marine mammals that may be killed … shall not exceed 78,000." The amendment also authorized the Director, NMFS, to determine the date of prohibition for encircling tuna/porpoise schools. The Circuit Court noted, in its opinion of August 6, 1976, that the NMFS had conceded that the Act required that the general permit contain a fixed number by amending the regulations in June to impose a limit of 78,000.

The NMFS obtained information that the limit of 78,000 porpoise mortalities by the U.S. tuna seiner fleet would be reached earlier than expected. "The total mortality for 1976 which was projected on August 31, 1976, had been below 70,000; however, due to unusually heavy porpoise fishing which occurred in September, the limit is now projected to be reached by October 19, 1976." The NMFS estimates of "total porpoise mortality" were based upon mortality determined by NMFS observers. A random survey of observer reports completed after May 1976 showed that 35 to 40 percent of "observed mortality" was caused by three vessels and that one of these vessels had been responsible for 15 percent of "observed mortality."[15] The prohibition on fishing tuna/porpoise schools became effective at 0001 hours on October 22, 1976. 41 FR 45569 (October 15, 1976).[16]

On October 21, 1976, the U.S. District Court, Southern District of California, Judge William B. Enright, issued a 10-day temporary restraining order on the NMFS from enforcing a porpoise mortality quota.[17] This order was based upon lawsuits filed by the ATA and owners of five tuna seiners.[18] The lawsuits contended, among other claims, that the NMFS had not met statutory procedures for promulgating and modifying the quota regulations. On November 2, 1976, Judge Enright denied the motions for a preliminary injunction; however, the temporary restraining order was continued until noon, November 5, 1976. The court rejected government requests that the lawsuits be stayed and transferred to the District of Columbia.[19]

Federal Courts Reject Agency Relief Requests

On December 23, 1976, U.S. District Judge Charles R. Richey denied a motion for an extension of the stay, and on December 30, 1976, the U.S. Court of Appeals for the District of Columbia also rejected the NMFS motions for emergency relief and reversal of Judge Richey's order.

Judge Richey's ruling stated in part: "The government estimates that it will not be able to begin implementation of the 1977 regulations until April 1977. Accordingly, it proposes to amend the 1976 regulations to make them identical to the proposed regulations for 1977. The amended regulations would then govern during an 'interim regime,' while the 1977 draft regulations remain under administrative consideration." Since the stay expires on January 1, 1977, thereby making the 1976 regulations and amendments void on that date, the NMFS asked "for another four month stay, or until the final regulations are implemented." The request was rejected, with Judge Richey noting that the "government in effect asks the Court to short-circuit the administrative process." However, the Court did suggest an option "to avoid imposing unnecessary hardships upon the industry," by allowing an interim period take of approximately 10,000 porpoise, a taking that was proportional to the proposed total mortality quota for 1977.

These refusals to grant a stay by the two courts in Washington, D.C., resulted in a series of the immediate judicial actions in California, and were the subject of discussions in hearings held by the Senate and House. These rulings contributed to the severe economic harm and distress suffered by all segments of the tuna industry during the first five months of 1977.

Conflicting Federal Court Decisions

JANUARY 1977 ADMINISTRATIVE LAW JUDGE (ALJ) RECOMMENDED DECISION

After 14 days of hearings in San Diego and Washington, D.C., during November and December 1976, involving a record of 3,391 pages of transcript, about 90 exhibits, and numerous officially-noticed documents, including environmental impact statements, Administrative Law Judge (ALJ) Frank W. Vanderheyden, issued a recommended decision to the Director, NMFS, on the regulations proposed to govern the taking of tuna/porpoise schools by the U.S fleet. His findings of fact and conclusions of law that the lower bound of OSP was 50 percent of the unexploited population of the species or stock and therefore, the eastern spinner porpoise stock was not "depleted," as defined by the MMPA, were rejected by the Director, NMFS. In addition, the ALJ's recommendation that an unintentional incidental take be permitted only in mixed schools of eastern spinner until the quota was met was also rejected. The ALJ recommended a total porpoise mortality quota of 96,100, including a quota of 64,393 of spotters, 6,587 eastern spinners, and 17,000 whitebelly spinners. The Director, NMFS, reduced the total quota to 59, 050, zero take of eastern spinners, a reduced quota of whitebelly spinners to 7,840, and a reduced quota of spotters to 43,090. [20]

The ALJ also made the following findings, which were not disputed by the Director, NMFS:

"Since 1971, (foreign nations) have increased significantly their involvement with yellowfin caught on porpoise. In addition to the United States, 14 other countries fished for tuna in the ETP [eastern tropical Pacific] ... Thus, as foreign participation increases effective control over porpoise mortality at this time by the U.S. is decreasing." (pp. 9-10)

"The evidence is persuasive, and it is so found, that the regulations as proposed by the NMFS would encourage transfer of seiners to foreign flags under appropriate circumstances. (p. 120)

"It is found that the proposed regulations in 1977 will result in a decline in the supply of all tuna, domestic and foreign, particularly yellowfin." (p. 113)

JANUARY 1977 CALIFORNIA FEDERAL COURT RULINGS

The plaintiff's attorneys in Civil Case No. 76-963-E (The Motor Vessels Theresa Ann, et al.) presented this ALJ decision to Federal District Court, Judge William B. Enright. Also submitted to the Court were the NMFS regulations that proposed establishing an interim regime (January 1 to April 30) for the taking of tuna/porpoise schools by tuna seiners and a notice to the ATA that its 1976 general permit had been modified. 42 FR 1034 (January 5, 1977). These regulations established a porpoise mortality quota for the interim period of 9,973 and zero take for Spinners and Coastal Spotters, and made reference to proposed rules and Notice to the ATA. 41 FR 49859 (November 11, 1976).

Judge Enright issued a Memorandum Opinion that noted "it is unlikely that a 1977 permit can issue prior to April 1977, but concluded that "it is virtually certain that a quota of some measure will be imposed for the calendar year of 1977." He asserted a right to grant this "limited injunction relief under the authority conferred by Federal Rule of Civil Procedure 65 and the general powers of equity vested in the discretion of the District Court," and found "justification for this equitable relief in the Act itself and its legislative history." He also found "that under the unusual circumstances of the instant case, the delay in promulgating regulations and issuing permits has impaired plaintiffs' property interest in violation of due process of law, and further finds this preliminary injunctive relief to be an appropriate remedy."

On January 28, 1977, the U.S. Court of Appeals, District of Columbia, after considering a motion of the Committee on Humane Legislation, Inc. (CHL) for injunctive relief, ordered a number of actions, including the following: (1) that the NMFS and ATA apply forthwith to the California District Court for a stay of the preliminary injunction and related orders entered by that Court on January 21, 1977; (2)

that the government be restrained from issuing any permit pursuant to the MMPA authorizing the taking of tuna/porpoise schools by tuna seiners, and to rescind any permits that may be outstanding; and, (3) that the ATA, its officers, members, agents, servants, employees, and attorneys, and all persons and organizations in active concert, be and hereby are restrained from taking porpoise incidental to tuna seining.[21]

On February 3, 1977, the U.S. Court of Appeals for the District of Columbia, acting upon the motion of CHL issued restraining orders on the Secretary of Commerce, ATA, and related individuals and persons. As to the ATA, the order extended to the "instituting or participating in any new litigation seeking" to enable the taking of porpoise by tuna seiners. To ensure compliance with its restraining orders, the Court issued 10 orders, which included directions to the Secretary of Commerce, Attorney General of the United States, and the ATA, including a direction that the Secretary request the assistance of the Federal Bureau of Investigation (FBI).

On February 7, 1977, Judge Enright denied the applications for stay of the preliminary injunction that he issued on January 21, 1977. They had been filed in compliance with an order issued on January 28, 1977, by the Court of Appeals for the District of Columbia. In addition, Judge Enright denied a motion of the government to dissolve such preliminary injunction. In this order, Judge Enright invited "an appeal of this Court's ruling to the Court of Appeals for the Ninth Circuit in an effort to promptly resolve the conflict in a higher forum."

On February 24, 1977, the U.S. Court of Appeals, Ninth Circuit, ruled that the preliminary injunction issued by the District Court for the Southern District of California was stayed subject to further order of the court. The ruling stated in part the following:

> "Severe economic hardship to the tuna fishing industry is being imposed by the operation of the [MMPA]. However, promotion of the public interest, as reflected in the Act, must also be weighed. When this is done we are constrained to hold that the issuance of the injunction by the District Court constituted an abuse of discretion.

> "We so hold in full awareness that the effect of the legislative and executive actions affecting the tuna fishing industry imposes substantial economic hardship on the appellees. Our stay of the district Court's preliminary injunction only reflects our belief that those hardships have their origin in the terms of the (MMPA), which we can neither amend nor ignore.

The Court of Appeals did not stay all proceedings in the District Court "but do observe that the District Court in proceeding to hear the constitutional claims should exercise its equitable powers in a manner that will not interfere with the complete and final disposition of the proceedings still pending in the District of Columbia." Noting that the 1977 regulations have not as yet been promulgated, the Court of Appeals did not foreclose the right to test their validity in courts other than in the District of Columbia.[22]

The NMFS published the final regulations applicable to the fishing of tuna/porpoise schools based upon the decision of the Director, NMFS. 42 FR 12010 (March 4, 1977).[23] On March 2, 1977, CHL and other persons, filed a motion for Preliminary Injunction and Memorandum In Support of the Motion with the U.S. District Court for the District of Columbia, claiming that the NMFS regulations promulgated on March 1, 1977, were in violation of the MMPA, and seeking declaratory, injunctive, and mandatory relief to restrain the Secretary of Commerce, *et al.*, from implementing administrative regulations that permitted the taking of marine mammals by tuna seining and issuance of a general permit to the ATA.[24] On June 30, 1977, Charles R. Richey, U.S. District Judge for the District of Columbia, ruled that the "1977 regulations and permit issued under the MMPA were promulgated in accordance with all procedural requirements and are supported by substantial evidence in the administrative record."

On March 4,1977, the U.S. Court of Appeals for the District of Columbia acted upon a motion of the federal government and supported by the ATA, that further court orders are required to assure compliance with its order of February 3, 1977, such as: (1) that "ATA and its consorts" are restrained from having more than one speedboat engine above deck on a tuna vessel when not in port; (2) that "ATA and its consorts," upon request of the NMFS, are to report their position daily via radio; (3) that upon reasonable cause to believe a violation of the MMPA or court orders has occurred, "ATA and its consorts" are to return to port, allow the NMFS to inspect vessels and log books and question crewmembers.[25]

Punitive Agency Regulations

On March 16, 1977, the NMFS published in the Federal Register statements noting the order of stay issued on March 8, 1977, by the U.S. Court of Appeals for the District of Columbia.[26] It was further announced that U.S. tuna seiners could commence fishing certain tuna/porpoise schools at 0001 hours March 14, 1977, and that such fishing was subject to the regulations recently published in the Federal Register on March 1, 1977, and on January 5, 1977. 42 FR 14733 (March 16, 1977). Two days later, the Court of Appeals granted a stay of the District Court's judgment of May 11, 1976.[27]

These NMFS interim regulations provided for a zero take of spinners (eastern, Costa Rican, and whitebelly), a zero take of coastal spotters, and an aggregate mortality take of not to exceed 9,972. Encirclements by U.S. tuna fishermen of mixed or pure schools of coastal spotters or spinners were prohibited. Necessarily, U.S. tuna fishermen operating in the EPO could encircle only pure schools of offshore spotters and common porpoise (northern, central, and southern). These restrictions on the encirclement of tuna/porpoise schools were not applicable to foreign-flag tuna seiners.

In Review

This 1977 episode of unusual court rulings and orders and of delayed agency regulatory actions and decisions caused a record loss of income for the U.S. tuna industry. The ATA advised the United States International Trade Commission (USITC) that these government actions, occurring during the first five months of

1977, caused the fleet to experience unprofitable fishing trips and delays in commencing fishing trips, resulting in lost revenue of some $40 million to $50 million.[28] We have no information on the losses sustained during this period by the tuna processors and cannery workers.

After 1976, the discretionary actions of the Secretary of Commerce in determining the issues of estimating the existing and future levels of porpoise populations in the EPO by species and stock, and of estimating their current optimum sustainable populations in accordance with the MMPA, would substantially contribute to the removal of the U.S. tuna seiner fleet from its traditional fishing grounds in the EPO and to the closing of all major tuna canneries in California and Puerto Rico.

It would be the uncertainty as to how the "Optimum Sustainable Population Regime" would be administered by the Secretary of Commerce/NOAA/NMFS that caused serious concerns about the future of the U.S. tuna seiner fleet operating in the EPO. The industry was advised that the administration of this regime could be successfully challenged only if a federal judge found that the Secretary of Commerce had abused his or her discretion in promulgating regulations to implement the "Regime."

The industry was very concerned and disappointed by the regulatory views of the Secretary of Commerce, as expressed to the House Committee on Merchant Marine and Fisheries in her letter dated May 16, 1977.[29] Individuals in the industry believed that this letter, which represented the position of President Carter's administration on resolving the tuna-porpoise controversy, was influenced by persons representing various non-profit organizations called by the media as "environmentalists" in Washington, D.C.[30] The ATA considered the Secretary's letter discouraging and overreaching in that it asked for changes to the MMPA that would allow regulators to do the following:

- limit the1980 porpoise mortality quota to no more than 50% of that authorized for 1977, and thereafter, have the quota "be reduced by at least 50% every second year;"[31]

- give "cop-like" authority to observers placed aboard commercial fishing vessels to monitor compliance with the MMPA regulations and permits;

- place observers aboard Class-III tuna seiners (vessels with fish-carrying capacities greater than 400 short tons) on every fishing trip during 1978, and for years beyond, give the Secretary discretion to place observers aboard these vessels subject to determinations by the Secretary and whether standards of performance established by the Secretary were satisfied;

- authorize the Secretary to charge fees for permits and certificates of inclusion to recover all or part of the cost of observer coverage and the cost of chartering one or more commercial fishing vessels to be used for research "as the Secretary deems appropriate;"

- authorize the Secretary to establish fees "on the basis of the number and kind of marine mammals authorized to be killed or seriously injured," and to provide an incentive to masters, owners, operators, and crews of individual fishing vessels to reduce the incidental taking of such mammals by returning these fees "in whole or in part if the Secretary determines, in his discretion, that the return of such fee or portion thereof would further the purposes and policies" of the MMPA;

- authorize the Secretary to place the following conditions upon the transfer of tuna vessels to foreign registry: (1) obligate the buyer to comply with United States standards for the incidental mortality and serious injury of marine mammals, (2) allow observers approved by the Secretary to board and accompany such vessels, and (3) file a bond with the Secretary in amount and form determined by the Secretary;[32]

- require the holder of the General Permit (ATA) "to make reports in such form and in such times and containing such information concerning the economic impact of the terms and conditions imposed by such permit," and authorize the Secretary to regulate the keeping and availability to the Secretary "such records as may be required by the Secretary for the verification of such reports;"

- develop and promote a solution to the tuna/porpoise enigma so as to eliminate the need for purse seining tuna/porpoise school.[33]

The regulations for 1977 and the final decision of the Director, NMFS, were issued on March 1, 1977. The Agency made a determination of optimum sustainable population (OSP) on all but 5 of 17 species and stocks, resulting in a total mortality take quota for 1977 of 59,050. The new rules prohibited the setting on tuna/porpoise schools that included individuals of any of these five stocks. This decision rejected the findings of the ALJ in the following areas:

On the issue of the lower bound of OSP and application of the term "depletion as defined by the MMPA:" the ALJ found and concluded that it "is 50 percent of the unexploited population of the specie [sic.] or stock." (p. 73) The NMFS had advised the ALJ that the lower bound of the OSP was not greater than 60 percent (p. 72). By finding the lower bound of OSP at 50 percent, the ALJ found that the eastern spinner and other stocks were not "depleted" and therefore, available for taking by the tuna fleet. By ruling that the lower bound of OSP was not greater than 60 percent, the NMFS proposed that fleet's quota of spotted porpoise would be 21,783, zero for eastern spinners, and zero for whitebelly spinners.

On the issue of annual mortality quotas: the ALJ recommended 96,000 (including 64,393 for offshore spotters; 17,000 for whitebelly spinners, 7,600 for common dolphins, and 6,587 for eastern spinners. The ALJ recommended no takes of coastal spotted dolphin and Costa Rican eastern spinner. The NMFS established a total limit of 59,050 (including 43,090 for offshore spotters, 7,840 whitebelly spinners, and 7,600 for common dolphins). No take of eastern spinners was allowed. In explaining this regulatory ruling, the Director, NMFS, stated:

> **"The proposed U.S. quotas were developed by subtracting the estimated foreign mortality from a proposed total mortality by all fleets.** ... Because I must be assured that the total mortality of individual species and stocks will not be to their disadvantage, I have considered the estimated foreign mortality in setting U.S. quotas."[34] (emphasis added)

In accordance with the regulations and subject to the availability of funding and observers, NMFS observers were scheduled to be aboard each large U.S. tuna-seiner (greater than 400 short tons of frozen tuna capacity) for at least one trip during the remainder of 1977. On September 12, 1977, Congress enacted H.R. 4740, as amended, a bill that extended the authorization period for the MMPA through fiscal year 1978 and increased the authorization level under the Act for fiscal year 1977.[35] The report of the Committee on Merchant Marine and Fisheries, dated May 16, 1977, stated:

> "This was an emergency authorization intended to enable the Secretary to meet expanded responsibilities mandated by the Federal courts in the tuna-porpoise controversy. ... In order to satisfy these rulings, the Department of Commerce must greatly expand its observer program to monitor the porpoise population levels. In addition, observer data is necessary to determine compliance with the Act and regulations promulgated under the Act. **The committee considers this supplemental authorization as vitally necessary to enable Commerce to comply with the court decisions and prevent wholesale disruption of the American tuna industry.**"[36] (emphasis added)

On April 15, 1977, a general permit was issued to the ATA. However, the fleet remained in port until approximately the middle of May 1977. In a Federal Court decision filed June 30, 1977, the MMPA regulations promulgated by the NMFS for 1977 were upheld.[37]

---

[1] *Committee for Humane Legislation, Inc. v. Richardson,* 414 F. Supp 297 (1976)

[2] To view copies of statements and affidavits of tuna industry officials in support of economic harm for failure to stay the court's order, see: May 1976 House Subcommittee Hearings-SN-94-29: 238-253 and 430-450.

[3] *Committee for Humane Legislation, Inc.* v. *Richardson,* 540 F. 2d 1141 (1976)); To view a copy of the decision by the Court of Appeals for the District of Columbia, see: Sep 1976 House Subcommittee Hearings-SN-94-45: 167-189.

The NMFS had conceded that the Act required that the general permit contain a fixed number by amending the regulations in June to impose a limit of 78,000 porpoises. To view copies of documents filed by the plaintiffs in support of the motion for summary judgment in the district court case, see: May 1976 Subcommittee Hearings-SN-94-29: 303-351.

[4] "The greatest incidence of take of marine mammals involves dolphins (porpoises) and pygmy killer whales in the eastern tropical Pacific purse-seine fishery for yellowfin tuna. Estimates of porpoise loss by U.S. fishermen were 214,000 in 1970, 167,000 in 1971, and 238,000 in 1972. **The importance of these kills in relation to optimum sustainable populations is not known due to lack of knowledge of the sizes of porpoise populations and other population dynamics factors.** Population modeling studies underway are scheduled to provide information on population sizes by October 1974. Data being gathered by observers aboard tuna fishing vessels are designed to provide accurate data on the composition (numbers, age, sex, size) of the porpoise kill," 39 FR 9685-9686 (March 13, 1974). (emphasis added)

This Notice indicated that the populations of the spotter, spinner, striped, and common porpoise were unknown to the NMFS. The importance of the NMFS statistics of annual porpoise mortality by the tuna purse-seine fleet during 1970-1973 "in relation to optimum sustainable population is not known due to lack of knowledge of the sizes of porpoise populations and other population dynamics factors." 39 FR 9685 (March 13, 1974) A later Notice corrected a typographical error indicating that the estimated population of spotted porpoise was "unknown-rare" by appropriately deleting the word "rare." 39 FR 11936 (April 1, 1974).

[5] The agency's Notice of September 8, 1975, provided information that the population of spotted porpoise in the eastern Pacific Ocean (EPO) ranged from 3,100,000 to 3,500,000, that the spinner porpoise population ranged from 1,100,000 to 1,200,000, and that the populations of the striped dolphin and common dolphin were unknown. On the issue of issuing a permit to "take" porpoise in the tuna-seiner fishery, the NMFS stated:

> **"Optimum sustainable population levels have not been determined; therefore, no statement can be made as to the effect of the proposed action on optimum sustainable populations.** The estimated annual incidental mortality rate on spotted dolphin for 1974 is 2.1 percent to 2.3 percent of the estimated population and for eastern spinner 1.8 percent to 2.8 percent. **At these levels of incidental porpoise mortality, the present population stocks are either stable or increasing or decreasing slightly.**[5] There is no evidence that the porpoise populations would substantially increase or decrease as a result of the regulations and re-issuance of the general permit." 40 FR 41536 (September 8, 1975). (emphasis added.)

The amendments to the regulations governing the incidental taking of marine mammals during commercial fishing operations were published by the NMFS became effective on December 19, 1975. 40 FR 56899-56907(December 5, 1975) The NMFS presented a number of reasons for its regulatory decisions, including its current view on the status of the affected porpoise populations, as follows:

> "Our best scientific estimate is, at the present time, that porpoise stocks involved in the yellowfin tuna fishery are either stable, or increasing or decreasing slightly ... In summary, the NMFS has concluded that the course of action delineated above will best serve the objectives of reducing incidental porpoise mortality without destroying the economic viability of the U.S. tuna fleet—both of which are mandates under the (MMPA) and its legislative history."

[6] "Report of the Workshop on Stock Assessment of Porpoises Involved in the Eastern Pacific Yellowfin Tuna Fishery (La Jolla, July 27-31, 1976)" September 1976; Southwest Fisheries Center Administrative Report No. LJ-76-29. 53 pp. and 7 Appendices.

[7] For a discussion of the findings of the OSP Workshop and related matters: Statement and testimony of Dr. William W. Fox, Jr, see: Sep 1976 House Subcommittee Hearings-SN-94-45: 46-79; For a discussion about why the MMPA used the term "OSP" rather than Maximum Sustainable Yield (MSY), see: Testimony of Lee Talbot, Assistant to the Chairman for International Scientific Affairs, Council of Environment Quality: Sep. 1976 House Subcommittee Hearings-SN-94-45: 80-86; For a reaction of the tuna industry to the report of the OSP Workshop: Statement and testimony of Gordon Broadhead, President, LMR, Inc., see: Sep. 1976 House Subcommittee Hearings-SN-94-45: 106-109 and 327-329.

[8] Sep 1976 House Subcommittee Hearings-SN-94-45; 208-211.

[9] In amending 50 CFR § 216.3, the NMFS published a definition of "Optimum Sustainable Population," 41 FR 55536 (December 21, 1976).

[10] September 1976 House Subcommittee Hearings-SN-94-45: 211.

[11] September 1976 House Subcommittee Hearings-SN-94-45: 269.

[12] On October 21, 1975, the Director. NMFS, testified before a House Subcommittee on the tuna/porpoise issue, and made comments "about needed changes in the act in general terms," as follows:

> "First: On tuna and porpoise, the law and the legislative history says: Protect the mammals but don't shut down or seriously curtail the industry. Two basic problems we see are that the law is not all that clear and the goals are not readily obtainable. A second point and a major problem, is at this time we simply do not have enough information to do the job as precisely as many of us want to. This doesn't mean we cannot do it, but we cannot do it as well as we would like to. We are working on both of these aspects ... We know that yellowfin and porpoise are found together, but we are not sure why they are. We are trying to find out collectively with the industry and other interested parties how to catch and keep tuna in the nets and release the porpoise caught, or not catch the porpoise at all, recognizing that they are found together much of the time ... The act caused us all, including our agency, to become more concerned about them, and one thing absolutely essential was to find out how many there were. And that is what we are trying to do. And in that big an area, although our procedures are being refined, there are specific areas which resist estimates, and so we are trying to get figures for these populations." 1975 House Subcommittee Hearings-SN-94-16: 31.

[13] This need for more data was also revealed by the agency to the Circuit Court: (explaining that the Circuit Court stay of the District Court decision on June 1, 1976) "was founded in part on the assertion that if ongoing research being conducted with the tuna fleet were permitted to continue figures could be obtained by autumn of this year (1976). **The court is now informed that '[I]t will take three to seven years for a scientifically valid figure ..."** (emphasis added)

[14] The NMFS published proposed regulations to replace those voided by the District Court order: 41 FR 45015 (October 14, 1976). The maximum mortality quota proposed for 1977 was 29,920 and limited to marine mammals that did not include spinners and coastal spotters.

[15] For testimony by Tuna Captains on the reasons for the high porpoise mortality caused by these three vessels, see: 1977 Senate Committee Hearings-SN-95-12: 212-213, 215-216.

For an ALJ explanation of the shortened 1976 fishing season: "The 1976 open season was characterized by a big run of school fish in the early part of the year in which very little porpoise were involved. After this run was over, the fleet resorted to fishing on porpoise for the rest of the open season. The result was that the large U.S. seiners caught about 85,000 tons of yellowfin in the open season and less than 60 percent of it was caught on porpoise. The relatively low percentage of open season yellowfin caught on porpoise reflects a combination of early open season small yellowfin-skipjack school fishing and late open season fishing on porpoise associated with yellowfin. The problem of fishing porpoise on yellowfin is essentially one for the large Class III seiners [vessels with fish-carrying capacities of more than 400 short tons]. These vessels have the capacity of going great distances, for example, outside the CYRA [Inter-American Tropical Tuna Commission's Yellowfin Regulatory Area] in search of tuna. In such an area, much of the yellowfin associate with porpoise." January 1977 ALJ Decision: 104.

[16] To read modification of the methodology used for determining the prohibition date, see: 41 FR 43726 (October 4, 1976).

[17] 41 FR 47254 (October 28, 1976). Facts about the impact of this litigation was published by NMFS.

[18] *Motor Vessels Theresa Ann et al. v. Krebs,* 548 F.2d 1382 (1977)

[19] On October 30, 1976, the U.S. District Court for the District of Columbia was aware of these cases and noted: "that District is fully capable of deciding which, if any, of the issues raised in those cases could and/or should have been raised in this litigation; and whether those cases should be transferred to this Court, as the governmental defendants in the California cases have apparently requested."

[20] NMFS published a notice that it had received the recommended decision of the ALJ. 42 FR 3886 (January 18, 1977). March 1977 House Subcommittee Hearings-SN-95-8: 22, summary of ALJ-recommended decision and the NMFS final decision with comments.

[21] See: Report of Secretary of Commerce Report dated June 20, 1977, at 42 FR 38982, 38988 (August 1, 1977).

[22] *Motor Vessels Theresa Ann et al., v. Krebs*, 548 F.2d 1382, 1383 (1977).

[23] To view a summary of the ALJ-recommended decision and the NMFS final decision, see: March 1977 Subcommittee Hearings-SN-95-8: 22-23.

[24] 1977 Senate Committee Hearings-SN-95-12: 203-207 and 197-203; Mar. 1977 House Subcommittee Hearings-SN 95-8: 250-266: view copies of Motion and Memorandum in Support of the Motion for Preliminary Injunction filed by Petitioner Committee for Humane Legislation, Inc., (CHL) in this action. May 1976 House Subcommittee Hearings-SN-94-29:303: testimony and copy of written Statement of CHL representatives.

[25] The term "ATA and its consorts" was defined in the Order: "the American Tunaboat Association, its officers, members, agents, servants, employees and attorneys, and all persons and organizations in privity, active concert or participation with them who have actual notice of this order." To view a copy of the enforcement plan submitted by the Department of Commerce, see: Mar. 1977 House Subcommittee Hearings -SN-95-8: 20.

[26] The ATA filed its application for a General Permit; notice of receipt was published by NMFS. 42 FR 13147 (March 9, 1977).

[27] On March 18, 1977, the U.S. Court of Appeals for the District of Columbia ordered that the judgment of the District Court issued on May 11, 1976, "be and hereby is stayed to allow the taking of porpoise incidental to yellowfin tuna purse seining pur-

suant to the 1976 permit, as modified, from the date of this order to and including April 30, 1977, or until a permit for 1977 is issued, which ever occurs first. Taking of porpoise pursuant to the modified permit shall be governed by the 1977 regulations, except as to term of permits and quota of porpoise, and may commence upon issuance of modified certificates of inclusion. Any and all porpoise taken under the modified permit shall be counted as a part of the total allowable take for 1977." The Court acted because it found that the Secretary made findings required by the MMPA as to the expected impact of the proposed regulations on the optimum sustainable population of the affected mammal species; has established a quota for the period January 1 to April 30, 1977, has adopted new regulations establishing a quota of 59,050 for the calendar year 1977, and other rules, and has "conditionally modified the 1976 permit to the ATA to extend its term through April 30, 1977."

[28] Certain Canned Tuna Fish. Report to the President on Investigation No.TA-201-53, Under Section 201 of the Trade Act of 1974. United States International Trade Commission (USITC) Publication 1558 (August 1984), p. A-10. In 1977, the value of the tropical tuna (yellowfin, bigeye, and skipjack) landings by U.S. tuna vessels was about $156 million. *Fisheries of the United States, 1977* (April 1978) Current Fishery Statistics No. 7500, DOC/NOAA/NMFS: 09. In 1976, the value of tropical tuna landings by U.S. tuna vessels for a restricted season was about $173 million. *Fisheries of the United States, 1976*, (April 1977). Current Fishery Statistics No. 7200, DOC/NOAA/NMFS:10. In 1979, the value of tropical tuna landings by U.S. tuna vessels was about $195 million. *Fisheries of the United States, 1979*, (April 1980). Current Fishery Statistics No. 8000, DOC/NOAA/NMFS, p.10.

[29] May 1977 House Committee Hearings -SN-95-3, pp. 29-38, at 32. Senator S.I. Hayakawa, California, who introduced S. 373 (95th Congress., 1st Session.) on February 10, 1977, explains during a Senate Committee oversight hearing that it was the intent of his bill to reduce incidental porpoise mortality "in significant annual increments." 1977 Senate Committee Hearings-SN-95-12: 122-123,

[30] In support of this opinion, reference is made to the statement of Rep. Bob Wilson, California, when he voiced his opposition to the Carter Administration "ratchet-down" quota amendment to H.R. 6970, proposed by fellow Republican Rep. Paul R. McClosky, Jr., California Rep. Wilson strongly supported Democrat Rep. John Murphy, New York, and explained why he differed with Rep. McClosky: "Mr. Chairman, I have been following this debate so far with great interest. My colleague, the gentleman from California, I am sure is trying to follow the dictates of some of the environmentalists in his area, of which there are many. I am concerned and I have more interest, I must admit, in my district (San Diego), which is the main fishing center for tuna." *Congressional Record-House*, June 1, 1977, p. 17158. "Those who allege that H.R. 6970 is anti-environmental clearly miss the point. Environmental interests were given extensive consideration by this committee. Important provisions, suggested by environmentalists were adopted in this legislation." Remarks of Rep. Mario Biaggi, New York, *Congressional Record*, June 1, 1977, p. 17148.

[31] Letter of Secretary of Commerce dated May 16, 1977: "(C) (i) Subsequent to calendar year 1977 ... The incidental mortality and serious injury of marine mammals allowed shall be progressively reduced to insignificant levels approaching zero. The Secretary shall achieve this reduction by establishing annual quotas for affected species and populations that accomplish significant reductions in the total incidental mortality and serious injury each year and that ensure that no such species or populations will be reduced below its

level of optimum sustainable population. The total incidental mortality and serious injury authorized in calendar year 1980 shall be limited to no more than 50% of that authorized for calendar year 1977, and the total limitation authorized thereafter shall be reduced by at least 50% every second year." (For 1977, the porpoise mortality quota was 59,050) This "ratchet-down" concept was partially rejected by the House as part of a compromise effort to obtain passage of HR 6970. Rep. Don Bonker, Washington, explained that his compromise amendment: "eliminated that provision that calls for a 50 percent reduction by 1980." *Congressional-Record*, June 1, 1977, Bonker amendment at p. 17159, quote at p. 17161, and debate and vote at p. 17162. On June 8, 1977, Rep. Bonker further explained his amendment, *Congressional Record*--Extension of Remarks, June 8, 1077, p. E 3624.

[32] The portion of the Secretary's proposal rejected by a vote during the House Floor Debate on HR 6970 concerned the requirement of observer placement. *Congressional Record*, June 1, 1977, pp. 17163-17164.

[33] The following proposal of the Secretary was included as an amendment to H.R. 6970: "(7) . . . While substantial efforts have been undertaken to reduce the incidental mortality and incidental serious injury of marine mammals in the course of commercial fishing operations for yellowfin tuna, **this mortality and serious injury should be further reduced and measures be taken to develop and promote fishing techniques which do not result in the incidental taking of marine mammals.**" (emphasis added)

[34] 42 FR 12018, (March 1, 1977).The best available estimate of the foreign mortality was approximately 41,000. The NMFS workshop assumed "that the non-U.S. death rate for 1973-1975 was the same as the 1972-73 U.S. average or approximately two and one-half (2-1/2) times the current U.S. rate." 42 FR 12020, (March 1, 1977).

[35] "Marine Mammal Protection Act Authorization," Fiscal Year 1978, *Congressional Record—House*, pp. H 9246-9246, September 12, 1877.

[36] Report No. 95-336, 95th Congress, 1st Session, Marine Mammal Protection Act of 1972 Authorization, dated May 16, 1977, To accompany H.R. 4740: 4. The report, at page 5, also noted that: "The court found that the Department of Commerce had granted the tuna industry an unrestricted general permit, without limitation as to the number or kind of porpoise which might be killed, in contravention of the Act. The court found that the department failed to comply with the provisions of the Act which require the agency to determine and publish reasonable estimates of the existing population levels of each species affected by the regulations, the optimum sustainable population of each of those species, and the expected impact of the regulations on the effort to achieve an optimum sustainable population level for each species ..."

[37] *Committee for Humane Legislation, Inc., vs. Juanita M. Krebs, et al.*, C.A. No. 77-0564, Order signed by Charles R. Richey, United States District Judge and filed on Jun 30, 1977. Judge Richey concluded "that defendants' 1977 regulations and permit issued under the MMPA were promulgated in accordance with all procedural requirements and are supported by substantial evidence in the administrative record. Accordingly, plaintiff's request for declaratory, injunctive and mandatory relief specified in its complaint must be denied, and judgment herein will be issued for defendants."

"Much credit must go to the skippers of the vessels ... Although most of the changes in the design of the equipment are **evolutions from previous gear and not radical new design**, each change in the nets make it perform differently, and the skippers must become accustomed to the changes in the behavior of the nets." (emphasis added)

Richard McNeely, NMFS Fishery Gear Specialist

PART VI

THE "MMPA JOINT VENTURE" ENDS

23

RICHARD L. McNEELY

Dick McNeely was known in the U.S. tuna fleet as the author of the celebrated and respected article "The Purse Seine Revolution in Tuna Fishing." This report, published in the June 1961 issue of the trade magazine *Pacific Fisherman*, was based upon his fishing trip aboard the converted tuna seiner DETERMINED during 1960.[1] Born in Huntington, West Virginia, in 1922, McNeely has an impressive history of working out practical solutions to fishing gear problems. For instance, in 1955, he designed, constructed, and field-tested a remote-controlled underwater television vehicle used by the research staff of the U.S. government's Exploratory Fishing and Gear Research Base in Miami, Florida. Prior to his work with the tuna fleet, he was recognized as an authority on the following subjects: (1) mid-water trawling; (2) echo sounding; (3) heavy-duty electrical towing cable; (4) research vessel deck gear; (5) depth telemetry; (6) underwater observation techniques; and, (7) fishing gear design. His at-sea experience includes sailing aboard nine government research vessels off the United States, in the Arctic Sea, and in the Central Pacific Ocean, and fishing trips aboard 30 commercial fishing vessels.

McNeely's describes how he helped find ways to mitigate porpoise mortality associated with the tuna/porpoise problem:

> "After a reasonable time of brainstorming the problem by the porpoise committee, I was detailed to San Diego for first hand observation of the problems at sea aboard several tuna seiners during commercial fishing operations. ... After completion of a list of all the ways porpoise died during fishing operations, attempts were made to devise methods and gear to totally eliminate each and every cause. ...

> "Many concepts of possible ways to reduce moralities [sic] were tried and abandoned. A few ideas tended to show promise and research in these fields was accelerated. Eventually a total system was developed which involved (among other things) use of the speedboats to serve as "little tugboats" to hold the net open after completion of their chasing maneuvers. The speedboats were incapable of opening a collapsed net but were totally effective in preventing collapse [aggregation of por-

tions of the cork line that can cause porpoises to become entangled in the net] before it started.

"More effective release of porpoise without fear of loss of fish was made possible by [sic] major modification of the seine net by addition of a tapered fine mesh section in the back down area (SUPER APRON). The apron took advantage of observed difference in behavior of fish and porpoise. The fish tended to stay in the deeper sections of the net while the porpoise tended to stay closer to the surface; the SUPER APRON provided a fine mesh and shallow escape route out of the net which the fish rarely visited in quantity.

"Minor causes of mortality were eliminated by totally closing up "hand holds" and use of a small one man rubber raft to cruise around the net to release porpoise that somehow became entangled for unknown reasons."[2]

As a result of his team's accomplishments while working with the captains and crews of the U.S. tuna fleet during 1973-1977, McNeely received the Department of Commerce Gold Medal Award and the "Man of the Year" award from the American Cetacean Society.[3] After working on the Porpoise/Tuna Interaction program for five years, McNeely was transferred back to the NMFS Northwest and Alaska Fisheries Center.[4] When asked why the transfer in June 1977, he said that his objective of developing gear and methods to reduce porpoise mortality to significantly low levels had been accomplished. The "hard lifting" had been done, and he felt that further reductions would be that of "fine-tuning" the existing methods and gear.

The judicial and regulatory decisions that adversely impacted the "joint venture" between the NMFS gear team and the U.S. tuna seiner fleet during most of 1976, and during the first four months of 1977, were discouraging, if not to McNeely, certainly to the fishermen. The fishermen believed that the at-sea experiments in 1976 had recorded significant porpoise mortality reductions, and that this record supported McNeely's opinion that he and his team had substantially achieved their objectives.

The American Tunaboat Association (ATA) and the captains and crews of the U.S. tuna fleet found Richard McNeely to have been the right man at the right time. Lou Brito, a highly-respected tuna captain, gave his evaluation as follows: "McNeely would come up with ten ideas during the fishing trip, nine of them were impractical, but the tenth idea made sense." In this way, his attributes of persistence and curiosity were recognized and greatly appreciated by the fleet. Tuna captains consistently expressed praise to ATA officials about the work and dedication of McNeely and his staff.

McNeely believes that his most important contribution in reducing porpoise mortality was in developing a system of using speedboats routinely to prevent net collapses prior to the "Back-down." His instruction to tuna captains, developed from data collected from the fleet in 1976, stated: "Don't wait until collapse of the net is imminent before hooking up speedboats to hold the net open. If the size of the porpoise school number between 500 to 1000, then have one speedboat hook-up and pull at 10 o'clock. If the porpoise school involve [sic.] 1000 to 2000 mammals, use one speedboat hook-up and pull at 10 o'clock, and one at 12 o'clock. If the porpoise school numbers greater than 2000 mammals, then use one speedboat at 10 o'clock, one at 12 o'clock, and one at 2 o'clock."

Experimentation by McNeely and his team of gear specialists during charter cruises in 1973 and 1974 resulted in a 1975 system of using three speedboats "to hold the net open in the approximate shape of a large pentagon ... [giving] considerably more surface area for containment of fish and porpoise than is normally available after pursing is completed and prior to backing down."[5] McNeely's idea of using a three-speedboat system to prevent net collapse was first used aboard the tuna seiner JOHN F. KENNEDY (Captain Lionel Sousa) during May 1973. A simulated net collapse was created during the fishing trip so as to permit the three speedboats equipped with specially-installed low-pitch propellers to be deployed. The purse seine was held open with an area equivalent to three football fields, thereby allowing the porpoise and tuna to move in separate areas, reducing the possibility of porpoise entanglement, and allowing the fishermen to proceed as rapidly as possible to the "Back-down."

McNeely and his team were convinced that this system of using speedboats would prevent net collapses, and thus reduce porpoise mortality. Further, with more room being available for both tuna and porpoise movements, there was less chance of tuna-porpoise contact. Also, the system would prevent the creation of net and cork-line movements that would cause porpoise to be entangled in pockets of loose webbing and canopies of webbing. Most sets needed the use of two speedboats rather than three, to hold the net open satisfactorily.[6]

A NMFS analysis of the first 20 field technician trips of 1975 showed that in sets involving 50 or more porpoise mortalities, 8% (51 of the 624 sets) resulted in the loss of 6,189 porpoise or 59% of a total mortality of 10,509 porpoises. Further, the analysis showed that of these 51 sets, net collapse was involved in 17, or 33%, of these problem sets. The analysis showed that 9%, or 57 of 624 sets that involved net collapse, resulted in a loss of 3,032 porpoise, or 29% of the total observed porpoise mortality.

McNeely understood that NMFS regulations were required to reduce porpoise mortality, but he also recognized that regulations concerning fishing gear and procedures needed to be carefully considered by both the fishermen and the NMFS. For example: on December 19, 1974, he addressed a memorandum to the Director of the Southwest Fisheries Center of the NMFS on the subject of "Porpoise-tuna regulations," which stated, in part, the following:

> "In my opinion, solution of the porpoise problem by regulation of gear is warranted but should be reasonable, not punitive, and backed with solid evidence of mortality reduction capability."

In this memorandum, McNeely provided reasons why the 1975 regulations, mandating handhold closures throughout the net, the use of speedboats on every set, and the use of anti-torque purse lines, required amendment.[7] The final 1976 regulations responded positively to McNeely's memo. [8]

McNeely's program of research was perceived by the fishermen as "the government" wanting to help them to perfect existing fishing gear and procedures developed by the fishermen to safely release porpoise from the purse seine. This outlook was strengthened in 1973, when the NMFS proposed interim regulations to govern the incidental taking of marine mammals "in the course of tuna purse-seining operations." These rules required the insertion in the tuna purse seine the net panel arrangement developed by Captain Harold Medina, and required the captains to use the "Back-down" procedure in releasing all live mammals from the net.[9] For most tuna fishermen, this perception changed to resentment toward the federal government after NOAA/NMFS proposed Draconian-type regulations on the fishing of tuna/porpoise schools and the imposition of a prohibition of fishing on such schools in October 1976. Tuna captains, crewmembers, and representatives of organizations representing them expressed disappointment and concern when McNeely departed California in mid-1977 for Seattle and his work at the NMFS Northwest Fisheries Center.

"Much credit must go to the skippers of the vessels," says McNeely, "Although most of the changes in the design of the equipment are **evolutions from previous gear and not radical new design**, each change in the nets make it perform differently, and the skippers must become accustomed to the changes in the behavior of the nets." (emphasis added)[10]

McNeely and his staff showed that smaller tuna purse seiners inflicted higher porpoise mortality when fishing large tuna/porpoise schools, explaining that this was probably the result of their use of shorter (less than 400 fathoms in length), shallower nets, defined as nets with 10 or fewer strips of netting (one strip is 6 fathoms deep).[11] Their studies showed that these nets created less volume or area for large tuna/porpoise schools. The larger converted and new purse seiners of San Diego were able to work with longer (greater than 400 fathoms in length), deeper nets (12 to 14 strips). In addition to reducing the mortalities of porpoises, the use of longer, deeper nets made the larger vessels more efficient at catching tunas than the smaller "regular" purse seiners operating from San Pedro. This fact, plus the experience and knowledge of fishing tuna/porpoise schools by San Diego baitboat fishermen, explains why, by 1970, the San Pedro "regular" tuna purse-seine fleet became an insignificant factor in fishing tuna/porpoise schools. As substantial numbers of new tuna purse seiners entered the U.S. tuna fleet during the 1970s, they created strong competitive pressures on the older "converted" tuna purse-seine fleet. These vessels, such as Captain Harold Medina's new seiner, the KERRI M., introduced new fishing technology, such as bow-thrusters, stabilizers, and satellite navigation. They were equipped with improved purse-seine winches, power blocks, and deeper and longer nets, all of which made them more efficient in fishing tuna/porpoise schools. More importantly, these new seiners of the 1970s were in the hands of captains and crews who had, as baitboat fishermen, acquired knowledge about the behavior of tuna/porpoise schools that enabled them to successfully purse seine tuna during the 1960s.

Some tuna captains believe that McNeely's ideas of using a large-volume net with its modifications of the Medina Panel, of reducing thread size and the "bulk of mesh webbing" was an important gear development that was ahead of its time. Today, deep, large-volume tuna purse seines are a necessity in fishing tuna in the central and western Pacific Ocean. Unfortunately, the NMFS "Large Volume Purse Seine" constantly required changes in design after trials by different captains, not only in fishing tuna/porpoise schools outside the IATTC's Commission Yellowfin Regulatory Area,[12] but also in conducting exploratory fishing for schools of skipjack and yellowfin in the central and western Pacific Ocean, where oceanographic conditions (*e.g.* a deeper thermocline) allows tuna schools to live and feed at greater depths. In 1976, after determining that the experimental net would require expensive repair and rebuilding, the NMFS terminated its research effort to further develop a "large-volume" net as a way to reduce porpoise mortality.

---

[1] For an interesting report on this trip, see: "Little Squeak from Dunbar (Memoirs of Richard L. McNeely)," pp. 162-170. Of McNeely's report on the only set of the trip on a tuna/porpoise school on page 167-"There may have been 5,000 porpoise in the school but we only caught 150 to 200. However, our catch of tuna far exceeded the 60 tons we needed to fill up."

[2] "Little Squeak from Dunbar (Memoirs of Richard L. McNeely), p. 176. See: McNeely, Richard L. and David B. Holts. "Methods of Reducing Porpoise Mortality in the Yellowfin Tuna Purse Seine Fishery," NOAA, NMFS, Southwest Fisheries Center Administrative Report No. LJ-77-13: 18 pp.

[3] The individuals from the Northwest Fisheries Center serving with McNeely during the period of November 1972 to October 1974: Jerry Jurkovich, Fred Wathne, Daniel Twohig, William High, Robert Loghry, and Gary Loverich.

[4] McNeely describes his participation in the "Porpoise Tuna Controversy" in his memoirs at pages 174-177. Attached is documentation describing the highest award given by the U.S. Department of Commerce in 1977, the Gold Medal, biographical information, and a list of the tuna fishing vessels and captains that he sailed with: BOLD CONTENDER (Capt. John Gonsalves); DETERMINED (Capt. John Cvitanich); EASTERN PACIFIC (Capt. Joseph Freitas); INDEPENDENCE (Capt. Vince Guarassi); J. M. MARTINAC (Capt. Sullivan); JOHN F. KENNEDY (Capt. Lionel Sousa); MARGARET L. (Capt. Joe Scafidi); SOUTH PACIFIC (Capt. Joe Scafidi), and TRINIDAD (Capt. John Gonsalves).

[5] SWFC-1975: 52.

[6] The observers recorded "a six-fold increase in the use of speedboats to tow the net in 1976," reducing the incidents of "net collapse" to about half and the reduction of porpoise mortality to about two porpoise per set. The NMFS claimed that "towing with speedboats probably has accounted for about 60 percent of the 21 percent drop in standardized kill per set between 1975 and 1976." SWFC-1976:40-41

[7] 39 FR 32117 (September 5, 1974).

[8] 40 FR 56899 (December 5, 1975).

[9] Proposed regulations: 38 FR 31180 (November 12, 1973). Final Regulations: 39 FR 2481 (January 22, 1974), and corrected 39 FR 5635 (February 14, 1974). The provisions of the regulations requiring that a certificated vessel be equipped with a Medina Panel by a certain date became subject to a waiver by the Regional Director, NMFS, Terminal Island. Limited supplies of nylon netting prevented vessel owners from complying with the regulation. "As a result of the petroleum shortage, it was determined on March 13, 1974, that nylon netting, a petroleum based product which is required for the safety panel, was not readily available to all persons and vessels affected by these regulations." 39 FR 20106 (June 10, 1974).

[10] Gerald D. Hill, Jr., "Saving The Porpoise-Ingenuity Made Him A Gold Medal Winner," *NOAA Magazine* (October 1978) 8 (4): 16 at 17.

[11] When discussing the depth of the net, Captains do not refer to the total number of strips in the net but only to those strips that each stretch to 6 fathoms. Since the cork line selvedge strip and the lead line selvedge strip do not stretch to a depth of 6 fathoms, these "strips" are not included. For an explanation of the tuna net used by a converted tuna seiner that is of about 425 fathoms in length and with a depth of about 42 fathoms (7 strips): Richard L. McNeely, "Purse Seine Revolution In Tuna Fishing," *Pacific Fisherman,* June 1961, pp. 27-58, at 38-39.

[12] See IATTC Special Report 13: Figure 1.

24

NEW AGENCY MMPA ENFORCEMENT POLICY

During the summer of 1975, the operation of the Observer Program was transferred from the Southwest Fisheries Center (SWFC) to the NMFS Southwest Regional Office at Terminal Island, California. "The observers, who are biological technicians, continue to collect specimens for use in the SWFC Biological Studies Task and they continue to record the same types of information collected in 1975, plus regulation compliance data for the Regional Office."[1]

In addition to all of the legal and economic troubles enveloping the tuna fleet during the period of October 1976 through May 1977, the ATA was informed that NOAA Counsel had commenced work on the issuance to tuna seiner captains and owners of Notices of Violations of the MMPA and NMFS regulations during 1977. Written reports of NMFS observers on compliance with regulations were to be used to support these Notices.[2] After being told of this new development, tuna captains and others in the tuna industry were concerned that the "Industry/NMFS Joint Venture" was all but closed down. These concerns increased after the June 1977 departure of Richard L. McNeely and his team of gear specialists and after the Secretary of Commerce had decided to impose greater regulatory constraints on the U.S. fleet by establishing a "ratcheting down program" of reduced porpoise mortality quotas.

The key to the success of the NMFS/industry "joint venture" in gear research projects was the mutual trust that existed aboard the U.S. tuna seiners between the fishermen and their government guests, the NMFS fishing gear specialists and scientific technicians. For decades, the U.S. tuna fleet had worked with onboard scientists conducting tuna fishery investigations. During the 1950s, fishery biologists of the Inter-American Tropical Tuna Commission (IATTC) and the California Department of Fish and Game made numerous trips aboard tuna vessels. Federal fishery scientists were also permitted to make fishing trips aboard tuna baitboats during this period. During the 1960s, increased numbers of federal fishery scientists and gear technicians were permitted to observe and record data on fishing operations and conduct studies aboard U.S. tuna seiners. Because of the development of new tuna fishing grounds in the Atlantic Ocean, charters were arranged with U.S. tuna seiners to explore the Gulf of Mexico and the South Atlantic Ocean off South America. These explorations, and also fishing operations by U.S. tuna seiners off West Africa, were observed and recorded by federal agency observers.

Commencing in 1970, the tuna industry worked successfully with NOAA/NMFS in persuading tuna captains to allow NMFS employees to conduct fishing gear studies, porpoise tagging, porpoise mortality counts, and other research work aboard their vessels. During this period of voluntary cooperation, it was understood that the role of these NMFS employees was not to collect information on compliance with government regulations. Their role was recognized by the captains and crews as being the same as that of IATTC personnel, who recorded data on tuna fishing operations for scientific purposes. In conversations with NMFS officials, tuna industry representatives were assured that NMFS agents would document tuna/porpoise fishing operations of U.S. tuna seiners as scientists, rather than as NOAA enforcement officials.[3] In 1975, the NMFS confirmed this understanding on two occasions:

> "It should be noted that observers are not enforcement officers, but are principally involved in gathering data on the cause of porpoise kills and basic biological information regarding the porpoise opulations. The information collected is of major value in evaluating the effectiveness of measures being taken to reduce incidental porpoise mortality in the yellowfin tuna purse seine fishery."[4]

> "Some have misconstrued the role of observers and characterized them as enforcement officers. However, the Notice makes it clear that the role of the observers will be, among other things to gather scientific data and monitor compliance with the regulations. Certain data collected by observers may, if requested by the public, be made available under the provisions of the Freedom of Information Act. The observers, however, will have no enforcement authority."[5]

During a Congressional hearing in 1975, Robert W. Schoning, Director, NMFS, NOAA, Department of Commerce, was asked by a House member of the Committee, Rep. Glenn M. Anderson, California, "What is your impression, in your conversations with the skippers of the way the skippers and owners of the tuna boats would react to having a government observer on every boat?" The Director answered:

> "... I think that there will be real difficulty in getting observers aboard if, and this is very important if, if they go aboard under the conditions that they are to record everything that happens, including violations of regulations. **However, if they go aboard only under the framework in which they initially went aboard in the last couple of years when we first put observers aboard as scientific observers recording scientific biological information to help us improve the situation, and if their findings will not be used to cite people for violation of regulations, I do not think there would be nearly the problem of getting people aboard.** However, if it is in the other framework then there is [sic] some real problems to have our people out there recording things on regulations. . . . "(emphasis added)

Mr. O. William Moody, Administrator, Seafarers International Union of North America, AFL-CIO, stated before a Congressional Committee: "We are also deeply concerned that the concept of "cop aboard every vessel" would be accepted by the committee or the U.S. government as the means by which compliance with this law could be ascertained. We feel that this concept is repugnant to the basic concepts of freedom and individual rights upon which our nation has long been based and should be rejected. ... if we continue a single standard of enforcement, not only in the matter of the tuna porpoise issue, but also enforcement of tuna conservation agreements ... with other nations; to the extent we are going to travel further down the road to the eventual extinction of our tuna fishing fleet ..."[6]

Poor performances by three tuna captains and their crews helped cause an un-expected and early porpoise mortality quota closure on the U.S. tuna fleet in October 1976. These performances were later found by the NMFS to have caused 35 to 45 percent of the "observed" porpoise mortality recorded for the entire U.S. tuna fleet. Thereafter, representatives of "protectionist" groups and others demanded that the NMFS take enforcement action against tuna captains who recorded poor performances in reducing porpoise mortality when fishing tuna/porpoise schools. The low porpoise mortality (4 deaths) attributed to fish-ing operations aboard the 1976 experimental cruise of the ELIZABETH C.J. was used by these groups to support their demands on the NMFS and Con-gress. The performance of the Captain and crew of the ELIZABETH C.J. in re-cording low porpoise mortality with high tuna catch came as an unexpected surprise for the onboard marine biologists. These scientists had been told by various persons prior to the cruise that they would see a "slaughter" of porpoise by the tuna fishermen.

A representative of Friends of Earth testified before a Congressional Committee:: "Given the fact that a disproportionate percentage of the kill of porpoise is in-flicted by a comparatively small number of captains, it seems almost patently ob-vious that administration of the act should aim at forcing incompetent captains to either retire from the fisheries, or improve their performance ...[7] The representa-tive of the Society for Animal Protective Legislation, stated: "Observers must re-port the violations of regulations which they observe for the purpose of law en-forcement by the Department of Commerce. This is the most important of their functions and it should not be limited in any way. ..."[8]

---

[1] SWFC-1976: 14.

[2] Report of the Secretary of Commerce dated June 1978, covering the period April 1, 1977, to March 31, 1978; on page 19, it is stated: 29 of the alleged violations were tuna-porpoise related."

[3] 1975 House Subcommittee Hearings-SN-94-16: 56-57

NMFS Field-Technicians, were termed "observers" by tuna fishermen. "Observers are GS-5 Biology Technicians, college graduate, most with sea experience. They are hired on a not to exceed one year temporary basis, and given 2 to 3 weeks of full-time orienta-tion and training in the class rooms and laboratory." 1975 House Subcommittee Hear-ings-SN-94-16: 258-259. The NMFS Observer Program began in 1966; porpoise mortali-ty data were first collected by an agency scientist in 1968. There were 6 observer trips in 1971, 13 in 1972, 24 in 1973, and 41 in 1974.

[4] "Report on the National Marine Fisheries Service Program to Reduce the Incidental Take of Marine Mammals," (1977) NMFS-SWFC: 1.

[5] 40 FR 56899 (December 5, 1975). See: January 1977 ALJ Decision: 149. "Mr. Winfred H. Meibohm, Assistant to the Director of the NMFS, stated that the observers are not en-forcement agents; they are essentially scientific observers, though their reports may be a source of possible infractions."

[6] 1975 House Subcommittee Hearings-SN 94-16:175-178. At the same hearing, representatives of groups concerned with animal protection were urging effective enforcement of NMFS regulations governing tuna seiners, stating: "Next year, I hope we will have a listing of substantial fines resulting from the enforcement of the regulations to protect dolphins." 1975 House Subcommittee Hearings-SN 94-16: 115. During these hearings, representatives of organizations, some of whom wanted total and absolute protection of marine mammals from commercial fishing, testified that their investigation of selected summaries of NMFS observer reports showed that tuna captains holding certificates of inclusion under the ATA general permit were committing regulatory violations. These summaries of NMFS observer reports were limited to sets by tuna seiners in which 50 or more porpoise died. The Freedom of Information Act was used by these organizations to conduct the investigation. 1975 House Subcommittee Hearings-SN 94-16 : 118. Two persons representing the Environmental Defense Fund reviewed the NMFS observer data. The review took place at the SWFC on July 30 and August 1, 1975. "A cursory examination was made of approximately 16,000 pages of data which constitute the first twenty observer cruises made during 1975." 1975 House Subcommittee Hearings-SN 94-16: 318-324.

[7] May 1977 House Committee Hearings-SN-95-3: 88.

[8] May 1977 House Committee Hearings- SN-95-3: 84.

25

THE "DEDICATED VESSEL" IN 1978

A Hope to Solve the "Enigma"

Dr. William W. Fox, Chief of the Oceanic Division, SWFC-NMFS, in response to a congressman's question on the possibility of continuing improvement in reducing porpoise mortality by perfection of gear and procedures during an oversight hearing on the MMPA in September 1976, stated:

> "I think that with some experimentation, perhaps with the system that we are developing now, it can become efficient. **Our real hopes are in getting into a new area of research by looking at tuna and porpoise behavior; their sensory systems, looking into methods of capturing tuna without capturing porpoise in the net or better ways of removing or segregating the animals in the net and removing porpoises from the net without having to back down."**[1] (emphasis added)

After explaining the mission of the experimental cruise of the ELIZABETH C.J. during a 1976 House Oversight hearing, Dr. Kenneth S. Norris, principal investigator and in overall charge of the experimental cruise, stated:

> "If the powers to be had responded to the continued call on the part of the [Marine Mammal Commission (MMC)] and its Committee of Scientific Advisors for a dedicated vessel to solve this problem, we might have reduced the kill to less drastic levels than we see today. ... I have outlined a program for such a vessel that would productively consume more than a year's time at sea ... [this program] would change the entire complexion of the problem ... A dedicated platform would serve to drive the program—no longer would all science be jammed together in a disorganized way on cruises only scheduled at very sporadic intervals in less than ideal circumstances. Gentlemen, if you really want to solve this problem, you will listen carefully to this suggestion, and you will act upon it. The result of inaction on this repeated request has resulted in a threatened industry, an enraged public, and a terribly frustrated scientific community who would like very much to help with every resource at their command. Thank you."[2]

In 1978, the tuna industry responded to the challenge made by Dr. Norris by providing the tuna seiner QUEEN MARY with its captain and crew for a "dedicated" year-long scientific research program to be conducted by the NMFS and MMC.[3]

Five Experimental Cruises

The Dedicated Vessel Program was a cooperative tuna/porpoise research program under the joint direction of the MMC, the NMFS, and the United States Tuna Foundation (USTF). Research funds and/or support were provided by the NMFS, the USTF, the National Science Foundation (NSF), and the MMC. The tuna seiner QUEEN MARY, chartered for the calendar year 1978 by the USTF, was used for this research. The vessel and its captain and crew were to make five cruises in waters of the eastern Pacific Ocean (EPO) of about 50 days each. In command of the QUEEN MARY was Ralph F. Silva, Jr., of San Diego, a highly-respected and successful tuna captain.

The research goals were: "A. Continue to reduce incidental and/or accidental porpoise mortality by: 1. transfer to the fleet of technological improvements in existing fishing systems, while 2. scaling down research emphasis on alternative fishing systems not requiring pursuit and/or encirclement of marine mammals. B. To generate additional data which will lead to refined estimates of status of porpoise stocks and impacts of the fishery on porpoise."[4]

Captain Ralph Silva and the QUEEN MARY
Photo Courtesy of Captain Ralph Silva

The QUEEN MARY (O/N 520 243) was owned by Marilyn M. Fishing, Inc., and managed by Captain Joseph (Joe) Medina, Jr., shareholder and Managing Officer. She was built in 1969 at Alameda, California, and her homeport was San Diego. The vessel's registered length, breadth, and depth were 136.8', 34.4', and 12.8', respectively. Her gross registered tonnage was 509 tons, with a frozen tuna carrying capacity of 520 to 550 short tons, depending on the size of the fish. She had twin Caterpillar diesel engines, 1125 horsepower each, allowing a top speed of 12.5 knots. She was equipped with a Caterpillar 333 bow-thruster, a Marco # W1062 main winch, and a 42-inch power block. The purse seine was 560 fathoms (3360 feet) long, 11 standard 4 1/4-inch mesh strips deep (about 65 fathoms or 390 feet), with 190 fathoms (1140 feet) of double Medina Panel (1 1/4-inch mesh) and a Super Apron.

Cruise One had two legs (26 January to 1 March 1978 and 3 to 16 March 1978). One of the eight objectives of this cruise was "to develop and enhance fishing methods which do not require the chase or capture of porpoise." Sound recordings were made of fish found in the vicinity of flotsam ("logs"), and the preliminary results justified further recordings on other cruises. The idea was to attach acoustical listening devices to floating objects (logs or man-made fish-aggregating devices (FADs)) so that the fishermen could monitor many logs or FADs, and then travel to the ones that had a strong tuna presence.[5]

During Cruise Two (17 April to June 5, 1978), a NMFS device known as the "Porpoise School Impoundment System (PSIS), was used to handle and release porpoise.[6] The PSIS was attached to the cork line of the net in the "porpoise release area," allowing the transfer of the porpoise from the net into the PSIS. The objective was to develop a way to examine whole schools of porpoise, and for scientists, "to carry out studies of school structure, population density and migration, and physiological parameters."

On the first leg of Cruise Three (22 June to 15 July, 1978) the objectives were to study the bio-acoustics of tuna-common dolphin schools, to detect log-associated tuna acoustically with passive listening devices, to test the use of a device ("Shark Field") that would generate pulsed, high-voltage electrical fields and cause control of tuna movements within the net, and to test the effectiveness of the "Shark Field" in protecting the contents of the net from shark attacks during sack-up and brailing. It was found that the "Shark Field" did not affect tuna behavior, and that passive listening devices could not detect the tunas. The Report expressed the view that future research efforts should be directed at both remote sensing and remote monitoring devices to locate tuna, and that acoustics held "considerable promise for remote detection of the tuna schools, but the simple listening devices tested to date have proved ineffective."[7] On the second leg of Cruise Three (20 July to 18 August, 1978), research was conducted on porpoise behavior in the net and on the efficacy of tuna olfactory attractants.[8] The olfactory attractants were found to be successful for only a short period of time. The behavioral investigators made a total of 135 five-minute recorded observations, sufficient for developing a "dictionary" of porpoise behavioral events and patterns while in the net.

During Cruise Four (12 September to 31 October, 1978), the PSIS device was used on 9 of 17 porpoise sets to tag porpoise.[9]

On Cruise Five (11 November to 10 December, 1978), research was directed primarily toward porpoise stock assessment. The first part of the trip focused on describing and measuring the "parameters of tuna purse seining, including the interaction of the net, seiner, and net skiff."[10] During the second part of the trip, about 7,000 feet of movie film of the fishing operations were taken for producing a "20 minute skipper/observer training film."

After reading a review of the NMFS administrative reports on the five cruises, Captain Silva stated that in his view nothing of value in reducing porpoise mortality was produced during these five experimental voyages. He recognized that much of the experimental work and collected data did not relate to improving the "existing fishing system." However, he strongly voiced his view that nothing was achieved during these cruises that would help him and other tuna captains become more efficient in saving porpoise. He recalled the day during Cruise One when, after reviewing a proposed research list "of about a hundred items," he told the scientists that most, if not all, of the ideas were unrealistic. He said that he appreciated the work of Frank T. Awbrey (San Diego State University) during Cruise One and Cruise Three, of William E. Evans (Hubbs-Sea World Research Institute) on the first leg of the Third Cruise, of Ms. Karen Pryor (New

York University) during the second leg of the Third Cruise, and of Franklin G. Alverson (Living Marine Resources) during Cruise Five. He stated that the radio-tracking of porpoise during Cruise Four was educational, in that it confirmed his views about how the composition of tuna/porpoise schools would change from mainly spinners to mainly spotters within a short time and within a small geographical area.[11]

Very little, if any, information about the "Enigma" was obtained by the studies conducted by the marine mammal scientists during the five experimental cruises. Efforts by the NMFS to develop modifications to the "standardized net" to reduce porpoise mortality by testing them aboard chartered U.S. tuna seiners during 1977, 1979, and 1980 were not productive.[12] During Cruise One, however, the QUEEN MARY caught more tuna in sets on floating objects (63 tons of yellowfin and 307 tons of skipjack in 17 sets) than in sets on fish associated with porpoise (159 tons of yellowfin in 10 sets). During the 1990s and 2000s, FADs were extensively used to attract fish, and most of the skipjack caught by purse seiners during that period were taken in association with floating objects. Unfortunately, however, substantial amounts of juvenile yellowfin and bigeye are also caught in sets on floating objects, which has apparently reduced the total catches of those two species. "From 1978 to 1981 a substantial portion of the funds for the mortality reduction project was spent to study and develop a computer–based, interactive numerical simulation of purse-seine behavior and to establish field measurements with which to verify the results of the simulation program."[13]

---

[1] SEP 1976 House Subcommittee Hearings-SN 94-45: 77

[2] SEP 1976 House Subcommittee Hearings-SN 94-45: 115. Two U.S. tuna seiners were chartered by the NMFS during 1977: MARGARET L. (19 May to 11 September and 27 October to 11 November) and the MARLA MARIE (2 November to 25 December). During 1979, two U.S. tuna seiners were chartered by the NMFS: CABRILLO (19 May to 19 July and 18 August to 7 October) and MARIA C.J. (17 September to 22 November). The final charter of a U.S. tuna seiner for gear research to reduce porpoise mortality occurred in 1980: MARIA C.J. (22 September to 28 December).

[3] For comments about the "dedicated vessel" by an administrative law judge (ALJ): January 1977 ALJ Decision: 46-48.

[4] DeBeer, J., F. Awbrey, D. Holts, and P. Patterson, 1978. Research Related to the Tuna-Porpoise Problem: Summary of Research Results from the First Cruise of the Dedicated Vessel, 26 January-16 March, 1978. SWFC Admin Rep. LJ-78-14, at pp. iii-iv. Scientific personnel on voyages: David B. Holts, NMFS, Cruise Leader, Dive Master; Richard W. Butler, NMFS; Paul Patterson, LMR; Frank Awbrey, San Diego State University (1st Leg); Donald Ljungblad, Naval Ocean Systems Center, (1st Leg); John DeBeer, Program Manager, 1st Leg, and Dale Powers, NMFS (2nd Leg).

[5] DeBeer, J., F. Awbrey, D. Holts, and P. Patterson, 1978. Research Related to the Tuna-Porpoise Problem: Summary of Research Results from the First Cruise of the Dedicated Vessel, 26 January-16 March, 1978. SWFC Admin Rep. LJ-78-14.

[6] Coe, J. M., J.G. Jennings, C.B. Peters, and J. DeBeer, 1979. Research Related to the Tuna-Porpoise Problem: Summary of Research Results from the Second Cruise of the Dedicated Vessel, 17 April to 5 June 1978. SWFC Admin. Rep. LJ-79-6. Scientific personnel on voyage: James M Coe, NMFS, Cruise Leader; Jacqueline G. Jennings, NMFS; Warren E. Stuntz, NMFS; James F. Lambert, NMFS; William A. Walker, NMFS Contractor, and Charles B. Peters, LMR.

[7] Awbrey, F.T., T. Duffy, W.E. Evans, C.S. Johnson, W. Parks, J. DeBeer, 1979. Summary of Research Results from the First Leg of the Third Cruise of the Dedicated Vessel, 22 June to 15 July 1978. SWFC Admin. Rep. LJ-79-11, at page 27. Scientific personnel on voyage: Frank T. Awbrey, San Diego State University; Thomas Duffy, NMFS; William E. Evans, Hubbs-Sea World Research Institute; C. Scott Johnson, Naval Ocean Systems Center; Wesley Parks, LMR, and John DeBeer, Program Manager.

[8] Bratten, D., W. Ikehara, K. Pryor, P. Vergne, J. DeBeer, 1979. Summary of Research Results from the Second Leg of the Third Cruise of the Dedicated Vessel 20 July to 18 August 1978. SWFC Admin. Rep. LJ-79-13. Scientific personnel on voyage: Dave Bratten, NMFS, Cruise Leader; Walter Ikehara, University of Hawaii, Karen Pryor, New York University; Philippe Vergne, LMR; John DeBeer, Program Manager.

[9] Powers, J.E., R.W. Butler, J.G. Jennings, R. McLain, C.B. Peters, J. DeBeer, 1979. Summary of Research Results from the Fourth Cruise of the Dedicated Vessel 12 September to 31 October 1978. SWFC Admin Rep. LJ-79-14. Scientific personnel on voyage: Joseph E. Powers, NMFS, Cruise Leader, Richard W. Butler, NMFS; Jacqueline G. Jennings, NMFS; Rodney McLain, LMR; Charles B. Peters, LMR, and John DeBeer, Program Manager.

[10] Holts, D.B., R. McLain, F.G. Alverson, J. DeBeer. 1979. Summary of the Research Results from the Fifth Cruise of the Dedicated Vessel 11 November to 9 December 1978. SWFC Admin. Rep. LJ-79-20. Scientific personnel on voyage: David B. Holts, NMFS; Rodney McLain, Contractor to LMR, Franklin G. Alverson, LMR, and John DeBeer, Program Manager.

[11] Personal conversation with Captain Ralph Silva, Jr., on August 24, 2006.

[12] Two U.S. tuna seiners were chartered by the NMFS during 1977: MARGARET L. (19 May to 11 September and 27 October to 11 November) and the MARLA MARIE (2 November to 25 December). A "bubble screen" to separate the tunas from the porpoise was tested with negative results during the fall cruise of the MARGARET L. Also tested with negative results was a device attached to the Super Apron called an "Apex Flapper."

[13] James M. Coe, David B. Holts, and Richard W. Butler, "The Tuna-Porpoise Problem: NMFS Dolphin Mortality Reduction Research, 1970-81," Marine Fisheries Review, 46 (3): pp. 18-33.

PART VII

THE FLOGGING CONTINUES, 1978-1980

26

RATCHETING-DOWN REGULATORY PROPOSALS, 1978-1980

With the failure of the 95th Congress to pass a legislative amendment to the MMPA, the Secretary of Commerce decided to implement the policy of President Carter's administration by regulation. This decision was supported by the adoption of a compromise amendment to H.R. 6970 that affirmed the idea of requiring progressive reductions in porpoise mortality by establishing a schedule of ratcheting down the annual quotas.

Differences in the Estimation of Porpoise Populations: Impact on the "Optimum Sustainable Population" (OSP)

During a Tuna-Porpoise Oversight Hearing conducted by the House Committee on Merchant Marine and Fisheries on August 1, 1977, Chairman John Murphy was introduced to the newly-appointed Administrator of NOAA, Richard A. Frank. He advised Mr. Frank and his aides that he sought answers to the following subjects: (1) A report prepared by his staff about a document containing a chart that was distributed during the 34th meeting of the IATTC, held on June 27-29, 1977, in San Diego, showed "considerable differences between the Commission's dolphin population estimates and those made by the NMFS.[1] He asked what NMFS had done to resolve these differences;" (2) status of the promise by the tuna industry to provide a "dedicated vessel;" and, (3) the progress, if any, on the implementation by the IATTC of the resolution adopted at the San Diego meeting regarding the placement of observers aboard selected foreign tuna seiners.

On the issue of why the difference in opinions by the IATTC and NMFS on the abundance of porpoise populations, Congressman Murphy was told by Dr. William Fox, Chief, Oceanic Fisheries Division, SWFC-NMFS, **that the NMFS had evaluated the IATTC chart, and that the IATTC "came up with population estimates that are considerably larger than the ones that the (NMFS) has adopted to date."** (emphasis added) This exchange with Dr. Fox on estimating porpoise populations from aerial surveys provided Chairman Murphy with the opportunity to report his experiences aboard the JEANNINE, as follows:

> "However, I do appreciate the disparity of data concerning dolphin populations. I spent Memorial Day aboard the tuna boat JEANNINE and observed firsthand the setting on dolphin for tuna and the dolphin rescue procedures used by the industry. I was most impressed with the "Back-down" techniques, the fine mesh paneling and with the genuine interest of crew members to reduce mortality.

"On the JEANNINE, the mast is about 87 feet above the water level and the bridge about—I guess about 25 feet, and there were three power scopes [binoculars]. These experts, who were ocean masters, trying to locate dolphin from all four points of reference. The dolphin were finally located and these experts were trying to make an accurate count of the dolphin as the vessel approached them. This is a very, very difficult task, because I asked about eight different people there to give me their estimate as to the dolphin numbers, and this is virtually on the surface with a fairly decent angle of observation, not 1,000 feet up, and we had totally different estimates on each of these schools.

"It was not until I got in the water after the dolphin had been encircled with a net and observed the dolphin from the bottom up that I realized there were layers of dolphin in schools....

"I think our colloquy pretty well points out there can be differences of opinion as far as the numbers of dolphin in any given setting vis-à-vis the total populations of the different sizes. These estimations have built-in inaccuracies an[d] a lack of scientific depth, and when I see IATTC and NMFS differing, I can easily see where there could be honest differences because of my firsthand experience with those people on board the ship."

Administrative Law Judge Hearings and Final Agency Rules

On July 20, 1977, the NMFS proposed regulations governing the U.S tuna seiner fleet in fishing tuna/porpoise schools for 1978, 1979, and 1980. Administrative Law Judge (ALJ) Frank W. Vanderheyden was selected again to conduct the public hearings on the 11 major proposals to amend the existing NMFS tuna/porpoise regulations.[2] They were held in San Diego on August 22-30, 1977 (excluding August 28), and in Washington, D.C., on September 6-8, 1977. The record of eleven days of hearings consisted of 1,915 pages of transcript, 60 exhibits, and 32 officially-noticed documents.[3]

In his November 1977 Recommended Decision, the ALJ provided a helpful explanation as to how the Medina Panel concept evolved into various types of small-mesh configurations in the "Back-down" area of the purse seine. For the ALJ, this report clarified the effectiveness of the three modifications of the net's "Back-down" area that had been developed prior to the 1976 experimental cruise of the ELIZABETH C.J. He identified the 2-inch small-mesh, single "Medina Panel" as the "Conventional System" (CS), the 1-1/4-inch fine-mesh, double "Medina Panel" with attached 1-1/4-inch small-mesh "Apron" as the Bold Contender Apron System (BCS), and the 1-1/4-inch fine-mesh Double-Medina Panel without an apron appendage as the Fine-Mesh System (FMS). Although the ALJ found that the ramp-like shape developed by the apron appendage of the BCS during "back-down" was more helpful in reducing porpoise entrapment than the FMS, which had no apron appendage, he also noted that the BCS had operational problems not experienced by the FMS.

The ATA and its consultants did not consider the new gear requirements unduly burdensome and costly to the US fleet. However, the new rule requiring that by July 1, 1978, all Class-III tuna seiners (vessels with fish-carrying capacities greater than 400 short tons) be equipped with the "Super-Apron" developed during the 1976 experimental cruise of the ELIZABETH C.J. was objectionable to many tuna captains and crew members. The Judge noted: "The results of the 1977 fishing season, to date, have confirmed that the SAS (super-apron system) represents the best technology available now. As of the time of the hearing, 18 Class-III tuna seiners have installed the SAS voluntarily ... Porpoise mortality data from May through August 1977, confirm the excellence of the SAS."[4] During the hearing, the ALJ noted: "The Industry is firm in its thinking that the SAS should not be mandatory, but optional equipment. Why it is asked, should a captain who has experienced low mortality rates with the FMS be required to convert to the SAS? It is also argued that the compulsory nature of the SAS denies the fishermen flexibility to experiment with new equipment and techniques."[5] The ALJ set aside these points by noting that the fleet's tuna nets should be standardized because the fleet has a history of captains and crews being changed frequently for a variety of reasons, and that the proposed regulations allow flexibility for innovation because applications for experimentation with new gear and procedures are allowed subject to the discretion of NMFS.[6]

The tuna captains who were very successful in recording low porpoise mortality without having an "Apron" or "Apron-chute" or "Super-Apron" strongly question the need for the government to compel them to install the "Super-Apron." Their objection to this "standardization rule" did not include the small costs of materials and labor for installation. They asserted that the fleet needed freedom from regulation, freedom in this area of net development to promote individual innovation and imagination, and that government-imposed standardization of nets would hinder the flexibility needed at sea by captains and crews to develop new gear technology to reduce porpoise mortality. They questioned the practicality of the regulatory proposal that the fishermen could petition the NMFS to experiment on the ground that this option involved "officialism" that tended to discourage innovative fishermen.

During the six-year period of 1971-1976, the average tonnage of yellowfin tuna caught on tuna/porpoise schools was about 112,000 short tons. Based on the NMFS quotas for 1978 (51,945), 1979 (41,610), and 1980 (31,150), the ALJ estimated that the fleet would have to achieve kills per ton of 0.44 animals for 1978, 0.35 animals for 1979, and finally 0.26 animals for 1980 in order to maintain this average annual catch of tuna. "The regulations seek a 50 percent reduction in porpoise mortality over three years."[7] In response to the Tuna Fleet's objections to the proposed regulatory regime, the ALJ stated in part:

> "A thought concerning technological feasibility. The NMFS owes a debt to the fleet for developing much porpoise saving equipment and techniques ... Understandably, fishermen, as others, tend to resist change, preferring to do things at their own pace... The record shows that much of the resistance to the proposed equipment and techniques has its roots in misunderstanding, distrust of government regulations generally, and suspicion of the unfamiliar. While there is empathy for the fishermen's attitudes, it is outweighed by the fate of the marine mammals, where continued delay results in increased mortalities."[8]

On December 16, 1977, the Administrator of NOAA, rather than the NMFS Director, made the final decision establishing the regulations to govern the taking of tuna/porpoise schools in the eastern Pacific Ocean (EPO).[9] This decision of the Administrator, Richard A. Frank, established declining individual species and stock porpoise quotas totaling 51,945 for 1978, 41,610 for 1979, and 31,150 for 1980. It was explained that this ratchet-down approach was taken because a rule prescribing level annual quotas for three years "would not conform to the goal of the Act if lower annual quotas are economically and technologically achievable."[10]

The negatives of this Final Decision were perceived by many in the US Tuna Industry as follows:

(1) The probable policy of the Secretary of Commerce was to "progressively" reduce the take of marine mammals by the US tuna seiner fleet after 1980 by reducing the annual quota by at least 50 percent every second year. The only defense to that would be the difficult task of proving in litigation that the Secretary's judgments were arbitrary; therefore, he had abused his discretionary power;

(2) The NMFS would be engaged in trying to take a "census" of porpoise populations in the EPO so as to estimate the "optimum sustainable population" (OSP) of all affected porpoise species and populations; therefore, the risk of further claims by the NMFS that, in addition to the eastern spinner stock, other affected species/stocks were not at or above the bound of OSP or 60 percent of initial stock size. The option available to the industry would be another lengthy and expensive ALJ hearing to engage experts on population dynamics and statistics to challenge the validity of the "depleted" findings;

(3) The affirmation in two successive Final Decisions by NOAA/NMFS that OSP was in the range of 50-70 percent of initial stock size, and that the MMPA term "depleted" means a porpoise population not at or above the lower bound of OSP or 60 percent of initial stock size, and

(4) That NOAA Counsel would use observer reports and the new regulations to strictly prosecute all violations of regulations, rather than exercise discretion in those cases in which tuna captains would violate technical regulations to protect and save porpoise during fishing operations.[11]

About nine years later, on January 3, 1986, the NMFS published in the Federal Register a Final Rule that made changes in tuna seiner vessel gear and procedural requirements for fishing tuna/porpoise schools.[12] The NMFS explained that "several regulations concerning required fishing gear and fishing practices will be modified or deleted in recognition that they are excessively restrictive or have become unnecessary. To "provide greater flexibility in the application of porpoise saving gear and techniques by operators and crews on U.S. (tuna seiners) ... fourteen regulatory items were identified for changes."[13] Importantly, tuna captains were given the option of using either the "super apron" system or the "fine mesh" system. The NMFS had found that both systems were effective, and noted that "the skill of the skipper and crew in using porpoise safety gear and procedures is the critical element in preventing mortality." The tuna captains who had objected to requirements that their gear be standardized were vindicated when the standardization approach was replaced by NMFS guidelines. The reasoning behind the regulatory change was explained by the NMFS, as follows:

"Up to this time, the U.S. Marine Mammal Regulations have prescribed in considerable detail the porpoise safety gear to be used and the procedures for its use.
Years of experience under those regulations revealed that although the gear and
procedural requirements typically had the desired effect of reducing porpoise kill
and injury, there were some limited circumstances under which it appeared that
departures from the strict requirements of some of the regulations might have resulted in less hazard to marine mammals. As a result of this experience, beginning in 1986 some regulations were reduced to guidelines to allow flexibility for
unusual circumstances and to encourage the development of further porpoise saving measures. Thus, the opportunity to reduce porpoise mortality can be enhanced without the fear of prosecution for technical violations of the U.S. Marine
Mammal Regulations."[14]

The Expert Skipper Panel and the Porpoise Rescue Foundation [15]

Every set of the tuna purse seine is unique. This is because there are too many
elements—human and natural—at work to allow such an event to be duplicated.
The fishermen identify a set without problems in catching tuna as a "regular set"
or a "normal set." A "problem set" occurs when some event involving gear, the
tuna/porpoise schools, sharks, the ocean environment, or human failures, inter-
venes to delay or prevent the captain from commencing or completing the "back-
down" procedure. If the event creates a "net collapse," then the captain has the
option of aborting the set to prevent hundreds of porpoise mortalities. No captain, crew, or vessel is immune to having a "problem set." The term "skunk set"
is used by the fleet to identify a set in which few or no tunas, other species of
fish, or porpoise are caught. IATTC records show that during the 1970s about 16
percent of the sets on tunas associated with porpoise and about 50 percent of
those on non-porpoise schools were skunk sets.

The idea of transferring the technology or "trade secrets" of fishing tuna/porpoise
schools for the purpose of reducing porpoise mortality occurred at the ATA during discussions with Franklin G. Alverson of Living Marine Resources (LMR). He
suggested that a confidential meeting of certain "top" skippers be held as soon as
possible in early 1971 for the implementation of this "idea." Gradually, the success of this first meeting developed into a second idea of having, in addition to
confidential meetings with skippers, regular ATA workshops on the subject of tu-
na/porpoise fishing to help the skippers help themselves. After the MMPA was
enacted, NMFS personnel participated in a large number of ATA-sponsored
workshops involving many tuna captains and crew members. Thereafter, the
NMFS established its own skipper training workshops.

After the Porpoise Rescue Foundation was organized, with LMR as its manager, the process of meeting with skippers became more formalized, and these
meetings of selected tuna captains became known as the Expert Skipper Panel. The ALJ noted in his Recommended Decision dated January 17, 1977, that
the Expert Skipper Panel was a "group involved in an effort to reduce porpoise
mortality" that it was organized in April 1975, that "it has as its immediate objective the formulation of procedures that would result in a 30 percent reduction in
the kill rate of porpoise per ton of yellowfin caught among problem vessels,"
and that the "group consists of the more highly qualified tuna boat captains

whose vessels experience low mortality rate. The ALJ also noted: "Aside from a few meetings, nothing concrete was accomplished in 1976 prior to the time of the hearings." (p. 48)

The ALJ was correct in noting that the Expert Skipper Panel had no authority, and operated only by persuasion and peer pressure. The General Permit was granted to the ATA by the NMFS, but the ATA had no power to revoke a certificate of inclusion.

In his Recommended Decision dated November 4, 1977, the ALJ noted that "there is great potential in the Skipper Panel (SP) for reduction of porpoise mortality. As presently constituted, however, the SP represents a stellar example of exclusivity. It is difficult to see how a NMFS representative could damage the potential of the SP . . . Though the SP is not part of the proposed regulations, there has been evidence on the subject, and it is again recommended to the Director that at the nearest appropriate time, steps be taken to have the SP include a NMFS representative." (pp. 88-90) The Final Decision of the Administrator of NOAA did not adopt the ALJ's recommendation because "an NMFS representative on the skipper's panel would compromise its purpose, and explained:

> "This panel should be a peer group that can correct a skipper's performance whether or not they are related to formal regulatory requirements. If the peer group feels that the individual skipper has serious problems, then they may recommend to the NMFS that his certificate be revoked ... Also, the ALJ appeared to have misunderstood the NMFS sponsorship of the present skippers training workshops. NMFS people participate directly in the skipper training sessions, data gathering and analysis, and have effective liaison with the Porpoise Rescue Foundation, Living Marine Resources, and individual skippers. Therefore, I do not believe that a NMFS representative on the skipper's panel will improve its function."[16]

The most important contribution of the Expert Skipper Panel was in helping tuna captains become more skillful and productive by being more knowledgeable in reducing porpoise mortality. This help took place in confidential meetings held in the ATA boardroom. The tuna captain would meet with at least two or three members of the Expert Skipper Panel and an officer of the ATA. Prior to the confidential meeting, a representative of the Porpoise Rescue Foundation (PRF) would review the important sections of the NMFS observer's reports concerning the sets made by the tuna captain that caused high porpoise mortality. After this review, PRF representatives would leave, allowing the tuna captain to enter the boardroom for a confidential discussion with the panel. Most meetings would last about two hours because of the need to review the observer documentation regarding the "problem" sets. A follow-up of the tuna captain's performance would be made by PRF. The co-authors were members of the Expert Skipper Panel; they do not recall any instance in which a tuna captain had to return for a second session with the Expert Skipper Panel on the ground that the captain had again recorded a poor performance in rescuing porpoise after his first session.

On December 13, 1978, members of the Expert Skippers Panel met with many industry representatives and others for the purpose of discussing and documenting operational procedures for "normal sets" on tuna/porpoise schools. The 20 tuna captains present at this meeting stressed "that each set is somewhat unique due to the great number of variables associated with fishing operations. Skillful maneuverings of the vessel, power skiff, power block, and cable winches are required to counteract the many physical forces which tend to close the net, create canopies, and entrap porpoise and block their escape through the "Back-down" channel during fishing operations."[17] The 10-page technical bulletin produced by PRF staff member Charles Peters, which was based upon the meeting's discussion, contains photographs and drawings showing how to set the purse seine, how the skiff is to tow the tuna seiner, how to perform certain operations during the pursing or closing of the seine, rolling of the net, and the "back-down."

This PRF bulletin was distributed throughout the fleet with the intent "to present many of the features of good tuna/porpoise fishing techniques so that new or younger skippers may benefit from the [Expert Skipper] Panel."

The interaction between the porpoise and fishermen was producing results in saving porpoise once they were encircled by the net, but the porpoise were also learning how to evade the purse seine:

To create motivation and an incentive for the tuna captains, the ATA established an annual presentation called the "Golden Porpoise Award." A brass statuette of a spotted porpoise was presented to the captain who recorded the lowest porpoise mortality rate during the year. It was presented to the captain in December during the annual ATA dinner meeting, at which representatives of all segments of the tuna industry were in attendance. Captain Lou Brito proposed this award during a 1979 meeting of the ATA Board of Directors and, also volunteered to donate the statuette each year. NMFS observer data were used by the PRF to determine which captain had the lowest porpoise mortality rate during the year.[18] To be awarded the "Golden Porpoise" by his peers became very meaningful and valuable to a tuna captain.[19] During the period 1980-1990, Captain Manuel Jorge received the award in 1980 and 1990, Captain Roman Rebelo in 1988 and 1989, John Balelo in 1981, and Joe Da Luz in 1984.

After 1977, the Expert Skipper Panel worked directly with a newly-created NMFS extension group. This NMFS team helped the captains and crews of the fleet to properly install required net modifications. Working with the Expert Skipper Panel to become aware of the latest techniques and methods to reduce porpoise mortality helped this team communicate to the fishermen new and proven developments in saving porpoise. This was important because, on average, a tuna seiner was at sea 200 to 220 days a year, working in an ocean area five times larger than the continental United States. Tuna captains customarily communicated with one another at sea by radio; vessels met bow to bow on the fishing grounds infrequently, and usually only to transfer supplies, fuel, or personnel.

---

[1] See: Annual Report of the IATTC 1977: 7-9 During the 34th meeting of the IATTC, held in San Diego, California, on June 27-29, 1977, the commissioners adopted a resolution directing the IATTC to "undertake activities to evaluate the populations of porpoise in the (EPO) ..." This was done after Commissioners reviewed and discussed the report of the

Director of Investigations on the problems arising from the tuna-porpoise relationship. The IATTC also approved a porpoise research budget of $640,427 for fiscal year 1978-1979. Funds for this purpose were not received by the IATTC until 1979. At the time of the adoption of this resolution, the member nations of the IATTC included Costa Rica, the USA, Panama, the United Mexican States, Canada, Japan, France, and Nicaragua. (Ecuador adhered to the IATTC Convention in 1961, but then withdrew effective 1968.) Representatives of Colombia, Guatemala, Korea, Peru, and Spain attended the meeting as observers. See also: Clifford L. Peterson and William H. Bayliff. 1985. Organization, Functions, and Achievements of the Inter-American Tropical Tuna Commission, Inter-Amer. Trop. Tuna Comm., Spec. Rep.5: pp. 7, 19-20

[2] United States Department of Commerce, National Oceanic and Atmospheric Administration, National Marine Fisheries Service, Recommended Decision. In the Matter of Proposed Amendments to Regulations to Govern the Taking of Marine Mammals Incidental to Commercial Fishing Operations for the Years 1978 through 1980, Docket No. MMPH No. 1-1977, (November 4, 1977), (cited hereinafter: "November 1977 ALJ Decision").

[3] Final Decision of Administrator, NOAA: 42 FR 64548-64551 (December 23, 1977). Final Rule: 42 FR 64551-64560 (December 23, 1977).

[4] November 1977 ALJ Decision: 36.

[5] November 1977 ALJ Decision: 36-37.

[6] November 1977 ALJ Decision: 37. "Also, there is mobility among the skippers of tuna-boats. Assuming a skipper has been using FMS with good results, he could be replaced by one having a poorer record with such system. For example, on observed trips, from January 1974 through July 15, 1977, there were 41 changes of captains out of a potential of 75, resulting in a 55 percent chance of a different captain. This mobility problem is answered by standardizing the equipment and thereby minimizing the time it takes a skipper to adjust to new gear." Changes may have been caused by a skipper's decision to command a new U.S. or foreign-flag tuna seiner.

[7] For information on the formula used to arrive at the "Kill Rate per Ton," see: November 1977 ALJ Decision: 39. View the ALJ's reasoning on the issue of whether the proposed quotas met the requirements of the MMPA as to conforming to its goal of technological feasibility: November 1977 ALJ Decision: 40-51. Conclusions of the ALJ on the issue of economic feasibility of the regulations: November 1977 ALJ Decision: 68-69.

[8] November 1977 ALJ Decision: 50.

[9] The authority of the Secretary of Commerce to administer the MMPA and to make final decisions on regulations concerning the taking of marine mammals incidental to the course of commercial tuna fishing operations was delegated to the Administrator of NOAA, including the authority in make the final decision on the Final Rule. See: 42 FR 64548 (December 23, 1977)

[10] Proposed regulations, amending the NMFS regulations were promulgated on March 1, 1977. 42 FR 12010 (March 1, 1977): 42 FR 37217 (July 20, 1977). On August 12, 1977, the Draft Environmental Impact Statement (DEIS) was circulated. In accordance with the MMPA and procedural regulations, hearings were conducted by Administrative Law Judge (ALJ) Frank W. Vanderheyden: 42 FR 35967 (July 13, 1977). ALJ hearings were

held in San Diego, California, on August 22-27 and 29-30, 1977, and in Washington, D.C., on September 6-8, 1977. Oral closing arguments were heard in Washington D.C., on October 5, 1977. Notice of the delivery of the ALJ's Recommended Decision to NOAA/NMFS: 42 FR 58419 (November 9, 1977). Notice of the issuance of the General Permit to the American Tunaboat Association (ATA) on December 27, 1977: 42 FR 65237 (December 30, 1977).

[11] "Something appears to be awry with enforcement of the current regulations ... during 1976, infractions occurred on 29 of 54 cruises ... that where fines have been issued they were low considering the potential earnings of the vessel per voyage, and ... that as yet, there are no penalty points for repeaters of violations ... Notwithstanding, regulations to be effective must be enforced with a will." November 1977 ALJ Decision: 90.

[12] 51 FR 197 (January 3, 1986).

[13] 51 FR 197 (January 3, 1986): 199.

[14] Mendes, Norman A, J. Brent Norberg, John A. Young, David R. Cormany, and Ben S. Meyer, "Protecting Porpoise A Guide for Tuna Seiners," Tuna/Porpoise Management Branch, February 1986, Southwest Region, NMFS: 2

[15] For comments about the work of the Porpoise Rescue Foundation and the Expert Skipper Panel during 1976 and 1977, see: January 1977 ALJ Decision: 45, 48-54. For a description of the activities of the Expert Skipper Panel and of the work of the Porpoise Rescue Foundation during the 1980s: Hearings before the National Ocean Policy Study of the Committee on Commerce, Science, and Transportation, United States Senate, 100th Congress, 2nd Session, on The Reauthorization of the Marine Mammal Protection Act, April 13 and May 19, 1988, S.Hrg.100-711, (hereinafter cited Senate Committee Hearing 100-711): 138-141.

[16] 42 FR 64551 (December 23, 1977).

[17] Charles Peters, "Operational Procedures of a Normal Set on Yellowfin Associated with Porpoise," Technical Bulletin, Porpoise Rescue Foundation (1979):1.

[18] In early 1980, the ATA obtained a report from the PRF regarding the performance of the top 10 Captains in the fleet in saving porpoise alive from the net during the previous three-year period (1977- 1979). The result was based upon NMFS reports covering the performance of 85 captains on 32 fishing trips. The government observers recorded 997 sets on tuna/porpoise schools, an estimated 1.2 million porpoise pursued, of which about 755, 000 were encircled after pursuit, and 536 porpoise mortalities. The top 10 Captains in order of top performance: Manuel Jorge, John Balelo, Louie Romani, Belchoir Mauricio, Chris Da Rosa, Ralph Silva, Maurice G. Correia, Spiridione Brunetto, Anthony Sabella, and Joe Da Luz.

[19] Based upon available ATA records, the annual Golden Porpoise Award was given to Captain Manuel Jorge in 1980 and 1990, to Captain Roman Rebelo in 1988 and 1989, to Captain John Balelo in 1981, and to Captain Joe Da Luz in 1984. Information on the Award has not been found in ATA and PRF records for 1982, 1983, 1985, 1986, and 1987.

27

REGULATORY ABUSE OF DISCRETION, 1980

During 1976-1977, segments of the U.S. tuna industry had developed serious concerns about the high risk of adverse porpoise "depletion" determinations by the NMFS based upon changing interpretations of the controversial MMPA phrase "optimum sustainable population" (OSP). In 1979, these concerns became reality when NMFS scientists participating in a workshop filed a report supporting a finding of "depletion" for the extremely important northern coastal spotter and offshore spotter porpoise stocks.[1] This finding would prohibit the U.S. fleet from fishing tuna/porpoise schools that were composed entirely or in part of either of these "depleted" porpoise stocks.

The findings in the 1980 Decision of the Administrative Law Judge (ALJ) were favorable to the industry.[2] However, portions of the Final Decision of the Administrator of NOAA (hereinafter cited "1980 NOAA Decision"), combined with other political and economic events affecting the industry, supported the concern of some in the industry that the U.S. tuna seiner fleet operating in the eastern Pacific Ocean (EPO) was fast becoming an unreliable source of tuna to the U.S. canners. The negative aspects of the 1980 NOAA Decision raising these concerns are found in its articulate explanation of how the application of OSP requires **continuing** estimates of the current abundance of the affected porpoise stocks and of their pre-exploitation stock size in 1959.[3] The "uncertainty" of fishing tuna/porpoise schools in the future by the U.S. fleet was made manifest by this decision.

The 1980 NOAA Decision stated: "I find that the ratio of present population of northern offshore spotted (3.15 million to their pre-exploitation population (5.03 million) is above the lower end of OSP (60%)."[4] **The NOAA Administrator also noted that the MMPA does not require a formal ALJ hearing to address quota mortality or other adjustments.[5] [and] that "[t]he disadvantage test is a continuing obligation of the agency." ... and that "[s]o long as there is an assurance that the populations will not be disadvantaged by the proposed takings, there is no need to adjust the taking regulations except for modifications to the existing quotas to achieve the Act's immediate goal objective."[6]** (emphasis added)

The NOAA Administrator also acknowledged that the significant costs and burdens to the parties in compiling a record in ALJ proceedings, and the argument of the American Tunaboat Association (ATA) that a multi-year permit should again be issued because of the costs to the NMFS and industry in preparing for the hearing.[7] The hearings were held in San Diego, California, from March 31 through April 5, 1980, and in Washington, D.C., on April 14, 15, and 18, and May 19, 1980. The Administrative Hearing Record included a transcript of about 1,674 pages, 155 exhibits, and extensive post-hearing briefs. It is believed that this ALJ hearing was the longest and most expensive in the history of the U.S commercial fishing industry. The ATA was later advised that the legal fees, expert fees, and other charges associated with the preparation for, and participation in the 1980 ALJ hearing had cost the industry slightly over $1 million.

Faulty Estimates of Optimum Sustainable Population (OSP)

The NMFS considers OSP as the "standard by which a determination of disadvantage to a porpoise stock is made." This standard was expressed as a range during the NMFS's 1976 Workshop, namely from 50 to 70 percent of the original porpoise stock size, and the mid-point (60%) of this range "was used to determine if the stock was depleted (42 F.R. 64548, Dec. 27, 1977)." The NMFS decided that the upper range of OSP to be the maximum number of porpoise that the ecosystem can support, and the lower end of OSP as a level of the original porpoise stock size that "will produce the maximum net increase in population." The NMFS contends that this lower end of OSP—a range within a range—can be determined theoretically. The NMFS asserted: "Every population of animals has a size at which it will increase at a maximum rate," that this level is "known as the Maximum Net Productivity Level (MNPL)," that it "is expressed as a range to reflect uncertainties in the data," and "is the lower end of OSP." 45 F.R. 72185, (Oct. 31, 1980).

Based upon a report of the 1979 Workshop, the NMFS claimed that the OSP had a range of 65-80 percent.[8] In his Final Decision,[9] the NOAA Administrator explained:

> "The report compares porpoises to other mammals and abandons the 1976 workshop approach of the linear relationship between stock growth and reproductive rates. This more conservative approach is based on the observation that larger mammals are longer lived and reproduce later in life and, therefore, require a large population to achieve MNPL, than smaller animals such as rodents. ..."

The ALJ found that the lower bound of OSP was between 50-70% of the original stock size. He found that the 50-70% range was already conservative and that a change to 65-80% range based on a change in population dynamics theory, rather than new data, was unwarranted, (Findings 144-50) ... "Despite my agreement with the workshop's theoretical approach, I cannot conclude that the range used by the workshop (66-70%) is the best. There is no direct evidence that porpoise populations fit the theoretical model. ... Therefore, I conclude that the best scientific evidence in the record is that 60 is the point where the lower range of OSP should be set." 45 F.R. 72185, (Oct. 31, 1977)

The Estimation of OSP: Current Abundance (45 FR 72180-183)

The Final Decision of the NOAA Administrator clarifies the methods used by the NMFS to estimate the original porpoise population size of an affected porpoise stock, a level critical to the estimation of OSP and of its lower range or the MNPL. On the issue of the present abundance of the affected porpoise stocks, the decision showed that all five factors used to compute such levels were in dispute during the ALJ Hearing.[10] The four basic data sources used to make population estimates: observer records, tuna vessel records, aerial surveys, and research vessel surveys.

In his Recommended Decision, the ALJ found that, "The best scientific evidence available consists of a combination of data from aerial survey, research vessel, and federal observers on tuna vessels." The Administrator of NOAA agreed with the 1979 Workshop Report that the NMFS observer data be excluded in computing the five factors used to estimate the population level of each porpoise stock. The ATA agreed with the ALJ's finding, and later obtained federal rulings against the Secretary of Commerce that found that NOAA "acted arbitrarily in failing to utilize the best scientific evidence in arriving at porpoise population and range estimates."[11] The June 1985 Annual Report of the Secretary of Commerce stated: "It is not expected that the decision in ATA v. Baldrige will affect the ongoing implementation of the tuna porpoise program. The decision, however, will have a bearing on the methodologies used in arriving at future estimates of population size."[12]

The Estimation of OSP: Pre-Exploitation Abundance (45 FR 72183-185)

The lack of any estimates of the abundance of porpoises in the EPO for 1959 required the 1979 Workshop participants to make a "back calculation" "in order to estimate the abundance of each stock in the year the stock was exploited to a significant extent. 1959 is the year that the industry began using purse seines on a large scale, and most of the porpoise stocks are assumed to have been at their maximum size (by number and area) in that year." The 1980 Final Decision explains that "back calculation" requires "a theoretical addition to present abundance of all porpoises incidentally killed since 1959 and a subtraction of the number of net recruits added to the stock in the interim years." To estimate the "addition," three types of data were required: (1) the number of sets made by tuna seiners on tuna/porpoise schools; (2) the number of porpoises killed in each set; and, (3) an apportionment of the mortalities by species. The "subtraction" is a number, "R_{max}," to be added to the population annually. R_{max} is the maximum annual rate of net production by porpoises in the EPO. Again, in the hearing, all of these issues were in dispute.

The ALJ covered the issue of "back calculation," advising in Finding 46: "Candor compels the conclusion that considerably more guesswork, and therefore considerably more uncertainty, is involved in the estimates of pre-exploitation size."[13] On the issue of R_{max}, the Administrator of NOAA and the ALJ agreed that the maximum net reproductive rate of 4 percent, based upon the 2-6 percent range adopted by the 1976 Workshop, was the best available estimate. In his Recommended Decision, on page 20, the ALJ noted: "The observational data from all sources reflect a large, healthy population apparently in excess of 3,000,000 creatures in the particular stock ... The experience with the stock is not depressing; the indications, even with respect to recovery, are strong. Implementing a change in theoretical approach is neither necessary nor desirable."[14]

Final NOAA/NMFS Decision and Regulations

In his Final Decision, the NOAA Administrator made three critical rulings. First, that an annual quota of 20,500 porpoise mortalities was economically and technologically feasible for a five-year period, 1981 through 1985. The ATA had requested a permit for a mortality take of 31,000 a year for a five-year term. Second, agreement with the ALJ that the northern offshore porpoise spotted stock was not depleted.[15] Third, rejection of the ALJ's recommended acceptance of a proposed regulation prohibiting the setting on a tuna/porpoise school at and after sundown "only if there was concurrently adopted a program of observer placement on all [tuna seiners]." The ALJ had made a finding that his prohibition "may reduce the catch of yellowfin on porpoise by approximately 10 percent." In adopting this proposed change, the Administrator knowingly reduced opportunities for the U.S. fleet to catch tuna in competition with foreign fleets, and reduced the mortality quota from 22,320 to 20,500.[16]

Importantly, the Administrator of NOAA also rejected a recommendation of the ALJ that responded constructively to the industry's continuing "request for broader freedom and flexibility for permitting operators to experiment with different gear and techniques." The Administrator explained that he did not want to compromise the methodology for monitoring of porpoise mortality that relied "on fishing gear and procedural requirements that are standardized for the entire U.S. fleet."[17]

The hearings on the proposed 24 regulatory changes were conducted by ALJ Hugh J. Dolan, an employee of the Department of Commerce, experienced in conducting hearings on "Tuna/Porpoise Enforcement Cases."[18] The fascinating feature of this regulatory episode was the unique story told by the ALJ, and his style of presentation. To illustrate, we quote extensively from Judge Dolan's decision, as follows:

> **"This rulemaking may, in some respects, be likened to a wake or a death watch over the U.S. tuna industry. (p. 96)** (emphasis added)

> "In the course of numerous regulatory proceedings considered since enactment of the Marine Mammal Protection Act of 1972, much publicity and sometimes virulent criticism has been made against the regulators and regulations. The cry of wolf has been frequently heard from the articulate and outspoken representatives of the industry to the point where they may now be ignored. The facts are that the salutary environmental concerns of the statute have been met and the fishermen have not been seriously hampered by the regulations presently in effect. The situation with respect [to] the depletion determination involving the Northern Offshore Spotted Stocks is significantly different for the stated reasons. The expressions of concern are not exaggerated. . . . The outlook is dismal. (pp. 96-97)[19]

> "If a finding is made that the stock in question is in fact depleted, I recommend that consideration be given to the Department of Commerce promptly sponsoring appropriate Congressional action to assure the continued viability of the United States participation in the fishery in order to provide for the survival of the domestic industry, the tuna stocks, and all of the affected species of porpoise particularly for the three million or so Northern Offshore Spotted Porpoises that will be adversely effected [sic.] by such a favorable determination." (p.97)

The ALJ explained why the 1979 Workshop on Status of Porpoise Stocks (SOPS) made errors in determining that the Northern Offshore Spotted Porpoise stock was "depleted." First, in contrast to the 1976 Workshop, it rejected the use of observer data "for significant portions of estimations, *e.g.* mean school size and proportion of target schools to all schools." The ALJ went into detail on the value of observer data and the "indefinite" reasons given by the Workshop to exclude these data:

"For the government to reject the very substantial data which it has compiled with the cooperation of the industry over many years on such inadequate representation[20] is not permissible [p. 9]. ... The government may not simply dismiss the most comprehensive data base which it has accumulated, with substantial effort by all parties, or to pick and choose when it will and will not use such information. How can it be said that the other, almost fragmentary by comparison, surveys from fixed wing aircraft and research vessels are creditable that the agency scientists condemn, without adequate explanation, the basic data collection which they have supervised and which is similar to the data collected and utilized by such international organizations as the International Whaling Commission (IWC) and the Inter-American Tropical Tuna Commission (IATTC)? If anything, that data should be accorded a higher degree of acceptability since it is accumulated in a scientifically prescribed format by trained, disinterested persons, rather than crew members who might be considered biased in such reporting. (p. 10) ... I conclude that such data must be considered as the primary validated informational source for the various population estimates of porpoises in the eastern tropical Pacific, including, but not limited to, stock assessments, school sizes, species proportion, density of schools, population size, areas inhabited, proportion of each species, stock and target schools, as well as any other formulation relevant to the regulatory determinations. I also find and conclude that the fractional data from the research vessels and aircraft sightings is also appropriate to consider, though I would accord a lesser level of reliability to the accuracy and validity of such surveys (p.11).

"... I do not accept the representation that observers in a fixed wing aircraft traveling at 130 or so miles per hour at a 900 foot elevation see all schools under all conditions. [pp. 12-13]. ... The basic assumption, that there is a high density band [of porpoise] near the coast and a lower uniform density throughout the balance of the range, appears to be justified only if the large mass of tuna vessel data is discarded. Such warping of the data to fit the theory is not permissible. [p.13]

"As a compromise approach for this proceeding I would at least combine the three data sets for porpoise school size. That is how I arrive at the 328 school size figure recognizing, however, that that estimate is low even if all the data is accepted." [p. 15]

The ALJ made 193 findings. The last 42 of these findings related to the various adverse impacts of the proposed regulation prohibiting the taking of northern offshore spotted porpoise stock by the U.S. tuna seiner fleet, including harm to the yellowfin tuna conservation and management efforts of the IATTC, and serious economic injury to the U.S. tuna industry. A selection of these findings is offered in summary form, as follows:

"The agency's proposed ban on setting on northern offshore spotted porpoise will also harm yellowfin tuna conservation efforts. ... If the proposal is adopted, a stress on the yellowfin tuna resource would be caused by the resulting change in fishing strategy. . . . Young, small yellowfin, normally not in association with porpoise, are found in greatest numbers in the inshore grounds. ... The expected impact of the proposal would be that United States fisheries on the outside of the CYRA would probably disappear completely simply because in that region the fishing is virtually all on porpoise stocks that are proposed to be prohibited. ... This change in fishing strategy would present a substantial threat to conservation of yellowfin tuna. ... Inshore schools of small yellowfin not associated with porpoise would probably be the source for much of the catch. ... The proposal, if implemented, will tend to have a negative effect on yellowfin tuna production. ... The effect of such implement will also be contrary to effects under the IATTC to afford maximum sustainable catch of tuna and therefore tends to run contrary to "existing international treaty and agreement obligations of the United States.' [16 U.S.C. Section 1373(b)(3)].

"The proposal is economically disastrous to the United States-flag tuna industry. . . Historically, tuna caught in association with porpoise have comprised, on the average, about 45 percent of the annual landings of the purse seine vessels. ... Over 70 percent of the yellowfin tuna catch taken on porpoise involves offshore spotted porpoise. ... The U.S. catch could decrease by as much as 53,000 tons and fleet revenue by as much as $71,400,000 per annum. Canneries may increase dependence on imported fish, and flag transfers may increase. ... The proposed reductions in porpoise quotas and the zero quota for northern offshore spotted dolphins stock, will have a major adverse impact on the harvest sector of the U.S. tuna industry.

"Tuna canneries account for a significant amount of direct employment. Some 6,215 employees in California and 6,834 employees in Puerto Rico, and the number of indirect jobs affected by this industry more than double this amount. ... It is probable that Puerto Rican and United States canneries could not operate under the unstable supply conditions created by curtailing ETP [eastern tropical Pacific] yellowfin supplies and would eventually have to cease their operations. The short and long term effects on socio-economic effects particularly upon the Puerto Rican communities will be very severe. ... At best, under the proposed regime, a 20 percent reduction in supply would be realized, at its worst, probably in excess of 40 percent, in the near term. A 20 percent reduction in the supply of yellowfin tuna to these plants would mean severely curtailed plants utilization, loss of direct employment would equate to 1300 workers, and shipments to the United States would decline drastically. In addition, canned tuna prices would rise sharply to the consumer from a reduced supply of canned lightmeat tuna. ... Implementation of the proposed changes would hasten and encourage the movement of these United States vessels to foreign flag registry. ... The proposed regulations are not economically feasible to implement not only for the United States tuna fishing fleet but also for the United States canning industry."

Relatively little gear research and development was carried out by the NMFS during the Carter administration (1977-1980). During this period, it was the policy of the NMFS to reduce U.S. fishing effort on tuna/porpoise schools by ratcheting downward annual quotas and by imposing restrictions on when, where, and how the fleet was to fish tuna/porpoise schools. Fortunately, the extension service of the NMFS worked closely and well with the fleet, the Porpoise Rescue Foundation, the ATA, and the Expert Skipper Panel. As a result, changes to the "Back-down" area of the nets to small mesh were implemented and the captains and crews worked to make the modified nets reduce porpoise mortality. During 1978-1980 NMFS observers monitored 4,849 sets fishing tuna/porpoise schools and recorded 17,362 mortalities, or about four porpoise per set. About 52,066 tons of yellowfin tuna were caught, or about one porpoise mortality per three tons of tuna. NMFS observers recorded that about 94% percent of the porpoise encircled by the 4,314 successful sets on tuna/porpoise schools were successfully released from the nets.[21]

During the 1971-1976 period, an annual average of about 112,000 short tons of yellowfin tuna was caught by the U.S. Tuna Seiner Fleet on tuna/porpoise schools. During 1977-1979, the average catch of yellowfin tuna declined to about 69,000 short tons, a 38-percent reduction. After the1980 Final Decision of the Administrator, NOAA, and new rules were published, speculation on the San Diego waterfront was that during the next five-year period (1981-1985) further substantial reductions in the annual porpoise mortality quota of 20,500 and/or prohibitions on the taking of various stocks of porpoise would be imposed by the NMFS. Members of the ATA expressed confidence that they would be able to further reduce porpoise mortalities. Observer records showed that the U.S. fishermen were improving their ability to prevent pre-back-down net collapse and canopies during back-down. Other causes of porpoise mortality occurring in the back-down channel still represented a problem, as were gear malfunctions. Importantly, captains and crews were reporting that offshore porpoise stocks were adapting to encirclement and to the "back-down" by remaining quietly in the net until the back-down commenced, and then swimming through the back-down channel to freedom.[22]

During the 1980s, no significant gear research directed at improvement of tuna purse-seine gear or fishing techniques to reduce porpoise mortality were undertaken jointly by the U.S. tuna captains and the NMFS. The most important innovation came from Captain Harold Medina when, in 1981, he designed and supervised the construction of the purse seine for the new super seiner OCEAN PEARL. He modified the "cork or float line" located in the "back-down" area so that the floats would be free to flop downward when pressed by wave action or by a porpoise moving out of the small mesh segment of net. This change from the traditional way that the cork line was installed allowed the porpoise to help themselves out of the net more easily during the back-down. In addition, Captain Medina retained the basic design of the net in the back-down area, which had proven highly successful in saving porpoise aboard the super seiner CAROLYN M. Specifically, the small-mesh segment was attached in a pattern that involved two different sized large-mesh segments. This arrangement would cause the small-mesh segment to be stretched in a manner that was more effective in preventing porpoise entanglement during the back-down. Also, the net of the OCEAN PEARL was composed of a new synthetic material that would sink more-rapidly than nylon, thereby increasing the likelihood of capturing a school of tuna. Although this third innovation was tested successfully aboard the OCEAN PEARL, this fact was not sufficient to cause other vessel owners to replace nylon webbing with webbing composed of this new synthetic material.

1981 Amendment of the MMPA: Help from Congress

By modifying Section 101(a)(2) of the MMPA, Congress helped the U.S. Tuna Industry. The original goal set forth in the MMPA with respect to the "incidental kill or incidental injury of marine mammals in the course of commercial fishing operations" was expressly and singularly changed for the U.S. tuna purse-seine fleet, as follows:

"… In any event it shall be the immediate goal that the incidental kill or incidental injury of marine mammals permitted in the course of commercial fishing operations be reduced to insignificant levels approaching a zero mortality and serious injury rate; provided that **this goal shall be satisfied in the case of the incidental taking of marine mammals in the course of purse seine fishing for yellowfin tuna by a continuation of the application of the best marine mammal safety techniques and equipment that are economically and technologically practicable**. ..." (emphasis added)[23]

Section 1 of this amendment, which concerned Section 3 of the Act (16 U.S.C. 1362), was entitled "Optimum Sustainable Population."[24] The terms "depletion" and "optimum carrying capacity" were affected. Section 5 of this amendment changed Section 110(a) of the Act of 1972 (16 U.S.C. 1380(a), by directing the Secretary of Commerce to undertake research in new methods of locating and catching yellowfin tuna without the taking of porpoise.[25]

A continuing problem for the fishermen was the ability of the porpoise to find and use new ways to avoid the chase and net encirclement. What concerned the U.S. fleet most about the future was the increasing number of foreign-flag tuna seiners fishing tuna/porpoise schools and the porpoise mortality resulting from the operations of these seiners. Why the concern? This porpoise mortality would be taken into account by the NMFS in setting porpoise mortality quotas for the U.S. fleet. More importantly, the NMFS would have to determine whether a combined mortality (U.S. and foreign) was working to the disadvantage of a particular porpoise stock, as required by the MMPA.[26] Finally, if the captains of the foreign-flag vessels were less careful than the captains of the U.S.-flag vessels, the abundance of porpoises could decrease to the extent that it would become more difficult to find tunas associated with porpoises.

Unfortunately, other natural and economic events were starting to affect the U.S. tuna industry. In time, they would overshadow the fleet's concerns about fishing tuna/porpoise schools in compliance with NMFS regulations.

---

[1] The Workshop, designated as the "1979 Status of Porpoise Stocks (SOPS)," was held in La Jolla, California, on August 27-31, 1979. The General Permit issued to the American Tunaboat Association (ATA) on December 23, 1977; the regulations applicable to this Permit were due to expire on December 31, 1980. In anticipation of these events, the NMFS commenced the preparation of a Draft Environmental Impact Statement (DEIS) on August 9, 1979, and convened a workshop for the purpose of developing the scientific basis for considering the re-issuance of the General Permit to the ATA and proposed regulations for 1981 and beyond. Background information and importance of the Workshop:
45 FR 72179 (October 31, 1980).

[2] United States Department of Commerce, Office of the Secretary, Washington, D.C. 20230. In The Matter of Proposed Regulations to Govern the Taking of Marine Mammals Incidental to Commercial Fishing Operations: Docket No. MMPAH 1980-1, Recommended Decision of July 18, 1980, (cited hereinafter: "1980 ALJ Decision").

[3] 45 FR 72180 (October 31, 1980) "However, in the event that new evidence is discovered or that the continuing refinement of the NMFS resource assessment data suggests

that takings may disadvantage any of the stocks, I am prepared to propose further amendments to the regulations, as was done in 1980. To insure that there will be no disadvantage to the stocks I am directing NMFS to continue to monitor and assess the status of all stocks in the ETP and to make a complete assessment of these stocks no later than 1984. ..."

[4] 45 FR 72180 (October 31, 1980.

[5] 45 FR 72179 (October 31, 1980) "Although the Act does not require a formal hearing to address adjustments for the 1980 season, NMFS determined that this was the best means of reviewing the Report and other relevant information."

[6] 45 FR 72186 (October 31, 1980).

[7] Although many modifications have been made by the NMFS to regulations governing the taking of tuna/porpoise schools by U.S. tuna seiners in the eastern Pacific Ocean since 1980; a formal ALJ hearing on such matters was never again conducted.

[8] 1980 ALJ Decision: 38, Findings 81: "The 1979 SOPS Workshop consisted of 17 participants, principally government employees and contractors. No industry representatives were invited to participate, though some were present as observers or in preliminary study meetings. The principal qualification for participation was specialized scientific expertise in population dynamics of mammals, particularly marine mammals of which little is known."

[9] 44 FR 67194 (November 23, 1979): An "Advanced Notice of Proposed Rulemaking" published by the NMFS/NOAA/DOC advising that a formal hearing would be conducted by an ALJ to consider whether the existing regulations should be changed for 1980, with the regulations to apply in 1981. This was done because the Report of SOPS Workshop contained information suggesting that the northern offshore spotted porpoise stock was "depleted," as that term is defined in the MMPA. Notices of the proposed regulations, availability of the DEIS, of the ALJ hearing, of expedited hearing procedures, and of the ALJ appointment, were published: 45 FR 10552 (February 15, 1980). The Recommended Decision of the ALJ was issued on July 18, 1980. The Final Decision and Final Rule of Richard A. Frank, Administrator of NOAA, was made on October 31, 1980. 45 FR 72178 (October 31, 1980).

[10] The five factors: (1) the mean size of porpoise schools; (2) the density of porpoise schools in the inhabited area; (3) the area inhabited by stocks in the ETP [eastern tropical Pacific (4) the proportion of schools that are "target" schools (*i.e.* spinner or spotted porpoise (5) the proportion of target species within target schools.

[11] American Tunaboat Ass'n v. Baldrige, 738 F.2d 1013 (1984). The Secretary of Commerce was required in 1982 to provide a reassessment of certain porpoise populations that supported a finding that the eastern spinner stock was above its OSP and not depleted as defined by the MMPA. For comments about this lawsuit in annual reports on the administration of the MMPA prepared by the U.S. Department of Commerce, NOAA, NMFS: Annual Reports 1981: 82; June 1982: 26; Annual Report 1982/83, June 1983: 17; Annual Report 1983/84, June 1984: 20; Annual Report 1984/85, June 1985: 21-22.

[12] U.S. Department of Commerce, NOAA, NMFS: Annual Report 1984/85, June 1985: 21-22, 22. 16 USCS § 1373 (f) "... and every twelve months thereafter, the Secretary shall report to the public through publication in the <u>Federal Register</u> and to the Congress on

the current status of all marine mammal species and population stocks subject to the provisions of this Act. ..."

[13]1980 ALJ Decision: 31, Finding 44: " The estimates of pre-exploitation population data size are based on a variety of data that was collected at various times for diverse purposes not relating to porpoise population size." 1980 ALJ Decision: 31, Finding 45: "Because that data was not generated in a systematic sort of way, it is uneven in scope, sparse, or altogether missing for many years, and certain of its [data] is of marginal quality."

[14] 1980 ALJ Decision: 38, Finding 82: "The 1979 workshop report acknowledges (pp. 53-54) the difference in population estimates is not the result of increased mortality of porpoises caused by fishermen since 1977, but rather is the result of differences between the method of estimating the stocks used in the 1979 workshop and those determined to be used by the NMFS in the 1976 and 1977 proceedings. 1980 ALJ Decision: 39, Finding 83: The 1979 workshop report recognizes (NOAA 52) that the net annual increase in the total offshore spotted porpoise population (northern and southern components) could well be between 0 and 132,161 animals annually." 1980 ALJ Decision 51-52, Finding "153: "Since these stocks carry few tuna ... The experience with the spotted population indicates a degree of patterned reaction or receptivity to encirclement and a developed facility for escape at "Back-down," probably indicating less stress to this species, a phenomena [sic.] which will not exist with the target species."

[15] 45 FR 80855 (December 8, 1980): A five-year General Permit (1981-1985) was issued to the American Tunaboat Association. Legislative authority for multi-year permit: 1981 amendment to the MMPA (Public Law 97-58). Public Law 97-58, 97th Congress, October 9, 1981. 95 STAT. 979. Legislative History: H.R. 4084: House Report No. 97-228, Committee on Merchant Marine and Fisheries; *Congressional Record*, Vol. 127 (1981), September. 21, 1981, considered and passed House, and on September 29, considered and passed Senate.

[16] 45 FR 72186 (October 31, 1980) ".. I find that the 1977-79 period is the best period from which to apportion the modified replacement yield to arrive at individual stock quotas. This figure is multiplied by a kill/ton rate of .24 results in a quota of 22,320. This quota is further modified by 8.5% to reflect the lost catch due by adoption of the ban on sundown sets. This results in a quota of 20,500."

[17] 45 FR 72187 (October 31, 1980). "To compromise this standardization in any substantial manner would remove the existing basis of extrapolating known incidental porpoise takings reported by observers to those fishing trips that are not assigned an observer."

[18] 1980 ALJ Decision: 10-11: "As stated in the proceedings, I have seen and heard the testimony of more than 30 of the college graduate observers who were trained in biology, and in data collection techniques by the agency. I have repeatedly heard the representation of other government counsel respecting the scientific nature, validity and accuracy of their observations. I have also seen and reviewed the detailed records and reports made incident to the performance of their duties. ..."

[19] In his Recommended Decision, ALJ Dolan made 193 findings. 1980 ALJ Decision, Findings 151-193 stated various negative impacts associated with a finding that the northern offshore spotted stock was "depleted" as defined by the terms of the MMPA. For instance: 1980 ALJ Decision, Finding 177: "The U.S. catch could decrease by as much as 53,000 tons and fleet revenue by as much as $71,400,000 per annum. Canne-

ries may increase dependence on imported fish, and flag transfers may increase." 1980 ALJ Decision, Finding 159: "The agency's proposed ban on setting on northern offshore spotted porpoise will also harm yellowfin tuna conservation efforts." 1980 ALJ Decision, Finding 170: "The effect of such implementation will also be contrary to effects under the IATTC to afford maximum sustainable catch of tuna and therefore tends to run contrary to 'existing international treaty and agreement obligations of the United States' 16 U.S.C. Section 1373 (b) (3)."

[20] 1980 ALJ Decision: 8-9: The Workshop's reasoning to exclude the Observer data to determined mean school size was rejected by the ALJ: "The tuna vessel observers estimates were not used because tuna vessels may selectively search for larger vessels [sic.-schools] which are likely to be associated with tuna." This claim that larger porpoise schools will always contain more tuna than smaller porpoise schools is not true.

[21] Coe, James M., David B. Holts, and Richard W. Butler, "The 'Tuna-Porpoise' Problem: NMFS Dolphin Mortality Reduction Research, 1970-81, *Marine Fisheries Review*, 46 (3): 22, Table 3.

[22] IATTC 1985 Annual Report: 55-56. "Tuna fishermen have noted that dolphin behavior has changed over the years, presumably as a result of fishing pressure by tuna boats. In areas where fishing has been conducted for many years, it was once fairly easy to herd and capture the dolphins, but some species are now more difficult to capture. In areas where the fishery is relatively new, however, dolphins are still relatively easy to capture. Changes over time in the behavior of dolphins inside the net also have been noted. ... [Studies] suggest that spotted and whitebelly spinner dolphins which are relatively naïve to fishing operations are more vulnerable to mortality because of their more active behavior inside the nets. With more experience with the fishing process, however, they become less active." The effect of different fishing areas (new fishery area vs. old fishery area) on behavior was found to be non-significant for the eastern spinner dolphins.

[23] MMPA Amendment, Public Law 97-58-October 9, 1981; 95 STAT. 979-980;

[24] MMPA Amendment, Public Law 97-58-October 9, 1981; 95 STAT. 979

[25] MMPA Amendment, Public Law 97-58-October 9, 1981; 95 STAT. 986-987. "In carrying out this subsection, the Secretary shall undertake a program of, and shall provide financial assistance for, research into new methods of locating and catching yellowfin tuna without the incidental taking of marine mammals. The Secretary shall include a description of the annual results of research carried out under this section in the report required under section 103(f)."

[26] As stated by the Administrator, NOAA : "Optimum Sustainable Population (OSP) is the standard by which a determination of disadvantage to a porpoise stock is made." 45 FR 72185 (October 31, 1980)

EASTERN PACIFIC OCEAN

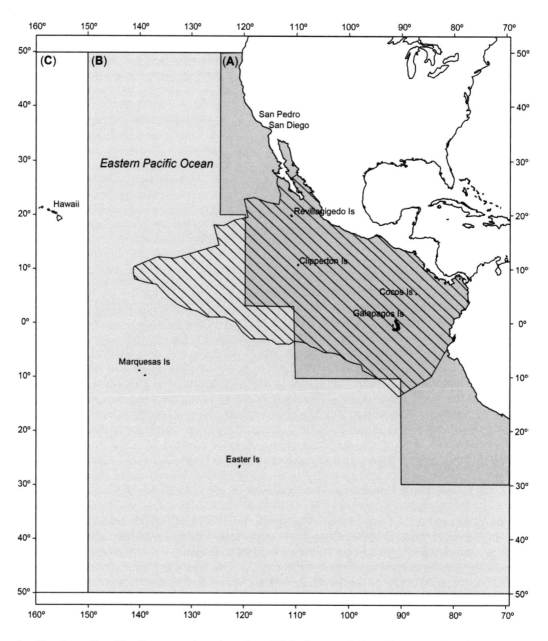

A. Eastern Pacific Ocean, showing the ATA General Permit area (160°W to the coast of the Americas)

B. Area of jurisdiction of the IATTC (150°W to the coast of the Americas)

C. The Commission's Yellowfin Regulatory Area (CYRA).

Hatch marks indicate the area in which sets on tunas associated with porpoises were made during 2008.

Photos courtesy of

WILLIAM BOYCE PHOTOGRAPHY

Underwater photo of yellowfin tunas and spinner porpoises

Yellowfin tunas

Yellowfin tunas

Yellowfin tuna with spinner porpoises

Spotter porpoises

Whitebelly porpoises

Yellowfin tunas swimming right under the surface

A "shiner" Yellowfin tunas

Spotter porpoises

Vessel midway in a set prior to "backdown"
Photo courtesy of William Boyce

Vessel in a backdown with porpoises swimming away from the net.
Photo courtesy of William Boyce

Chaseboat used to herd porpoise.
Photo courtesy of William Boyce

"Big" Skiff used to brail tuna aboard vessel.
Photo courtesy of Co-Authors

ELIZABETH CJ in a "backdown" configuration
Photo courtesy of National Marine Fisheries Service (NMFS)

Porpoises swimming away from backdown
Photo courtesy of William Boyce

WILLIAM BOYCE BIOGRAPHY

William Boyce, born February 21, 1956, in Granada Hills, California, is a 1979 graduate of Humboldt State University, California, with a B.S. in Fisheries. After graduation, he was hired as a fisheries biologist by the U.S. Forest Service, Tahoe National Forest. In 1982, he started working for an agency of the U.S. Department of Commerce, the National Marine Fisheries Service (NMFS). He served for 12 years as a shipboard observer and biologist to work on projects concerned with the management and conservation of the tunas, porpoises, sharks, and other pelagic species harvested in the Eastern Pacific Ocean. He made 23 trips as a federal observer aboard U.S. Flag Tuna Seiners, taking photos of their fishing operations as well as collecting scientific data. The average length of these fishing trips was about 60 days; his first and longest trip was 113 days, his shortest was 37 days. He considers his 1997 presentation of his tuna/porpoise collection of photos and fishing information to Members of Congress to be the "pinnacle of his career." Presently, Mr. Boyce is an internationally recognized photo/journalist. His photos have been published monthly in many national and international sportfishing publications. His filming activities for TV companies have taken him on numerous ocean expeditions throughout the world. Presently he is involved with the World Fishing Network, WFN, for the purpose of producing and hosting a TV network series on saltwater fishing/travel that will begin in April 2011.

PART VIII

RECESSION, GLOBALIZATION, EL NIÑO, AND THE SOUTHEAST ASIAN TRADE COMPETITION

28

GLOBALIZATION OF TUNA SEINING

During the 1960s, the U.S. tuna seiner fleet was proving to the world of fisheries that purse seining, as practiced in the eastern Pacific Ocean (EPO), was an exceptionally productive and reasonably profitable means of supplying tuna to canners. Vessels that had fished successfully in the EPO shifted their operations to waters off the east coast of the United States and, experimentally, to the Gulf of Guinea off West Africa during the early 1960s. During this period, tuna seiners based in Puerto Rico and San Diego were successful in harvesting bluefin tuna off New England and skipjack tuna off the mid-Atlantic States. Explorations by tuna seiners in the Gulf of Mexico, the Caribbean Sea, and off the northern coast of Brazil indicated that the tuna resources in these areas were limited. Within a few years, it was recognized that substantial amounts of tuna for canning could not be obtained by purse seining in the western Atlantic Ocean off the United States, in the Gulf of Mexico or the Caribbean Sea, or off South America. However, experimental fishing by a few small tuna seiners sent by a major U.S. tuna canner to fish in the tropical waters off West Africa produced encouraging results. Judgments were made by experienced U.S. tuna cannery officials and fishermen that the tuna fishing conditions off West Africa, particularly in the Gulf of Guinea, were favorable for the introduction of the California style of tuna purse seining. The question was how to convince talented U.S. tuna captains that they should leave the EPO, where they had been fishing successfully, to become "explorers" in waters off West Africa.

In 1967, the measures recommended by the Inter-American Tropical Tuna Commission (IATTC) staff to prevent the overfishing of yellowfin tuna were approved and implemented by the United States government in accordance with treaty obligations and statutory law. These measures resulted in an "open" season and a "closed" season within a regulatory area that bordered the Western Hemisphere from California to Chile, encompassing a part of the Pacific Ocean about five times the size of the continental United States. As the "open" season was reduced from 12 months to 9 months to 6 months, the pressure on the U.S. tuna industry to develop fisheries for tuna outside the IATTC's "Commission Yellowfin Regulatory Area" (CYRA) increased. This pressure was reduced for U.S.

tuna seiners based in Puerto Rico after they developed a successful seasonal tuna fishery from June to December off the coast and islands of West Africa from Angola to Senegal, especially, after they found that skipjack could be caught in commercial quantities off Angola. (The canneries in Puerto Rico had been constructed with the intention of utilizing tunas caught in the eastern Pacific and of albacore and yellowfin tunas caught in the Atlantic by Asian longliners) Not unexpectedly, this success influenced Spanish and French tuna entrepreneurs, with the help of their governments, to build their own fleets of U.S. style tuna seiners. The mid-East oil crisis of 1974 plus other operating problems made fishing off West Africa difficult for the U.S. tuna seiners, causing vessel owners to turn their attention back to the Pacific Ocean.

In another effort to adjust to the stringent IATTC conservation controls, U.S. tuna seiners based in California searched for new tuna fishing grounds west of the CYRA. In 1970, a fleet of six San Diego-based tuna seiners proceeded toward the western Pacific Ocean, with the objective of developing a purse-seine fishery off Palau, the Philippines, and islands near American Samoa. Instead, they found new areas of abundant tuna/porpoise schools in the EPO closer to San Diego and Hawaii than to American Samoa. This new tuna/porpoise fishery in the area called "the Outside," because it was outside the CYRA, was later used to help venturesome U.S. tuna seiners to participate in a new skipjack tuna fishery established off New Zealand and in searching for tunas on the track to and from American Samoa, such as in waters off New Caledonia. During the "closed season," a vessel could make a trip to "the Outside," unload its catch at a port in the eastern Pacific, then make a trip to New Zealand and unload its catch at American Samoa, and then arrange to bring a NMFS observer aboard so that it could fish in "the Outside," and then unload its catch in California. By the late-1970s, some vessel owners had decided to use American Samoa as their base of operations. After harvesting skipjack tuna off New Zealand from November to March, they would explore waters off various South Pacific islands for new tuna grounds in the western Pacific, rather than fish for tuna/porpoise schools in "the Outside" area. Also during this period in the 1970s, U.S. tuna seiners were chartered by a non-profit entity, the Pacific Tuna Development Foundation (PTDF), to test the effectiveness of the tuna purse-seine technique in the western Pacific. It was discovered that deeper nets, having depths of at least 15 strips or 90 fathoms, were required in the western Pacific, whereas in the eastern Pacific nets having a depth of 12 strips or 72 fathoms were employed.[1] It was also found that the yellowfin schools in the central and western Pacific did not school with porpoise, so tunas could be caught only in free-swimming schools or in schools associated with flotsam ("logs") or man-made fish-aggregating devices (FADs). In addition, some U.S. fishermen adopted unique fishing techniques used by Japanese tuna purse seiners to catch the deep-swimming tunas.[2]

It was no secret in the U.S. tuna industry that foreign and domestic entrepreneurs who were aware of the success of the "California Tuna Purse Seine Revolution" were engaged in efforts to transfer this technology to as many foreign fishing interests as possible. Also, San Diego tuna fishermen were not ignoring this opportunity to sell their technology. To finance the building of new "super" tuna seiners, many owners sold their old and tired converted tuna seiners to foreign buyers in Latin America and Asia. Much of this transformation from "old" converted seiners to new "super" seiners occurred during the late 1970s, a period of troubled economic times, when tuna entrepreneurs were hit with exceptionally high interest rates, rising fuel costs, and inflation.

By the early 1980s, fleets of Spanish and French tuna seiners had expanded from their traditional grounds off West Africa to newly-discovered and highly-productive tuna fishing areas in the Indian Ocean, especially in the tropical waters about the Seychelles. After disappointing years of trial and error in the eastern Pacific and off West Africa during the early 1970s, a growing fleet of Japanese tuna seiners was experiencing considerable success in the western Pacific by the mid-1970s, especially off Papua New Guinea, Palau, and around the Equator. This fleet was joined by a productive fleet of South Korean tuna seiners. Meanwhile, entrepreneurs in Latin America began acquiring large new purse seiners. The IATTC reported that during 1980, the fleets of Costa Rica, Ecuador, Panama, Peru, and Venezuela included 22 large tuna seiners and that Mexican citizens were operating 36 large tuna seiners.

By 1983, an estimated 346 "super" seiners, with carrying capacities of 500 or more metric tons of frozen tuna were afloat in the world. A 1984 report compiled by a U.S. Tuna Canner best illustrates the growing changes in the world's canned tuna industry wrought by the "California Tuna Purse Revolution." A table in this report listed 100 tuna purse seiners by name, flag, frozen tuna capacity, ocean fishing area, and an estimated total catch of tuna during that year. The total catch of this international tuna seiner fleet was approximately 460,000 short tons. About 2000 men caught enough tuna in 1983 to process about 28 million standard cases of tuna (1.4 billion cans), enough to supply the total consumption of "lightmeat" canned tuna in the United States during 1983. (Lightmeat tuna is almost entirely yellowfin, skipjack, or bigeye; albacore is sold as "white meat" tuna.) Tuna seiners of nine countries (USA, Spain, Mexico, South Korea, Japan, Taiwan, France, Venezuela, and Panama) were represented on the list. All operated in the tropical waters of the world's major oceans. Signaling a future trend in the processing of canned tuna, most of these seiners had fished in the western Pacific, making their harvest available to low-cost tuna canners located in Thailand, Taiwan, and the Philippines.

During the late 1970s, the U.S, Department of State conducted negotiations with other governments for the purpose of establishing an international fishery organization that would conserve and manage the tuna resources of the western Pacific Ocean. The negotiated final document was not found acceptable by a number of South Pacific island governments. Following this failed effort, segments of the Japanese tuna industry successfully worked out bilateral fishing access arrangements with entities of the U.N. Trust Territory of the Pacific Islands as administered under a U.S. trusteeship. The American Tunaboat Association (ATA) was contacted by representatives of the Palau Maritime Authority concerning its interest in negotiating a tuna fishing license agreement patterned after the agreements worked out with the Japanese fishing organizations. The ATA responded that it could not negotiate a bilateral arrangement on tuna fishing licensing, but that it would be interested in working out a multilateral agreement with the Palau Maritime Authority and other similar government organizations representing Micronesia and the Marshall Islands. The ATA desired to prove the practicality of a regional license approach for a tuna purse-seine fishery based upon concepts described by the Delegation of the United States during the Third United Nations Conference on the Law of the Sea. Two regional fishing license agreements were negotiated. The 1981 regional license agreement was with the Maritime Authorities of Palau, Micronesia, and the Marshall Islands. The 1983 regional license agreement included the Republic of Kiribati and the Maritime Authorities of Palau and Micronesia. As these events were occurring in the western Pacific, law of the sea problems with the governments of Mexico, Costa Rica, Ecuador, and Peru, were adversely affecting access to traditional tuna grounds by the U.S. tuna fleet in the EPO. Efforts by the United States to work out a regional diplomatic solution to these confrontations were unsuccessful. In addition, the regulatory controls imposed by the NMFS on the U.S. tuna purse-seine fleet under the Marine Mammal Protection Act were nearing the regulatory tipping point. Some in the U.S. tuna industry were finding more and more reasons to seek an expansion of their operations into the central and western Pacific, rather than in the eastern Pacific.

Data produced by a tagging program conducted by scientists of the South Pacific Commission between October 1977 and August 1980 in the southwest Pacific Ocean indicated that there was a standing stock of about 3 million metric tons of skipjack in that area.[3] In 1981, the world's commercial catch of tuna was estimated to be 2 million tons, of which 1.3 million tons was used to produce canned tuna. Two major U.S. canners were initiating major investments in the construction of new vessels that were designed to take advantage of the western Pacific tuna resources. In the fall of 1980, Van Camp Seafood Company ("Chicken of the Sea") announced a boat-building program that involved investments by well-known San Diego fishing families in seven super seiners being built in Port Arthur, Texas.[4] Star-Kist was also involved in the building of super seiners for the western Pacific and in shifting large tuna seiners from the eastern Pacific to the western Pacific.

---

[1] The "Converted Purse Seiner" (CPS) ALPHECCA operated with a net of 550 fathoms or 3,300 feet in length, and with 8 strips having a depth of 48 fathoms or 288 feet. The "New Purse Seiner" (NPS) KERRI M. operated with a net of 750 fathoms or 4,500 feet in length, and with 12 strips having a depth of 72 fathoms or 482 feet. The "super" New Purse Seiner" (NPS) OCEAN PEARL operated with a net of 1000 fathoms or 6,000 feet in length, and with 15 strips having a depth of 90 fathoms or 540 feet. In addition, tow line cable was available to stretch out the length of the net.

[2] For an excellent paper on the U.S. Tuna Seiner Fleet high seas development beyond the eastern Pacific Ocean during the period 1976-1990, see: Coan, A.L., 1993. USA distant-water and artisanal fisheries for yellowfin tuna in the central and western Pacific, p. 138-152. *in:* Shomura, R.S.; Majkowski, J.; Langi, S. (eds.) Interactions of Pacific tuna fisheries. Proceedings of the first FAO Expert Consultations on Interactions of Pacific Tuna Fisheries, 3-11 December 1991. Noumea, New Caledonia. Volume 2: papers on biology and fisheries. FAO Fisheries Technical Paper, No. 336, Vol. 2,: 439 pp.

[3] Kleiber, P, A.W. Argue, and R.E. Kearney. 1987. Assessment of Pacific skipjack tuna (*Katsuwonus pelamis*) resources by estimating standing stock and components of population turnover from tagging data. *Canadian Journal of Fisheries and Aquatic Science*, 44 (6): 1122-1134.

[4] ATA records show that in 1979 five super seiners were built; of which four were fishing for Star-Kist. In 1980, five super seiners were built, four of which fished for Chicken of the Sea. During 1981-1983, 16 super seiners were built, of which 7 were controlled by Chicken of the Sea. No new seiners were built in 1984 or 1985.

29

CONSUMER'S CHOICE:

"BETTER TASTE" (TUNA IN OIL)
OR
"BETTER FOR YOU" (TUNA IN WATER)

By the late 1970s, the skipjack and yellowfin tuna resources of the western Pacific were being successfully fished by a growing Japanese tuna purse-seine fleet and by a smaller fleet of South Korean tuna seiners. The Spanish and French tuna purse-seine fleets were expanding their operations off West Africa, and, in the early 1980s, to the Indian Ocean, particularly around the Seychelles Islands. In addition to these major foreign sources of tuna supply for U.S. tuna canners, Mexican tuna seiners and new U.S. tuna seiners financed by domestic entrepreneurs supported by U.S. tuna canners entered the fishery in the eastern Pacific Ocean.

This expansion of the world's tuna purse-seine fleets operating in the Pacific, Atlantic, and Indian Oceans occurred during a period when the market for canned tuna in the United States was growing. For example, to supply the domestic market the U.S. canners produced 26.3 million and 29.0 standard cases of tuna in 1978 and 1979, respectively. The fight for dominance in the world's biggest market for canned tuna was mainly between the two largest tuna canners in the world. The three leading labels in the canned tuna market of the United States were "Chicken of the Sea," "Star-Kist," and "Bumble Bee." For the next three 52-week periods, commencing on May 1, 1978, the leader was "Chicken of the Sea," followed by "Star-Kist," "Bumble Bee," and then a group of supermarket and private brands known in the trade as "Private Label." However, in 1981, "Star-Kist" overtook "Chicken of the Sea."[1] "Bumble Bee" showed steady growth—from 9.9% to 14.7%. The "Private Label" share also grew significantly—from 14.5% to 19.8%.

Star-Kist was successfully implementing a national marketing program that promoted preference of tuna canned in "spring water" over the traditional tuna canned in vegetable oil. Star-Kist's advertising suggested to the consumer that tuna canned in "spring water" was healthier than the tuna canned in oil. In short, it was a spin between: "It is better for you" versus "It tastes better." As a result, significant trends in the consumption of canned tuna were introduced into the U.S. marketplace. They also caused a crushing competition with Southeast Asian tuna canners because existing tariffs were much higher for tuna canned in oil than for tuna canned in water.[2]

With the onset of the 1980 recession and the burden of high interest rates in the United States, tuna canners reduced their shipments to the marketplace. This was caused by an apparent reduced consumer demand. Major supermarket chains were using computer technology to control their canned tuna inventories and thereby to reduce their purchases and other related costs. For example, the purchases of canned lightmeat tuna by supermarkets during the first quarter of 1981 were 29% less than during the same period of 1980. Apparent canned tuna consumption in the United States declined by 13% during 1981-1982. To reduce their costs, U.S. tuna canners ceased their purchases of frozen tuna from Asian-flag (Japanese, Korean, and Taiwanese) vessels and slowed down the unloading of U.S. tuna seiners.[3] In reaction to the U.S. canners' actions, many foreign-flag tuna operators searching for new markets sold their frozen tuna to seafood canners in Thailand, the Philippines, Indonesia, and Malaysia. This resulted in a surge in imports into the United States of tuna canned in water by canneries in those countries, and then problems for the owners of U.S.-flag tuna vessels.

By late 1980 and early 1981, some owners of U.S. tuna seiners were keeping their vessels in port. During 1981, 10 vessels were tied-up in San Diego.[4] In 1982, 16 tuna seiners became inactive and 5 others that had been idle were sold to foreign owners in South Korea (2) and Mexico (3). On February 10, 1982, the NMFS proposed the removal of the conditions imposed in 1977 on the transfer of documented U.S.-flag purse-seine vessels to foreign flags. The NMFS explained that these conditions were imposed because "**there was concern that the promulgation of porpoise protection regulations would cause U.S. tuna boat owners to transfer to foreign flag to avoid these regulations. Since that concern no longer exists, and since most of the purse seining nations have been determined to be fishing in substantial compliance with U.S. porpoise protection regulations, this policy is not longer necessary.**"[5] (emphasis added) The NMFS explained its action, which was later approved, by advising that during the 1977-1981 period, about 25 U.S.-flag tuna seiners had been transferred to foreign flag, but that 11 of these had re-registered to U.S. flag, and that 6 of the 14 vessels remaining under foreign flag were no longer fishing in the eastern Pacific Ocean. The NMFS also reported that since 1977 about 17 tuna seiners had been built in U.S. shipyards for foreign citizens and that these vessels could be transferred without conditions.

In early 1982, the Ralston Purina Company of St. Louis, Missouri, owner of the "Chicken of the Sea" brand, decided to go to direct sales, rather than sales through food brokers. It was reported that this would save some $6.0 million in annual brokerage commissions. In addition, promotional allowances were reduced, and steps were taken to test a new low-sodium pack that would highlight a 50% reduction in salt content. The American Tunaboat Association was informed that officials of the Van Camp Seafood Division objected to parts of these decisions, citing that the bypassing of food brokers had been tried in the past with unfavorable results. The action taken by the management at Ralston-Purina Company resulted in declining sales for "Chicken of the Sea" and a significant loss in market share.

---

[1] In 1978, "Chicken of the Sea" had a 31% market share, dropping to 26% in 1982. "Star-Kist" had a 28.9% share in 1978, increasing slightly to 29.3% in 1982. The United States

International Trade Commission (USITC) reported that in 1981 the management of Van Camp Seafood Division, Ralston Purina Co., was moved from San Diego to St. Louis "in conjunction with a major reorganization of Ralston Purina's operations." USITC Publication 1558 (August 1984), p. A-14.

[2] The history of the rates of duty applicable to imports of canned tuna is available in the August 1984 and October 1986 reports of the USITC. Canned tuna not packed in oil, that is, in water or "brine," was first introduced to American consumers by the Japanese during the early 1930s. During those times, the product failed to compete with tuna canned in oil. American consumers liked the taste of tuna packed with olive or other vegetable oil. The reason the Japanese introduced canned tuna in brine was to avoid the tariff increase imposed in 1933 on tuna canned in oil, from 30% *ad valorem* to 45% *ad valorem*.

[3] See: USITC Publication 1912 (October 1986): 47

[4] "Adverse conditions in the processing sector of the U.S. tuna industry at the end of 1981 filtered downward to U.S. tuna fishermen in the form of substantially lower ex-vessel tuna prices and difficulties and delays in selling their catches. Further, canneries were anxious to divest themselves of interests they held in tropical tuna vessels and to cut back their financial support to independently-owned vessels. Under these circumstances many vessels were unable to participate in the fisheries. In addition to weakened ex-vessel markets, U.S. tropical tuna fishermen faced continued uncertainty in terms of access to traditional eastern Pacific fishing grounds, decreased availability of tropical tuna resources in the eastern Pacific attributed to *El Niño*, and increased competition from foreign fishermen." Samuel F. Herrick, Jr., and Steven J. Koplin, "1983 U.S. Tuna Trade Summary," (June 1984), NMFS Southwest Region Administrative Report, SWR-84-1: p 17.

[5] Annual Report of the Secretary of Commerce, MMPA, 1981/82, June 1982: 42-43.

30

RECORD "EL NIÑO"

As more U.S. tuna seiners became idle in U.S. ports, Japanese and South Korean tuna seiners were achieving great success in fishing the tropical tunas in the western Pacific. American tuna seiners were finding fewer porpoise schools associated with tunas in the eastern Pacific Ocean (EPO). As the imports of canned tuna in water from Southeast Asian tuna canners penetrated the U.S. market during 1982, an exceptional act of nature occurred in the EPO. By October 1982, the most intense El Niño episode of the 20th century became fully developed. The Annual Report of the Inter-American Tropical Tuna Commission (IATTC) for 2006 explains the causes and effects of an El Niño event as follows:

> "Easterly surface winds blow almost constantly over northern South America, which causes upwelling of cool, nutrient-rich subsurface water along the equator east of 160°W, in the coastal regions off South America, and in offshore areas off Mexico and Central America. El Niño events are characterized by weaker-than-normal easterly surface winds, which cause above-normal sea-surface temperatures (SSTs) and sea levels and deeper-than-normal thermoclines over much of the tropical eastern Pacific Ocean (EPO). In addition, the Southern Oscillation Indices (SOIs) are negative during El Niño episodes. (The SOI is the difference between the anomalies of sea-level atmospheric pressure at Tahiti, French Polynesia, and Darwin, Australia. It is a measure of the strength of the eastern surface winds, especially in the tropical Pacific in the Southern Hemisphere.) Anti-El Niño events, which are the opposite of El Niño events, are characterized by stronger-than-normal easterly surface winds, below-normal SSTs and sea levels, [and] shallower-than-normal thermoclines. ..."[1]

The IATTC reported that fishing success was reduced markedly in the Commission's Yellowfin Regulatory Area (CYRA) during the period of October 1982 through about October 1983, most probably because forage was not available to the tunas.[2] This unusual event caused about 60 of the large U.S. tuna seiners in the 127-vessel fleet to transfer their area of operations to the western Pacific. The catch of this fleet represented about 60% of total domestically-caught cannery receipts for 1983, a historic record. By the end of 1983, 37 tuna seiners had became inactive, and docked in California and Puerto Rican ports. Of this group of idle vessels, three were sold during the year, two to Venezuela and one to Taiwan.

During 1980-1983, the catch of the U.S. tuna seiner fleet in the western Pacific increased dramatically from 14,000 to 170,000 short tons. As the El Niño receded during the latter half of 1983, and fishing conditions became more normal in the EPO, many of the vessels returned to the eastern Pacific. In 1984, the fleet's total catch was estimated to be about 228,000 tons, valued at about $132 million, of which about 30,000 tons was exported to Asian canners. Many tuna captains reported that they enjoyed the diversity and excitement of the competitive fishing in the EPO, and that they considered the 1982-1983 fishing operations of the central and western Pacific to be more routine and less "challenging."

The westward movement of vessels resulted in many operating changes for vessel owners deciding to base their vessels in American Samoa or Guam, such as in crew composition and hiring, the absence of union collective bargaining agreements, and a reduction in the filing of personal injury lawsuits by crewmembers.[3] This new presence of U.S.-flag fishing vessels in the Central and Western Pacific also gave rise to law of the sea disputes between the governments of the United States and Pacific Island nations.

---

[1] Annual Report of the Inter-American Tropical Tuna Commission (2006): 21.

[2] For a report on this El Niño: Annual Report of the IATTC, 1983: 66-71. "The 1983 total catch of yellowfin in the CYRA was 24 percent below the 1982 catch, but in 1984 the estimated catch was approximately 57 percent greater than during the peak El Niño year, 1983 ... The skipjack catch was markedly depressed in 1983 in the CYRA, with a 48 percent lower catch than in 1982. In 1984, the skipjack catch showed a 17 percent improvement over 1983, but remained approximately 39 percent below the 1982 catch." Annual Report of the IATTC, 1984: 73.

[3] The insolvency of a major insurance company caused changes in the way lawsuits involving personal injuries of crewmembers were defended by vessel owners. See: August Felando, "U.S. Tuna Purse Seine Fleet and the P & I Problem" presented at the 4th annual Fishing Industry Conference (23 May 1983), sponsored by the Fishermen's Insurance Service, Inc., Seattle, Washington.

31

UNITED STATES INTERNATIONAL TRADE COMMISSION (USITC)

The August 1984 Decision[1]

In the United States, canned skipjack, yellowfin, bigeye, and bluefin tuna must be labeled as "lightmeat tuna," whereas albacore can be labeled as "whitemeat tuna."[2] Other species, such as bonito, cannot be labeled as either lightmeat or whitemeat tuna. During the early 1980s, canned tuna from canneries in Southeast Asian countries were making inroads on the growing canned lightmeat tuna-in-water market in the United States. In 1977, the market share of imported canned tuna was 6%; this share had more than doubled to 14% by 1982. For 1983, imports of canned lightmeat tuna in water recorded a 40% increase over those of 1982. The total volume of imported canned tuna increased 72% from 1981 to 1983. The tariff schedules for canned tuna explains one incentive for importing canned tuna in water to the United States; the other was to take advantage of the fast-growing market for canned tuna in water. A U.S. government report explained: "Tuna in oil is subject to a 35% ad valorem tariff, thus imports are negligible. Canned tuna not in oil is under a tariff rate quota which allows imports up to 20% of the previous year's domestic production, excluding the production by canners located in American Samoa, to enter at 6% ad valorem, with a higher rate, 12.5% ad valorem, imposed on imports above the quota level."[3]

This continuing surge of imports from Asian tuna canners created the first concrete sign of a lightmeat canned tuna in water import problem for the U.S. tuna industry, when, in 1982, Castle & Cook, Inc., through its Bumble Bee Seafood Division, closed its San Diego Tuna processing facility, but kept its U.S. plants operating in Honolulu, Hawaii, and Mayagüez, Puerto Rico, and sold its interests in U.S. tuna seiners.[4] A facet of the "import problem" existing in 1983 was explained by a U.S. National Marine Fisheries Service (NMFS) report:

> "Import prices (for canned tuna) were still $3.00 to $5.00 per case below domestic prices. Lower prices and a strong U.S. dollar abroad have made foreign produced canned tuna very attractive to U.S. importers since early 1982. Furthermore, since the ad valorem duties on canned tuna imports are determined by their price, the lower the price of imported canned tuna, the lower the customs duty. The current high value of the U.S. dollar acts to further reduce the effective tariff on imported canned tuna. Even if the dollar weakens against foreign currencies in the near term, U.S. producers will continue to face stiff competition from foreign processors."[5]

A new trend of canned tuna consumption was firmly established by the U.S. consumer in 1984, when the 6.5-ounce can of chunk style, lightmeat tuna in water represented over 45% of all tuna sales. During 1982 and 1983, some major U.S. tuna canners responded to the challenge of imported canned tuna-in-water products by marketing low-salt canned tuna products. For a brief period, this innovation was widely accepted by U.S. consumers. However, the advantages provided by a tariff difference between canned tuna in oil and canned tuna in water were too great for a new canned tuna product that merely stressed health benefits, rather than a price advantage.

It was the expectation of the American Tunaboat Association (ATA) that the USITC would provide a remedy to the U.S. tuna canners by raising the duty on tuna canned in water on the ground that the existing duty rate did not equalize the differences in the costs of this product to the U.S. canners versus the low-cost foreign canners in Southeast Asia, and that this fact was causing economic hardship to the California tuna industry. This view was supported by the negative changes occurring in the San Diego tuna industry; the 1981 management changes in the Van Camp Seafood Division by Ralston Purina Company, the 1982 decision by Castle & Cook, Inc., to close its San Diego cannery, the increasing number of idle tuna seiners, the increasing number of vessels being sold to foreign citizens, and the failure to replace the ships lost at sea.[6] For these and other reasons, on February 15, 1984, the ATA joined with other organizations representing all segments of the industry in filing a petition for import relief. Unfortunately, not all U.S. tuna canners had signed the petition.[7] The relief desired was an increase in the rate of duty for canned tuna not in oil, to 35% ad valorem for five years.[8] To add further evidence in support of the ATA's concerns about the future of the California tuna industry, Ralston Purina (Van Camp) implemented an "indefinite" closure of its eight-year-old San Diego cannery—the World's most modern—effective July 1, 1984.

On August 15, 1984, the majority of the USITC (three Commissioners) found: "that imports are increasing and that the domestic industry is facing economic difficulties, if not suffering serious injury. However, we find that the third condition, the causation condition is not satisfied and therefore have made a negative determination ... Having found that the requirements of section 201 of the Trade Act of 1974 are not satisfied, we have made a negative determination and do not recommend to the President that import relief be provided."[9]

Vice Chairwoman Susan W.Liebeler of the USITC presented her own analysis on the issues of injury and causation, after stating her concurrence with the Commission majority in the determination "that the increased importation of canned tuna is not a substantial cause of serious injury or threat of injury to the domestic industry."[10]

Chairwoman Paula Stern presented her views, finding "that imports of canned tuna are a substantial cause of serious injury to the domestic tuna industry."[11] Her views on relief, however, did not agree with the petitioners, explaining:

> "Given the substantial labor cost advantages of some of the leading foreign suppliers of canned tuna, and the fact that labor costs are a critical cost component in this high-volume, low-profit-margin canned tuna industry. It is clear that domestic processors face a long-term fundamental competitive disadvantage. ... I am not persuaded that any of the various plans offered by petitioners would allow the industry to meet the fundamental and irreversible competitive advantage posed by imports. **Rather, a temporary tariff increase would simply delay the inevitable shifting**

of production to foreign locations. It would do little to arrest the irreversible decline of production and fish landings in California. Even if temporary import relief were granted, it would be just that—temporary. (emphasis added)

"The close of California plants will mark the end of an era for California, the century-old home of the tuna processing industry and the U.S. tuna fleet. It also will mark the end of a lifestyle for many fishermen and their families. The Commission cannot recommend import relief based upon sentiment or sympathy alone. But it can recommend needed assistance for the victims of economic forces beyond their control. Therefore, had the majority voted affirmatively, I would have recommended trade adjustment assistance as the appropriate remedy. ..."

As stated above, in July 1984, Van Camp Seafood Division closed its San Diego cannery. At the time it announced its intention to close the San Diego plant (April 11, 1984), Van Camp also announced plans to close its cannery in Pago Pago, American Samoa, for purposes of renovation and expansion. Star-Kist closed its Terminal Island, California, tuna cannery in October 1984, announcing that it had closed the plant "in response to continued high costs and the government's failure to provide relief from low-priced canned tuna imports." (Van Camp had not referred to the decision made by the USITC in the announcement that it would close its San Diego cannery.) As a result of changes in purchasing policies by U.S. tuna canners in 1984, the U.S. tuna fleet exported a substantial amount of frozen tuna (65 million pounds) to foreign tuna canners during that year.

Restructuring Industry Assets After 1984

In 1985, Star-Kist increased the capacity of its Mayaguez, Puerto Rico, cannery by 22%, claiming that this plant was now the largest in the world. Also in 1985, Star-Kist reported that it increased the capacity of its American Samoa plant by 40%, and that this expanded plant was now the second largest in the world. C.H.B. Foods-Pan-Pacific Fisheries continued to operate its cannery at Terminal Island, California, making its operation the only major tuna cannery servicing commercial fishing vessels in continental United States.

The apparent quantity of canned tuna consumed in the United States increased by 16% from 1981 to 1985, while its value declined by 19% during that period. For the U.S. canners, however, the quantity decreased by 12% and the value by 34% during that period. During 1985, the imports of canned tuna increased 202% in quantity and 80% in value. The exports of frozen tuna caught by U.S. vessels increased from 2.8 million pounds in 1981 to 71 million pounds in 1985.[12]

During 1985, 35 U.S. tuna seiners were listed by the ATA as inactive, including 6 that were sold to citizens of other countries (3 to Chile and 1 each to the Republic of Korea, Venezuela, and the Cayman Islands), and for 4 for entry in other U.S. fisheries.

In June 1985, Castle & Cooke, Inc., sold most of its assets in its Bumble Bee Seafoods Division, including its trademark, to an independent entity owned by a group of former management personnel. Later, to complete its divestment of tuna-related assets, it closed its tuna-canning facility operated by Hawaiian Tuna Packers, Ltd., in Honolulu, Hawaii. Also during 1985, an ownership change occurred with respect to C.H.B. Foods, Inc., resulting in a name change to California Home Brands, Inc., as owner of Pan-Pacific Fisheries. By the end of 1985, the number of tuna-processing plants had declined from 20 in 1981 to 8 in 1985. Six firms operated these eight plants, and the three largest firms (Star-Kist Foods, Inc., Van Camp Seafood Division, and Bumble Bee Seafoods, Inc.) accounted for 81 percent of U.S. canned tuna production. Five of these plants were located in Puerto Rico, two in American Samoa, and one in Southern California.[13] The other remaining four tuna firms were: Star-Kist Foods, Inc., a division of H.J. Heinz; Van Camp Seafood, Inc., a division of Ralston Purina Co.; Caribe Tuna, Inc., a subsidiary of Mitsubishi Foods (MC), Inc., and Neptune Packing, Inc., a subsidiary of Mitsui and Company (USA), Inc.[14]

In 1985, canned tuna-in-water products of U.S. tuna canners accounted for 62% of total canned lightment shipments and 78% of canned whitemeat shipments. A 1986 USITC Report concluded that the U.S. tuna processors, as a whole, outperformed the larger U.S. food-products industry in 1985 and that the financial health of the six tuna canners "improved substantially from its depressed state in 1982-83."[15] This recovery was attributed in part to the decline in the price of frozen tuna. Frozen tuna, as a share of cost of goods, fell from 71% in 1981 to 56% in 1985. "Clearly, the decline in the cost of frozen tuna to the processors played a major role in explaining their return to financial health despite significant declines in prices of canned tuna."[16] It was also noted that the tuna canners had incurred significant expenses in closing plants and selling fishing vessels, particularly during 1984. The USITC Report stated that these non-operating expenses totaled $66 million in 1984, compared with an annual average of $22.5 million for the 1979-85 period. The USITC commented: "While this restructuring of the industry's assets was costly in the short run (and forced the industry to sustain a net loss in 1984), the disposal of inefficient assets may significantly improve the future performance of the industry."[17]

The 1986 USTIC report found that during 1979-85, the net income before taxes earned by the average purse seiner was consistently negative, "ranging from the largest annual loss of $691,000 in 1982 to the smallest loss of $43,000 in 1980. As a share of net sales, pre-tax net losses suffered by the average purse seiner ranged from 1.9 to 33 percent during 1979-85."[18] Subject to the condition that ownership interest exceeds 33% in a vessel, the USITC reported that 26 of 29 vessels that U.S. tuna canners had ownership interests in during 1985 recorded operating losses.[19]

The number of vessels in the U.S. seiner fleet declined, through sales to foreign owners, losses at sea, and transfers to other U.S. fisheries, from 141 vessels in 1976 to only 58 in 1985.[20] During 1981-85, 34 were transferred to foreign citizens, 15 were lost at sea, and 8 were transferred to other U.S fisheries or trades. These removals were partially offset by the addition of 15 new seiners and 15 transfers of foreign-flag vessels to U.S. registry,[21] but none of these acquisitions took place in 1984 or 1985. During 1981-85, the U.S. fleet sustained a net loss of 27 vessels with a total fish-carrying capacity of 20,158 short tons. During the last quarter of 1985, the NMFS reported that 23 U.S.-flag tuna seiners, representing about 30% of the total fleet capacity, had been inactive.

The number of vessel name changes and transfers during this five-year period was remarkable. One tuna canner sold seven converted seiners to citizens of Chile and two to citizens of Venezuela. Other sales were made to citizens of Venezuela (eight), Mexico (five), Costa Rica (two), the Philippines (four), South Korea (three), Taiwan (one), Vanuatu (three), Cayman Islands (five), and Netherlands Antilles (one). In a temporary effort to reduce operating costs, eight U.S. seiners were chartered during 1984 to citizens of Venezuela and Ecuador. These charters required name changes, but not transfers of ownership or changes of registry.[22]

Commenting on transfers of U.S. tuna seiners to foreign buyers during the early 1980s, a study reported: "Most of the flag countries involved in re-registration required a minimum of 51% ownership and control of the property by their citizens to qualify for flag registration. Furthermore, U.S. tuna vessel owners had no tradition of using flags of convenience. Their vessels were built and financed in the USA, where they qualified for benefits that would be forfeited with foreign registration. ... The downsizing of the U.S. purse-seine fleet and the transfer of U.S. vessels to foreign flags in the 1980s occurred because of changes in the economic climate of the industry, not because of government tuna-dolphin regulations. The transfers were the result of the sale of vessels to foreign interests and not a ploy to circumvent U.S. tuna-dolphin regulations."[23]

The authors agree with the conclusion of this study that the sales of U.S. tuna seiners to foreign citizens were not made to evade the MMPA regulatory regime. Some sales were made to finance new vessels or because it was judged that the vessel was no longer competitive under the U.S. flag for operations in the eastern Pacific Ocean (EPO), and that its carrying capacity was insufficient for fishing in the central and western Pacific Ocean. Other owners of U.S.-flag tuna seiners recognized that U.S. laws protected them from illegal seizures and harassments on the high seas by foreign naval forces. This protection would not be available to U.S. citizens owning a tuna seiner flying a "flag of convenience."

The authors agree that the burden of complying with NMFS regulations concerning gear and equipment requirements promulgated under the MMPA was not in itself justification for the sale of a U.S. tuna seiner to foreign owners. However, we strongly believe that the other sections of the NMFS tuna/porpoise regulatory regime that existed on January 1, 1981, were part of the "changes in the economic climate of the industry." The decisions by canners and vessel owners to move away from the uncertainties created by the MMPA regulatory regime in the fishing of tuna/porpoise schools in the EPO reflected one change. The industry was signaling the United States government that the regulatory tipping point had been identified.

On January 1, 1986, the U.S. tuna seiner fleet numbered 90 vessels with a fish-carrying capacity of about 97,131 short tons. A reduction of 34 vessels (27%) and about 27,033 capacity tons (21%) from a record high fleet of 124 vessels of 126,164 capacity tons on January 1, 1984. "The number of U.S. tuna purse seiners declined from 90 in 1986 to 63 in 1989. The capacity of the fleet declined

40 percent during that period. Most of the decline resulted from the sale of vessels to foreign-flag fleets."[24]

Meanwhile, consumption of tuna canned in water in the United States increased from 45 percent of the market in 1979, to 74 percent in 1986, and to 82 percent in 1989.

---

[1] The petition was filed on February 15, 1984, on behalf of the United States Tuna Foundation, C.H.B. Foods, Inc, the American Tunaboat Association, the United Industrial Workers, AFL-CIO, the Fishermen's Union of America, AFL-CIO, and the Fishermen's Union, ILWU, No. 33.

[2] Albacore tuna looked and tasted like baked chicken when first cooked experimentally in 1903-1906 by a sardine packer in San Pedro, California Since it was the first tuna to be canned in the United States, this may explain why only albacore tuna can be labeled as "whitemeat tuna." All other tunas must be labeled as "lightmeat tuna." With the exception of large individuals that spawn in tropical waters of the mid-Pacific, and their offspring, albacore tuna do not occur in the tropics. During the summer, albacore travel along the coasts of California, Oregon, Washington, and British Columbia, and then head toward Japan. They are followed in this migration by another "lightmeat tuna," bluefin.

[3] Samuel F. Herrick, Jr., and Steven J. Koplin, "U.S. Tuna Trade Summary, 1984," NMFS, Southwest Region (June 1985) Administrative Report SWR-85-6: 15.

[4] Another indicator of a serious problem with imported canned tuna: the success of an investigation in 1982-1983 that resulted in a countervailing duty of 0.72% being levied against Philippine exporters to offset production subsidies they received. The petitioner seeking relief was a major U.S. tuna canner.

[5] Samuel F. Herrick, Jr., and Steven J. Koplin, "U.S. Tuna Trade Summary, 1983," NMFS, Southwest Region (June 1984) Administrative Report SWR-84-1: 19.

[6] In 1980, two seiners, representing about 1% of the total fleet capacity, were idle; in 1983, the number jumped to 34 vessels, representing 23% of the fleet's total capacity. In 1984, 37 vessels were idle, and 9 vessels were sold to other countries (3 to Chile, 5 to Venezuela (5), and 1 to the Grand Cayman Islands), and 3 to other U.S. trade and fisheries. During the 1980-83 period, 47 seiners were removed from the U.S. tuna seiner fleet due to losses at sea (11), transfers to other U.S. fisheries (1), and transfers to foreign flags (35). See: Competitive Conditions in the U.S. Tuna Industry Report to the President on Investigation No. 332-224 Under Section 332 of the Tariff Act of 1940, as Amended. USITC Publication 1912, October 1986: 158. (Cited herein as: "USITC Publication 1912 October 1986").

[7] Representatives of Bumble Bee Seafoods Division, Castle & Cook, Inc, publicly stated: "that Bumble Bee does not agree with all the statements and conclusions in the petition." See: Certain Canned Tuna Fish Report to the President on Investigation No. TA-201-53 Under Section 201 of the Trade Act of 1974, USITC Publication 1558, August 198)": A-16. (Cited herein as: **"USITC Publication 1558 August 1984"**)

[8] The correct identity of canned tuna fish for purposes of tariff treatment: tuna fish in airtight containers, prepared or preserved in any manner, not in oil, provided for in items

112.30 and 112.34 of the Tariff Schedules of the United States (TSUS), and tuna fish in airtight containers, prepared or preserved in any manner, in oil, provided for in TSUS item 112.90.

[9] For the views of Commissioners, Alfred E. Eckes, Seely G. Lodwick, and David B. Rohr: USITC Publication 1558 August 1984: 3-21.

[10] See: USITC Publication 1558 August 1984: 23 Views of Vice-Chairwoman Susan W. Liebeler.

[11] See: USITC Publication 1558 August 1984: 31 Views of Chairwoman Paula Stern.

[12] Prior to 1984, the historical record shows that almost the entire catch of the U.S. tuna fleet was sold to U.S. tuna canners. Commencing during the late 1960s, some vessel owners became export-minded, and marketed small quantities of frozen tuna to European canners. However, it was not until the mid-1980s that a significant number of American tuna vessel owners sold their catches to foreign canners.

[13] Star-Kist closed its cannery in Terminal Island, California, in October 1984, causing the loss of about 1,200 jobs.

[14] At this time, "Approximately 20 percent of the total world-wide sales of Heinz during 1982-85 was accounted for by tuna and tuna related products, the single largest component of the company's sales." USITC Publication 1912 October 1986: 22. The USITC Report also states that Van Camp Seafood accounted for about 5% of total sales by Ralston Purina Co.

[15] USITC Publication 1912 October 1986: 33.

[16] USITC Publication 1912 October 1986: 34.

[17] USITC Publication 1912 October 1986: 34-35.

[18] USITC Publication 1912 October 1986: 16.

[19] In 1982, after Castle & Cooke closed its San Diego tuna cannery, it sold all of its interests in 12 tuna vessels to persons other than the new owner of Bumble Bee Seafoods, Inc. In 1985, Van Camp Seafood, Inc, had equity ownership interests in 15 tuna purse seiners, 8 of which were wholly owned, and one was leased." The USITC did not report the number of tuna seiners that were owned by Star-Kist and C.H.B. Foods, Inc

[20] All seven San Pedro "regular" seiners listed by the NMFS as in the fishery on December 31, 1976, were no longer listed by NMFS on December 31, 1985, as actively engaged in the fishery. Of the 27 baitboat conversions and 6 military hull conversions on the 1976 NMFS list, only 4 converted seiners and one military hull remained active in 1985. Of the 84 tuna seiners newly built with a frozen tuna carrying capacity of 1,200 short tons or less, 39 vessels were no longer on the 1985 NMFS list, and of the 14 vessels having a capacity greater than 1,200 short tons, only seven remained listed.

[21] During September/October 1980, a group of 9 tuna seiners built in the United States, some registered foreign flag, were sold to Mexican interests. In November 1981, most of these vessels were transferred to U.S. flag. The vessels involved: BOLD ADVENTU-

RESS (ex Aventurera); CALYPSO; GANN DISCOVERER (ex Zapata Discoverer; ex Descubridor); BOLD PHOENICIAN (ex. Maria Elena, ex Fenicio) ; BOLD FLEET, (ex Carol Virginia, ex Intrepido); SOUTH SEAS (ex Mar Del Sur); BOLD PRODUCER (ex Productor); SOUTH WIND (ex Viento Del Sur), and ROSA OLIVIA. In addition, the vessel CARIBE (ex Captain Steven Scott), which was sold to Mexico in 1978, was transferred from Mexican flag to U.S. flag in November 1981. The SOUTH SEAS, BOLD PHOENICIAN, BOLD FLEET, and SOUTH WIND were built in U.S. shipyards, but registered as flag vessels of Netherlands Antillies at the time of transfer to Mexican flag.

[22] This provided the vessels with the opportunity to reduce their operating costs by purchasing low-cost fuel in Venezuela. The following six vessels and their new names were believed involved in this venture: CAPTAIN FRANK MEDINA to Caroni, CAROLYN M to Apure, FRONTIER to Neveri, KERRI M to Guanipa, MONTANA to Arauca, and SEA WOLF to Manzanares. For purposes of reducing fuel and other operating costs, at least two U.S.-flag tuna seiners were temporarily chartered to citizens of Ecuador.

[23] Gary T. Sakagawa, "Are U.S. Regulations on Tuna-Dolphin Fishing Driving U.S. Seiners to Foreign-Flag Registry?" North American Journal of Fisheries Management, 11 (3): 241-252. "During the period 1977-1981, 82 vessels were involved in transfer of flag transactions, some including a few reversions back to U.S. documentation. During the period the 1980-1981, 21 former U.S. flag tuna seiners were sold to Venezuela; 11 to Mexico, 11 to South Korea, 7 to Vanuatu, 4 to Panama, and 4 to Cayman Islands."

[24] Tuna: Competitive Conditions Affecting the U.S. and European Tuna Industries in Domestic and Foreign Markets Report to the Committee on Finance, U.S. Senate, and the Committee on Ways and Means, U.S. House of Representatives, Investigation No. 332-291 Under Section 332 of the Tariff Act of 1930 USITC Publication 2339, December 1990: xi.

A table showing the decline of the U.S. tuna purse-seine fleet operating in the Eastern Tropical Pacific Ocean from a high of 155 vessels in 1976 to a low of 7 vessels during 1992-94, and the rise of foreign-flag tuna seiners from low of 48 vessels in 1971 to a high of 132 vessels in 1980 and 75 foreign flag vessels operating in 1994: Marine Mammal Protection Act of 1972, Annual Report, January 1,1994 to December 31, 1994, U.S. Department of Commerce, NOAA, NMFS, Office of Protected Resources: Appendix C. Estimates of Total Incidental Dolphin Mortality for U.S. and Foreign Purse Seine Vessels in the Eastern Tropical Pacific Ocean, 1971-1994.

PART IX

GOVERNMENT AND INDUSTRY ACTIONS
1984-1989

32

1984 AMENDMENTS TO THE MMPA

Most of the 1984 amendments to the MMPA concerned the tuna purse-seine fishery, reflecting concerns that the participation of foreign vessels in the fishery of the eastern Pacific Ocean (EPO) was increasing while that of U.S. vessels was declining.

Amendments to Section 104(h) made the American Tunaboat Association (ATA) general permit valid for an indefinite period, but subject to a number of conditions.[1] This permit, with its annual porpoise mortality limit of 20,500 animals, could be modified if the Secretary determined "on the basis of the best scientific information available" that fishing on tuna/porpoise schools "is having a significant adverse effect on a marine mammal stock ..." This information would include the data collected during the five-year monitoring program.

The 1984 amendments strengthened the requirement that the Secretary of the Treasury "ban the importation of commercial fish or products from fish which have been caught with commercial fishing technology which results in the incidental kill or incidental serious injury of ocean mammals in excess of United States standards."[2]

Also, commencing on January 1, 1985, the Secretary was directed to "undertake a scientific research program to monitor for at least five consecutive years, and periodically as necessary thereafter, the indices of abundance and trends of marine mammal population stocks" involved in the commercial purse-seine tuna fishery in the EPO.

The amendments were the result of compromises negotiated between the interested parties, with the assistance of Senator John Breaux of Louisiana. Senator Breaux explained how this was done during hearings conducted on April 13, 1988, before the National Ocean Policy Study of the U.S. Senate Committee on Commerce, Science, and Transportation, as follows:[3]

> "Senator Breaux ... The U.S. tuna industry has a quota which was painfully negotiated and agreed to by the industry, by this Congress, by the administration, and by environmental groups that sat at that table. ...

"Mike Bean (Environmental Defense Fund), who is sitting at this table, knows what I am talking about, because those quotas were not easily arrived at, 20,000 was a figure that was difficult to come to an agreement on, and the industry has been below those takes. ..." (p. 125)

"... Now let me tell you something else. In 1984, when we agreed to the quota and wrote it into the law, and Mr. Bean can comment on that, the agreement was 20,500 porpoises that could be taken. There were 34 boats in the U.S. industry at that time when this group and others agreed to the 20,000 quota. (p. 126)

"Last year, there were 35 boats. So at the time that the groups agreed to the 20,000, not when we agreed to it at first in 1981 but when it was written into law with everybody's agreement in 1984, we had 34 U.S. boats. Now we have 35.

" ... So it is not a 65-percent reduction in the vessels from the time that it was written into the law and everybody agreed to that 20,000 quota. Does anybody differ with that?

"Mr. Bean. I do not remember the precise numbers, but the thrust of your remarks is, I believe, correct. (p. 126)

"If I could just add a bit, Senator Breaux, I agree with the basic thrust of your remarks, and that is why my testimony this morning has focused on what I believe to be the most important problem, the foreign fleet's killing of porpoise. (pp. 126-127)

"... So while agreeing with you that the U.S. fleet has certainly made dramatic progress since this act was passed in reducing its killing of porpoise, I personally subscribe to the view that it would be highly desirable to reduce it still further. One of the ways in which that might be done is through the development of alternative fishing techniques that you and others in Congress said was to be done in 1981." (p. 127)

During 1971-75, NMFS observers aboard U.S. tuna seiners reported that during each set of a tuna purse seine, an average of 32 porpoise deaths was recorded. This count dropped to about 6 mortalities per set during the next five-year period, 1976-1980. For the next five-year period, 1981-1985, a time of economic distress for the U.S. tuna fleet, this average decreased to 5 mortalities per set. **Zero porpoise mortality sets** averaged over 58% during the 1981-1990 periods, a significant improvement from the previous 10-year period, 1971-1980, for which NMFS observers recorded a 44% average of zero porpoise mortality sets.[4] These data, collected to monitor the performance of American tuna fishermen, showed that tuna captains and their crews were continually improving their techniques and procedures in saving porpoise while harvesting greater catches of tuna.

---

[1] See: Public Law 98-364-July 17, 1984; 98 STAT. 440-441. "(2)(A) Subject to subparagraph (B), the general permit issued ... to the American Tunaboat Association is extended to authorize and govern the taking of marine mammals incidental to commercial purse seine fishing for yellowfin tuna during each year after December 31, 1984." The conditions included the following: "(1) that the fishermen be required to use the best porpoise safety techniques and equipment available; (2) that adjustments may be made with respect to fishing gear, fishing practice requirements, and permit administration, provided that such terms and conditions are based on the best scientific information available; and

(3) annual quotas of 250 coastal spotted dolphins and 2,750 eastern spinner dolphin, and that these quotas are to be included in the overall annual quota established by the Secretary of Commerce." See: Annual Report 1984-85, MMPA, Secretary of Commerce, June 1985: p. 6.

[2] Public Law 98-364-July 17, 1984; 98 STAT. 440. "(B) in the case of yellowfin tuna harvested with purse seines in the eastern tropical Pacific Ocean, and products there from to be exported to the United States, shall require that the government of the exporting nation provide documentary evidence that--- (i) the government of the harvesting nation has adopted a regulatory program governing the incidental taking of marine mammals in the course of such harvesting that is **comparable** to that of the United States; and (ii) the average rate of that incidental taking by the vessels of the harvesting nation is **comparable** to the average rate of incidental taking of marine mammals by United States vessels in the course of such harvesting." (emphasis added)

[3] Hearings before the National Ocean Policy Study of the Committee on Commerce, Science, and Transportation, United States Senate, 100th Congress, 2nd Session on The Reauthorization of the Marine Mammal Protection Act, April 13 and May 19, 1988, S.Hrg.100-711. (cited hereinafter as "1988 Senate Hearing 100-711"): 125-127.

[4] See: 1988 Senate Hearing 100-711: p. 138.

33

1988 AMENDMENT TO THE MMPA

During the 1986-1988 period, the regulatory program of the U.S. National Marine Fisheries Service (NMFS) was changed in a constructive manner by encouraging tuna captains to be more innovative and accountable in taking actions to reduce porpoise mortality. In addition, the extension service provided to the fleet by the NMFS and the Porpoise Rescue Foundation (PRF) was assisting tuna captains and crews in using the gear and procedures proven to reduce porpoise mortality more effectively. Importantly, the NMFS and the PRF established procedures to improve the relationships between the tuna captains and the expanded observer program now provided jointly by the NMFS and the Inter-American Tropical Tuna Commission (IATTC). "Of the 4,116 observed sets capturing porpoise in 1987 by the U.S. fleet, 60 percent had zero mortality and sets with a kill of 5 porpoise or less accounted for 89 percent of the total sets. ... In contrast, "disaster sets"— sets with more than 50 mortalities—represented less than 1 percent (35 of 4,116) of the sets capturing porpoise, but accounted for almost 34 percent of the total observed mortality.[1]

Also, during this period the IATTC porpoise program was improving the collection of data by expanding its observer program and by implementing an excellent educational and training program to instruct tuna captains and crews of foreign-flag seiners on the use of gear and procedures developed by the U.S. tuna fleet to reduce porpoise mortality.

The 1988 amendments to the MMPA were directed mainly toward the problem of increased porpoise mortality caused by growing foreign tuna seiner fleets in the eastern Pacific Ocean (EPO).[2]

The provisions of the Act dealing with the duty of the Secretary of the Treasury to ban imports of fish or fish products caught by methods harmful to porpoises were substantially changed by the 1988 amendments to the MMPA.[3] The Secretary was restrained from making a finding of comparability in five areas, including the following: (1) if a foreign nation's 1990 regulatory program did not include prohibitions applicable to U.S. vessels against encircling pure schools of certain species of marine mammals, conducting sundown sets, and other activities ; (2) if the vessels of the harvesting nation during the 1989 and subsequent years are not monitored by a porpoise observer program of the IATTC or by an equivalent international program in which the U.S. participates or by a program proposed by the Secretary. In addition, the Secretary was required to obtain "from the government of any intermediary nation from which yellowfin tuna or tuna products will be exported to the United States to certify and provide reasonable proof that it has acted to prohibit the importation of such tuna and tuna products from any nation from which direct export to the United States of such tuna and tuna products" is banned under the provisions of the MMPA. Further, subject to factual findings, the Secretary is required to undertake a certification to the President for the purposes of section 8(a) of the Fishermen's Protective Act of 1967 (22 U.S.C. 1978(a).

A NMFS document provided to the Chairman of the U.S. Senate National Ocean Policy Study concluded that import restrictions of yellowfin could impact the U.S. tuna canners, as follows:[4]

> "A shortage of raw product or increased price of raw product to the U.S. processors,
>
> "Loss of considerable investment of time and capital that the U.S. processors have extended developing shipping and processing centers in eastern tropical Pacific countries,
>
> "A serious adverse impact on local communities in Puerto Rico where U.S. processors maintain five tuna canning facilities."

The actions taken on imports also reflected the continuing interest of Congress and others in government to seek alternatives to the use of purse seines to catch tunas associated with porpoises and as answers to the national publicity campaigns continued by "protectionist groups" to prohibit the use of purse seines to fish tuna/porpoise schools. Unfortunately, some of the 1988 amendments reduced the competitive capacity of U.S. tuna seiners. For the first time, Congress adopted specific rules that prohibited American fishermen from using proven fishing techniques to encircle tuna/porpoise schools.

During hearings before a U.S. Senate Subcommittee on May 19, 1988, the record of the U.S. tuna seiner fleet in saving porpoise was recognized: Senator John Breaux of Louisiana stated:

> **"The program is working in the United States. The problem is not with our tuna industry. The problem is with the foreign fishermen, who take four times more porpoises than our industry does, who have very little recognition of the problem, and absolutely no real interest, I think, in trying to do anything to resolve it.** We in Congress recognized that problem four years ago when we established some standards that we said foreign fishing fleets would have to follow if they were going to export their product to the United States. **They simply have not done that. And, even equally as bad, our government has not done anything about it.** ... They have not even issued the regulations to institute the program that Congress passed. "[5] (emphasis added)

The Deputy Assistant Administrator for Fisheries, National Oceanic and Atmospheric Administration, presented data before this Senate Subcommittee showing that during 1986-1987, the total estimated porpoise mortality for foreign fleets was 168,410 animals, while that of the U.S. fleet was 34,684 animals, and advised: "We are, however, quite concerned over porpoise mortality in the foreign segment of this fishery."[6]

Dr. William W. Fox, Jr., Commissioner, Marine Mammal Commission, also testified before this Senate Subcommittee on April 13, 1988. He stated:

> **"A critical fact is that more than 60 percent of the tuna taken and more than 80 percent of the porpoise now being killed or seriously injured in the Eastern Tropical Pacific are being taken by foreign purse seiners.** In many cases, they

are not required to employ the porpoise-saving measures required of U.S. purse seiners, and they have not demonstrated the ability to meet the performance standards being met by the domestic fleet. Thus, efforts by the United States fishing industry and the US Government to reduce overall mortality and serious injury are being seriously compromised by foreign activities."[7] (emphasis added)

Dr. Fox also testified that "as the numbers [of porpoise] killed have decreased with the domestic tuna purse seine fleet, the levels of incidental kill and serious injury have increased substantially for the foreign fleet. We now have a situation where the estimated take by the foreign purse seine fleet exporting yellowfin tuna to the United States has risen to levels that have exceeded 100,000 animals in a year."[8]

---

[1] 1988 Senate Hearing 100-711: 138.

[2] Public Law 100-711-November 23, 1988, [H.R. 4189]; 102 STAT. 4755.

[3] Public Law 100-711-November 23, 1988, [H.R. 4189]; 102 STAT. 4766.

[4] 1988 Senate Hearing 100-711: 137.

[5] 1988 Senate Hearing 100-711: 04. "Regulations to enforce the 1984 MMPA amendments pertaining to import restrictions were not adopted until April 1988. Between 1984 and 1988, embargoes were only imposed or in force against the former Soviet Union, El Salvador, and Mexico, and the embargoes relating to Mexico related to a dispute over the seizure of U.S. tuna vessels. In October of 1988, embargoes were imposed against tuna imported from Venezuela, Vanuatu, Panama, and Ecuador. These embargoes were lifted in November 1988." See: "Tuna: Current Issues Affecting the U.S. Industry Report to the Committee on Finance, United States Senate on Investigation No. 332-313 Under Section 332(g) of the Tariff Act of 1930 as Amended, USITC Publication 2547 (August 1992): 3-4, 3-6. (cited hereinafter as "USITC 2547 August 1992").

[6] 1988 Senate Hearing 100-711: 12.

[7] 1988 Senate Hearing 100-711: 53.

[8] 1988 Senate Hearing 100-711: 47. See: Annual Report of the IATTC for 2006 (2008): 63, Table 7, annual estimates of porpoise mortality, by species and stock, for 1979-2006. Only 1986 showed total mortalities (by U.S and non-U.S. fleets) over 100,000, namely 132,169. The estimate for 1987 was 98,882. The estimates for 1988 and 1989 were 81,129, and 98,451, respectively. During 1990-1993, the estimates decreased dramatically—53,874, 27,127, 15,539, and 3,601, respectively.

34

YANKEE TUNA CANNERS EXIT

By 1985, the principal countries involved in the harvesting of tuna, in order of importance, were Japan, the United States, Spain, the Philippines, Indonesia, France, Taiwan, South Korea, Venezuela, and Mexico. The principal countries involved in the canning of tuna, in order of importance, were the United States, Japan, France, Thailand, Spain, Italy, the Philippines, Taiwan, Canada, and Mexico. Japan was first in the consumption of tuna, fresh, canned, or otherwise preserved. The principal consumers of canned tuna, in order of importance, were the United States, Japan, France, Spain, Italy, the United Kingdom, West Germany, Canada, Mexico, and Australia.[1]

This growing globalization of canned tuna production and consumption was reflected by ownership changes in firms operating U.S. canneries. During 1988-1989, the assets of two major U.S. tuna canners, Van Camp Seafood Company, Inc., and Bumble Bee Seafoods, Inc., were sold to foreign tuna firms in Southeast Asia,[2] and two of the four canneries in Puerto Rico, Van Camp Seafood Company and Neptune Packing Corporation, were closed by their foreign owners by the end of 1990.[3] By 1989, dominance of the tuna fishery in the eastern Pacific had clearly shifted from U.S.-flag seiners to fleets of Ecuador, Mexico, and Venezuela.[4] During 1986-1989, the tuna fishery in the western Pacific had become critically important to a U.S. tuna seiner fleet that was restricted to 50 vessels by the terms of the world's first government-to-government regional tuna fishing access agreement, the South Pacific Tuna Treaty.[5] Tuna canners in Southeast Asia expanded their markets in Europe,[6] as well as in the United States, providing economic strength in competing with the remaining U.S. tuna canners.[7] Southeast Asian tuna firms became established as the world's lowest-cost processors of canned tuna, and as the world's leaders in the exportation of canned tuna.[8] This achievement was aided by the fact that firms based in Thailand and Indonesia were now in the marketplace in the United States with two purchased brands of canned tuna familiar to the U.S. consumer, "Chicken of the Sea" and "Bumble Bee." Competition during this period caused major U.S. canners to increase the use of precooked, frozen tuna loins for processing, reduce full-scale production capacity in Puerto Rico, and change cooking and other procedures to increase production yields. In the marketing of canned tuna, U.S. firms sought advantages by decreasing the retail can size from 6.5 ounces to 6.125 ounces, increasing promotional and discount activities, and increasing purchases of imported canned tuna for use in their brands.

In our view, the 1988 decision by Ralston Purina Company, the owners of Van Camp Seafood Company, Inc., to sell its interests in the tuna industry to a Southeast Asian firm, combined with the subsequent failure of Star-Kist to acquire Bumble Bee Seafoods, accelerated adverse long-term changes in the U.S. tuna industry.[9] We believe that these actions created serious competitive and leadership problems for the two remaining U.S. tuna canners, Star-Kist and Pan Pacific Fisheries, not owned by Asian citizens.

For American tuna fishermen looking for opportunities to become tuna vessel owners, the sale of Van Camp Seafood Company helped end the traditional way that most innovative and entrepreneurial American tuna fishermen had become tuna vessel owners, that is, by having tuna canners venturing as co-owners. The operating premise: you don't build a tuna seiner and then look for a captain; you build a tuna seiner because you are or have a talented and proven tuna captain. Now, Star-Kist was the only U.S. tuna canner available to offer that opportunity. During the 1979-1985 period, some U.S. tuna canners implemented the premise that it was "more economical for vertically-integrated processors to let independent tuna vessel owners bear the financial risk of operating vessels."[10]

In competition with the Southeast Asian tuna canners who were not engaged in the advertised-brand retail sector, Star-Kist had learned the value and importance of marketing the Star-Kist brand or label to the U.S. consumer.[11] Now, it was faced with competition in this extremely important market sector from two Southeast Asian tuna canners who owned successful advertised brands: "Chicken of the Sea" and "Bumble Bee."

Star-Kist also recognized the absolute necessity of obtaining low-cost frozen tuna from as many reliable sources of supply as possible in order to be competitive with the low-cost Southeast Asian tuna canners. Now, Star-Kist was faced with the reality that its two new competitors in the advertised-brand sector were proven buyers of low-cost tunas from growing fleets of purse-seine vessels fishing in the western Pacific. Also, that the new owner of Van Camp Seafood Company, Inc. was planning to close its cannery in Puerto Rico and concentrate its canning operations in American Samoa and Indonesia. It must have been apparent to Star-Kist that these two competitors were in a position to market their advertised brands of canned tuna in the United States and make the claim that the tunas processed were not harvested by fishing tuna/porpoise schools in the eastern Pacific Ocean. Other signs of dramatic changes in the canning segment of the U.S. tuna industry were occurring: waterfront talk was that Mitsui, the Japanese company that operated a subsidiary that was the largest importer of canned tuna in the United States, was planning to have another subsidiary close its tuna cannery in Puerto Rico.[12] It could be argued, at this time in early 1990, that the U.S. tuna industry could no longer be united in its views on political and economic matters; the fleet was divided, with more vessels and capacity fishing in the western Pacific than in the eastern Pacific, and with more tuna canners, in number and capacity, owned by citizens of Asian countries, than canneries owned by U.S. citizens.

---

[1] Charles J. Peckham, "The United States Tuna Industry: an Overview of Changing Patterns in Production, Imports and the Market," presented at the Infofish Tuna Trade Conference, Bangkok, Thailand, February 26, 1986. Vice President, Living Marine Resources, Inc, San Diego, California

[2] "On November 15, 1988, P.T. Management Trust, a privately held Indonesian concern, purchased Van Camp Seafood Company, Inc. and its "Chicken of the Sea" canned tuna brand from Ralston Purina for $260 Million." USITC Publication 2339 (December 1990): 2-17. "In September 1989, Bumble Bee Seafoods, Inc. was purchased by Uni-Group, a company whose shareholders included Unicord Co., Ltd., the largest processor and exporter of tuna in Thailand for $269 million. USITC Publication 2339 (December 1990): 2-16. In a letter dated May 1, 1990, addressed to the Chairman of the House Subcommittee on Fisheries and Wildlife Conservation and the Environment, the President of Van Camp Seafood Company, Inc., advised that P.T. Management Trust was its major shareholder.

[3] Van Camp Seafood Company, Inc., closed its plant in Ponce, Puerto Rico, on June 29, 1990, but continued its operation in Pago Pago, American Samoa. Neptune Packing Corporation, a subsidiary of Mitsui (U.S.A.), New York, NY., closed its cannery in Mayaquez, Puerto Rico, in August 1990. Also, during the summer of 1990, Star-Kist Foods, Canada, closed its tuna cannery in St. Andrews, New Brunswick. The closure explanation provided to the USITC: price cuts by canners using Asian imports.

[4] In 1991, the share of all catches of tunas in the eastern Pacific Ocean for the fleets of Ecuador, Mexico, and Venezuela totaled about 71%, while that of the U.S. was down to 11.6%. As to landings, the U.S. share was only 8.8%; the combined share of Ecuador, Mexico, and Venezuela was over 54%. See: IATTC Annual Report for 1992: 167. IATTC Annual Report for 1991: 153. In 1989, the U.S. fleet's share of the tuna catch in the eastern Pacific was 25.2%, and the U.S. share of landings was 37.4%. See: IATTC Annual Report for 1990: 153. Data showing the growth of the Ecuadorian, Mexican, and Venezuelan tuna fleets during 1981-1987 is provided at 1988 SENATE HEARING 100-711: 30.

[5] The Treaty of Fisheries between the governments of certain Pacific Island States and the government of the United States of America, was signed at Port Moresby, Papua New Guinea, on April 2, 1987.

[6] During 1985-1989, the apparent European consumption of canned tuna rose 63 percent, placing Europe as second only to the U.S. market in the consumption of canned tuna. "Although accounting for only 5 percent of the European total, consumption of canned tuna by non-EC European nations rose 75 percent during 1986-1989 ... Virtually all canned tuna supplies in this market are provided by imports." USITC Publication 2339 (December 1990): 4-4.

[7] The remaining U.S. tuna canners were as follows: Pan Pacific Fisheries, Inc., a wholly-owned subsidiary of Marifarms, Inc., Terminal Island, Los Angeles Harbor, California, the only remaining tuna cannery servicing tuna seiners in the continental United States. Star-Kist Foods, Inc., a subsidiary of H.J. Heinz, Pittsburgh, Pennsylvania, operated canneries at Mayaquez, Puerto Rico, and in Pago Pago, American Samoa. Bumble Bee Seafoods, Inc., operated a cannery at Mayaquez, Puerto Rico, and in 1990 opened a plant to process tuna loins exclusively at Santa Fe Springs, Los Angeles County, California Mitsubishi Foods, Inc., (Caribe Tuna), a subsidiary of Mitsubishi Corporation, Tokyo, Japan, operated a plant in Ponce, Puerto Rico. Van Camp Seafood Company, Inc., operated a cannery in Pago Pago, American Samoa.

[8] "Asian producers gained the lead in world canned tuna trade as a result of competitive advantages afforded by relatively inexpensive labor, proximity to raw fish resources, and

export-oriented national government and business environments." USITC Publication 2339 (December 1990): xv.

[9] Star-Kist Foods, Inc., failed in its efforts to purchase Bumble Bee Seafoods. The American Tunaboat Association opposed this effort in the belief that its membership would be placed at a disadvantage if Star-Kist were allowed to have more than a 50% share of the canned tuna market in the United States. It is believed that the opposition to this merger by the Department of Justice probably caused Star-Kist to drop its purchase effort. Thereafter, Pillsbury Corporation purchased Bumble Bee Seafoods, retaining current management. In January 1989, Pillsbury was merged into Grand Metropolitan PLC. In August 1989, Pillsbury sold Bumble Bee Seafoods to a Thailand tuna processor.

[10] USITC Publication 1912 (October 1986): 27.

[11] During 1979-1985, the share of the advertised-brand retail market sector by the U.S. tuna canners ranged from 94 to 98 percent. "U.S. processors have maintained their position in this market segment because of brand recognition that has been developed over a long period of time. For this reason, direct entry into this market segment is difficult for imports." USITC Publication 1912 (October 1986): xxiii.

[12] The largest importer of canned tuna during the period of 1979-1983 was a subsidiary of Mitsui & Co, U.S.A., Inc., New York, N.Y. ("Mitsui"). Neptune Packing Corporation of White Plains, New York, another subsidiary of Mitsui, operated a tuna cannery in Mayaguez, Puerto Rico. This plant was acquired 1n 1973 by Mitsui from Inter Basic Economy Corporation (IBEC), a firm founded by Nelson Rockefeller in 1971. This tuna cannery had been built by IBEC. USITC Publication 1558 (August 1994): A-16. Neptune was the second tuna firm to close a tuna cannery in Puerto Rico after the "Dolphin Safe" purchasing policy was announced on April 12, 1990. The tuna cannery operated by Van Camp in Ponce, Puerto Rico, was closed in June, 1990, and the Neptune plant in Mayaguez was closed in August 1990. As of December 1990, only three firms were operating tuna canneries in Puerto Rico: Star-Kist in Mayaguez; Bumble Bee in Mayaguez, and Caribe Tuna, Inc; a plant operated by a subsidiary of Mitsubishi Foods, Inc., in Ponce. USITC Publication 2339 (December 1990): 2-16.

35

TUNA AND ECONOMICS

In 1992, Roger Lyman Corey, Jr., submitted a dissertation to the University of Rhode Island entitled "Technology and Competition in the Tuna industry."[1] Significantly, Mr. Corey was an employee of the United States International Trade Commission (USITC).[2] The two goals of Mr. Corey's work were to describe the "economic history of the U.S. tuna industry, with a particular emphasis on the nature of competition and technological change," and to evaluate "the extent to which the nature of competition in the tuna industry" has been affected by technological changes in both the harvesting and processing segments of the industry.[3]

Mr. Corey concluded that there is indeed a TCL [technology-competition link] in tuna—a Schumpeterian link between the dynamic, long-run forces of competition and technological changes in tuna harvesting and processing.[4] In the harvesting sector, he referred to the development of the modern tuna purse-seine fleet by citizens of the United States, noting that this change "propelled the U.S. industry to technological and economic supremacy. Yet within a few decades that dominance was dissolved at the hands of foreign rivals that, having adopted the best technology, at first competed with and now appear to be engulfing the ever diminishing U.S. industry." In the processing sector, he noted that all tuna canners have the same technology; therefore, "economic success comes to those that have lower costs of labor and other significant inputs ... Thailand, for example, will outperform the United States as long as both nations' industries use the same technology and as long as Los Angeles labor continues to command ten times the wage rate that prevails in Bangkok."[5] In 1992, Mr. Corey found that the canned tuna industry was in "equilibrium," awaiting an unforeseen technological change in competition that would go beyond impacting only "simple cost" advantages but that would land a new and decisive advantage for the risk taker.

Mr. Corey's dissertation claimed that this "foundational" technological change of the future was born in the processing segment of the U.S. canned tuna industry when in 1989-1990, Bumble Bee Seafoods built a 122,000-square foot tuna loin-canning plant in Santa Fe Springs (Los Angeles County), about 25 miles from the Pacific Ocean. The imported tuna loins were shipped to the low-cost canning facility in airtight containers for processing into canned products for shipment to customers in the nearby Los Angeles and other markets.

In 1989, Unicord PCL, Thailand's largest tuna processor, in a highly-leveraged acquisition, purchased Bumble Bee Seafoods from Grand Metropolitan PLC for $283 million. A short time after the purchase, Patrick Rose, the CEO of Bumble Bee Seafoods, advised the CEO of Unicord, Mr. Dumri Konuntakiet, of a feasibility study directed by Patrick Rose and implemented by his staff that examined the profitability of a new tuna loin plant project for the important Los Angeles canned tuna market. Mr. Rose explained that the study examined the costs and benefits of two ideas: (1) taking advantage of the low tariff applicable to the importation of tuna loins packed in airtight containers, and (2) taking advantage of the low labor and other production costs involved in producing tuna loins at the firm's facility in Manta, Ecuador. Mr. Konuntakiet was very enthusiastic about the idea of a new tuna loin plant near Los Angeles, and told Mr. Rose to move forward with the new project. After further discussions with Mr. Konuntakiet, the concept was expanded to include the importation of tuna loins shipped from Unicord's plants in Thailand.[6]

Despite the limited information available about Bumble Bee Seafood's new tuna loin plant, Mr. Corey made following prediction in 1992 about the plant's future impact on the industry's harvesting and processing sectors:

> "Eventually, it seems apparent to me, the tuna industry will return to the west coast, although in a dramatically altered form that will not include the harvesting sector. The reason for this is the canning of imported loins, on which Bumble Bee has taken the lead ... unforeseen factors may loom up to slow the development of loin canning, but continued efforts in this area seem inevitable in view of the vast labor-cost advantage ..."

Mr. Corey's 1992 predictions of about the future of canning tuna loins in the United States seem to be coming into fruition.

At a press conference, on May 7, 2009, representatives of Chicken of the Sea International and Samoa Packing announced plans to shut down the tuna cannery in American Samoa on September 30, 2009, which would affect the jobs of an estimated 2,041 employees in American Samoa. The two companies explained, in a written statement, that

> "[We] have been partners with American Samoa since 1954 and have worked diligently for decades to ensure Chicken of the Sea remains competitive—in today's global economic environment that is no longer possible. Ceasing canning operations in American Samoa and opening a U.S. domestic canning operation in Lyons, Georgia, ensures Chicken of the Sea will remain viable and competitive for the long term."[7]

On May 1, 2009, a press release by Chicken of the Sea International stated:

> "The Georgia canning facility will receive high-grade tuna loins for canning, meaning less processing time, quicker turn-around in developing the same high end product, and a much-reduced inventory—giving our customers and their consumers, the same high quality Chicken of the Sea products they expect from us. For Lyons, GA., this means the immediate creation of 220 jobs and up to 310 new jobs in further years ..."

On May 4, 2009, a press release from Sonny Perdue, governor of Georgia, stated:

> "Chicken of the Sea International plans to return tuna canning to the United States and open a domestic canning operating in Lyons ... [in] a 200,000 square-foot facility in Lyons, where workers will process frozen tuna loins into shelf stable Chicken of the Sea canned tuna to be shipped throughout the United States."

Effective May 14, 2010, reductions in the employment of cannery workers by Star-

Kist at its American Samoa plants were again announced. Additional 600-800 jobs will be eliminated over the next six months. In 2008, Star-Kist employed a high of more than 3000 people; by the end of 2010, employment will be reduced to about 1200 people. In explanation, Star-Kist officials stated the following:

> "Our competitors have been using a model that moves the labor-intensive fish clean-ing process to low-wage countries. We have vigorously resisted this model, but it has become difficult to compete with wages nearly ten times those of Thailand and elsewhere, especially when combined with rising utility and shipping costs and the decreased value of duty protection ... Our market share and business is vulnerable to competitors that have adopted the lower cost model. We must therefore continual-ly evaluate the cost-effectiveness of our long term operations in American Samoa."[8]

During the May joint meetings with American Samoan government officials, Star-Kist President and CEO Donald Binotto advised: "I'm here to tell you that we will be bringing in [our operations] more loins to reduce our costs. It's unfortunate [but] that's something we have to do."

During October 2010, a six-year lease of the former Chicken of the Sea Interna-tional tuna cannery was negotiated between the government of American Samoa with a joint venture reportedly named "Samoa Tuna Processors." Waterfront talk is that this new operation may process imported tuna loins and frozen tuna in the round unloaded by tuna vessels.

If it is correct to say that the top three major tuna brands in the United States are presently canning imported tuna loins, then it also proper to conclude that in 2010, a fundamental change has occurred in the U.S. tuna processing sector. To what extent has this new technology affected the harvesting sector of the U.S. tuna Industry that operates in the Central and Western Pacific?

It is our view that in the central and western Pacific Ocean, the "tuna loin" con-cept is founded upon the requirement that tuna vessel operators transship their catch to locations that process low cost tuna loins and canned products. Compe-tition on the tuna fishing grounds requires vessel operators to reduce costs by avoiding delays at cannery docks. Presently, trips made by seiners to a cannery in American Samoa are more likely to increase costs than trips made by seiners to transshipment locations because, more often than not, transshipment locations are closer to tuna fishing grounds than is American Samoa. The scheduling of transshipments requires the tuna seiners to meet the schedule of freezer ships, regardless of fishing conditions. To operate under this "transshipment model," significant changes in tuna seiner operation at sea are occurring.

Tuna economics have not changed; the harvesting and processing sectors are under continuing pressure to seek lower labor and operating costs by the intro-duction of new technology and competition. Nor has canned tuna consumption changed; it continues to be recognized as a desirable food product by consumers world-wide. However, the implementation of tuna conservation and management needs to change world-wide.[9]

[1] Roger Lyman Corey, Jr (1992) "Technology and Competition in the Tuna Industry," A dissertation submitted in partial fulfillment of the requirements for the degree of Doctor of Philosophy in economics—Marine Resources Option, University of Rhode Island (hereinafter referred to as "Corey dissertation.")

[2] The descriptions, views, and opinions of Mr. Corey on the U.S. tuna industry, as expressed in his 1992 dissertation, are relevant. He is an employee of the United States International Trade Commission (USITC), and was selected to help prepare the following three publications for the USITC: (1) Report to the President: "Competitive Conditions in the U.S. Tuna Industry," USITC Publication 1912, October 1986; (2) Report to the Committee on Finance, U.S. Senate, and the Committee on Ways and Means, U.S. House of Representatives: "Tuna: Competitive Conditions Affecting the U.S. and European Tuna Industries in Domestic and Foreign Markets," USITC Publication 2239, December 1990, and (3) Report to the Committee on Finance, United States Senate: "Tuna: Current Issues Affecting the U.S. Industry," USITC Publication 2547, August 1992,

[3] Corey dissertation, page viii

[4] Corey dissertation, page 331

[5] Personal conversations with Patrick Rose, former CEO of Bumble Bee Seafoods, during May 2010, at San Diego, California

[6] Fili Sagapolutele fili@samoanews.com May 2, 2008

[7] Fili Sagapolutele fili@samoanews.com May 14, 2008

[8] Fili Sagapolutele fili@samoanews.com May 14, 2008

[9] Allen, Robin, James Joseph, and Dale Squires (editors). (2010) Conservation and Management of Transnational Tuna Fisheries, Wiley-Blackwell: xvi, 343 pp.

PART X

THE TUNA "CATCH 22"

36

TUNA CONSERVATION VS. "DOLPHIN SAFE"

A House Divided by a Canned Tuna "Label"

On April 12, 1990, three major U.S. tuna canners announced a new purchasing policy, called "dolphin safe."[1] This meant that they would not purchase tuna caught in the eastern Pacific Ocean (EPO) on a fishing trip by any purse seiner that had made one or more sets during that trip on tuna/porpoise schools, even if no tunas were caught in association with porpoises on that trip. Why was the U.S. canned tuna industry in early 1990 no longer unified on the issue of fishing tuna/porpoise schools by tuna seiners in the EPO as it had been in 1980?

A review of the Administrative Law hearings conducted by the Office of the Secretary of Commerce in 1980 shows that the entire U.S. tuna industry—canners, vessel owners, fishermen, and their representatives—opposed proposals by the U.S. National Marine Fisheries Service (NMFS) to prohibit the purse seining on tuna/porpoise schools in the EPO. The reasons provided by the industry as to why these proposals should be rejected were accepted by the Administrative Law Judge and by the Administrator of the National Oceanic and Atmospheric Administration (NOAA). The Administrative Law Judge agreed with industry and others that the NMFS proposal to a **limited ban, even though it was** not a **total prohibition**, on the seining of certain tuna/porpoise schools would (1) probably cause a shift of "economic fishing technology to non-U.S. controlled interests"; (2) threaten yellowfin tuna conservation and production, (3) be "economically disastrous to the United States-flag tuna industry", and (4) cause tuna cannery closures in Puerto Rico and California.[2] Why did some U.S. tuna canners change their positions in 1990?

In the years following the declaration of the "dolphin-safe" policy by the U.S. tuna canners, the establishment of that policy by federal legislation, and the enforcement of the law by regulation, the U.S. government undertook diplomatic and legislative efforts to persuade Latin American governments to also prohibit their fishermen from making sets on tuna/porpoise schools in the EPO. The United States failed in these campaigns because scientific evidence and common sense indicated that this policy, if implemented, would severely damage the efforts of the IATTC to properly manage the yellowfin tuna resource at sustainable levels and greatly increase the "waste" of species other than tunas, such as billfishes, sharks, dorado, wahoo, and many other species that would be discarded at sea. This bycatch of seining on non-tuna/porpoise schools would be wasteful, especially since many of these species are exploited by artisanal and recreational fishermen in Latin America and California.

On April 12, 1990, StarKist Seafood Company ("Star-Kist") announced a new purchasing policy that was taken "independently and without prior consultation with any other tuna canner." This "dolphin-safe" purchasing policy was immediately followed by similar announcements from the two major competitors of StarKist: Bumble Bee Seafoods ("Bumble Bee") and Van Camp Seafood Company ("Chicken of the Sea"). Prior to these announcements, no official of StarKist, H.J. Heinz, Bumble Bee, and Chicken of the Sea had consulted with the American Tunaboat Association (ATA) on this new buying policy.

Why did these three major tuna canners embrace the "dolphin-safe" policy? During Congressional hearings held on October 4, 1989, and as late as April 3, 1990, the tuna industry was presumably united, along with the NMFS, in testifying that the tuna industry was opposed to the legislation introduced to require that tuna products be labeled with information on the method used to catch the tunas.[3] Immediately after the announcements, in April 1990, meetings were held at the ATA to seek information about this surprising change in a once-united industry.

ATA members were told by individuals representing tuna canners that H.J. Heinz, the corporate owner of Star-Kist, was threatened with a national boycott of all of its non-tuna products by a group of radical environmental organizations and their supporters, and that this national boycott was to be implemented on Earth Day (April 22, 1990). It was explained that H.J. Heinz was singled out because the other major tuna canners were foreign owned, and did not have significant sales of non-tuna products in the United States. In addition, certain radical environmental organizations and their supporters had purchased stock in H.J. Heinz for the purpose of bringing a stockholder lawsuit against the officers and Board of Directors of H.J. Heinz. And, that these individuals had hired a law firm for the purpose of determining whether a refusal by the officers and board of directors of H.J. Heinz to adopt a "dolphin-safe" purchasing policy, in view of threatened national boycott, could be used as a basis for a stockholder lawsuit. Finally, that the management of H.J. Heinz knew that its foreign-owned competitors were developing a "dolphin-safe" label, so it decided it had to take a leadership role on moving ahead with a "dolphin-safe" label.

Only the U.S. tuna canners who made their announcements on April 12, 1990, know the real reasons for their actions. Some individuals in the industry stated that it was a reaction to a "marketing problem," which may be true. In 1989, the press reported that a tuna canner in British Columbia, Canada, was claiming that consumers were willing to pay more for a can of tuna with a "dolphin-safe" label than for a can of tuna without this label. During the 1970s, Star-Kist was highly successful as the first tuna canner to market tuna canned in water by persuading the consumer of its diet and health benefits. Maybe Star-Kist believed that it would increase its market share and profits by marketing "dolphin-safe" canned tuna by persuading the consumer that the purchase would promote "environmentally-safe" fishing practices. Who knows? Maybe officers of H.J. Heinz were influenced to take their actions by the 1978 Hollywood movie, "Heaven Can Wait," a fantasy involving a Heaven-sent angel (actor James Mason), and a professional football player (actor Warren Beatty). Presumably, God orders the football player's spirit to enter and restore life to a murdered millionaire businessman. Then, the football player-millionaire businessman buys the Los Angeles Rams football team in order to play quarterback, wins the game and championship and later, as CEO of a tuna cannery, orders a purchasing policy similar to that announced by Star-Kist on April 12, 1990.

After announcement of the "dolphin-safe" buying policy, some in the tuna industry voiced the opinion that Hollywood stars and others in that community influenced some officers of H.J. Heinz to unilaterally declare their leadership to "save the environment" and to protect and enhance their competitive position in the industry by strongly supporting labeling legislation proposed by a member of Congress representing a district in Northern California.

Others expressed the opinion that the new buying policy by the major American tuna canners would severely damage the competitive capacity of the U.S. tuna seiners based in Southern California to fish on their traditional fishing grounds in the EPO. Others claimed that the new policy would cause the closure of the remaining small tuna cannery operation in California by preventing that cannery from obtaining a reliable supply of tropical tunas provided by a viable U.S. tuna fleet operating in the EPO.[4]

On May 3, 1990, a hearing was conducted on H.R. 2926 (Dolphin Protection Consumer Information Act; DPCIA) by the Subcommittee on Fisheries and Wildlife Conservation and Environment of the House Committee on Merchant Marine and Fisheries. This bill would require the labeling of tuna products for the purpose of identifying which of those products involves the use of technologies known to be harmful to dolphins. During his testimony in support of furthering the passage of H.R. 2926, the president of Star-Kist explained how its new policy would be implemented: "Star-Kist will not purchase tuna caught by the targeting or intentional encirclement of dolphin in a purse seine net in the Eastern Tropical Pacific (ETP) fishery. ... we will only buy from the catch of boats whose observers (NMFS or Inter-American Tropical Tuna Commission (IATTC)) certify "zero" intentional encirclements of dolphins during the trip."[5]

On July 10, 1990, the Committee on Merchant Marine and Fisheries reported favorably on an amended H.R. 2926 with a recommendation that it pass, together with additional and dissenting views.[6] The Department of Commerce opposed the passage of H.R. 2926, stating:

> "The only way to verify whether tuna were caught with dolphin would require tracking and separation measures before canning. ... Since most of the canned tuna is from foreign sources, the burden to verify the accuracy of how the tuna was caught ultimately would fall on U.S. tuna importers and processors. Implementing such segregation measures would be impractical if not impossible. ... H.R. 2926 also could

undermine our Congressionally mandated efforts to reduce dolphin mortality in the ETP. ... The U.S. tuna industry will likely be affected to a greater degree by H.R. 2926 than would the foreign industry. ... The Department also is concerned that labeling cans "Dolphin Safe" may imply to uninformed consumers that the contents of a can of tuna might actually contain dolphin meat with the label designating that such is safe to eat. Alternatively, it could imply that the contents of cans not labeled "Dolphin Safe" may pose a human health hazard rather than just indicating that the tuna were caught using fishing methods than can kill dolphins. We strongly recommend against the use of a "Dolphin Safe" label."[7]

Congressman Don Young of Alaska, a member of the Committee, submitted a dissenting view to H.R. 2926, stating in part the following:

"There is no evidence that consumers will react to labels reflecting fishing practices—even if they are fully 'informed" from the environmental special interest point of view about those fishing practices—as long as a price differential exists. In fact, in spite of a massive campaign against tuna conducted by a variety of special interest groups last year, the American consumption of canned tuna **increased** by over 8% and is still rising! Americans like canned tuna because it is an inexpensive, healthy food product that is easy to prepare, serve, and store. Simply slapping a "dolphin unsafe" label on a can of tuna will not keep the consumers away.

"What, then, will be the effects of this bill? We have seen some already. The decision to change buying practices made by canning companies—under intense pressure from special interest groups—has shut down one processing plant in Puerto Rico, throwing 5,000 workers out of jobs. It has idled one third of the U.S tuna fleet. Tuna cannery officials have testified that the price of canned tuna will increase to U.S. tuna consumers. **Yet, the bill will do nothing to save dolphins which are killed in the tens of thousands by foreign tuna vessels over which the U.S. Congress has no control. Further, if tuna fleets must now concentrate on harvesting smaller tuna, which don't associate with dolphins, there are indications that tuna populations will be adversely affected, since tuna will be caught at a younger age and thus not contribute to sustaining populations. In other words, we may, or may not, depending on foreign reactions—save the dolphins at the expense of the tuna."[8]** (emphasis added)

On July 25, 1990, the President of Star-Kist testified in support of H.R. 2926 before the House Subcommittee on Commerce, Consumer Protection, and Competitiveness of the Committee on Energy and Commerce, explaining that Star-Kist supported H.R. 2926 because:

"... **as a practical matter, if there is no legislation passed and others do not follow the same definition of dolphin-safe that we do, then we will perhaps be at a competitive disadvantage.** And certainly the consumer, if she thinks she is buying dolphin-safe tuna from a company other than Star-Kist and getting the same thing as if she buys Star-Kist dolphin-safe tuna, she will be misinformed. ... What I was speaking of in terms of a competitive disadvantage is simply a processor that is buying fish that is not caught in a dolphin-safe manner, perhaps, at a lower price and selling it as dolphin-safe in the marketplace, and being able to charge less simply because their costs are less."[9] (emphasis added)

In response to questions by the Subcommittee, the president of Star-Kist Seafood Company stated that the passage of the H.R. 2926 "would not affect the continued viability of the U.S. Fleet in the eastern tropical Pacific,"[10] and "it is only real speculation as to what is going to happen in terms of the total catch coming out the eastern tropical Pacific."[11]

The Star-Kist policy of not purchasing, processing, or selling any tuna caught in tuna/porpoise schools was quickly recognized within the U.S. tuna industry as divisive and harmful to those segments of the industry dependent primarily upon canning facilities in Southern California and Puerto Rico. The adverse economic consequences of denying the U.S. tuna seiners access to tuna/porpoise schools in the EPO had been thoroughly vented and explained by a **united** U.S. tuna industry during the Administrative Law Judge hearings held in 1980. Now, it became clear that a permanent schism had occurred within the U.S. tuna industry. In the western Pacific, the three major U.S. tuna canners (Star-Kist, Bumble Bee, and Chicken of the Sea) were positioned to operate efficient and low-cost canning facilities, and to have access to inexpensive tuna supplies from highly-productive U.S and foreign tuna seiners. In addition, this ocean region was estimated by fishery biologists to contain millions of tons of tropical tunas.[12] Furthermore, since these tunas did not associate with porpoise, the catch of tuna seiners in this region could be labeled as "dolphin-safe." Further, American tuna seiners based in the western Pacific were operating pursuant to a tuna treaty providing access to tuna grounds within the 200-mile Exclusive Economic Zones (EEZs) of numerous South Pacific island countries and free of any tuna conservation measures, adding to their reliability as suppliers of frozen tuna. No such treaty was applicable to American tuna vessels in the EPO.

For the U.S. tuna canners dependent upon operating canning facilities in Puerto Rico and Southern California, the "dolphin-safe" announcement made them dependent on tuna seiner fleets operating in the EPO that would have serious problems in being a reliable source of supply. Reliability would be a problem because tuna seiners, particularly U.S.-flag vessels, would be at risk of seizures at sea by as many as 11 Latin American governments enforcing their claims of 200-mile EEZs. This was likely because at that time tunas not associated with porpoises were caught mostly within the EEZs claimed by the Latin American countries. This risk of seizure-related losses became more unwelcome after the ATA advised its membership that financial support from U.S. tuna canners in seizure incidents was becoming more questionable because some canners were being financially impacted by the increasing competition in the U.S. canned tuna market. The Convention that created the IATTC in 1949 did not give it the authority to establish a regional fishing license arrangement to provide tuna fishing access to the 200-mile fishery zones claimed by the coastal Latin American nations fronting the EPO. The prospect of diplomatic success in achieving a treaty in the EPO patterned after the South Pacific Tuna Treaty, which authorized vessels of the United States, Australia, and New Zealand to fish within the EEZs of 14 island nations [13] of the southwestern Pacific Ocean, was slim to none. Other serious supply problems confronted the U.S. tuna canners having facilities only in Southern California or Puerto Rico. The source of supply from the Mexican and Venezuelan tuna seiner fleets was adversely affected by the development of canned tuna markets in those countries and export markets for frozen tuna to canners in Spain and Italy.[14]

During the hearings held on May 3, 1990, a member of the House Subcommittee asked whether the passage of H.R. 2926 would cause tuna fisheries management and conservation problems in the EPO due to the fact that the purse-seine fishermen would be required to target small and immature yellowfin tuna not associated with porpoise in order to comply with the canneries' dolphin-safe policy. The counsel for the Wildlife Policy Defenders and Chairman of The Dolphin Coalition responded: "If this bill happens to be associated with causing a problem later on, we could return to that. But there is no reason to believe now that requiring accurate labeling will affect that."[15]

Efforts by the U.S. Congress were unsuccessful in establishing a five-year moratorium on fishing of tuna/porpoise schools in the EPO.[16] These unilateral and unwise legislative actions failed because the scientific staff of the IATTC had produced data indicating that a policy of total protection of porpoise would create serious and unacceptable mismanagement of the yellowfin resources in the EPO.[17] Biological data showed that the yellowfin tuna associated with porpoise are almost exclusively large (averaging about 20 to 90 pounds), sexually-mature yellowfin. (Skipjack and smaller yellowfin and bigeye are incapable of maintaining the cruising speeds of the porpoise.) Large bigeye tunas rarely, if ever, associate with porpoise, possibly because they inhabit greater depths than do porpoise and yellowfin. Yellowfin tuna in unassociated schools and in schools associated with floating objects are usually smaller (about 5 to 20 pounds), and mostly sexually immature. Yellowfin weigh about 5 pounds at age 1 year, 15 pounds at age 1.5 years, 35 pounds at age 2 years, 60 pounds at age 2.5, years, and 100 pounds at age 3 years.[18] IATTC scientists have estimated that the "critical size" (the size at which the losses due to natural mortality of a cohort of fish balance the gains to that cohort by growth) of yellowfin tuna of about 65 pounds. Therefore, the maximum sustainable yield could theoretically be obtained by catching all the fish at 65 pounds. This would not be possible, of course, unless an infinite amount of fishing effort were exerted with a method of fishing that avoids catching fish less than 65 pounds but is successful in catching all tunas weighing 65 pounds or more. The next-best thing would be to use a method of fishing that avoids catching fish weighing considerably less than 65 pounds, but is most efficient at catching fish with weights not too much less than 65 pounds— say 30 to 100 pounds. The fishing method that most closely meets this requirement is fishing for fish associated with porpoise. At age 1.5 years about 10% of female yellowfin are sexually mature, and at ages 2 years, 2.5 years, and 3 years these percentages increase to about 50, 80, and 90, respectively.[19] In general, for highly-fecund fish such as tunas, recruitment of young fish into the fishery does not seem to be related to the abundance of spawning fish at the time that those recruits were hatched, but nevertheless the abundance of spawners should not be permitted to be reduced drastically. Fortunately, most of the fish caught in association with porpoise have already reached sexual maturity and begun to spawn.

The data collected by the IATTC also showed that a policy of total protection for the porpoise would result in the mortality and waste of many other marine living resources. The data showed that while a set on a tuna/porpoise school would, on average, result in the death of one porpoise (in recent years, about 0.1 porpoise), a set on a floating object directed at skipjack would result in the capture of thousands of juvenile tunas (mostly bigeye, but also some yellowfin) and other species, such as mahi-mahi, wahoo, rainbow runners, sharks, marlin, triggerfishes, and other small fish.[20] Some of the bigeye and yellowfin, along with the skipjack, are sold for canning, but the smaller bigeye and yellowfin, plus most of the other fish, are discarded at sea. The amounts of bycatch taken by sets on "pure" or unassociated schools of tuna are greater than those taken in sets on tunas associated with porpoise, but less than those taken in sets on tunas associated with floating objects.[21] "As the "logs" or floating objects are drifting, fish of all sizes and body configurations, slow or fast-moving, aggregate under them. On the other hand, groups of tunas and dolphins cruise at high speeds, and prior to setting there is a chase at even higher speeds, so that when the group is encircled almost no small or slow-moving species of fishes or other animals are encircled. Aside from dolphin, catches of dolphin sets consist of a few sharks and occasionally, billfishes, mahi-mahi, wahoo, and/or sea turtles. The billfishes may have been traveling with the tuna-dolphin aggregation, but others were probably by chance in the water encircled.[22] The data show conclusively that seiner sets on tuna/porpoise schools are the "cleanest" in terms of bycatch.

These are some of the facts that influenced Dr. James Joseph, Director of the IATTC, in responding to the "conservation dilemma" confronting the IATTC in September 1990. After the unilateral action taken by the U.S. tuna canners to shut down the market for tuna caught by seiners fishing tuna/porpoise schools in theEPO, the then member nations of the IATTC (Costa Rica, France, Japan, Nicaragua, Panama, the United States, and Vanuatu) had the option of adopting a resolution to prohibit the seining of tuna/porpoise schools and thereby eliminate porpoise mortality. If this were done, Dr. Joseph and his scientific staff knew that the result would be "adverse long-term consequences for yellowfin tunas and possibly harm the ecosystem of the eastern Pacific as a whole." This was a realistic statement because they knew that the fishermen would have to shift their effort to "logs [flotsam] and schools for predominately smaller, sexually immature yellowfin and skipjack tunas closer to shore." This action would "lead to overexploitation of the resource and also give rise to political problems over access in areas under national jurisdiction."[23]

Fortunately, the member nations of the IATTC and other governments having tuna seiner fleets worked with the staff of the IATTC in continuing its efforts to reduce porpoise mortality "without incurring heavy ecological costs to the yellowfin population or the ecosystem of which they both form a part."[24] To their discredit, the Congressional committees considering the "dolphin-safe" bills did not seek consultation from the scientific staff of the IATTC.

Congress Creates a Tuna "Catch 22"

On November 28, 1990, a bill passed by Congress in October 1990 entitled "Fishery Conservation Amendments of 1990" became law. It contained provisions amending the Magnuson Fishery Conservation and Management Act (MFCMA) that, effective January 1992, asserted fishery jurisdiction over tuna species found within its 200-mile EEZ.[25] In addition, it included provisions that amended the Marine Mammal Protection Act (MMPA) and the DPCIA, which created the "dolphin-safe" label for tuna products.[26]

The Fishery Conservation and Management Act of 1976 (FCMA), declared that the fishery management jurisdiction of the United States extended seaward to all species of fish within a 200-mile EEZ, with the **exception** of highly-migratory species, such as tuna. This exclusion required that U.S. tuna vessels be protected by their government when other nations seized or harassed them on the basis of a claims not recognized by the United States. The United States did not recognize its right or the rights of other coastal states to assert fishery jurisdiction over tuna resources occurring within an ocean region. Section 103 of the FCMA stated: "The exclusive fishery management authority of the United States shall not include, nor shall it be construed to extend to, highly migratory species of fish." The term "highly migratory species" was defined by this Act to mean "species of tuna which, in the course of their life cycle, spawn, and migrate great distances in waters of the ocean."[27]

Concerns about the status of Atlantic tuna stocks within the 200-mile EEZ of the United States were the subject of a hearing held on December 8, 1981, before the National Ocean Policy Study of the U.S. Senate Committee on Commerce, Science, and Transportation. The bill (S. 1564) discussed at this hearing proposed that the MFCMA be amended by changing the definition of the term "highly migratory species" and by striking out Section 103 of the MFCMA. This bill received support by senators from Maine, Delaware, and New York, by the Massachusetts Marine Fisheries Advisory Commission, by a national sportfishing group, and by a New Jersey-based fish processor of bluefin tuna. The U.S. Department of State, the United States Tuna Foundation, the ATA, Living Marine Resources, and others representing a united U.S. tuna canning industry, opposed passage of S. 1564. During the hearing, Theodore G. Kronmiller, Assistant Secretary of State for Oceans and Fisheries Affairs, testified and provided written testimony, which included the following:

> "Mr. Chairman, it is the view of the Department of State that, if the U.S. were to assert jurisdiction over highly migratory tuna, it would have a very detrimental effect on ongoing negotiations aimed at the conclusion of an international regime which would assure the effective conservation and management of tuna stocks in the eastern tropical Pacific. ... such a radical change in our law and policy would entail severe consequences for U.S. tuna fishermen operating off Latin America. ..." (p. 7)

> "The tuna exclusion in the FCMA is both symbolic and practical evidence of the U.S. government support of our tuna industry. If the United States extended its 200-mile jurisdiction to tuna, the embargo provisions of the MFCMA and the compensation programs of the Fishermen's Protective Act (FPA) would, in effect, be eliminated, insofar as they relate to the tuna industry. These provisions of law provide the United States with important negotiating leverage and without them, the U.S. tuna fleet would be at the mercy of the Latin American coastal states in the 200-mile zones ..." (p. 8)

"Without the MFCMA embargo sanction and the FPA compensation programs, the coastal states with whom we must negotiate would be convinced that, if they simply had the patience to wait, a negotiated settlement would go their way, since the U.S. government would not in the long run stand behind our industry. ... Without these legal protections, the U.S. tuna fleet would soon decide that there is no future in attempting to operate on a commercially viable basis under the U.S. flag. U.S. tuna vessels would be compelled to buy very expensive coastal State licenses and to adhere to whatever arbitrary or discriminatory regulations were imposed by the coastal States, or indeed to remain outside certain zones entirely, without regard to the location and abundance of this rich resource. Recently, Ecuador and Peru doubled their license fees, so that it now would cost the average U.S. vessel almost $100,000 simply to search for tuna, for 50 days, inside 200 miles. Mexico, despite the great abundance of tuna off its coast, refuses to make licenses available to U.S vessels for fishing outside 12 miles under any terms and conditions."[28] (p.402)

In late 1990, a report of the United States International Trade Commission noted the following:

"... disputes have put pressure on the United States to concede and include tuna among the fishery resources suitable for unilateral jurisdiction. To date, the United States has maintained its position in the face of this foreign pressure and instead has successfully negotiated some important multilateral fishery agreements, first, among some Latin American nations and, more recently, among a group of nations and island states in the southern and southwestern Pacific. ...

"Recently, however, domestic pressure to include tuna within the 200-mile limit has surfaced from sports fishermen, charter boats, and from other interests with a stake in the tuna fisheries of the East Coast and the Gulf of Mexico. These fisheries are not targeted by vessels supplying the cannery section. Rather, they support recreational fishermen, as well as the small (but growing) U.S. restaurant demand for fresh tuna and sushi (raw tuna). ..."[29]

The Report of the Senate Committee on Commerce, Science, and Transportation, stated that the purpose of its bill (S. 1025) was "to improve the conservation and management of U.S. marine fishery resources" by amending the MFCMA "to extend the management authority of that Act to cover tuna species."[30] The Report noted the following about the management of "highly migratory species":

"Several main fish species, including tunas, swordfish, marlins, sail-fishes, and pelagic sharks, migrate through broad ocean expanses and traverse the coastal waters of many nations. ... tuna stocks in particular support major fisheries and are among the most highly valued of marine resources. Over the past two decades, landings of commercially important tuna species (albacore, bigeye, bluefin, skipjack, and yellowfin) have increased about six percent each year, and world tuna fleets have continued to grow in size and capacity.

"Our distant water tuna fleet supports one of the largest and most important fishery-based industries in the United States. Tuna fishing and canning operations presently employ about 20,000 people in the United States. In 1989, Americans ate almost 700,000,000 pounds of canned tuna, worth over $1,000,000,000. During the same period, the U.S. fleet landed 541,000,000 pounds of tuna with an ex-vessel value of [sic.] $309,000,000. Approximately 90 percent by weight of the U.S. catch comes from foreign or international waters.

"In addition to the distant water fleet, U.S. fishermen have focused increasing effort on tuna resources within our EEZ. About 500 longline vessels currently fish for tuna along the Gulf and Atlantic coasts. In the Western Pacific, the size of the longline fleet has doubled in less than 2 years, and now numbers over 100 vessels. While catches in the EEZ are relatively small, the fish command a high price, and this sector of the fishery now harvests about 26 percent of the total value of U.S. tuna landings. In addition, the tuna longline fleet catches significant quantities of swordfish.

"Due to the nomadic nature of the fish, efforts to conserve and manage highly migratory species require a high degree of international cooperation and coordination if they are to be effective. The longstanding U.S. policy has been to negotiate international agreements for managing and securing access for U.S. fishermen to highly migratory stocks, particularly tuna. Using the rationale that such agreements provide the sole basis for effective management, the United States presently does not claim or recognize jurisdiction over tuna beyond the territorial sea. Consistent with that policy, tuna species were specifically excluded from the management authority of the Magnuson Act when it was enacted in 1976."

The Report explains the reason for changing this "long standing policy" by referring to the following concerns: (1) that "the tuna exclusion has hampered conservation and management of other species that are under the Magnuson Act authority"; (2) that the current "U.S. tuna policy appears to have been a factor in reducing the effectiveness of swordfish management efforts"; (3) that with "respect to the Western Pacific, the need for authority to manage tuna in our EEZ also has been raised," and. (4) that concerns exist about the Council System established in the Magnuson Act because it is not designed to regulate highly migratory species, particularly swordfish, that span several Council regions.

Importantly, the Senate Report does not comment on how the proposed amendment to change the "long standing U.S. policy" to conserve and manage tuna would affect the canned tuna industry of the United States. In our opinion, this failure may find a partial explanation in the disunity and division of interests that existed within the U.S. canned tuna industry during 1990. To illustrate: Section 105 of the Fishery Conservation Amendments of 1990 directed the U.S. government to begin negotiations with the South Pacific Forum Fisheries Agency to extend the existing South Pacific Tuna Fisheries Treaty for 10 years. Thus, Congress adopted legislation that protected the interests of the U.S canned tuna industry based in the western Pacific, but fatally damaged the interests of that segment of the U.S. canned tuna industry dependent upon a reliable supply of tuna from a fleet of U.S. tuna vessels fishing in the EPO.

When U.S. fishery management jurisdiction was extended to cover tuna within its 200-mile EEZ, the U.S. tuna fleet was no longer protected from seizures made by foreign nations claiming that they had jurisdiction over the fishing of tuna within their 200-mile EEZs. The main protections lost were the embargo provisions in the MFCMA and the compensatory programs of the FPA of 1967. Although this new MFCMA amendment mandated that the Secretary of State, in cooperation with the Secretary of Commerce, initiate negotiations "with respect to obtaining access for vessels of the United States fishing for tuna species within the EEZs of other nations on reasonable terms and conditions," since 1990 no agreement has been negotiated with any other nation to provide access for tuna vessels of the United States in the EPO. In view of the negotiating leverages, such as embargoes, lost by the MFCMA tuna exclusion amendment, this result is not surprising.

By the end of 1990, the "Catch 22" for the U.S. tuna seiner fleet was now complete: If you fish tuna/porpoise schools in waters beyond the 200-mile zones claimed by nations bordering the EPO, you cannot sell your catch as "dolphin-safe" in the U.S. market because of the provisions of the DPCIA in the MMPA or to foreign canners who have a "dolphin-safe" policy. If you fish for tuna that is not associated with porpoise within those 200-mile zones without a fishing license (assuming that a license is available and affordable), you risk seizure and penalties that would be recognized by your government as legal. Therefore, the U.S. tuna seiners that remained active became restricted to finding and fishing tuna schools not associated with porpoise in fishing areas outside the 11 existing 200-mile EEZs claimed by the coastal Latin American countries and of the claim of France over the uninhabited Clipperton Island. By 1992, the U.S. tuna seiner fleet operating year-round in the EPO had dwindled to six vessels.[31] (emphasis added)

In 1998, the PDCIA was significantly amended.[32] This law changed the definition of "dolphin safe" by requiring certifications by the vessel's captain and approved observer stating that "no dolphins were killed or seriously injured during the sets in which the tuna were caught." The prior law required statements by the captain and approved observer that the vessel's purse seine net was not intentionally deployed on or to encircle a school of tuna and dolphin during the entire fishing trip. (The prior law was written to ban the encirclement of a school of tuna/dolphin by deploying a purse seine during the entire fishing trip.) Despite the changes in the 1997 law, it failed to stimulate a return to the tuna/porpoise fishery of the EPO by a fleet of U.S.-flag tuna seiners. The IATTC reported that of the 227 tuna purse seiners fishing in the EPO during 2007, only 3 were of U.S. Flag.[33]

---

[1] Fishermen refer to the marine mammals that associate with tunas as "porpoises," and marine mammalogists did the same until the late 1970s. Thereafter, marine mammalogists began to use the word "dolphin" for these animals. They explain that dolphins are members of the family Delphinidae, which always have cone-shaped teeth, usually have a beak, and usually have a hooked or curved dorsal fin, whereas porpoises are members of the family Phocoenidae, which always have spade-shaped teeth, never have a beak, and usually have a triangular dorsal fin. (When fishermen use the word "dolphin," they are referring to a fish usually marketed in the United States as "mahi mahi" and in Latin America as "dorado.")

[2] U.S. Department of Commerce, Office of the Secretary, In the Matter of Proposed Regulations to Govern the Taking of Marine Mammals Incidental to Commercial Fishing Operations, Docket No. MMPA H 1980-1, Recommended Decision of ALJ (Administrative Law Judge) Hugh J. Dolan, July 18, 1980, (cited hereinafter as "1980 ALJ Decison"): Findings 154-171 and Findings 175-187.

[3] Hearing on Marine Mammal Protection Amendments before the Subcommittee on Fisheries and Wildlife, Conservation and the Environment of the House Committee on Merchant Marine and Fisheries, 101st Congress, First Session on H.R. 2926 and H.R. 2948, October 4, 1989, Serial No. 101-58, (cited hereinafter as "1989 House Subcommittee Hearing-SN-101-58"): 32-33; 135-142. Also: 28-30; 98-115.

Hearing on Marine Mammal Protection Act Amendments Part II before the Subcommittee on Fisheries and Wildlife Conservation and the Environment of the House Committee on Merchant Marine and Fisheries 101st Congress, Second Session on H.R. 2926, April 3, 1990, and May 3, 1990, Serial No. 101-80, (cited hereinafter as "April/May 1990 House Subcommittee Hearing-SN-101-80"): Testimony on April 3, 1990: 8-10; 100-113 Also see: 11-13;157-174.

[4] In February 1990, Bumble Bee opened a plant in Santa Fe Springs, California, for the purpose of processing tuna loins imported mainly from Thailand. USITC Publication 2339 (December 1990): 3-25. This plant's design and location prevents it from taking and processing frozen whole tuna from tuna vessels; therefore, it is not considered by the trade as a conventional tuna cannery servicing tuna vessels dockside.

[5] April/May 1990 House Subcommittee Hearing-SN-101-80: 47-48. Also see: Hearing before the Subcommittee on Commerce, Consumer Protection, and Competitiveness of the Committee on Energy and Commerce, House of Representatives, 101st Congress, Second Session on Labeling of Tuna Products, July 25, 1990, Serial No. 101-208, (cited hereinafter as "July 1990 House Subcommittee Hearing-SN-101-208"): 3-12. The "Dolphin-Safe" issue is fully discussed in USITC Publication 2547 August 1992: 3-1 to 3-22, and in USITC Publication 2339 December 1990: 1-2 to 1-4.

[6] Report 101-579 Part 1, 101st Congress, 2nd Session, House of Representatives. "Dolphin Protection and Consumer Information Act of 1990 (July 10, 1990), from the Committee on Merchant Marine and Fisheries, to accompany H.R. 2926, together with Additional and Dissenting Views, 27pp., (cited hereafter as "House Report 101-579, 101st Cong. 2nd Sess.").

[7] House Report 101-579, 101st Cong. 2nd Sess.: 20-22.

[8] House Report 101-579, 101st Cong. 2nd Sess.: 26-27.

[9] July 1990 House Subcommittee Hearing-SN-101-208: 109-110.

[10] July 1990 House Subcommittee Hearing-SN-101-208: 109. "*Question.* If this legislation is passed, will it eliminate the rest of the U.S. fleet in the eastern tropical Pacific? *Answer.* Passage of the legislation will not affect the continued viability of the U.S. fleet in the eastern tropical Pacific. ... failure to pass the legislation will not enhance the chances of the U.S. fleet to continue to operate in the eastern tropical Pacific." Responses of StarKist Seafood Co. to Questions of Congressman Howard C. Nielson.

The IATTC found in a study that seiners fishing on tuna/porpoise schools have a catch rate of about 55 percent higher than those that do not. "The difference is much greater when comparing gross earnings. Large yellowfin of the size taken in association with dolphins currently sell for about $907 per ton, while small yellowfin and skipjack of the size generally taken by the other modes of fishing sell for about $727." See: Joseph, J. 1994,

The Tuna-Dolphin Controversy in the Eastern Pacific, Biological, Economic, and Political Impacts. Ocean Development and International Law, Vol. 25: 22

[11] July 1990 House Subcommittee Hearing-SN-101-208: 112.

[12] Kleiber, P., A.W. Argue, and R.E. Kearney (1987) Assessment of Pacific skipjack tuna (*Katsuwonus pelamis*) resources by estimating standing stock and population turnover from tagging data. Canad. Jour. Fish. Aquatic Sci., 44 (6): 1122-1134.

[13] Cook Islands, Federated States of Micronesia, Fiji, Kiribati, Marshall Islands, Nauru, Niue, Palau, Papua New Guinea, Samoa, Solomon Islands, Tonga, Tuvalu, and Vanuatu. To view the federal statute implementing the obligations of the United States under the Treaty: South Pacific Tuna Act of 1988 (16 U.S.C. 973, et seq)

[14] See: USITC Publication 2339 December 1990: 5-18 to-5-21, and USITC Publication 1912 October 1986:112-113; 119-120.. During the 1975-1992 period, the consumption of tuna, canned and frozen, in Mexico rose from about 20,000 tons to about 100,000 tons. This experience of increased consumption of tuna was duplicated in other Latin American countries in the region, such as Costa Rica, Venezuela, and Ecuador.

[15] July 1990 House Subcommittee Hearing-SN-101-208: 110.

[16] International Dolphin Conservation Act of 1992; Public Law 102-523, October 26, 1992, 106 Stat. 3425 16 U.S. C. 1411, et seg. House Report 102-746, Part 1, 102nd Congress, 2nd Session, July 28, 1992, of the Committee on Merchant Marine and Fisheries, to accompany H.R. 5419. 34 pp. House Report 102-746, Part 2,102nd Congress, 2nd Session, Committee on Ways and Means, July 31, 1992. 13 pp. The Act authorizes (1) the Secretary of State to enter into an international agreement establishing a five-year moratorium on the seining of tuna/porpoise schools; (2) an international research program to find ways to fish tuna/porpoise schools without causing porpoise mortalities; (3) revokes the General Permit of the ATA effective on the date of the moratorium and (4) lifts existing embargoes on nations entering the moratorium agreement. After June 1, 1994, it would become unlawful to sell, purchase, offer for sale, transport, or ship any dolphin-unsafe tuna product in the United States.

[17] Dr. James Joseph was of the opinion that the moratorium idea, as proposed in the International Dolphin Conservation Act of 1992, was a response by the United States government to defuse the problem caused when a General Agreement on Tariffs and Trade (GATT) panel ruled in favor of Mexico on September 3, 1991. Mexico contended that the actions taken by the United States to impose MMPA embargoes and enforce the DCPA were not allowed under GATT. Joseph, J. 1994, The tuna-dolphin controversy in the eastern Pacific, biological, economic, and political impacts. Ocean Development and International Law, Vol. 25: 9-10.

[18] Maunder, M.N, and A. Aires-da-Silva. (2009) Status of yellowfin tuna in the eastern Pacific Ocean in 2007 and outlook for the future. Inter-Amer. Trop. Tuna Comm., Stock Status Report 9: Table 4.2.

[19] Maunder, M.N, and A. Aires-da-Silva. (2009) Status of yellowfin tuna in the eastern Pacific Ocean in 2007 and outlook for the future. Inter-Amer. Trop. Tuna Comm., Stock Status Report 9; Schaefer, K.M. 1998, Reproductive biology of yellowfin tuna (*Thunnus albacares*) in the eastern Pacific Ocean. IATTC Bulletin, 21 (5): Figure 13.

[20] Hall, M.A. (1998) An ecological view of the tuna-dolphin problem: impacts and trade-offs. Reviews in Fish Biology and Fisheries, 8: 25.

[21] IATTC Annual Report for 2006: Table 4.

[22] Hall, M.A. (1998) An ecological view of the tuna-dolphin problem: impacts and trade-offs. Reviews in Fish Biology and Fisheries, 8: 21.

[23] Joseph, J. (1994) The tuna-dolphin controversy in the eastern Pacific, biological, economic, and political impacts. Ocean Development and International Law, Vol. 25: 10. "The net effect of restricting the fishery to log and school fishing would be a reduction of between 30 and 60 percent in the catch of yellowfin, from recent levels of 300,000 tons to between 120,000 and 200,000 tons." Joseph, J. (1994) The tuna-dolphin controversy in the eastern Pacific, biological, economic, and political impacts. Ocean Development and International Law, Vol. 25: 20.

[24] Joseph, J. (1994) The tuna-dolphin controversy in the eastern Pacific, biological, economic, and political impacts. Ocean Development and International Law, Vol. 25: 10.

[25] See: U.S. Code Congressional and Administrative News-101st Congress, Second Session 1990. for Legislative history of Public Law 101-627; 104 Stat. 4436-November 28, 1990; 16 U.S.C. 1812. House Report (Merchant Marine and Fisheries Committee) No. 101-393, December 15, 1989 [To accompany H.R. 2061]; Senate Report (Commerce, Science, and Transportation Committee) No. 101-414, August 2, 1990 [To accompany S. 1025]; House Report (Merchant Marine and Fisheries Committee) No. 101-579, July 10, 1990 [To accompany H.R. 2926], and Congressional Record Vol. 136 (1990): Consideration by House: February 6, October 23, 27, 1990, and by Senate: October 11, 27, 1990.

[26] " Fishery Conservation Amendments of 1990, Public Law 101-627, title IX, § 901, Nov, 28, 1990; 104 Stat.4465-4467. "Almost all tuna resources of commercial importance to U.S. harvesters are found outside the U.S. EEZ, either in other nation's EEZs or in the high seas. Bilateral or multilateral agreements are necessary to allow U.S. tuna harvesters access to tuna as they pass through various EEZs along their migratory routes." USITC Publication 2547 August 1992: 1-4.

[27] Committee Print, 94th Congress, 2nd Session, "A Legislative History of the Fishery Conservation and Management Act of 1976 together with a Section-By-Section Index, Prepared for the Use of the Committee on Commerce and National Ocean Policy Study (October 1976) : 6-7. The citation of the "Fishery Conservation and Management Act of 1976" was changed to "Magnuson Fishery Conservation and Management Act" and currently, to the "Magnuson-Stevens Fishery Conservation and Management Act."

[28] Hearings on Atlantic Bluefin Tuna Stocks before the National Ocean Policy Study of the Committee on Commerce, Science, and Transportation, United States Senate, 97th Congress, 1st Session, on S. 1564 The American Tuna Act, December 8, 1981, Serial No. 97-85: 7-8. See also: Hearings before the Subcommittee on Fisheries and Wildlife Conservation and the Environment of the Committee on Merchant Marine and Fisheries House of Representatives, 97th Congress, 1st Session on Magnuson Fishery Conservation and Management Act Oversight September 24, 25, October 14, 1981, Serial No. 97-18: 402.

[29] USITC Publication 2339 December 1990: 1-3.

[30] Senate Report No. 101-414, August 2, 1990, of the Senate Committee on Commerce, Science, and Transportation, to accompany S. 1025: I, 3-5. The House bill (H.R. 2061) was passed in lieu of the Senate bill (S. 1025) after amending its language to contain much of the text of the Senate bill.

[31] USITC Publication 2547 August 1992: 4-2.

[32] Dolphin Protection Consumer Information Act, 16 U.S C. § 1385; Pub. L. 105-42, §5, Aug. 15, 1997, 111 Stat. 1125.

[33] IATTC, Fishery Status Report 6, Table A-11b: 53.

EPILOGUE

United States Senator Ernest P. Hollings, after listening to testimony from American Tunaboat Association (ATA) representatives during the 1971 legislative hearings on bills to provide protection to ocean mammals on the high seas, expressed doubt as to the wisdom of solving this international problem by having the United States unilaterally regulate its citizens:

> "... So, we think we legislate correctly in our enthusiasm to do the right thing, but in essence, you say we eliminate ourselves from the field. So nothing goes into research, nothing goes into development, nothing goes into conservation and from what you say now, the exact opposite of what is intended occurs."[1] (emphasis added)

The Record is Clear

Research by the Inter-American Tropical Tuna Commission (IATTC) has shown that large bycatches of juvenile tunas and of unmarketable marine life are taken in purse-seine sets on tunas in "pure" or unassociated schools and on tunas associated with floating objects, and that U.S. efforts to prevent the vessels of all nations from making purse-seine sets on tuna/porpoise schools would adversely affect the IATTC's efforts to properly manage the yellowfin tuna resource in the eastern Pacific Ocean (EPO). Therefore, a strict international enforcement of the "United States rule" would unduly jeopardize a proven program of conservation and management of the yellowfin tuna resource in the EPO and wrongfully encourage fishing practices that would cause an inexcusable waste of other marine life.[2]

It was wrong and unfair for the United States Government to sacrifice and punish the U.S. tuna seiner fleet operating in the EPO. It did this by enacting a law that implemented a tuna buying policy announced by three major tuna canners in April 1990–a policy of not purchasing tuna from tuna seiners that had made a "set" or encircled a tuna/porpoise school during its fishing trip. The fact that the "set" resulted in zero porpoise mortality was immaterial; the purchase policy forced rejection simply because of encirclement. We believe that this policy was cleverly devised to implement a de facto rule of prohibiting the purse seining of tuna/porpoise schools. In this way, the "Dolphin Safe" rule would circumvent a judicial interpretation of the Marine Mammal Protection Act declaring that the Act did not prohibit the seining of tuna/porpoise schools.

Congress, in enacting this "Dolphin Safe" law, decided that the U.S. tuna fleet operating from California and Puerto Rico was expendable—the losers. This is because the passage in 1990 of this labeling law, in concert with the law that changed this nation's law of the sea position regarding fishery management jurisdiction over tuna, created the "Catch 22" condition that caused this segment of the U.S. tuna seiner fleet to become an unreliable source of tuna supply for canners who operated plants in California and Puerto Rico, but not in American Samoa or elsewhere in the central and western Pacific. The choices for the American owners of seiners operating in the EPO: sell the vessel or fish for tunas in the central and western Pacific.

The unilateral action taken by the United States to enact the "Dolphin Safe" rule was not followed by other governments who had citizens operating fleets fishing tuna/porpoise schools in the EPO. Although it was argued that the United States was exercising "moral leadership" in enacting its canned tuna labeling law, and that other governments should also exercise the same leadership, other governments were not persuaded. The scientific facts concerning the tuna/porpoise mystery created the hard reality that the "dolphin safe" position of the United States was not complementary to the existing regime of tuna management and conservation established by the IATTC.[3] In our opinion, the U.S. government was arrogant in attempting to impose its marine mammal policy on other nations fishing for tuna/porpoise schools. In pursuit of this course of action, it acted unjustly in enacting laws and promulgating regulations that effectively destroyed the livelihood of the American citizens who developed the gear and procedures to fish tuna/porpoise schools responsibly.

With the removal of a meaningful U.S. tuna fleet in the tropical tuna fishery of the EPO and with the absence of significant landings of tuna from this fishery for processing by U.S. tuna canners, the U.S. government no longer represents important stakeholder interests as a producer, processor, or consumer of tuna from this region. Our nation is no longer a dominant factor in the IATTC, where decisions are made on tuna conservation and management and marine mammal research. Except for collecting data from research cruises to estimate porpoise abundance in theEPO, we have "eliminated ourselves from the field," a result not intended by Congress when it first enacted the MMPA.

In response to lobbying by special interests, Congress was influenced to wrongfully enact punitive legislation that reduced the ability of U.S. fishermen to compete with foreign fishermen. The U.S. tuna fishermen, who did the most to reduce porpoise mortality in the EPO were treated as expendable by their government and by a once united industry. Congress ignored the fact that it was the fishermen's time, talent, motivation, and sacrifices that developed the gear and procedures to save porpoise when seining tuna/porpoise schools. And that little, if any, of this achievement was the result of funding by Congress. Besides reducing the ability of American tuna fishermen to compete with foreign fishermen on the high seas, the laws enacted also destroyed the bargaining leverage that the U.S. Department of State could have used for obtaining a regional tuna fishing license treaty for the EPO similar to the one that was negotiated for the central and western Pacific. Were these two harmful legislative actions enacted for political reasons? We are of the opinion that politics involving U.S. Senate elections in California and Hawaii did play a part in the passage by Congress in October 1990 of these harmful amendments to the Magnuson Fishery Conservation and Management Act of 1976 and the Marine Mammal Protection Act of 1972. Perhaps, in time, historians will uncover the truth.

In 1983, the U.S. tuna seiner fleet totaled 124 vessels, 36% of the world total of

346 tuna seiners, but by 1991 the U.S. fleet had declined to 56 vessels, only 14% of the world total of 407 vessels.[4] In 1983, U.S. canners received 275,084 short tons of tropical tunas from the U.S. fleet; in 1991, landings fell to 174,598 short tons, a decline of about 37 percent.[5] During 2007, tuna vessels of over 24 nations fished in the EPO. This fleet included 227 tuna seiners, of which only 3 were of U.S. flag documentation. During 2009, only two U.S. flag tuna seiners operated year round in the EPO, and both vessels were based in ports of Ecuador.[6]

During 2009, a fleet of about 39 U.S.-flag tuna seiners fished for skipjack, yellowfin, and bigeye tunas in the central and western Pacific pursuant to the provisions of the South Pacific Tuna Fisheries Treaty. Presently, a majority of the vessels in this fleet is comprised of hulls built in foreign shipyards.

The Enigma Remains Unsolved

It has been difficult for many in the United States scientific community to accept the fact that man has not solved the tuna/porpoise enigma. Efforts by Congress to solve the tuna/porpoise enigma by financing various research projects authorized by amendments to the MMPA have failed. The 1981 Amendment of the MMPA, in Section 110 (a) [16 U.S.C. 1380(a), required the Secretary of Commerce to "undertake a program of, and shall provide financial assistance for, research into new methods of locating and catching yellowfin tuna without the incidental taking of marine mammals and annually report the results of this research." The 1988 Amendment to the MMPA, Section 4(e), amended Section 110(a) of the MMPA by adding a new paragraph that required the Secretary of Commerce to contract with the U.S. National Academy of Sciences (NAS) to conduct an independent review of information pertaining to the identification of "appropriate research into promising new methods of locating and catching yellowfin tuna without the incidental taking of marine mammals." This effort also failed.

During the 1990s, Congress authorized increased long-term funding for research to solve the tuna/porpoise enigma and find alternative methods of economically fishing tuna/porpoise schools. This effort also failed. The enigma remains, and no alternative fishing technology to the seining of tuna/porpoise schools in the EPO has been discovered. The 1997 Amendment to the MMPA, Section 304(b)(2), provided that specific research be carried out and that it may include:

> "(A) projects to devise cost-effective fishing methods and gear so as to reduce, with the goal of eliminating, the incidental mortality and serious injury of marine mammals in connection with the commercial purse seine fishing in the eastern tropical Pacific Ocean;

> "(B) projects to develop cost-effective methods of fishing for mature yellowfin tuna without setting nets on dolphins or other marine mammals ..."[7]

Millions of dollars have been authorized and appropriated by Congress to conduct the above research, and yet there exists no workable alternative to the seining on tuna/porpoise schools in the EPO.

The most recent estimates of the populations of porpoises in the EPO are 1,675,500 for offshore spotted porpoise, 1,209,300 for spinner porpoise, 2,551,717 for common porpoise, and 2,802,300 for other porpoise/dolphins, for a grand total of 8,238,817.[8]

The following data for 2000-2008 have been compiled by the IATTC [9]

Year	Sets on tuna/porpoise schools	Retained catches in short tons			Mortalities of porpoises
		Yellowfin	Skipjack	Bigeye	
2000	9,235	147,776	539	15	1,636
2001	9,876	238,145	1,808	6	2,140
2002	12,290	301,480	3,177	2	1,499
2003	13,760	264,035	13,354	1	1,492
2004	11,783	175,856	10,796	3	1,469
2005	12,173	166,163	12,078	2	1,151
2006	8,923	91,987	4,806	0	886
2007	8,871	97,351	3,285	7	838
2008	9,201	115,870	8,802	5	1,169

It is time to recognize and applaud the tuna purse-seine fishermen operating in the EPO for mastering many, if not all, of the mysteries of the tuna/porpoise enigma for the benefit of mankind, the tunas, and the porpoise.

---

[1] Hearings before the Subcommittee on Oceans and Atmosphere of the Committee on Commerce, United States Senate 92nd Congress, Second Session on Ocean Mammal Legislation, February 15,16, and 23, and March 7, 1973, Serial No. 92-56, Part 1, (cited hereinafter as: "1972 Senate Subcommittee Hearings-SN-92-56"): 482.

[2] Joseph, James. (1994) The Tuna-dolphin controversy in the eastern Pacific: biological, economic, and political impacts. *Ocean Development and International Law*, Volume 25: 1-30; Hall, Martín A. (1998) An ecological view of the tuna-dolphin problem: impacts and trade offs, *Reviews in Fish Biology and Fisheries*. Volume 8: 1-34.

[3] Some argued that the "Dolphin Safe" law represented a breach by the United States of its international obligations undertaken in the Convention establishing the IATTC. This argument may become moot with the expected ratification of the "Antigua Convention." "At its 70th meeting on 24-27 June 2003, the IATTC adopted the Resolution on the Adoption of the Convention for the Strengthening of the Inter-American Tropical Tuna Commission established by the 1949 Convention between the United States of America and the Republic of Costa Rica (the Antigua Convention). This convention will replace the original 1949 Convention 15 months after it has been ratified or acceded to by seven Parties that were Parties to the 1949 Convention the date that the Antigua Convention was open for signatures. "Annual Report of the IATTC (2007): 6. The Antigua Convention replaced the original convention on August 27, 2020. Article VII of the Antigua Convention describes the "Functions of the Commission." Article VII (f) refers to species affected by the fishing of fish stocks covered by the Convention, stating that measures adopted for such species be "with a view to maintaining or restoring populations of such species above levels at which their reproduction may become seriously threatened."

[4] Dirks, Douglas, H. and G. M. Hetherington. (1992) Tuna Clipper Design: A San Diego Perspective," Campbell Industries, San Diego, California: 38.   Douglas H. Dirks, Vice

President, Engineering/Sales, and Gary M. Hetherington, Chief Naval Architect, Campbell Industries, San Diego, presented their study at the February 6, 1992, meeting of the San Diego Section of the Society of Naval Architects and Marine Engineers. A table in this study listed the world's tuna seiner fleets of 1983 and 1991 that were comprised of vessels having a frozen tuna capacity of over 500 metric tons. The countries listed by name in the table and size of fleet in 1983 versus 1991 included USA (124; down to 56), Spain (43; up to 56), Mexico (43; up to 54), South Korea (10; up to 39), Japan (33; up to 37), Taiwan (0; up to 35), France (29; up to 32), Venezuela (7; up to 22), Panama (6; up to18), Vanuatu (0; up to 14), Ecuador (3; up to 8), and "other countries" (48; down to 36).

[5] USITC Publication 1558 (August 1984): Table 17, A-43, and USITC Publication 2547 (August 1992): Table D-32, D-24.

[6] Two seasonal tuna fisheries remain significant off the west coast of the United States, albacore and bluefin. These fisheries originated in waters off Southern California during the summers of 1903-1907 for albacore and during the summers of 1917-1918 for bluefin. The baitboat/troller fleets based in California, Oregon, and Washington unload their seasonal catch of albacore in ports of Oregon and Washington for canning or transshipment. The California coastal pelagic seiner (sardine, mackerel, and squid) fleet unloads its seasonal catch of bluefin caught off Southern California to fresh fish markets in San Pedro, California

[7] Much funding was provided by Congress: Section 304 (c) Authorization of Appropriations.— "(1) There are authorized to be appropriated to the Secretary, the following amounts, to be used by the Secretary to carry out the research described in subsection (a): "(A) $4,000,000 for fiscal year 1998" "(B) $3,000,000 for fiscal year 1999 ..." "(C) $4,000,000 for fiscal year 2000," "(D) $1,000,000 for fiscal year 2001.
"(2) In addition to the amount authorized to be appropriated under paragraph (1), these are authorized to be appropriated to the Secretary for carrying out this section $3,000,000 for each of the fiscal years 1998, 1999, 2000, and 2001."

Reports required by the Secretary of Commerce: "(1) results of research conducted pursuant to section 304; (2) a description of the status and trends of stocks of tuna; (3) a description of the efforts to assess, avoid, reduce and minimize the bycatch of juvenile yellowfin tuna and bycatch of non-target species; (4) a description of the activities of the International Dolphin Conservation Program [of the IATTC] and of the efforts of the United States in support of the Program's goals and objectives, including the protection of dolphin stocks in the eastern tropical Pacific Ocean, and an assessment of the effectiveness of the Program; (5) actions taken by the Secretary under section 101(a)(2)(B) and section 101(d); (6) copies of any relevant resolutions and decisions of the Inter-American Tropical Tuna Commission, and any regulations promulgated by the Secretary under this title; and, (7) any other information deemed relevant by the Secretary."

[8] IATTC Annual Report, 2006, Table 6 (p. 62). See also: IATTC Annual Report, 2008, Table 4 (p.51). The estimate of the populations of "other dolphins" noted in the 2006 Annual Report is not reported in the Annual Report, 2007,Table 4, (p. 61) and in the Annual Report, 2008,Table 4 (p. 51)).

[9] Numbers of sets and retained catches of tunas: IATTC Fishery Status Report 7, Table A-7 (page 46); for number of annual mortalities of porpoises: IATTC Annual Report for 2008, Table 5 (page 52); for 2008, the percentage of zero porpoise mortality sets was 92.4, Table 7 (page 54).

APPENDIX A

1974 Experimentation with a "Porpoise Apron" Placed Above the Medina Panel

The results of a charter cruise (June 25-September 14, 1974) aboard the new "Super Seiner" SOUTH PACIFIC, while encouraging, showed that a U.S. National Marine Fisheries Service (NMFS) net design attached to the Medina Panel required further modifications. On October 28, 1974, the SOUTH PACIFIC left Panama, under the new command of Captain Joseph Scafidi. Also aboard the chartered vessel were NMFS gear specialists Richard McNeely and David Holts.

During the voyage, Captain Scafidi proposed to change the NMFS net design by securing a "piece" of 1 1/4-inch mesh netting between the existing Medina Panel and the "float-line" or "cork-line." This "piece" (62 fathoms in length at the bottom and 34 fathoms in length at the top) was later named the "Porpoise Apron." In early 1975, a NMFS report written by Richard McNeely stated, in part, the following:

> "During the cruise of the SOUTH PACIFIC several innovations, including the apron, were tested but the most promising results appeared associated with the use of the apron. After initial trials, 22 consecutive sets using the apron resulted in a porpoise mortality rate significantly lower that [sic] the fleet average. . . . "The apron is a trapezoid shaped, tapered strip of small mesh webbing added to the existing porpoise safety panel (Medina panel) to improve the dynamics and shape of the "Back-down" area. Its principal functions are twofold: 1) the prevention of canopies of loose webbing which sometimes entrap porpoise during "Back-down"; and, 2) allow release of porpoise without significant loss of fish."[1]

Captain Scafidi explained that McNeely was experimenting with the idea of adding more slack in webbing just below the "cork-line." The objective of this was to reduce the opportunities for canopies to develop near the end of the "Back-down" channel, thereby preventing porpoise entanglement or entrapment. Experimentation with McNeely's idea showed that it created undesirable results. It caused the webbing in the apex area just below the "cork-line" to become "balloon-like." To correct this and other defects, Captain Scafidi developed the idea of creating a bump in the "cork-line" by inserting a strip or piece of 1 1/4-inch webbing. This ramp-like piece of webbing was tapered at both ends in connecting with the Medina Panel, giving rise to the description of a waist-type apron.[2] It is the recollection of Captain Scafidi that Richard McNeely coined the term "Porpoise Apron."

After obtaining the NMFS Report on the "Porpoise Apron" concept, the American Tunaboat Association (ATA), Living Marine Resources (LMR), and other members of the tuna industry strongly recommended to Richard McNeely that the idea be tested at sea by a group of tuna captains, rather than on another NMFS-chartered tuna seiner. Tuna industry representatives explained that this approach worked in testing the original Medina Panel, and that it was important to the tuna industry to achieve rapid success in finding new gear and methods to reduce porpoise mortality, especially, since the two-year research and development program prescribed by the Marine Mammal Protecton Act (MMPA) had ended. The industry representatives believed that further testing of the "Porpoise Apron" by one tuna captain aboard a NMFS-chartered tuna seiner every two months was not as helpful as having an evaluation based upon the views and experiences of 10 or 11 volunteer captains and crews within two months. In addition, the captains and their crews respected Captain Joe Scafidi as a proven innovator in encircling tuna/porpoise schools and in developing gear and methods to save porpoise.[3] This confidence in the reputation of Captain Scafidi that the "Porpoise Apron" would prove productive for them at sea in fishing tuna/porpoise schools explains, in part, why the volunteer captains and crews were willing to devote their time to participating in this unique trial at sea.

Within a short time, the captains and owners of 10 tuna seiners volunteered to cover the risk and costs of testing the "Porpoise Apron" concept during 1975. According to a survey conducted by the NMFS, all of the captains interviewed stated that they intended to continue to use the "Porpoise Apron," that they all believed that the device improved their ability to save porpoise, that most believed that, for some captains, time would be required to learn the proper use of the "Porpoise Apron," and that it made execution of the "Back-down" easier.

The analysis of the NMFS found the following: that mortality of porpoises per set using the "Porpoise Apron" was lower than the fleet average for all categories but one, and that, importantly, fewer porpoises were left in the net after "Back-down" in the sets by vessels that used nets with the "Porpoise Apron" than the average for all sets. The NMFS announced plans to conduct further tests on the "Porpoise Apron," develop design modifications, and "experiment with alternate configurations ... [because] the apron is not an automatic success. ... the apron has not always been properly centered in the "Back-down" area or the necessary changes in procedures have not always been made. ... an educational package [is being prepared]."[4] Meanwhile, Captain Scafidi and other captains were busy at sea experimenting with the "Porpoise Apron."

During 1975, NMFS observers were asked for the first time to record the locations of entanglement in their logbooks. In 1976, a net diagram was provided to allow the observers to better describe their findings. The NMFS analysis used data from 20 cruises and 154 sets, and concluded that entanglement "can be greatly reduced through the use of 1-1/4" mesh over a larger area of the "Back-down" area than the regulations presently require."[5]

Two experimental changes in the design of the "Porpoise Apron" occurred during charter trips in 1975. The NMFS analysis for the 1976 fiscal year (July 1, 1975-June 30, 1976), which took into account the increasing usage by U.S. tuna seiners of the "Porpoise Apron" or modifications (by September 1976, 16 vessels), the results of findings by NMFS personnel aboard eight commercial fishing trips and charters that tested the "Porpoise Apron," indicating that a configuration using 1 1/4-inch webbing in both the "Porpoise Apron" and the "Medina Panel" achieved the lowest average loss of porpoise, a clear decrease of individual porpoise entanglement in normal sets, a reduction of porpoise loss resulting from entrapment in folds or canopies of the net, fewer porpoise left alive in the net requiring manual release after "Back-down," and, when this modified "Porpoise Apron" is properly deployed, no tuna escaping from the net. This analysis also reported that "the 1-1/4" apron on the 1-1/4" Medina Panel "showed a very substantial decrease (in mortality per normal set) under standardized conditions."[6]

1975 Experimentation of Using a "Chute" Placed Above the "Porpoise Apron"

The new seiner BOLD CONTENDER (Captain John Gonsalves) was also chartered by the NMFS during the fall of 1975 to test a dramatically new concept later introduced to the interested public as the *Bold Contender System.*

The vessel's net was modified with a new piece of 1 1/4-inch webbing that was placed above the "Porpoise Apron," which was also constructed of 1 1/4-inch webbing. The "Porpoise Apron" was, in turn, attached above a double-depth "Medina Panel," also constructed of 1 1/4-inch mesh. (Each "strip" of netting measures about 6.5 fathoms in depth.) This two-strip "Medina Panel" was 180 fathoms in length; the one strip "Porpoise Apron" was 94 fathoms in bottom length and 26 fathoms in top length. The "chute" appendage, attached to the top of the "Porpoise Apron," had a bottom length of 26 fathoms, a top length of 3.5 fathoms. [7]

Richard McNeely and his team of gear specialists tested the idea of using a system approach or combination of six developments in gear and techniques to reduce porpoise mortality during the charter of the BOLD CONTENDER, as follows: (1) the use of the new configuration of the "Porpoise Apron" to reduce canopy formation during "Back-down" and to form "a shoaled area at the apex of the "Back-down" area; (2) the use of the new "Chute" to accelerate water flow over the cork-line and help "accentuate the shoal area at the apex of the "Back-down" channel."[8] (3) the use of speedboats to prevent "net collapse," rather than using them to reverse a "net collapse" that had already occurred; (4) the use of a manned rubber raft into the "Back-down" channel that would allow the men in the raft to assist the captain's operation of the "Back-down" and in sighting and rescuing live porpoise; (5) requiring the "Back-down" and other rescue operations to continue until all live porpoise were out of the net, and (6) the use of a NMFS-designed "porpoise grabber," a long pole similar to a shepherd's crook, allowing fishermen to rescue live porpoise by guiding them out of the net or by rescuing individual porpoise that could not be reached manually without the "porpoise grabber."

The "system" was tested on 25 sets, 15 of which produced no porpoise mortality. "Net collapses" were prevented by the use of one to three speedboats on 23 sets "under varying conditions of weather, current, and gear malfunctions." The results of the charter showed that the "Apron-Chute" did not work perfectly, requiring the use of a speedboat on 11 of the 25 sets to pull the "Apron-Chute" into proper shape just before "Back-down." To prevent the sinking of the "cork-line" along the tapered portions of the "Apron-Chute," adjustments were made prior to the start of "Back-down" in Sets 12 to 31.[9]

The question confronting the U.S. tuna fleet and the NMFS gear team was whether the low mortality rates recorded during the charter cruise of the BOLD CONTENDER resulted from the combination of "Apron-Chute" appendages of 1-1/4" mesh atop of double-depth Medina Panel using 1-1/4" mesh (*Bold Contender System*) or from the use of a modified "Medina Panel" that was of double depth and comprised of 1-1/4" webbing. To find the answer, a competition at sea involving 20 U.S. tuna seiners during 1976 was jointly developed and financed by the tuna industry and the NMFS.[10]

1976 At-Sea Competition between the Double-Depth Medina Panel System and the Bold Contender System[11]

The NMFS loaned complete *Bold Contender Systems* to nine tuna seiners; the system was already aboard the BOLD CONTENDER. NMFS gear specialists worked the two to four days required to install the small-mesh webbing (1 1/4 inch), with some help from the crews of the vessels. The NMFS required that the captains and crews of the vessels participate in a one-day training session on handling the modified gear. A half-day NMFS training session was required for the captains and crews of the ten vessels using the *Double-Depth Medina Panel System* with small-mesh webbing (1 1/4"). The NMFS absorbed the costs, including salaries, insurance, and related expenses, of placing gear technicians aboard the 20 vessels. The primary duty of these technicians was to collect data on gear performance, and, when practicable, to collect biological data and specimens.

The entity used to finance, develop, and monitor the effort of the industry was its newly-created Porpoise Rescue Foundation, which funded the provision of 1 1/4–inch mesh webbing for the *Double-Depth Medina Panel System*. It was required that this system be installed in the same position in the net as the *Bold Contender System*. This was done for two reasons: (1) because it would be easier to later add the Apron-Chute appendages if the tests indicated that the *Bold Contender System* was superior and (2) because the *Double-Depth Medina Panel System* had shown that it resists net collapse during "Back-down."[12]

The NMFS, the Marine Mammal Commission (MMC), and the industry concluded a cooperative research agreement: "the Government agreed to match industry funds on a two-to-one basis. The tuna Industry contributed $250,000, the NMFS $450,000, and the Marine Mammal Commission $50,000."[13]

To test the claims of some marine mammal behaviorists, who had observed captive porpoises in shore-side tanks, that such porpoise "show less avoidance to dark-colored objects than to brightly-colored objects," the NMFS required some vessels to darken the corks or floats located on about 10 fathoms of the cork-line in the apex of the "Back-down" area with black paint.[14]

All vessels were required to use speedboats as instructed by NMFS regulations to prevent "net collapse" and to deploy one crewmember on a rubber raft, wearing a face mask and snorkel, "to observe relative position [sic.] of porpoise and tuna during "Back-down" and assist in manual removal of porpoise during and after "Back-down" on every set possible."[15] The NMFS-designed "Porpoise Grabbers" were provided for use in rescuing porpoises in the net beyond hand-reach of rescuers during and after "Back-down," and from the net skiff during "sacking-up."

The following diagram, produced by NMFS-SWFC (Southwest Fisheries Center of the NMFS), illustrates the various designs that were offered to make the basic Medina Panel more effective in releasing porpoise alive during the "back-down" procedure:

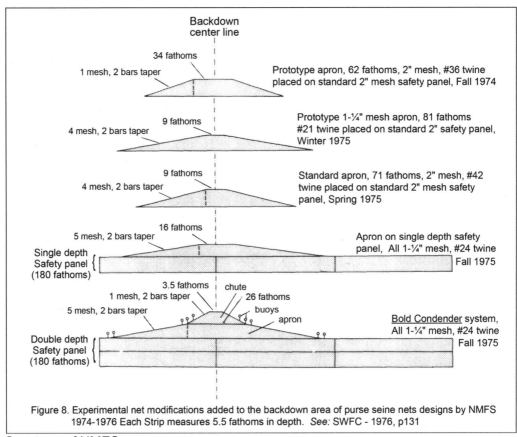

Figure 8. Experimental net modifications added to the backdown area of purse seine nets designs by NMFS 1974-1976 Each Strip measures 5.5 fathoms in depth. *See:* SWFC - 1976, p131

Courtesy of NMFS

Judicial Action Stops the 1976 At-Sea Competition

The joint NMFS/Industry experiment of the two systems was stopped effective May 31, 1976, because of a notice and the promulgation of various amendments to 50 CFR Part 216 published in the <u>Federal Register</u> by the NMFS on May 28, 1976. These amendments voided the regulations applicable to U.S. tuna seiners and prohibited the importation of yellowfin caught in association with marine mammals after May 30, 1976. By such publication, the ATA was notified that its

MMPA General Permit and Certificates of Inclusion were void.[16] The NMFS also advised that NMFS observers and gear technicians on board tuna seiners at sea may be returned to certain U.S. and foreign ports, either immediately or at the end of the voyage, at the discretion of the vessel captain. "All gear research which involves the taking of porpoise in the course of commercial fishing is to be terminated effective after May 30, 1976." [17] The NMFS took this action to conform to an order of Federal District Court Judge Charles R. Richey issued on May 11.

The NMFS filed motions to stay the court order pending appeal, but on May 26, the motions were denied by Judge Richey.[18] After the NMFS informed the fleet of Judge Richey's decision and refusal to stay his order pending appeal, six NMFS gear technicians were put ashore. "The effect was different with regard to the two systems—primarily affecting the vessels testing the fine-mesh-only system. The placement of the fine-mesh-only systems was also behind the schedule of placing the *Bold Contender System* which compounded the problem."[19]

On May 28, 1976, the U.S. Circuit Court of Appeals for the District of Columbia stayed Judge Richey's Order until 5:00 p.m., June 1, 1976.[20] A notice and amendment to 50 CFR §216.24 was published by the NMFS at 41 FR 23204 (June 9, 1976). It advised that on June 1, 1976, the stay of Judge Richey's order was extended until further ordered by the Circuit Court, making ATA's General Permit and the Certificates of Inclusion valid.[21] The new regulation amendment rescinded all amendments published in the Federal Register on May 28, 1976, and amended 50 CFR §216.24, by stating that the provisions of 50 CFR §216.24 in effect on January 1, 1976, remained in effect until amended by the NMFS or otherwise modified by order the U.S. Circuit Court of Appeals. The NMFS notified all Holders of Certificates of Inclusion under the ATA General Permit that NMFS scientific observers and gear technicians were to continue activities in accordance with prior plans aboard their vessels until further notice.

On June 11, 1976, the NMFS published in the Federal Register, an amendment to 50 CFR §216.24 (d) (3) (i) (A) of the regulations that was effective immediately on June 8, 1976.[22] This notice also advised that the number of scientific observers would be increased, and that NMFS would maintain the ongoing cooperative gear testing program on tuna seiners. [23]

As of September 7, 1976, the NMFS had obtained limited data on the two systems, as follows: For the *Bold Contender System*: of the nine trips tested inside of the Commission's Yellowfin Regulatory Area (CYRA), seven trips were complete and the other two were incomplete. For the *Double-Depth Medina Panel System*, of the five trips being tested inside the CYRA, data were available for one complete and three partial trips. A fifth trip was excluded because the data were unusable. Data were complete for one trip made outside the CYRA. "Simply as a matter of interest", a comparison based on this preliminary data showed that mortality per set by the *Bold Contender System* was one-third of the Fleet's average and that the Fine-Mesh-Medina Panel system was one-half of the Fleet's average ... The experiment is still in progress and definitive conclusions cannot be adequately supported at this time."[24]

The NMFS decided that "there was no significant statistical difference between the two systems. Since the *Bold Contender System* is more complex from both an operational and equipment point of view, NMFS will require the placement of a porpoise safety panel based on the Industry Fine Mesh system in 1977. This system has the advantage of easy convertibility to the *Bold Contender System* should further development and evaluation determine its desirability."[25]

---

[1] Richard L. McNeely (1975) "The Porpoise Apron." NOAA/NMFS-SWFC. This six-page document explains how the "Apron" idea was developed during a charter cruise aboard the SOUTH PACIFIC under the command of Captain Joseph Scafidi, providing information on the theory behind the "Apron" concept, the operation of the concept, and guidance on how the "Apron" is to be installed. Two diagrams were attached to the document.

[2] Conversation with Captain Joseph Scafidi on June 23, 2006.

[3] Captain Scafidi was the first to developed and introduce a tool known as a "Porpoise Grabber." The device "closely resembles a long-handle shepherd's crook, and is used to guide porpoise out of the net and to reach entangled porpoise that are out of arm's reach." (SWFC 1976: 77) During a 1975 House subcommittee hearing, testimony from a witness claimed that sharp-pointed gaffs were customarily used by tuna fishermen to remove live porpoise from the net during "Back-down" and sacking-up operations. Although Captain Scafidi was present at this hearing to explain the use of the "Porpoise Grabber," no subcommittee members asked him to testify. See: 1975 House Hearings-SN-94-16: 119-120. NMFS gear specialists explained the development and use of the "porpoise grabber" in SWFC-1975: 61-62. This "gaff" issue was mentioned in the written statement of William A. Walker (1975 House Hearings-SN-94-16: 67) Walker stated that as an observer on a tuna seiner "hundreds of porpoise were gaffed out of the net during back down. The gaffing of porpoise under these conditions can result in debilitating secondary skin infections and abscess formation. ..."

[4] SWFC-1975: 57-58.

[5] SWFC-1976: 39.

[6] SWFC-1976: 50.

[7] SWFC-1976: Figure 8, p.131, Figure 9, p. 132.

[8] SWFC-1976: 54.

[9] SWFC-1976: 55-56.

[10] Of the NMFS funding of the NMFS/Industry Cooperative Program, $290,000 was allocated to the "Mass Gear Test." SWFC-1976: 12

[11] John T. Everett, SWFC, "Cooperative Tuna Industry/Government Porpoise Mortality Reduction Experiment: a Brief Overview" February 27, 1976, (7 pp), (cited hereinafter as: "1976 Experiment Overview, NMFS." See: Report of the Secretary of Commerce, June 21, 1976, 41 FR 30152 (July 22, 1976): 30160-30161. For an excellent review and explanation of this experiment in terms of regulatory action, see: 1977 ALJ Recommended

Decision in Docket NO. MMPAH No. 1-1977, (cited hereinafter as "November 1977 ALJ Decision"): 28-29.

[12] 1976 Experiment Overview, NMFS: 5.

[13] Report of the Secretary of Commerce, June 21, 1976, 41 FR 30152, 30161.

[14] SWFC-1976:, p. 65.

[15] 1976 Experiment Overview, NMFS: 2.

[16] A renewal of General Permit (GP-1) had been issued to the ATA by the NMFS on December 19, 1975. It was valid "From 0001 hours, January 1, 1976 to 2400 hours, December 31, 1976 ..." 40 FR 59766 (December 30, 1975). This General Permit was impacted by the U.S. Court of Appeals Order dated May 28, 1976, staying Judge Richey's Order. 41 FR 23205 (June 9, 1976).

[17] 41 FR 21782 (May 28, 1976) See: Correction: 41 FR 22565 (June 4,1976)

General Permit No.1 was first issued to the ATA by the NMFS on October 21, 1974, 39 FR 38403 (October 31, 1974). The period of validity was from October 21, 1974-December 31, 1975. A modification to the ATA General Permit was made effective November 21, 1974, 39 FR 12936 (December 9, 1974). The first amendment to the General Permit was made on January 3, 1975, 40 FR 2852 (January 16, 1975).

The General Permits issued to the ATA in 1974 and 1975 did not contain any restrictions on the ocean location of the "takings" or fishing of tuna/porpoise schools. In the two applications filed by the ATA during 1974 and 1975, the NMFS was advised that takings could take place in the Pacific, Atlantic, and Indian Oceans. The General Permit issued to the ATA by the NMFS on April 15, 1977, stated in paragraph 2, the following: "Takings pursuant to this permit may be made **only** in the Pacific Ocean in the area bounded by 40°N latitude, 40° S latitude, 160°W longitude, and the coastline of North, Central, and South America." (emphasis added) This condition was continued in the three-year permit (January 1, 1978, to December 31, 1980) issued to the ATA by the NMFS on December 27, 1977, and in the five-year permit (January 1, 1981, to December 31, 1985), issued to the ATA by the NMFS on December 1, 1980.

[18] A footnote in Judge Richey's order denying the motions, stated: "Also, the Court's decision does not require a permanent ban against "on porpoise" tuna fishing; once the agency is able to determine the optimum sustainable population levels, it may then be able to authorize, consistent with the terms of the MMPA, the incidental taking of a limited number of porpoise, keeping in mind the general policy goal of reducing the incidental mortality rate to insignificant levels approaching zero."

[19] SWFC-1976: 57.

[20] On May 28, 1976, the NMFS filed an Affidavit by the Director stating, in part, the following: "The District Court has indicated that **the Agency**, although acting in good faith, **acted improperly in the issuance of the general permit without a specific limitation at the time of issuance**. Therefore, if a stay of the order of the District Court is granted pending appeal, the Agency will forthwith impose a quota for the full 1976 season of 78,000 porpoises as the total number of porpoises which may be killed by the U.S. fleet

in connection with commercial fishing for tuna by setting on porpoise." 41 FR 23680 (June 11, 1976). (emphasis added)

[21] After noting the prohibition on the encirclement of striped dolphin schools, the amended portion stated in part: "The number of all other stocks or species of marine mammals that may be killed ... shall not exceed 78,000." The amendment also authorized the Director of the NMFS, to determine the date of prohibition for encircling tuna/porpoise schools. {The methodology for determining that date was published in 41 FR 31227 (July 27, 1976), later modified as noted in 41 FR 43726 (October 4, 1976)}

[22] The NMFS explained: "Since this amendment is prescribed under sanction of a Court of the United States, it is effective immediately, in accordance the provisions of 5 U.S.C. § 553 (d)." 41 FR 23680 (June 11,1976) The ATA's application for re-issuance of its general permit for 1976 was granted, but its request for a 3-year term made during a public hearing was rejected by the NMFS. The application asked for a permitted kill of certain species of marine mammals, "of approximately 85,080 marine mammals." 40 FR 56899 (December 5, 1975).

[23] 41 FR 23680 (June 11, 1976)

[24] SWFC-1976: 58-59. Impact of the NMFS Prohibition on Fishing Tuna/Porpoise Schools on At-Sea Experiment in October-December 1976. Notice of the prohibition advised that "at the pleasure of the vessel captain" the NMFS scientific observers and gear technicians on board the vessels at sea may be returned to selected ports at no cost to the government. Because of various legal actions filed by the ATA and tuna vessel owners, the NMFS prohibition did not become effective until November 15, 1976; therefore, little, if any, adverse impact was experienced by the continuing at-sea research program aboard the ELIZABETH C.J October 1976 Quota Closure Distinguished: A proposed porpoise mortality quota, authorized in the 1976 amended regulations, was not imposed by the NMFS earlier during the year, because the U.S. tuna fleet "had met the conditions required by NMFS for continued fishing on porpoise." A "30% reduction in the U.S. kill during the early part of 1976 was obtained in comparison to the early part of 1975." Porpoise mortality had dropped about 67% (74,352 versus 24,199). " About two-thirds of this reduction was attributable to an increased catch of tuna not associated with porpoise and the balance was due to an improvement in releasing porpoise during porpoise sets." See: SWFC-1976:17-18. This result of not imposing a porpoise mortality quota for 1976 under the conditions set forth in the regulations became moot after the issuance of a Memorandum Opinion and Orders on May 11, 1976, by Judge Charles R. Richey, U.S. District Court for the District of Columbia.

[25] "Report on the National Marine Fisheries Service Program to Reduce the Incidental Take of Marine Mammals," p. 2. This three-page report was sent by the NOAA/NMFS-SWFC to the tuna Industry and interested public in 1977.

ACKNOWLEDGEMENTS

For his steady encouragement and guidance, we respectfully acknowledge our obligations to James Joseph, Ph.D. (University of Washington), former Director, Inter-American Tropical Tuna Commission (IATTC). Dr. Joseph's unexpected death in December 2009 was a great loss to us and to his many government, scientific, and industry friends in the world of tuna. We acknowledge the permission of Dr. Guillermo A. Compeán, Director, IATTC, for allowing the Commission's respected scientist, William H. Bayliff, Ph.D. (University of Washington) to perform the difficult task of reviewing and editing our manuscript from beginning to end. Others assisted in reading our early manuscripts or in providing helpful advice; these include Michael K. Orbach, Ph.D. (University of California at San Diego) Professor, Duke University, Antoni Trutanich of San Pedro, California, Mrs. Jan Loomis of San Diego, California, Mrs. Iris H. W. Engstrand, University of San Diego and co-editor, *The Journal of San Diego History*, San Diego History Center, Mrs. Juliann Ford of Rancho Santa Fe, California, Ray Ashley, Executive Director, Maritime Museum of San Diego, Mrs. Neva Sullaway, Managing Editor, *Mains'l Haul, A Journal of Pacific Maritime History*, Maritime Museum of San Diego, and Dale Squires, Ph.D. (Cornell University), Fisheries Resources Division, National Marine Fisheries Service, Southwest Fisheries Science Center, NOAA, NMFS, La Jolla, California.

For our research, we are indebted to the always graceful assistance of Mrs. Debra Losey, Librarian, Southwest Fisheries Science Center, La Jolla, California. We also used the facilities and helpful services of the San Diego County Public Law Library, Scripps Institution of Oceanography Library, San Diego Historical Center, Maritime Museum of San Diego, San Diego Yacht Club Library, San Diego Public Library, and the Portuguese Historical Center. We are thankful for the advice and information provided by John T. Gaffey, II, of San Pedro, California.

For their expert instruction and advice on how to bring our work to the public, we are especially thankful to William H. Bayliff, Mrs. Neva Sullaway, and Mrs. Christine Patnode.

This is to acknowledge the courtesies of persons representing the following entities in granting permission to use their photos and documentation, as follows: (1) Regional Administrator, U.S. Department of Commerce, NOAA, NMFS, Southwest Region; (2) Permissions Department, Editor & Publisher, *National Fisherman;* (3) Copyright Clearance Center, Inc., Publisher: Springer. Publication: *Reviews of Fish Biology and Fisheries*, Author Dr. Martín A. Hall, "An ecological view of the tuna-dolphin problem: impacts and trade-offs;" (4) Permissions Coordinator, Publisher: Taylor & Francis, Publication: *Ocean Development and International Law*. Author, Dr. James Joseph, "The Tuna-Dolphin Controversy in the Eastern Pacific, Biological, Economic, and Political Impacts."

This is to further acknowledge the courtesies of the following individuals in granting permission to use some of their treasured photos: (1) Mrs. Mary Brito, a picture of her husband, Lou Brito, and a photo of the converted tuna seiner

SOUTHERN PACIFIC; (2) Mrs. Carolyn Medina, a picture of her husband, Joe Medina, Jr., and photos of the new tuna seiners QUEEN MARY and CAROLYN M.; (3) Arnold Neves, a picture of his brother Manuel Neves at the time Manuel was in command of the converted seiner CONSTITUTION; (4) Ronnie Misetich and Anthony Misetich, a picture of their father, Anton Misetich, and the converted tuna seiner PARAMOUNT;(5) Gregory Scafidi and his father Joe Scafidi, in providing a photo of Joe Scafidi while in command of a tuna vessel; (6) Ralph F.Silva, Jr., a picture of himself at the time he was in command of the QUEEN MARY as a "dedicated vessel;" (7) Julius Zolezzi, a picture of himself at the time he was in command and co-owner of the tuna seiner JEANNINE, and (8) William Boyce, who made 23 tuna fishing trips as a NMFS observer aboard U.S. tuna seiners and provided photos of the fishing operations of these seiners.

To all who have worked in the U.S. tuna industry, we hope that our descriptions of the U.S. tuna fleet's efforts to fish tuna/porpoise schools in a responsible and innovative manner receive your approval. If we have failed in this task, we urge the submission of your written corrections and comments.

INDEX

This index includes words and phrases that are in the text, Appendix A, or the Acknowledgements, but not words and phrases that are only in the endnotes.